British Liberators in the Age of Napoleon

British Liberators in the Age of Napoleon

Volunteering under the Spanish Flag in the Peninsular War

Graciela Iglesias Rogers

B L O O M S B U R Y

LONDON · NEW DELHI · NEW YORK · SYDNEY

Bloomsbury Academic
An imprint of Bloomsbury Publishing Plc

50 Bedford Square
London
WC1B 3DP
UK

1385 Broadway
New York
NY 10018
USA

www.bloomsbury.com

Bloomsbury is a registered trade mark of Bloomsbury Publishing Plc

First published 2013
Paperback edition first published 2014

British Library Cataloguing-in-Publication Data
A catalogue record for this book is available from the British Library.

ISBN: HB: 978-1-4411-3565-0
PB: 978-1-4725-7533-3
ePDF: 978-1-4411-0374-1
ePUB: 978-1-4411-9321-6

Library of Congress Cataloging-in-Publication Data
A catalog record for this title is available from the Library of Congress.

Designed and typeset by Deanta Global Publishing Services, Chennai, India

Contents

Contents

Acknowledgements

To give adequate thanks to everyone who helped me with this book would probably take the equivalent of an additional chapter. Brevity and a few omissions, therefore, are a matter of regrettable necessity. My first debt of gratitude is to Professor Michael Broers (Lady Margaret Hall, University of Oxford), supervisor of the doctoral thesis from which this study originated, and to my examiners, Dr. David Hopkin (Hertford College, Oxford) and Prof. Brian R. Hamnett (University of Essex), for their insights, generous comments, encouragement and continuous support. I am particularly grateful to Lady Margaret Hall, not only for providing a friendly and intellectually stimulating environment for my work, but also for taking the unprecedented step of doubling the terms of the college's *Warr-Goodman Scholarship* for my benefit. I am also grateful to the neighbouring Wolfson College for awarding me the *Hargreaves-Maudesley Graduate Scholarship*, which I declined in view of LMH's generosity, and to St. Hilda's College and Rewley House for believing in my academic potential when I gambled on taking my first degree in History coming from a successful career in journalism. My research was also supported by several travel grants provided by the *Georges Labouchere Fund* (Faculty of History, Oxford), the *Royal Historical Society*, the *Abbey Santander Academic Travel Award* and the *British Association of Romantic Studies*.

Among the many persons who have assisted me with information, allowed me to quote from their unpublished work and provided helpful advice are Dr. Christine G. Krueger (University of Oldenburg) and Dr. Sonja Levsen (University of Freiburg); Prof. Agustín Guimerá Ravina (National Research Council of Spain); Prof. Laurence W. B. Brockliss (Magdalen College, Oxford); Prof. Robert Evans (Oriel College, Oxford); Prof. Charles Esdaile (University of Liverpool); Prof. Fransjohan Pretorius (University of Pretoria); Dr. Huw John Davies (Kings College, London); Dr. W. A. Speck (University of Leeds); Dr. Lynda Pratt (University of Nottingham); Dr. Diego Saglia (University of Parma); Prof. John Lynch (University of London); Dr. Matthew Brown (University of Bristol); Prof. Rafe Blaufarb (Florida State University); Imke Heuer (University of York); Andrew R. Nicoll (Scottish Catholic Archives); Dr. Simon Skinner (Balliol

College, Oxford); Dr. Bob Harris (Worcester College, Oxford); the convenors and participants of the Long Nineteenth Century European History seminar (Oriel College) and the Graduate History Seminar 1680–1850 (Lincoln College). I am also grateful to the anonymous readers and colleagues who commented on different aspects of this work.

I have incurred debts of gratitude to staff members at numerous archives, libraries and museums, but I would like to record special thanks to *subteniente* Javier Puentes, of the *Archivo General Militar de Segovia*; Juan Ramón Ramirez Delgado, director of the *Museos Municipales de Cadiz*; Norma Aubertin-Potter, of the Codrington Library, All Souls College, Oxford; Rachel Kennedy, General Manager of Duff House, Banff, Scotland; and to the ever-friendly and helpful staff of the *Archivo General Militar de Madrid*; the *Archives Nationales de France*; the Duke Humphries and Upper Reading Room at the Bodleian Library, Oxford; the Special Collections at King's College, University of Aberdeen; the Manuscripts and Rare Books Reading Rooms at the British Library and the National Archives at Kew.

I would like also to thank my former tutor at the Reuters Fellowship Programme (Oxford), Dr. Neville Maxwell, my friends David and Joan Potter, Isobel Watt, Dr. Belinda Beaton and my niece Charlotte Fereday for their moral and practical support. But my deepest gratitude is to my late husband, Arthur Frank Rogers, who encouraged me to embark in this project and who, since his untimely death, has become that inner voice that never ceases to urge me to strive for excellence and to never, ever give up.

Abbreviations

AAC	*Archivo del Ayuntamiento de Cadiz*
AB	King's College, Special Collections, Aberdeen University
AGM	*Archivo General Militar de Madrid*
AGMS	*Archivo General Militar de Segovia*, (unless stated, all entries refer to *Sección Primera*)
AHN	*Archivo Histórico Nacional*
AMO	*Archivo Municipal de Oviedo*
ANF	*Archives Nationales de France*
ASL	Codrington Library, All Souls College, University of Oxford
BCL	Bristol Central Library
BL	British Library
BL, Add.	British Library, Additional Manuscripts
BNE	*Biblioteca Nacional de España*
BOD	Bodleian Library
BOD North	Bodleian Library – North Collection
CU, Add.	Cambridge University Library, Additional Manuscripts
DNB	Oxford Dictionary of National Biography (on line and printed versions)
NA FO	National Archives of the United Kingdom – Foreign Office Papers
NA WO	National Archives of the United Kingdom – War Office Papers
NLS	National Library of Scotland

Illustrations

Introduction

Napoleon called it his 'unlucky war'.[1] Brutal and protracted, the conflict that engulfed the Iberian Peninsula between 1808 and 1814 has been categorized by historians among the first examples of modern total warfare, a sort of European laboratory for the combination of popular resistance, *guerrilla* and battlefield combat.[2] As such, it has been the subject of numerous studies, the majority focused on the military activities of the Anglo-Spanish-Portuguese alliance, those of their French opponents and of the insurgency.[3] Much has also been written about high politics and constitutional developments,[4] the French occupation and the Spanish *afrancesados* (pro-French collaborators),[5] the impact of the conflict on society, culture[6] and even on gender roles.[7] The activities of volunteers in the British forces have also been acknowledged, notably in Michael Glover's biographies of George Hennell and Sir Robert Wilson, the recruiter and organizer of British fighting units in Portugal.[8] Yet, neither in Britain nor in Spain, or, indeed, anywhere else, has any systematic attempt been made to investigate the presence of British volunteers embedded directly within the Spanish forces. This book addresses that challenge through the study of the role played by a group of men who, long before the International Brigades made its name in the Spanish Civil War, also found reasons to fight under the Spanish flag. Their enemy was not a forerunner of Franco's fascism, but what, at times, could be an equally overbearing ideology: Napoleon's imperialism.[9]

Extensive research in British, Spanish and French archives has revealed that, although small in number (42),[10] they exerted a surprisingly influential role not only on the conduct of war, but also in furthering the notion of social and gender equality in the Spanish military, in local politics, in cultural life both in Britain and Spain and even in relation to emancipation movements in Latin America. Some became prisoners of war in France, while a few served with *guerrilla* forces. Volunteers of English, Scottish and Irish origin included army officers who joined the Spanish army without necessarily relinquishing their British commissions; a seminarist turned warrior; a surgeon keen to put medical theory into practice; a bereaved Scottish nobleman with an eye for artistic talent;

and the frankly quixotic, such as the Romantic poet Walter Savage Landor who beat Lord Byron to become the first British writer to exchange his pen for the sword in a foreign cause. It might be difficult to understand how generations of historians could have overlooked this group of men, given that many attained the highest ranks in the Spanish army (three occupied leading positions in the military–political structure of post-war Spain)[11] and a few were the subject of individual case studies.[12] There are also tantalizing hints in a few contemporary Spanish sources of a prevailing impression that British volunteering in Spain was a widespread phenomenon. In 1810, for example, the Cadiz newspaper *El Diario Mercantil* carried adverts directed at Britons fighting with the Spanish forces, including one by the owner of the coffee-house *El Correo* offering them free food and accommodation,[13] and others by a language professor who claimed to be able to teach Spanish to the incoming Englishmen in less than 3 months.[14]

A plausible explanation is that, unlike British regular forces, many of the volunteers in the Spanish army became deeply embedded within Spanish society and the very nature of this close relationship served to obscure their involvement. Names often appear in documents naturalized into Spanish and frequently misspelled. For example, John Downie became *Juan Doume*[15] and Paul Palmer, *Pablo Palmés*;[16] Philip Keating Roche has been identified as *Felipe Qeating Roche*[17] and *Felipe de la Roche*;[18] Samuel Ford Whittingham was permanently renamed as *Santiago* (normally, the translation of James) with his surname turned at times into *Wittingam*,[19] at others *Witinga*[20] and even into *Güitinghan*.[21] The problem is compounded by the absence from the nineteenth-century Spanish alphabet of the letters 'K', 'Y' and 'W', and the consequent divergent phonetic approximations employed by generations of archivists. Thus, the English 'W' is variously conveyed as UU or VV (consequently, in the Spanish military archive of Segovia, the personal file of Whittingham remains catalogued under 'V' and that of Arthur Wavell, under 'U')[22] and K as Q, converting Kearney into *Quearney*.[23] Problems of faulty cataloguing and gaps in information resulting from such translations were only overcome by drawing from the knowledge of archival experts. Underlining the importance of *in-situ* research, in Segovia it was reported that many historians have tended to rely upon mail-order requests for copies of service record sheets (*hojas de servicio*) citing a catalogue published in 1959.[24] These records form only a fraction of substantial holdings of documentation, much of which is fragile, charred by a fire that in 1862 destroyed the *Alcazar* of Segovia where many of the files were already kept, and incapable of being photocopied. Therefore, the chances of locating material on many of the volunteers would have been highly reduced by research done at one remove. Further confusion may have arisen from ill-founded assumptions that Spanish officers with Irish-sounding names must have been drawn from the Irish community based in Spain since the 'Flight of the Wild Geese', the emigration of Catholic survivors of the Battle of the Boyne (1690). A century or so later, a bewildering number of Spanish-born generals had, indeed, Irish surnames. Among them, General Juan O'Donojú (O'Donohue), who headed the Patriots' War Department during part of the Peninsular War, and generals Joaquín Blake, Luis Lacy, and Enrique José O'Donnell.[25]

In the case of those volunteers who were also British military agents, historians have been unable or reluctant to uncover the true extent of their dual status. René Chartrand correctly described one of them, William Parker Carrol, as 'an Irish-born liaison officer of the Marquess de la Romana',[26] but made no reference to his British commission. Others simply dismissed them as 'hispanophiles who had made themselves popular with the Spaniards',[27] and consequently failed to disclose their full status and role within the ranks of the Spanish army. Perhaps such oversight was the inevitable result of observing the Iberian conflict from national perspectives. Successful efforts have been made to unite the divergent routes taken by British and Spanish historiographies since the nineteenth century, yet many of the works published during the last two decades have adopted an Anglocentric narrative which, at its worst, ignores the contribution made by Spanish historians, writes the Spanish forces out of victories or tends to present the war, not as won by the Anglo-Spanish-Portuguese alliance, but lost by the French.[28] This book takes a radically different approach. It sees this particular war as a transnational phenomenon that demands a similar frame of reference for its study. Material from and across multiple nations has been consciously sought and cross-examined, taking the Atlantic World as the geographical area of enquiry. Following on the footsteps of other historians who have embraced this method, attention has been paid to the movement of people, the links and flows of ideas as well as other issues that operated 'over, across, through, beyond, above, under, or in between polities and societies'.[29] On this basis, and by drawing on British, Spanish, French and Latin American sources, many previously untapped, it will be here suggested that victory was the result of a truly transnational effort: the combination of Spanish endurance and British (official and unofficial) interventionism.

In more than one way, this work ventures into uncharted territory. The phenomenon of war volunteering is attracting increasing academic attention,[30] but no transnational analysis has so far been undertaken in a European context for the early nineteenth century.[31] A conference organized by the University of Tübingen ('War volunteering in the nineteenth and twentieth centuries', Heinrich Fabri Institut, Blaubeuren, 6–8 September 2007) is believed to have held the first international discussions of the subject.[32] No precise definition of the term 'volunteer' emerged from that gathering, with historians unable to agree on the thorny issue of whether mercenaries could be validly viewed as volunteers.[33] As a starting point, this study has embraced the broadest and most consensual view of volunteering as a decision taken 'in the absence of pressure or coercion'.[34] For the precise identification of volunteers, the criteria applied have been far stricter: only those men who offered their services and had that offer accepted by the Spanish authorities, or made a contribution widely acknowledged, have been included. Those men who expressed a desire to volunteer, but failed to pursue that aspiration, have not been taken into account. This approach entailed other exclusions. For example, French intelligence reports intercepted by the Spanish army in the Basque country in 1812 made reference to the presence of around ten Englishmen fighting with the *guerrillero* Pastor.[35] In July 1810, the British agent and volunteer Charles William Doyle offered to a 'young Shelley' a rank in his Spanish regiment, the *Tiradores de Doyle*.[36] Months later, reporting on a successful landing on the Catalan port of Bagur, Doyle also mentioned 'a young Irishman, Galway, who accompanied me as a volunteer'.[37] Returning from 19 months imprisonment in France, fellow volunteer John Clarke claimed that he learnt of the death of a brother who 'had also served in the defence of the Spanish Nation'.[38] No personal file or any other record has been found corroborating that any of these men did, indeed, join Spanish regular or irregular forces. For that reason, they were not added to this survey.

The selection was tightened up even further for those volunteers who were originally dispatched to Spain by the British authorities to operate as military envoys. In the early years of the war, it became common practice for Spanish provincial and national authorities to confer ranks on British agents to encourage continued British support, yet with no expectation that this would result in military service under their banner.[39] For example, the first Patriot national government, the *Junta Central*, awarded the rank of *coronel*, soon upgraded to that of *brigadier*, to Major William Cox, one of the first British agents dispatched to confer with the Spanish authorities.[40] This was made in recognition of the friendly assistance he provided as representative of the British allies, first in Seville, and later in Cadiz.[41] Three years after the war ended, Cox made an attempt to have himself promoted to the rank of *mariscal de campo* with a view to securing a handsome pension.[42] His request was categorically refused after an examination of his file at the War Ministry established 'clearly that this English officer never served under the Spanish flags (sic)'.[43] In order to avoid misrepresentations, therefore, this study has only included those British agents for whom evidence was found of their involvement in the activities of the Spanish Patriots, irrespective of them having received a Spanish military rank.

This book consists of eight chapters, a conclusion and an appendix containing a glossary, a table and biographical notes where the volunteers' names, age, military background and record of service in the Spanish forces have been laid out in detail. The chapters follow on each other in chronological sequence, but each one deals with a different theme and forms a complete discussion in itself. The opening chapter sets the scene in Britain and in the Hispanic world prior to the outbreak of the war on the premise that the prevailing political, socio-economic, cultural and religious circumstances of the British Isles and the Spanish world largely conditioned the terms of the volunteers' engagement in the struggle against Napoleon. Chapter 2 examines why Britons decided to join the Spanish forces in the light of almost three centuries of Anglo-Spanish antagonism. This examination is complemented in Chapter 3 with a study of the 'Spanish cause', a set of views and ideals that encouraged participation in a conflict known in Britain as the 'Peninsular War', while for the majority of Spaniards it was, and to a large extent still remains, their *Guerra de la Independencia* (War of Independence). Both terms have been adopted in this book and the origins and implications of each are discussed in depth. Based on contemporaneous accounts, a reassessment of these concepts challenges recent historiography that has tended to question the existence of a Spanish national cause.[44]

A central argument of this book is that the British volunteers did not act as mere adventurers or soldiers of fortune. They behaved as liberators, driven, in many cases, by a romantic quest for adventure and a desire to fight in what they considered a popular war of national independence. It must be said, however, that they never referred to themselves as such. Save for religious references to Christ, the epithet appears not to have been coined in either English or Spanish until late 1813 when it was conferred on the Venezuelan liberator Simon Bolivar.[45] Yet, there can be no better word to describe these men whose objective was nothing less than Spain's outright liberation. Ascertaining the way in which they pursued this goal is of pivotal importance to forming an accurate idea of their role both in the war and in Anglo–Spanish relations. This is addressed in Chapter 4 through their intervention in the political arena where they appear to have exercised considerable influence at national level and, on at least one occasion, contributed to unseating a provincial government. Also considered is the extent to which they were acting on their own initiative and how far they risked entanglement in the manoeuvres of the Spanish politicians and British diplomats with whom they remained in contact. A trend to encompass all principles and accommodate all actions within the narrow aim of achieving Spain's liberation from the French yoke emerges from this analysis as a distinctive ideological force.

Chapter 5 explores their activities within the context of British and Spanish national traditions and mentalities in a period when, to quote a key exponent of the so-called 'Romantic' period, the 'spontaneous overflow of powerful feelings'[46] gained wide acceptability. Particular attention is paid to the issue of safeguarding one's honour; a concept deemed a hallmark of Hispanic identity. Drawing from anthropological and literary studies, in addition to archival sources, this chapter aims to highlight how the British volunteers' single-minded preoccupation with liberation could also lead them to play a significant role as propagandists of Spanish cultural exceptionalism in Britain. Further examples of unforeseen consequences are in evidence in Chapter 6, which looks at the British volunteers' foundation of two establishments that fostered social diversity – at least in the armed forces – by offering general education in addition to military training, innovatively to recruits from all social backgrounds. Other initiatives designed to boost morale and better prepare Spanish society to engage in a war characterized by the high involvement of civilians are also discussed.[47]

The status of the Britons within the Spanish forces afforded them opportunities to become immersed in Iberian society, but this created its own set of dilemmas. Chapter 7 opens with an examination of the circumstances that allowed the volunteers to socialize with Spaniards of all social ranks as well as with representatives of trading houses of British origin. Relations with their compatriots, particularly with British military leaders such as Sir John Moore and Lord Wellington, are studied in the context of an uneasy coalition between two countries whose objectives in the Peninsula did not necessarily coincide. This is followed by an appraisal of the potential effects of the duality of the volunteers' position – as Britons fighting under the Spanish flag – on their national loyalties and identities. The closing chapter records the circumstances of the volunteers in the turbulent period leading to the end of the war. This is a necessary prelude to a description of the extent and limitations of their legacy in the years that followed the restoration of Ferdinand VII in 1814. In search of signs of continuity in the liberating role of the British volunteers, this book unveils some material that sheds light on what could be described as a 'missing link' in the history of British–Iberoamerican relations. Certain volunteers established long-standing relations with Spanish officers of Latin American extraction, who themselves became liberators on returning to their homelands. A few volunteers went on to pursue military, diplomatic and mercantile careers in Latin America. These intriguing connections, along with some common patterns of behaviour that strengthen key arguments advanced by this book are briefly presented as a contribution to future research into the wider phenomenon of national liberation.

None of the British volunteers left an extended contemporaneous account of their experiences, such as a journal. Consequently, this study has drawn mainly on correspondence, dispatches, newspaper articles, family and census records, parliamentary debates, in addition to posthumously published memoirs, some edited by relatives, from which use was made only of those texts declared as literal transcriptions of correspondence, official papers and proclamations.[48] The availability of historical evidence has, in part, determined that some volunteers appear in this work more conspicuously than others. The author cannot but join the familiar chorus of historians' lamentations for the paucity and fragmentary nature of sources, particularly concerning lower-ranking officers, prisoners of war and members of the *guerrilla*. An explanation may be required at this point to allay potential methodological anxieties. This book is not a collection of individuals' life stories, so biographical notes and narratives have been limited to those relevant to the purpose and scope of the issues covered. This should not be interpreted as an effort to present a piece of depersonalized social analysis. The ambition here is to uncover and explore relationships of power, instances of cooperation and of cultural cross-fertilization. As Matthew Brown demonstrated in his highly perceptive study of British volunteers in Latin America, this task can only be properly accomplished by examining individuals as human beings, not as one-dimensional military machines.[49] Statistical methods are inadequate for the study of motivations, loyalties and issues of honour because they require labelling each individual under a particular category – an exercise that would produce a distorted and monochrome picture of reality. Instead, much use has been made of individual examples, mainly based on first-person accounts. The rationale behind this approach is not that testimonial evidence tends to enliven the text, but that it can often be more illuminating than generalizations based on little more than manufactured assumptions.

Finally, a note on the conventions and style adopted. All the personal files (*expedientes*) of the volunteers at the *Archivo General Militar de Segovia* (AGMS) consist of a summary of their military career (*hoja de servicio*) as well as other documentation, such as reports, reference letters and birth and marriage certificates. Unless stated, all references made under the AGMS relate to service records (*hojas de servicio*). All translations from Spanish are my own, except when an English version was already offered by the author of the source, as is often the case with the documents of Charles William Doyle preserved in the Bodleian Library (North Collection). Original spelling and punctuation have been retained in quotations; 'sic' has been used only where the original quotation could suggest an error of accuracy. Spanish military ranks are not translated into English, this for two reasons: First, in order to highlight the volunteers' affiliation to the Spanish army and thus, avoid confusion in the cases of those who still held ranks in the British army; second, because no comparative study of nineteenth-century British and Spanish military hierarchies has so far been undertaken, and so literal translations are misleading. A *mariscal de campo*, for example, was not a 'field marshal', but something approximating a major general in the British military scale.[50] Making matters even more bewildering, there were also subtle discrepancies in hierarchies between the Spanish infantry, artillery and cavalry.[51] Although these differences appear to have undergone a degree of harmonization towards the end of the war,[52] comparisons with British ranks have been avoided for the sake of rigour and clarity.

The World of the Future Volunteers

No study of voluntary military service in support of a foreign state could be deemed complete without first considering the situation in the volunteers' country of origin and in that of their destination. This section aims to meet that requirement through a *tour d'horizon* of the prevailing political, socio-economic, cultural and religious circumstances of the British Isles and the Spanish world as they related to the background and activities of the British volunteers. Their motivations for military service with foreign allies and their manner of enlistment will be examined in Chapter 2. The purpose here is to outline the complex background to the volunteers' engagement, in the likelihood that it served to shape their attitudes, irrespective of their widely divergent origins. At first sight, there is little to link, for example, the sons of Irish military families with a failed West Indies entrepreneur, a leading poet of the Romantic movement and an aristocratic Scottish adventurer, save that all were born and brought up under the Union flag. Beyond this fundamental common denominator, additional factors merit consideration prior to a detailed examination of the volunteers' role in the Spanish forces between 1808 and 1814.

Most immediately apparent in this overview are the advantages of education and some kind of property, which placed the majority of these men (at least 25 out of 42) within a privileged minority in an increasingly affluent Britain.[1] Theirs was a powerful country undergoing what traditional historiography has viewed as 'the first industrial revolution', now more accurately identified as the 'Great Transformation' or 'Great Divergence'[2] – a transition from an agrarian economy to one based on manufacture, machine production and mass consumption. These developments engendered an entrepreneurial culture that conferred social status through the patient accumulation of wealth. The volunteers' time was, indeed, the period of 'polite and commercial people',[3] when aristocrats, landed gentry, manufacturers and merchants could collaborate to promote shared interests. While progress was manifest, the benefits were unevenly distributed.

Numerically, the 'middling sort' dwarfed the gentry and the aristocracy. They formed, in turn, a small minority by comparison with the largely uneducated labouring poor.[4] They all functioned within the matrix of a fiscal-military state, which, through taxation, the development of national debt – which revolutionized the government's borrowing capacity – and the growth of an expanded public administration, canalized resources to war and imperial expansion.[5]

Yet, this did not suffice to prevent the definitive loss of the American colonies in 1783. Within a decade of that humiliation, Britain embarked upon a more dangerous war with revolutionary and Napoleonic France and her allies, conducted on a global scale and destined to drag on for twice the combined duration of the twentieth-century's two world wars. Resources were stretched to the limit. The British army, 40,000 strong at the time of the fall of the Bastille, would reach a quarter of a million in 1814 – at great economic and social cost.[6] Furthermore, Britain – with its traditional distaste for the concept of a standing army – feared invasion by forces raised by conscription, an apprehension heightened by two raids (Cork 1796; Fishguard 1797), French encouragement of the United Irishman Rebellion (1798) and the presence of the *Armée d'Angleterre*, from the summer of 1797 to the winter of 1798, a few miles across the Channel in preparation for a combined assault with Dutch forces.[7] In this climate, military and naval forces were supplemented by an array of part-time and voluntary units designed for both national defence and maintenance of civil order. By 1804, up to a third of all adult males had joined these units.[8] As Linda Colley observed, in a country where a fifth of young Britons were under arms, donning military uniform became *de rigueur* for any respectable gentleman.[9] So, it is unremarkable that almost all the subjects of this book (30 out of 42) had received some degree of military training prior to arriving in Spain.[10]

The Union flag, under which the majority of the volunteers had served, represented a state that was a relatively recent composite of four distinctive nations (England, Wales, Ireland and Scotland). The dynastic union, which linked England and Wales with Scotland in 1603, was reinforced in 1707 by parliamentary union. In 1800, Ireland's autonomous parliamentary institutions were dissolved and a new state, the United Kingdom of Great Britain and Ireland, was established. But unification by political dictate could hardly bring about immediate homogenization: the new British state encompassed multiple, often conflicting identities. In religion, for example, Anglicanism was the established church in England, Wales and Ireland, while Presbyterianism was that of Scotland. Catholicism was the religion of the majority in Ireland and remained influential in the Highlands.[11] Nor could a union that was largely a marriage of political and administrative convenience[12] assuage long-standing tensions between London and the constituent entities of the United Kingdom.

Nowhere were these tensions more evident than in Ireland, homeland of many of the volunteers. Under the aegis of the Privy Council, an Anglican 'Ascendancy' represented a colonial élite, ruling a Catholic majority as well as Nonconformists. Penal laws introduced in the years following the Glorious Revolution to eliminate the ethnic–religious imbalance had largely failed. The population of Dublin, a citadel of Protestantism in the 1700s, was nearly 70 per cent Roman Catholic by the end of the century, and many of the Protestants were Nonconformists. Some aristocratic Catholic families had managed to survive, and a substantial 'middling sort' was beginning to emerge in the legal and medical professions as well as from the ranks of merchants, traders and manufacturers.[13] Ties of kinship and religion underpinned networks on an international scale. It was common for the Catholic gentry of Dublin, Wexford, Waterford, Cork, Limerick and Galway to send their offspring to Irish colleges established in the sixteenth and seventeenth centuries in France and Spain (Salamanca, Seville, Alcalá, Santiago de Compostella and Madrid).[14] Trading houses established in Cadiz in the late eighteenth century, such as that of the Wiseman family, maintained their connections with Ireland.[15]

Certain members of these networks were debarred from returning home since, in one respect, sectarian restrictions had been relatively effective. After the mass emigration of Catholic survivors of the Battle of the Boyne in 1690 – the 'Flight of the Wild Geese' – the Irish Parliament enacted statutes prohibiting recruitment for foreign service (1722); precluding those already serving in the Catholic armies of France or Spain from holding property in Ireland (1746); and making service abroad treasonable (1756).[16] These measures sought to end the activities of clan-based 'regimental families' that kept alive a Gaelic network of kinship through foreign service, mainly in forces opposed to Britain.[17] The legislation had the effect of positively encouraging Irish emigration. Moreover, Irish preoccupation with genealogy proved helpful in meeting the condition stipulated by European monarchs that officers should be of noble birth.[18] In exile, emigrant families became naturalized, and over the generations, linguistic and cultural traditions were often diluted. Nonetheless, a good number of generals on the Patriot side of the Peninsular War had Irish surnames (such as Luis Lacy and Enrique José O'Donnell) and a few could communicate in English (Joachim Blake and Pedro Sarsfield).[19] Yet, the Napoleonic Wars produced a schism in the Irish diaspora, evidenced by the volunteers' awareness of Spaniards of Irish descent serving on both sides of the conflict.[20] At one point, General Juan O'Donojú (O'Donohue) headed the Patriots' war department at Cadiz, while General Gonzalo O'Farrell served King Joseph Bonaparte as War Minister in Madrid, aided by Irish veterans of the secessionist rebellion of 1798.[21]

Since the 1770s, successive British governments, particularly the first administration of William Pitt the Younger (1783–1801), had favoured Catholic emancipation despite opposition from George III and many in the Ascendancy. This was not achieved, but some concessions were granted: Catholics were permitted to hold commissions in the British army up to the rank of colonel (1793) and to serve as militiamen outside Ireland (1799).[22] But, by then, certain Irish regimental families had already opted for a more pragmatic approach. They took the view that, other than by entering the East India Company, which imposed no restrictions upon Catholic military service,[23] crypto-Catholics might secure advancement by exercising discretion on issues of faith and cultural identity, while publicly professing to subscribe to the 39 Articles of the Established Church. An ancestor of the future volunteer Charles Doyle, William '*Guillermo*' North y Gray, encountered no difficulties on returning home in 1727, having been promoted to the rank of *teniente general* in the Spanish army by the Bourbon King Philip V.[24] Leniency was probably exercised because, as one of his descendants later explained, his family had supposedly pledged allegiance to the Established Church 'some time ago, perhaps even before 1690'.[25] The family of another Peninsular volunteer, William Parker Carrol (1776–1842)[26] also transferred to the Ascendancy, probably in the early eighteenth century.[27] When he died, having been knighted by the Prince Regent, he was buried at an isolated location unconnected with any church, but recognized by the people in Tipperary as the traditional resting place of the clan Carrol, still known by its Gaelic name *Ui Cearbhaill Eli*.[28] The ability to balance with dexterity and discretion two seemingly incompatible identities, and their familiarity with the particularities, if not practice, of Catholicism, gave these men a qualitative advantage when serving abroad.

Scottish volunteers also had recourse to a dual identity, though of a less covert nature. During most of the eighteenth century, many educated 'North Britons' were enthusiastic Anglicizers. They subscribed and contributed, particularly through the works of Scottish Enlightenment *literati* such as David Hume, to the view of Englishness as an ideal to be universally embraced. To be English meant to be Protestant, to speak English, but also to be freed from despotism – a concept born out of the anti-papist Reformation and the interpretation of the Glorious Revolution as the struggle against the absolutism of the Stuarts.[29] Seven decades after the Act of Union (1707), Scottish elites enjoyed demonstrable benefits in terms of access to government appointments, army and naval commissions and East India posts, since the Act accommodated Scotland's juridical, religious and educational particularities, which was not the case for Ireland. High levels of literacy also gave Scots a competitive advantage. In proportional terms, they dominated the political and imperial structures of the British state, both at home and abroad, often in coordination with an influential private sector.[30] Thus, a cousin and namesake of the future Peninsular volunteer James Duff[31] established with his nephew William Gordon Duff, the 'Duff Gordon' sherry *bodega* in Cadiz (1772) and ran it profitably for over 50 years, while simultaneously serving as British consul and, at times during the Peninsular War, as Britain's sole representative in Andalusia.[32] Not everybody was so successful. Long before he decided to join the Spaniards in their resistance to Napoleon, John Downie (1777–1826), a native of Stirling, made and lost a fortune in the West Indies.[33] For the future volunteer James Arbuthnot, a Catholic background (and perhaps illegitimate birth into an aristocratic family as well) forced his transfer to the *Real Colegio de Escoceses de Valladolid* (Royal Scots College of Valladolid) where he was trained for the priesthood.[34]

Scots maintained their martial traditions by way of service in foreign armies (particularly after the Jacobite risings of 1715 and 1745) or by joining the British forces. In the 1750s, one in four of all army officers was a Scot.[35] For many Scottish grandees, involvement in national defence offered an opportunity to demonstrate their 'North Briton' credentials. In the wake of the Napoleonic invasion scare, James Duff's uncle, the second Earl of Fife (1729–1809) proudly claimed, as Lord Lieutenant of Banffshire, to have raised '21 companies of volunteers'.[36] He appointed James, his eventual heir, to a lieutenancy in the 2nd battalion of volunteers of Cullen and later promoted him to the rank of lieutenant colonel in the Invernesshire Militia. But the future officer of the Spanish army failed to share his uncle's enthusiasm and performed his tasks with little application.[37] Many in the younger Duff's generation were beginning to question the advantages of an Anglicized modernity and were drawn to ideas of a new form of British identity that celebrated indigenous particularism, including a sentimental appropriation of Scotland's Stuart heritage.[38] While the second Earl sought to deflect attention from his brother's participation in the 1745 rising, his nephew – as the fourth Earl – would eventually boast about his family's Jacobite

Figure 1 James Duff, Lord Macduff, fourth Earl of Fife (1776–1857), painted by Mons Richard (*circa* 1830), engraved by William Holl; published by Fisher & Co. © National Portrait Gallery, London.

past without jeopardizing his standing in British society.[39] As will become clearer in subsequent chapters, this recourse to an idealized, vernacular past would give British volunteers a language in common with Spanish patriots.

On a wider scale, notions of 'nation' and 'nationality' had been profoundly reassessed since 1776 when men who, for over a century, were considered 'Englishmen' declared themselves equal citizens of the newly created United States of America.[40] In revolutionary France, nationality was based not on ethnicity, religion or allegiance to a Crown, but on a theoretical compact among citizens. In the initial phase of the Legislative Assembly (1791–92), whoever showed themselves to be 'cosmopolitan was, therefore, French,' as the legislator François Chabot said when supporting the case for honorary nationality for the Englishman Joseph Priestly.[41] This enlightened, universalistic approach appealed to young British intellectuals, such as the poets Wordsworth, Coleridge, Southey and volunteer-to-be Walter Savage Landor.[42] In the years 1796–99, these writers considered Bonaparte the champion of the Revolution, the restorer of the hopes of a virtuous all-embracing republic seemingly extinguished by the Terror. But this admiration was short-lived. For Landor, Napoleon's *coup d'état* of November 1799 and his installation as Consul for Life in 1802 turned the erstwhile hero into a 'profaner of republics' who had left France with 'not an atom of liberty'.[43] Such repugnance had the wider effect of questioning the ideals of a new era of universal rights while it encouraged interest in national particularisms. Folkloric evocations of a world of ceaseless conflict, such as that of Macpherson's 'Ossian', carried topical appeal throughout a continent beset by an unprecedented war.[44] Chapter 5 will examine this cross-border cultural phenomenon of looking to the past for guidance and inspiration.

Since the Reformation, Britain and Spain had followed separate paths, often competing as rival powers, with Spain frequently the junior partner of France. In Britain, ignorance and aversion fostered a view of Spain – the old Catholic menace – as a power disfigured by despotism and religious bigotry.[45] Nonetheless, one branch of the British political establishment was relatively familiar with the realities of life in Spain, and found its headquarters at Holland House, residence of Whig grandee Henry Richard Vassall Fox, third Baron Holland of Holland (1773–1840). He had visited Spain in 1793. Returning after the Peace of Amiens (1802), Holland spent 3 years travelling the country with his wife and their family physician, John Allen. They befriended leading families and *ilustrados* such as Capmany, Blanco White, Floridablanca and, above all, Gaspar Melchor de Jovellanos.[46] Those most likely to gravitate towards Holland House would be those most sympathetic to the liberal (*avant la lettre*) Whig political orientation of their hosts. In Georgian Britain, political life was dominated by clusters of personal and family alliances, which found it hard to cohere in stable factions. In true Foxite style, the Hollands eventually saw Spanish resistance to Bonaparte as an example of a popular movement, undirected by kings or bishops, in pursuit not only of liberation but also of a transition to an English-style constitutional system. In short, the Patriots deserved to be recognized as 'Spanish Whigs'.[47] To witness events at first hand and perhaps even influence matters, the Hollands returned to Spain in October 1808, remaining until July 1809. On this visit, their itinerary crossed the paths of at least three of the volunteers.[48]

A further source of first-hand information about Iberia existed in the form of numerous British-owned trading houses operating in Spain, the exact number of which immediately prior to the Peninsular War is not known, though a study covering the years 1780–1850 suggested that British businesses in Spain ranked second in number behind France.[49] Their operations extended beyond those of basic trade to embrace activities such as freight forwarding agencies, money lending, maritime insurance brokerage and even commissary-related military supply.[50] Further information is emerging from ongoing regional studies.[51] Research undertaken for this book in census material held in the Cadiz municipal archives identified at least eight British traders operating between 1805 and 1813 in the port, which represented the main commercial gateway for

Spain's monopoly trade with Spanish America. The most prosperous seem to have been the Shaw, Strange, Wiseman and Costello families (part of the Irish network) and the British consul James Duff. All of them would have dealings with the volunteers.[52] On the other side of the country, a business owned by Richard Hart Davis, MP for Colchester, managed to prosper – despite the vicissitudes of warfare – in the long-established Spanish wool trade between Bilbao and Bristol.[53] Hart Davis was brother-in-law to the future volunteer Samuel Ford Whittingham who worked for him in Spain for a few years.[54] This gave Whittingham a good knowledge of Spain's diverse cultures and regional political particularities.

While the extent to which British business interests in peninsular Spain carried weight in London remains unclear, there was certainly an influential lobby pressuring the British government for access to South American markets. When deputies from the Spanish principality of Asturias arrived in London to seek support for their struggle against Napoleon (8 June 1808), Britain was assembling a force of 9,000 troops at Cork for a 'liberating' invasion of Spanish Venezuela to be led by Sir Arthur Wellesley, accompanied by the campaigner for South American independence Francisco de Miranda.[55] Such projects had long been part of the stock-in-trade of British foreign policy, to be dusted off whenever conflict with Spain occurred. Military operations were directed towards depriving Spain of the most profitable branches of her commerce. Territory was only acquired as a bargaining counter in future peace negotiations. If local elites demanded emancipation while guaranteeing open markets for British merchants, Britain would stand ready to assist, while encouraging the freely chosen adoption of a constitutional monarchy.[56] This strategy became pressing when Napoleon's Berlin Decrees (1806) prohibited commerce with Britain, ordered the arrest of British subjects found on French-controlled territory and the seizure of British vessels in continental waters. Yet, more draconian decrees ensued to choke off the flow of revenue into the Exchequer, which was already struggling to perform as the 'War Paymaster' of anti-Bonaparte Austrian and Prussian forces all too prone to defeat.[57] Britain reacted by accelerating the search for markets in the Far East and the Americas. 'Unauthorised' invasions of Buenos Aires in 1806 and 1807 exemplified this strategy.[58] Three future volunteers participated in the second of these ill-fated missions.[59]

In Britain, the emergence of Spanish popular resistance to Napoleon served momentarily to counteract old prejudices. The press rallied support in favour of the Patriots. British assistance, it was suggested, would help the country redeem itself in the eyes of the world after the Royal Navy's destructive bombardment of Copenhagen, a pre-emptive strike to deprive Napoleon of access to the Danish navy (1807).[60] The 'liberating' invasion of Spanish America was put on hold with a view to redirecting it to the Peninsula. The Portland administration was already contemplating this possibility, but needed further information. It rapidly transpired that Iberian experts were thin on the ground. Dispatches to London by Gibraltar garrison commander Lieutenant General Sir Hew Dalrymple and messages from consuls John Hunter (Oviedo) and Duff (Cadiz) tended to be overtaken by the pace of events.[61] Meanwhile, in Parliament, few in the Opposition shared Lord Holland's hispanophilia. The leader of the Grenville-Foxite faction between 1807 and 1817, William Wyndham, Baron Grenville (1759–1834), declared against British intervention on budgetary grounds. Privately, he was apprehensive about the wisdom of encouraging mass armed uprisings.[62] Some reservations were voiced in Cabinet, while the King urged caution.[63]

Despite such uncertainties and lack of sound intelligence, Britain's first large-scale expeditionary force to the continent since the War of the Spanish Succession (1702–13) was dispatched in early July 1808 – not to Spain, but to Britain's oldest ally Portugal. The Asturian deputies had refused to countenance a British landing on Spanish territory. Their mandate from the regional *junta* of Asturias was expressly confined to requests for money and *matériel*. A subsequent delegation of Galician deputies (30 June 1808) had been explicit in asking that British troops be sent to Portugal, which bordered Galicia. The government acquiesced, won over by the prospect of halting Napoleon and encouraged by a climate of domestic triumphalism.[64] Yet, in the minds of many Britons – not least a majority of the volunteers – the true objective could be nothing less than joining the liberation resistance movement in Spain. It was in this conviction that, in a tavern in Brighton, the poet Landor 'preached a crusade' to 'two Irish gentlemen'[65] and, on the spur of the moment, lacking a single word of Castilian, they set off 'to join the Spanish army immediately'.[66]

The target for liberation

Except as a cartographical entity, it could be argued that the volunteers' target for liberation – Spain – did not exist in 1808. There was no single, cohesive political and cultural unit responding to that name – a situation that could not solely be attributed to the chaos newly created by the Napoleonic invasion. Lured to

Bayonne by the French emperor, the Bourbon monarch Ferdinand VII and his father and predecessor Charles IV had never been the rulers of Spain, but of the *Monarquía Hispana* (Hispanic Monarchy).[67] Their royal decrees were always prefaced by a proclamation that clearly identified them as being 'By the Grace of God, king of Castile, Leon, Aragon, the two Sicilies, Jerusalem, Navarre, Granada, Toledo, Valencia, Galicia, Mallorca, Minorca, Seville, Sardinia, Cordoba, Corsica, Murcia, Jaen, Algarves, Algeciras, Gibraltar, the Canaries, Oriental and Occidental Indies, Lord of Biscay, Lord of Molina, & c'.[68] Although the accuracy of this long list is highly questionable, it is clear that Spain remained unnamed. Even the pragmatic invader, in attempting a synthesis, opted for a plural form used briefly by the Habsburgs, when Joseph Bonaparte was proclaimed king of 'las Españas y de las Indias'[69] (the 'Spains' and the Indies), a term that seemingly represented tacit recognition of diversity within the Peninsula while also marking a distinction between the 'motherland' and the colonies which, though long promoted by many within the Bourbon court, had never officially been acknowledged.[70]

The Crown was expected to bind together all the components of the vast Spanish world, which still extended across most of the Iberian Peninsula, the South American continent and the Philippines, but this requirement had never led to complete amalgamation. This was not for lack of trying. In 1707, the first Bourbon king on Spanish soil, Philip V, victor of the War of Succession, announced his intention of 'reducing all kingdoms to a common pattern of law, usages, customs and courts, all equally administered by the laws of Castile, which have won such praise and acceptance throughout the world'.[71] To make Castilian law applicable throughout the Spanish world had been in the minds of Spanish monarchs since at least the early seventeenth century, but it was the Bourbons who carried out the policy. The kingdom of Isabella *la Católica* (the Catholic), the template for colonization of American territories, was now to be applied across the Hispanic world. In 1709, the parliaments of Aragon, Valencia and Catalonia were dissolved. Their representatives were subsumed into a single chamber under the general banner of the *Cortes* of Castile. Catalan was replaced by Castilian as the official language of Aragon and the Levante whose governments were directly appointed by Madrid. But the intended Bourbon process of merging was never so wide-ranging as to engulf the entire Peninsula. There were numerous exemptions. The northern kingdoms of Navarre, the principality of Asturias and the *señoríos* of the Basque country, which had proved loyal to Philip, were permitted to keep much of their legal, political and cultural individualities.[72]

Indeed, their territories constituted an area known as *la España foral* where medieval laws and popularly based institutions of self-government (*fueros*) were preserved relatively free of interference from the central government, leaving their population out of the reach of national taxation, custom duties and national conscription.[73] There were other important provisions in the *fueros*. All the inhabitants of these regions were considered 'nobles', thus none could suffer demeaning punishment and had to be tried by their peers. Crucially, a procedure known as *pase* enabled their local governments (*Diputación*) to obey, but not to put into effect pending appeal, a royal order thought to contradict their freedoms.[74] This situation was expected to constitute a countervailing brake on the general Bourbon process of castilianization.

Far from being mitigated, however, the process of homogenization was promoted with increased vigour during the three decades that preceded the War of Independence. Local laws and customs became a target for abolition by a monarchy with increasing centralizing ambitions. The government's offensive was, on the whole, successfully resisted, often violently, as when First Minister Manuel de Godoy attempted to extend the system of conscription to provincial militias in the *foral* regions. The idea was abandoned after riots in Valencia in 1801 and in Biscay in 1804.[75] Isabel Burdiel has rightly noted that no correlation can be found between this sort of *foralism* and the nationalism that emerged in peripheral regions of the late nineteenth to early twentieth centuries because the latter phenomenon was secessionist in character, while *foralism* could function within a national sphere.[76] Nonetheless, harmony in the relationship between monarch and subjects, the essential key to the Rex-Regnum system, was often elusive.[77]

Discontent became even greater when homogenization began to be perceived as the wholesale importation of foreign political structures, practices and cultural aesthetics far removed from the proclaimed objective of castilianization. Indeed, in the view of the Bourbon court, France, and, to an extent, Naples – not Castile – represented the unquestionable beacons of modernity.[78] As Sánchez-Blanco has pointed out, the Spanish Enlightenment was not a mere process of imitation and translation of foreign authors,[79] yet it is clear that during the eighteenth century the concept of a general Spanish *decadencia* – that the years of Spain's glory were truly in the past – established firm roots among an élite troubled by the idea that there was little hope in home-made innovations.[80] Popular culture, however, remained attached to vernacular customs and traditional amusements, such as bullfighting. Castilian particularisms were robustly defended as demonstrated by the *majos* and *majas* of Madrid who publicly mocked all things perceived as French, such as powdered hair and the use of three-cornered hats.[81] This attitude was to be encouraged during the war by some of the British volunteers who, for example, made a point of wearing the traditional Spanish cloak.[82]

As victors of the War of Succession, the Bourbons had divided the Peninsula into ten military districts known as *Capitanías Generales* with seats in Malaga, Seville, Santa Cruz de Tenerife, Badajoz, Zamora, Corunna, Oviedo, Saragossa, Barcelona, Valencia and Palma de Mallorca. With the exception of Navarre and Spanish America, *capitanes generales* (captains general) replaced viceroys as the representatives of the King, as supreme chiefs of the local army in peacetime and as heads of civil administration. Consequently, it was during this period that an association came to be formed in people's minds between military uniforms and political authority. In everyday civilian affairs, captains general were expected to heed the advice of the *Audiencia* (a provincial high court with certain administrative and executive functions), although in troublesome Aragon, the captain general happened also to be the head of the *Audiencia*.[83] They were the recognized *jefes politicos* (political chiefs) while French-style *intendentes* were civil servants who acted as representatives of the central Treasury, collecting taxes, overseeing compliance with financial legislation and adjudicating in disputes over jurisdiction. Importantly, the *intendentes* also supported the army across a range of functions, including commissary services and recruitment.[84] In wartime, troops were mobilized into field armies commanded by specially appointed generals, who might or might not be captains general, while the *intendentes* remained responsible for the pay and supply of the forces; auditing military accounts; levying patriotic contributions; administering hospitals and magazines; and requisitioning billets and transport. The burden of these impositions fell on the population, as the *Monarquía* accepted no responsibility for provisioning its own forces.[85] This reliance upon the local population for supplies hampered the defence of the country during the French invasion of 1794 and was to prove even more disastrous when more than half of the Peninsula fell under Napoleonic control.

Whereas the armies of the Habsburgs had consisted of state-supported militias supplemented by foreign mercenaries on short-term contracts,[86] the Bourbons introduced what has been described as the *sine qua non* of absolute monarchies: a standing army.[87] In Spain, the members of this army were not only employed in wars, but also served as police officers and customs controllers.[88] They could also be summoned by civil magistrates to tackle fires and enforce *cordons sanitaires* during outbreaks of epidemics such as yellow fever.[89] Under the control of captains general acting as political chiefs, and with a large bureaucracy and law enforcement personnel in military uniform, Bourbon Spain had all the appearances of a 'gendarme State'. The Bourbons, however, were never able to satisfy the enormous budgetary requirements entailed by such a model. In times of war, such as in 1778, the army and navy could account for as much as 72 per cent of all government expenditure, yet they were unable to accomplish fully their allotted roles.[90] Military salaries failed to keep pace with inflation, a situation that became acute in the period 1780–1808 as the Spanish Treasury tried desperately to avoid bankruptcy. The rank and file was filled with the urban and rural poor, criminals and foreigners since the Bourbons were never able to enforce a system of conscription, not even one of quotas such as the *sorteo* form of balloting. People resorted to bribing magistrates, using influence, flight – and even marriage – to avoid recruitment into the lower ranks of the army, which were perceived as the most despised form of life in Spain. Large sectors of the population were already excluded from service, such as all bureaucrats, skilled workers, married men and those who provided the sole support of a widowed mother. Many of those who failed to avoid service reacted to hunger and boredom by deserting. In the period 1797–1801, of the 35,427 men removed from the army's list of active soldiers, 16,545 were deserters, outnumbering the dead and wounded.[91]

From the outset, the Bourbons sought to maintain the officer cadres of their underfunded standing army and foster their loyalty by exploiting what has been described as 'the structuring value'[92] of Spanish society, that of honour. Access to army commissions was confined to those who could demonstrate that they had inherited or otherwise acquired honour, normally through membership of the nobility. As they were assumed to be rich already, it was expected that they would be satisfied with the acquisition of yet more honour either by way of elevation to a higher grade of nobility or by promotion in rank – often both. Thus, honour in eighteenth-century Spain came to acquire, in a military context, a connotation of intangible reward. Recourse to wholesale distribution of promotions in place of remuneration had a perverse effect. The army became top-heavy with generals whose numbers grew from 150 in 1711 to 220 in 1770 and 538 in 1799. On the premise that service in the army was *per se* an ennobling activity, it was possible for a commission to be granted to the son of an officer who had attained the rank of at least captain or to regular soldiers with an exceptionally good record of long service. This element of the officer corps accounted, however, for only 12 per cent of the total.[93] Issues of ennoblement were so sensitive that the Bourbons introduced a system of personal files (*expedientes*) in which were recorded not merely service given to the Crown, but, crucially, social status, religion and profession of parents and relatives.[94] The *expedientes* meticulously perpetuated the distinction between the majority *honorables* (honourable) and the minority entrants of non-noble origin categorized as *honrados* (honest). The records were periodically reviewed, at which point officers could be graded under four categories: *valor, capacidad, aplicación* and *conducta* (courage, ability, diligence and conduct). Barely 6 per cent of promotions granted in the eighteenth century were awarded purely based on *capacidad* (ability). Promotion came slowly for the plebeians. While in the infantry it took an average of 6 years for a noble to reach the rank of *subteniente*, a soldier of non-noble origin had to wait 16 years. In the cavalry, progress was even slower: 8 compared to 23 years.[95]

Qualifying hurdles were also raised by the end of the eighteenth century. Mirroring the situation in the army of pre-revolutionary France with the Segur Ordinance,[96] it was decided in the 1790s that to get a commission in the Spanish navy it was necessary to demonstrate noble antecedence extending back at least four generations. Across the armed forces, this produced what Andújar Castillo has described as a process of 'aristocratisation'.[97] The forces were plagued by internal rivalries, corruption and afflicted by the same conviction of Spain's decadence that prevailed among the élite, as clearly emerges from reading contemporary satires such as Cadalso's *El buen militar a la Violeta*.[98] In theory, the army to which British volunteers were to offer their services was a professional army. In reality, considerations of honour and status held such sway that the character of the army was completely distorted. These views were so ingrained that a British volunteer of noble origin had to be accorded a senior rank.[99] Conversely, a British volunteer who gained high rank through service in the Peninsula was automatically assumed to enjoy aristocratic status.[100]

In the fall of 1807, as the first flakes of snow circled through the air, 25,000 French troops crossed the Pyrenees. They had been invited to traverse Spanish territory on the way to conquer Portugal by the terms of the Treaty of Fontainebleau. Such was the trust that the Spanish Bourbon monarchy placed in France, her traditional ally, that the incursion went ahead 9 days before the document would be formally signed (27 October 1807). The declared objective was to share the spoils of conquest and to wage total economic war against Britain by blockading her trade with the continent. In the Madrid court, expectations were higher. Charles IV and his *valido* (prime minister) Manuel de Godoy saw the deal as a first step in a dreamed refashioning of the 1761 Bourbon 'Family Pact' adapted now to the growing size of the Napoleonic imperial dynasty. Under orders based on this misconception, Spanish polite society offered the visitors a cordial reception. Not so the rest of Spaniards, who, guided by what a French reconnaissance officer described at the time as 'une espèce d'instinct national'[101] (a sort of national instinct), showed themselves profoundly ill-disposed.[102]

Controlling the Atlantic access to the Mediterranean and with vast overseas territories, Spain was politically and strategically too important to French interests to be left outside direct control. By March 1808, imperial forces had secured the ports of Barcelona and San Sebastian and occupied four important fortresses. But this was no walk over. Revolts sprung up in Pamplona and Burgos; two French soldiers were murdered in Vitoria and over a hundred were seriously wounded in clashes with the inhabitants of poor neighbourhoods of Barcelona.[103] The general of division Paul-Charles-François Thiébault bitterly complained that while the French were marching to fight 'Spain's natural enemy', probably meaning England, Portugal's traditional ally, he had seen along the route 'embaucheurs espagnols' (Spanish recruiters) actively fomenting desertion among his troops.[104] Rumours that Charles IV and his wife were to be spirited away to the safety of South America triggered a mutiny at Aranjuez (17–18 March 1808) that ended Godoy's rule and placed the untested Ferdinand VII on the throne. Months of uncertainty, tension and hostilities, heightened by the eventual kidnapping of the Royal family in Bayonne, culminated in an uprising in Madrid (2 May 1808) ruthlessly suppressed by Marshall Joachim Murat. Like ink on blotting paper, a wave of resistance spread throughout the rest of the Spanish world.

It might seem improbable that, barely 32 months after the Battle of Trafalgar (21 October 1805), and with the shattered remains of the Spanish navy still visible in the Bay of Cadiz,[105] British volunteers should have been accepted into the Spanish military resistance. Yet, it could not be otherwise, given the catastrophic situation into which Spain had descended in less than two decades. Wars with Britain (1796–1801; 1804–08) and a relatively stable alliance with France had encouraged successive Bourbon regimes to concentrate their energies on the navy,[106] allowing the hierarchy of the army to remain the preserve of noble courtiers.[107] Favouring maritime power seemed logical for an imperial power economically dependent on raw materials from, and manufacture of exports for her transatlantic colonies.[108] Napoleon's invasion and the Bayonne incident struck at the heart of the weaknesses in the Spanish economic and defence systems. It also gave a *coup de grâce* to Spain's central government, already in free fall since the events in Aranjuez. These events had been preceded by a demoralizing series of apocalyptic natural disasters: droughts (Alicante, 1806), earthquakes (Granada, 1807), floods (Lorca, 1807) and a plague of locusts (Segovia, 1807).[109] Nonetheless, the vast majority of Spaniards rose against the French. But the insurgents were unprepared for the challenge. Old age, casualties and desertions to the side of the *afrancesados* rapidly reduced the number of fit men in the higher echelons of their army. The Patriots became so desperate for expert assistance that they began to contemplate embracing any assistance offered, including that coming from recent foes.

Why Volunteer with the Spanish Forces?

Attempting to establish the precise motivations behind any human action is inevitably difficult, even more so in the context of war, when the life of the individual is placed at risk. The purpose of this chapter is, therefore, simply to explore a variety of topics that may explain why Britons, after three centuries of enmity, should choose to fight under the colours of Spain, a country widely despised in Britain as a dangerously exotic land, a once mighty power brought low by absolutism and religious bigotry.[1] No single cause for volunteering will emerge from this assessment, as it is probable that several overlapping factors were present to varying degrees in each individual. This has proved to be the case in the few existing academic works carried out so far on the subject of war volunteering in modern European history.[2] The point of the present exercise is to consider which reasons are more plausible than others and to look for common themes, even if these themes may not apply to all volunteers to the same degree.

After months of scattered outbreaks of resistance, full-scale opposition to French occupation erupted in Madrid on 2 May 1808 and spread rapidly. In those quarters of the British press which had predicted that 'Spain will soon become politically extinct, and no longer exist but as an appendix of France',[3] the events were hailed as potentially the first successful popular uprising anywhere in Europe against French expansionism. There had been revolts in the Vendée and in Calabria, but these were localized and, on the whole, contained affairs. The Spanish world would be a bite more difficult to chew. In the city where merchants had, for centuries, traded in Spanish sherry and Merino wool, *Felix Farley's Bristol Journal* made a U-turn in editorial policy to contend that, by assisting Spain against France, 'we shall be fighting our own battles; we shall be opposing a mound to the overwhelming tide of conquest before it reaches our shores'.[4] The defeat of Napoleon's forces at Bailén (19 July 1808) corroborated this impression by ending the myth of the Emperor's invincibility, which had grown out of victories over the years. In his caricature 'The Valley of the Shadow of Death' (24 September 1808), the satirist James Gillray depicted a terrified Napoleon confronted by the Spaniards represented as Death riding a mule of 'True Royal Spanish-Breed'.[5] This interpretation was not confined to the British Isles. News of the Spanish bravado dominated press headlines from Bombay to neutral America.[6]

The Spanish war soon captured the popular imagination and energized men to offer their services. Among them, no less than the brother-in-law of the man appointed to lead the British forces in the Peninsula, Sir Arthur Wellesley, future Duke of Wellington and of Ciudad Rodrigo. After a military career fighting Napoleonic forces in theatres as far flung as Copenhagen and Martinique, Lieutenant Colonel Edward Michael Pakenham revealed to his family the shocking news that he had returned to Europe with the sole object of joining the Spanish forces. 'My plans are considered; they may be strong, but they are not wild. They are composed of interest towards my family, good will towards my Land',[7] he told his long-suffering mother awaiting him in Ireland. He left no stone unturned until a friend helped him to secure a passage to the continent on a pretext of delivering despatches to his brother-in-law. But the feint backfired. All aspirations to link his 'fortunes to those of the Spanish Army' were frustrated by Wellington's decision to assign him to permanent staff duties at British headquarters.[8]

The impulse to engage in the Spanish war extended beyond military circles. This happened in a period that had witnessed a transformation in the role of artists. Instead of simply depicting heroic deeds, writers, painters and musicians aspired – and were also increasingly expected – to be heroic themselves.[9] Many expressed the desire to wear military uniform and test their mettle. In a diary entry for 29 January 1809, the painter Benjamin Robert Haydon declared:

> O God, grant I may astonish mankind as a great Painter and then die in Battle, and I shall die as I sincerely wish, and let me not die undistinguished, let me die in "the blaze of my [illegibly, possibly 'fame']". I fear it will be impossible for me to die in Battle – how it can be brought about I don't see, but I live in hopes as these are strange times.[10]

Months later, he confided to his diary the yearning to have been present at the Battle of Basque Roads (12 April 1809) and the unfulfilled determination to 'go out as volunteer one day or other'. His rationale was simple enough: he just liked the idea of seeing at first hand the 'fire, shot, shells, dying groans, tremendous explosions, enthusiastic huzzas, dying efforts, blazing fires, and all the horrors, terrors, fury, rage & smoke of a thundering battle'.[11] Lord Byron, regarded as the prototype of the would-be warrior artist engaged in a foreign cause, did travel to Spain in 1809, but with touristic rather than heroic ambitions.[12] He launched into a tour that would also take him to Portugal, Gibraltar, Malta, Athens and Constantinople. In a letter from Gibraltar in August 1809, Byron expressed admiration for the Spanish cause saying '. . . I like the Spaniards much, you have heard of the battle near Madrid [Talavera] . . . I should have joined the army, but we have no time to lose before we get up the Mediterranean & Archipelago'.[13] Although his brief visit to Spain would provide much inspiration for *Childe Harold's Pilgrimage*, composed on the way back to England, it would be fully 14 years before Byron took up arms and then to join the Greek liberation movement.[14]

Others responded more promptly, including the poet Walter Savage Landor, who could arguably be considered the first British writer to exchange his pen for the sword in a foreign cause. In search of a precedent, the author and courtier Sir Philip Sydney (1554–86), whose death at the siege of Zutphen, in the Spanish Netherlands, was mourned publicly by many fellow poets, including Sir Walter Ralegh and Edmund Spenser, should certainly be discounted. Sydney died while fighting under the English banner. He was dispatched to the Netherlands by Queen Elizabeth I who had him appointed governor of Flushing, in the former island of Walcheren, claimed at the time as English territory.[15] In one of his *Imaginary Conversations*, penned between 1821 and 1846, Landor took the trouble of highlighting the English imperialistic nature of Sydney's final mission through a dialogue in which a Warwickshire grandee (Landor was himself a Warwickshire landlord) named Lord Brooke said to the Elizabethan writer: 'Only some cause like unto that which is now scattering the mental fog of the Netherlands, and is preparing them for the fruits of freedom, can justify us in drawing the sword abroad'. To which Sydney retorted: 'We have nothing to dread while our laws are equitable and our impositions light: but children fly from mothers who strip and scourge them'.[16]

Liberty was, for Landor, a troublesome obsession. Originally a fervent admirer of Napoleon – the 'mortal man above all mortal praise'[17] of his poem *Gebir* (1796–98) – he was repelled by the Corsican's seizure of absolute power in 1802. Napoleon and the French in general became the objects of his opprobrium on grounds that they had betrayed the libertarian principles of the French Revolution. In a letter to his friend, fellow poet Robert Southey (and future

author of the first British history of the Peninsular War),[18] he announced his
determination to join the Spanish army in terms that displayed furious anti-
Gallicism:

> Nothing I do, whether wise or foolish, will create much surprise in those who
> know my character. I am going to Spain. In three days I shall have sailed. At
> Brighton, one evening, I preached a crusade to two auditors. Inclination was not
> wanting, and in a few minutes everything was fixed. I am now about to express
> a wish at which your gentler and more benevolent soul will shudder. May every
> Frenchman out of France perish! May the Spaniards not spare one! No calamities
> can chain them down from their cursed monkey-tricks; no generosity can bring
> back to their remembrance that a little while since they mimicked, till they really
> thought themselves, free men. Detestable race, profaners of republicanism, –
> since the earth will not open to swallow them all up, may even kings partake in
> the glory of their utter extermination![19]

There is little evidence, however, to suggest that extreme Francophobia such
as that expressed by Landor could have spurred other volunteers to join the
Spaniards. Antipathy was more sharply focused on the person of Napoleon and
on his imperial forces. British volunteers seemed to be able to disassociate French
nationals from the actions of the 'despot'. They tended to consider the French
invaders – but not the whole French community – as 'savages and plunderers'[20]
intent on forceful implementation of Napoleon's theory of amalgamation by
imposing their culture and values on their conquests, no matter how proudly
independent those nations might be. This was an attitude shared by the Spanish
authorities themselves who, through proclamations by their different provincial
juntas, stated from the very beginning of their struggle that it was not a 'war of
nation against nation', but that their concern was only to 'protect ourselves from
the oppression of a tyrant'.[21]

   Henry Milburne, a member of the Royal College of Surgeons, was determined
to help the Spaniards release themselves from the 'fetters of an infatiable (sic)
despot',[22] but this was not the only reason for his support. At the time, he was
writing a treatise on the treatment of gunshot wounds and saw the war in the
Iberian Peninsula as an opportunity to extend his knowledge on the subject.[23]
Recently appointed Assistant Surgeon in the York Rangers,[24] Milburne tried
to join Sir Arthur Wellesley's expedition to Portugal, but found all vacancies
in its medical department already filled. He offered his services gratis to José
María Queipo de Llano, Viscount de Matarrosa (later Count de Toreno), one of
the Asturian deputies who were in London soliciting aid for the liberation of

Spain. But he was to be disappointed again. The Asturians had already refused to countenance the landing of a British expeditionary force on Spanish territory. Their mandate from the regional *Junta* of Asturias was expressly confined to requests for money and *matériel*. Viscount Matarrosa had no authority from his government to engage the services of any British subject, so he declined his offer. Undeterred, Milburne decided to proceed to the war zone without any appointment. On the eve of departing, however, he was introduced to Sir William Gordon Duff, MP for Worcester and partner in the counting house of his uncle James Duff, consul at Cadiz.[25] Coincidentally, Gordon was looking for a surgeon to join the regiment that another partner in Cadiz, the Malaga-born *coronel* Juan Murphy, had just assembled in Castile.[26] The house of Gordon and Murphy had a commercial network that spread from Andalusia to Veracruz, Havana, St Thomas, New York, Boston and New Orleans, Lisbon, Hamburg and Copenhagen. In London, it was one of the largest firms, employing some 360 clerks. The founding stone of the business had been the wine trade, but the company's fortune depended on contracts signed with the Spanish and British governments for the import of Spanish-American bullion.[27] Napoleon's invasion of Spain now threatened its very existence. Murphy decided to fund, recruit and lead in person the *Regimiento de Infanteria Voluntarios de España* established under the auspices of the provincial *junta* of Castile. Surgeons were not easily available amid the chaos of war in Spain,[28] so Milburne was recruited immediately. He gathered every medical article and surgical instrument he thought likely to be useful, and on 10 December 1808, disembarked at Corunna ready to join the Spaniards' brave 'exertions in opposing the lawless and unprecedented pretensions of an overbearing tyrant'.[29]

Admiration of Spanish valour may be considered among the reasons to volunteer. Although the War of the Convention (1793–95) served to discredit the Spanish regular forces, many of the volunteers had been on the receiving end of popular risings in Spanish America, and thus had first-hand experience of how determinedly a nation could take up arms against a foreign invader. Three prominent volunteers, Samuel Ford Whittingham, Philip Keating Roche and William Parker Carrol, were veterans of the second of two disastrous British attempts to capture Buenos Aires in 1806 and 1807. This experience not only endowed them with a knowledge of Spanish defence tactics but, most notably in the case of Parker Carrol who had been left 18 months as a hostage in Buenos Aires, a familiarity with the language and manners.[30] In their testimonies at the court martial of Lieutenant General John Whitelocke, commander-in-chief of the expedition against Buenos

Aires, all three expressed admiration for the determined manner in which the British had been resisted by forces largely composed of civilians.[31]

A fourth leading volunteer, Charles William Doyle, the eldest son of Ireland's Master in Chancery William Doyle KC, a member of the politically influential North family, had also seen action against Spanish forces in Puerto Rico (1797) and in Cadiz (1799). As lieutenant colonel in his uncle's infantry regiment, the 87th of Foot garrisoned in Guernsey,[32] Doyle managed to get himself appointed British military agent before sailing to Spain in late June 1808. The appointment had been the result of 'wearing out the patience'[33] of Lieutenant Colonel James Willoughby Gordon, military secretary to the Duke of York, commander-in-chief of the army. Doyle had also pestered an Irish family friend, Under Secretary of State, Sir Charles Stewart, playing up his suitability to be sent to Spain, in meetings and letters. He described what, from archival research, seem to have been slightly exaggerated accounts of visits to Cadiz and Madrid, his wide circle of Spanish acquaintances and his 'knowledge of the Lingo'.[34] On 2 July 1808, War Minister Lord Castlereagh instructed him to travel to Spain, accompanied by Carrol, in what they might have liked to interpret as a first step in a mission of liberation – escorting several hundred Spanish prisoners of war released from British gaols back to their country. Yet, they were clearly told that in this short-term assignment, their duties were not to go beyond 'informing yourself of the state of affairs' and expressing the British 'desire' to assist the Patriots.[35]

At various points, Whittingham, Roche, Carrol and Doyle, all holders of British commissions, decided to join the Spanish army. In the case of Doyle, the decisive moment occurred when his efforts to foster unity among the Spanish Patriots were snubbed by the British authorities, whereas the Spaniards honoured him with the rank of *mariscal de campo*.[36] In December 1808, Doyle ended a letter to the *Junta* of Aragon with the emotional outburst: 'Europe will see that Spain, the Patriotic Spain, is loyal to her religion, to her King and that she will never be slave of a tyrant . . . *Viva España!*'.[37] Henceforth, Doyle would sign all his letters, including those he continued sending to Whitehall, with the styling of Spanish general. Equally inspired by admiration for Spanish valour, Doyle's cousin, Carlo Joseph Doyle, briefly joined *guerrilla* forces operating in northern Spain.[38]

Charles Doyle's reference to religion raises the question as to whether faith issues played any role in persuading Britons to join the forces of Catholic Spain. As Simon Bainbridge observed, Spanish Catholic resistance to 'atheist' French forces had the effect of elevating the war in Spain to 'a fight between good and evil'.[39] We have seen that in July 1808, over drinks in a Brighton tavern,

Landor spoke of having 'preached a crusade' to two companions, Irishmen identified by another source merely as Messrs O'Hara and Fitzgerald.[40] This was probably more a flight of rhetoric than a call to armed religious zealotry. Until this time, Landor had shown little personal interest in religion. If anything, he had been critical of the role of the organized Church both at home and abroad. He would not become attached to any faith until much later in life and that was to Anglicanism.[41] During his brief experience in Spain, he proclaimed his determination to fight 'in the defence of religion and liberty',[42] but in the sense of preserving the right of Spaniards to exercise their religious beliefs, rather than setting himself up to exterminate infidels. Among the volunteers there were, indeed, some Catholics. But only five felt able to declare themselves as such with equal frankness to both Spanish and British authorities. None expressed sympathy with Spanish Catholics as their primary motive for service. Nor did they join any of the *cruzadas* organized in a few provinces.[43] Even James Arbuthnot, a seminarist at the *Real Colegio de Escoceses de Valladolid* (Royal Scots College of Valladolid) seemingly saw the war as an opportunity to engage in a military career.[44] He was not completely unusual in choosing this path – at least three students at the same college had taken up arms in different armies in precedent years.[45] The other declared Catholic volunteers included a fellow Scot, Reynaldo Macdonnell,[46] two Irishmen, John Kearney Donnelan[47] and Timothy Meagher,[48] and a lone Englishman, Charles Silvertop, scion of a prominent Catholic family in the North East.[49]

Significantly, and counter-intuitively, there is no evidence to suggest that Irish Catholics were induced to serve in Spain as part of some spontaneous wave of support for Spanish co-religionists.[50] Research for this book has established that certain Irish volunteers may be considered crypto-Catholics: they were members of clan-based 'regimental families' that had succeeded in preserving Gaelic kinship networks despite having publicly subscribed to the established Anglican faith. We have seen that the families of Charles Doyle, Carlo Joseph Doyle and William Parker Carrol had ostensibly converted to Protestantism at unrecorded dates in the aftermath of the Glorious Revolution.[51] In a Spanish context, historians such as Agustín Guimerá Ravina have identified Irishmen settled in Spain who would cheerfully project themselves as either Irish or Spanish, as circumstances required. But they evinced no such ambiguity regarding their attachment to the Catholic faith.[52] Whatever their true religious affiliations, these volunteers – in common with many English and Scottish colleagues – emphasized their Christian faith in private correspondence and in public declarations directed exclusively to the Spaniards. Carrol had no qualms about presenting himself to the Spanish authorities as 'coming from one of the most distinguished Irish Catholic families'.[53] Such a confession publicly expressed in the United Kingdom would have harmed his family's social standing, particularly as it was linked by blood and fortune with that of the Hely-Hutchinsons, defenders of Catholic emancipation in the British Parliament, but nevertheless members of the Irish Ascendancy.[54] Charles William Doyle, who as nephew of the army officer and Irish Pro-Catholic Whig MP John Doyle,[55] had long since been promoted beyond the highest military rank normally attainable by Catholics – that of captain –[56] avoided such declarations. But his frequent appeals to defend the '*Santa Religión*'[57] (Holy Religion) suggest a degree of attachment to the 'old faith', which might have underpinned a decision to fight in Spain, though any such attachment was never expressed.

If anything, it seems that an important factor in encouraging service with the Spaniards was not faith *per se*, but the obstacles that flowed from affiliation to Catholicism in Britain. Captain Charles Silvertop, having attained the highest rank open to him, introduced himself to the *Junta Central* as an English national, 'descendant of an old and honourable Catholic family in the North of England'.[58] He was not bluffing. The Silvertops of Minster Acres, in the county of Northumberland, were members of the landed gentry since the fourteenth century and had amassed a considerable fortune from coal mining. His elder brother George, as key player in the campaign for Catholic emancipation in England, was in contact with the far-famed leader of their co-religionists in Ireland, Daniel O'Connell, and would eventually become British envoy to the Vatican.[59] By means of a statement written in the third person as it was the form in Spanish formal applications, Captain Silvertop told the Spanish authorities how 'having strong inclination for military service, when all liberal and enlightened persons of his country shared the opinion that the restrictive laws against Catholics would be abrogated', he had been persuaded to join the 14th Regiment of cavalry. There he served 7 years 'with the entire approbation of his superiors for his abilities and good conduct', but once he obtained the rank of captain it was made clear to him that his career would go no further. In a pragmatic tone, he explained that

> because the aforementioned restrictions against his beliefs subsisted with the same vigour and strength, he had resolved to transfer to Spain and take service there, as a country more congenial to preserve the religious principles he has received from his grandparents and because in this country, under current circumstances, there exist greater possibilities for him to distinguish himself.[60]

Indeed, the prospect of career advancement seems to have been a prevalent motivation among the volunteers. The French invasion generated demand for experienced soldiers. Not only did over 900 Spanish officers choose to serve under Napoleon,[61] but each provincial government organized the patriotic resistance with the creation of new regiments; consequently, there was an increased demand for experienced officers to coordinate their operations.[62] In Britain, threat of Napoleonic invasion had led to an unprecedented scale of mobilization, yet promotion remained largely dependent on personal contacts and purchase of commissions.[63] In Spain, Whittingham – a lowly captain – enjoyed meteoric progress to the rank of *mariscal de campo* (approaching the rank of major general on the British scale) in less than a year.[64] This should not be interpreted, however, as a mere flattering progression of honours. To placate his father, who had objected to Whittingham's youthful aspirations to a military career, he worked for a few years in the wool trade, including in the Bilbao office of the Bristol firm owned by his brother-in-law Richard Hart Davis.[65] He only ventured to return to Britain to begin life as a soldier at the age of 31, 2 years after his father's death in 1801. In 1804, Prime Minister William Pitt engaged him in a secret mission to Portugal intended to lure a 'Captain Rogers', an Englishman serving in the Spanish army, as a spy in preparation for a British expedition to South America.[66] This ended in failure, but his familiarity with Iberian culture led to deployment in Latin America – an experience he feared in 1808 would be repeated and that, he said 'would be completely reducing one to the situation of a civil agent, whose knowledge of the language might be considered convenient'.[67] Appointed, once again, to the position of deputy assistant quartermaster, Whittingham seized an opportunity presented by a stop over in Gibraltar of the vessel that was transporting him to join the staff of the army in Sicily. He voiced his frustrations to an old acquaintance, the governor of the colony Sir Hew Dalrymple, who put him in contact with the chief of the patriotic army of Andalusia, General Francisco Javier Castaños. In a letter to Colonel Gordon, military secretary to the commander-in-chief of the army, a personal friend, Whittingham stated:

> I have to conceive it possible that my good fortune may attach me to the advance guard of the Spanish Army, and in this glorious struggle between patriotism and tyranny, I should then acquire that experience of which I stand so much in need, or finish my career.[68]

His wishes were fulfilled that same day, 4 June 1808. Castaños appointed Whittingham his *aide-de-camp*.

While Spain provided the opportunity to acquire the experience that would justify promotion, denial of such recognition generated bitter disappointment, as in the case of Irish volunteer Rudolf Marshal. In a letter written in English to the Spanish General Joachim Blake, from the besieged Mediterranean town of Sant Feliu de Guixols, close to the foothills of the Pyrenees, Marshal, by now a *teniente coronel* in the Ultonia Regiment and commander of a group of *guerrilla* fighters, *somatens* and *miguelets* (Catalan militia and home guard forces), requested promotion while admitting that he had not been in the Spanish service for more than '7 or 8 months'.[69] During that 'very busy' period, he had been wounded in action on nine occasions, had disbursed his personal wealth without seeking reimbursement and yet had been denied the degree of advancement enjoyed by all others in the first wave of volunteers, such as *coronel* Carrol.

> My friend Mr. (Charles) Stuart the envoy who was in Spain, has since gone to Trieste and I hope is now in St. Petersburg in his letter asks me if I am not a Spanish Colonel & offers me his letter of recommendation. But I will owe nothing in war but to a warrior. My letter is full of an Egotism which disgusts myself but I thought I ought to state my reasons to Y. E. (Your Excellency) for this application.[70]

Marshal was justified in expecting some degree of recognition, as his commitment to the Spanish cause was such that he would lose his life a few months later defending the besieged city of Gerona.[71]

Yet, there were also a few Britons who imagined that the very act of volunteering would entitle them to a rank higher than that which they already held. This seems to have been particularly the case among Catholics who assumed that their religious affiliation would enhance their eligibility for higher rank. This was an expectation in which Charles Silvertop himself was initially disappointed as the *Junta Central* accepted his offer of service, while granting him only the rank of *capitán* for which he already held a similar British commission. In his case, in the early stages of the war, a single letter to the Spanish Minister of War emphasizing that he had 'incurred some personal sacrifices in coming to this country'[72] was sufficient to gain him immediate promotion to the two levels higher rank of *teniente coronel*.[73] In other cases, however, the Spanish authorities were more selective, particularly with regard to applications predicated on the assumption that volunteering would qualify for immediate promotion – or even advance payment. This was the case of an Irishman, William Mac Veagh, who requested in January 1810 the rank of *capitán*. The Spanish attempted without success to verify through the British ambassador his claim to hold a commission in the British army at the rank of lieutenant, but nevertheless offered Mac Veagh the lesser position of *segundo teniente* in the Hibernia Regiment. In April 1810, however, he decided to try his chances and demanded two months' payment as *capitán*. The Spaniards rejected his claim and told him to take the rank offered, advising his superiors that 'si no le acomoda que se marche a Inglaterra' (if this does not suit him, let him go back to England).[74] Mac Veagh's response remains unknown.

Monetary demands appear to have been the exception, given the weight of evidence that other volunteers waived their entitlement to payment, as in the case of James Duff, heir to the earldom of Fife, one of the richest in Scotland. Duff was accepted, and rapidly promoted to the rank of *mariscal de campo*, on the strength of his assurances that he would not draw any pay and that he would withdraw from the service – and thereby impose no long-term obligations on the Spanish purse – as soon as the objective of liberation had been achieved.[75] In cases where payment was drawn, the proceeds were often used to provision the military units in which the volunteers were serving – or even donated, as in the example of Charles Doyle, to causes such as the relief of the victims of the sieges of Saragossa, Tortosa and Tarragona.[76] On transferring to the Spanish army in February 1809, the Scot Patrick Campbell agreed to forego the daily allowance to which he was entitled as a member of the British garrison in Gibraltar inspired, he later said, by

> the most lively feelings of justice and attachment to such a heroic Nation on seeing it under attack and invaded by the Tyrant of Europe (. . .) he ran without delay to join those who fought against those who were depriving them of their liberty, expressing his desire to share in their company all the dangers and glories of the campaign in which they were engaged.[77]

In the event, Campbell subsequently managed to re-secure his Gibraltar entitlements and over 3 years he used this cash flow not merely to defray his own expenses, but also to underwrite the costs of a journey to Britain on a mission assigned by the Spanish government in 1811.[78] The prospect of booty may have proved attractive to some volunteers, but, so far, no evidence has come to light to support the suggestion that this could have been a motivation to join the Spaniards. None of the men studied here emerged from their war service significantly wealthier than before. In only one instance, a volunteer, Philip Keating Roche, became the target of unproven accusations that he used his position as *mariscal de campo* and later *teniente general* in charge of the defence of Alicante for self-enrichment.[79] Another volunteer, the Scot John

Downie relinquished his commissariat post in the army of Sir John Moore – a non-combatant position considered at the time as full of hardship, but ideal for profiteering –[80] to join the Spaniards.

Downie offers probably the most outstanding example of the volunteers' 'death or glory' approach to seeking the status of hero in their own lifetime. Most volunteers had reached an age at which they might fear they would never attain that aura of immortality that Romantic poets and writers would make a *sine qua non* of human existence.[81] They still yearned for excitement and were prepared to seek it out. As the third son of a less than wealthy family of landowners in Renfrewshire, Downie followed the path taken by many cadet sons – that of seeking his fortune in Britain's expanding empire. Having made – and lost – a fortune in the West Indies, Downie switched to a military career initially as an officer in a colonial force under the auspices of the governor general of Trinidad, Sir Thomas Picton. In Trinidad, Downie had come into contact with the would-be liberator of Venezuela, General Francisco de Miranda, and served as his second-in-command during Miranda's ill-fated Leander expedition in 1806. Enthused by the idea of becoming a leader of a liberation enterprise, Downie was accorded the rank of colonel of the 'army of Colombia' – a country that had yet to exist.[82] By the autumn of 1807, Miranda had returned to London with a handful of followers, including Downie. Immersed in debt, a plight that led to a period of imprisonment, Downie once again turned to Picton for assistance. His benefactor not only secured his freedom, but was also instrumental in securing a post in the commissariat, an office not yet under the control of the military, but the Treasury.

After a few months in Portugal, Downie was clearly unhappy with his 'desk job' and openly hinted to his superiors that he wanted to relinquish it. In a letter from Castello Branco, 16 June 1809, he confessed to his superior, Deputy Commissary General Sir Charles Dalrymple, that on entering Spain, he had 'passed myself as an officer of General Cuesta's army, sent out for information and to reconnoitre the enemy and was taken in by every one as such from speaking Spanish'.[83] He sought to justify this bravado, which had entailed neglect of his commissariat duties, by pleading that he had left 'a person of confidence in charge'.[84] He must have received a cool response because in a further letter, annotated as a postscript, he told Dalrymple that 'should I err, I claim the justice of it being atributed (sic) to the head not to the heart'.[85] Wellington praised his efforts, but although considering him 'active and intelligent',[86] he never went beyond recommending his promotion to the position of assistant commissary.[87] On 22 July 1810, Downie

worthy of emulation. Spirits rose so high that upon the arrival of a Spanish government vessel in Trieste on 27 November 1808, a rumour was circulated to the effect that the Spanish Crown had been offered to Archduke Charles.[104] Spain would return to the halcyon days of Habsburg imperial rule. Thus, the balance of power in Europe could be restored. The dream proved short-lived. The Spaniards had never made any move towards a return to the times when it was at the heart of the Holy Roman Empire, and Austria's declaration of war against Napoleon on 9 April 1809 would end in defeat and the evacuation of Vienna. Earlier in that year, and despite pleas from Duff's in-laws, the influential Manners family, that he should return to a promising political career, the Scottish Earl-in-waiting decided to seek more adventures in a land of which he knew little except that a distant cousin and namesake, James Duff, was British consul in Cadiz.[105] Before leaving Vienna, he told a friend, John Sinclair Jr, that he wanted to satisfy his curiosity about the situation in Spain.[106] Having seen some military service as a lieutenant colonel in the Invernesshire Militia stationed in Edinburgh,[107] Duff (now holding the subsidiary dignity of Viscount Macduff)[108] offered his services to Gaspar Melchor de Jovellanos, then a leading member of the *Junta Central*, in a letter dated 23 March 1809. He said nothing about his personal reasons to enlist with the Spaniards, professing only that his greatest desire 'has been and will be to demonstrate the attachment I feel to the welfare of the Spanish Nation'.[109] Any misgivings on the part of the authorities seem to have been set aside in view of the Patriotic armies' need for experienced officers – and Duff's offer to serve unpaid.[110]

In his study of volunteers in the Boer War, Fransjohan Pretorius found that disputes with the military authorities in their home country could drive men to serve abroad.[111] In the Peninsula, there seems to be only one such case, that of Richard Lee, a captain in the Waterford Regiment who had, in effect, been suspended from service and placed on half-pay as a result of a 'a juvenile prank, due perhaps to excessive drink'.[112] Lee tried to join the Spanish army in order to return to active service. Although his former commander, General William Carr Beresford, now head of the allied armies in Portugal, supported the application, the Spanish authorities declined the offer.[113] They were not keen to recruit potential troublemakers.

Family-based loyalties were also a factor for enlisting abroad. Patrick Campbell encouraged his nephew, Neil MacDougall, to quit his native Scotland. Initially, the 23-year-old lieutenant in the 75th Regiment was granted leave by the commander-in-chief of the army, Sir David Dundas, to join the *Legión de Extremadura*, a regiment founded by John Downie.[114] But Campbell persuaded his young relative to join him instead in the Mallorca garrison. MacDougall lost his life within months of arrival while fighting alongside the *guerrillas* in the Battle of Castalla in which Campbell also saw action. Downie himself brought his brother, Charles, and his 16-year-old nephew, Benjamin Barrie, to join his legion.[115] William Parker Carrol enrolled his brothers Charles Morgan and Richard, as well as a cousin, Michael Carrol, in the Hibernia regiment of which he was then commander.[116]

From this examination of motives for service with the Spanish forces, it is now possible to form certain general conclusions. War volunteering seems to have been predominantly inspired by a combination of a desire to advance in a career – including the possibility of realizing the dream of becoming a hero or, as in the case of Henry Milburne, of extending medical knowledge – and admiration for the spirit of resistance among the Spaniards. The prevalence of these motivations seems to be reinforced by the lack of expressed interest in prospects of material gain. Although financial motives alone are insufficient to define a soldier as a mercenary,[117] their absence makes it difficult to place these British volunteers under that category, much less to brand them as soldiers of fortune. It is worth noticing that when it came to define the terms of their engagement, informality was the rule. No contract was ever signed with the Spanish authorities that guaranteed the payment of a specific amount of money, bounty, the offer of promotions or even of continuous employment. An agreement was certainly implied by the mere act of enlistment, often formalized through the granting of a commission, which included the promise of salary according to the pay scale of a particular rank. But if that commitment was not honoured, the chances of successfully pursuing a demand through the military courts of war-torn Spain were minimal. This chapter should perhaps also serve to illustrate the risk of over-reliance on assumptions regarding the weight that religious considerations might have exercised as a motivation to repulse the Napoleonic invasion in Spain. For Catholic British volunteers, the issue of religion appears to have been a minor factor – except where attachment to their faith constituted an obstacle to progress in the British military. If there is anything remarkable, it is the absence of any mention of wanting to advance an agenda of political or social change, particularly when the radical press in London adamantly demanded that British assistance to Spain should be made conditional to the adoption of fundamental reforms, including the adoption of constitutional representative government.[118] No proof has been found that the subject was even raised by Daniel Robinson, a first lieutenant in the Royal Navy and *teniente coronel de los Reales Ejércitos*, who has been identified as the author of the first full English translation of the Spanish Constitution of 1812, considered as the Liberal Codex of early nineteenth-century Europe.[119] While anti-Bonapartism was frequently voiced, it is also worth noticing that Landor's expressions of Francophobia were exceptional among men determined to fight a defensive war against a tyrant seen as having violated the liberty of a proud nation. A man such as James Duff could even correspond with figures close to the French forces, yet he was prepared to risk his life in a foreign land to challenge what was seen as the juggernaut of Napoleonic expansionism. There is little doubt that the war in Spain, a country unexpectedly recast in the role of a British ally, suddenly presented prospects of adventure and immersion in an exotic culture. But this should not be overstated. These men were not joining a pleasure cruise or looking for an experience in war tourism. They were prepared to kill and to die for the Spanish cause. Whether idealistic impulses always outweighed self-interested concerns is impossible to say; nonetheless, from all the evidence, there are no reasons to doubt that the sentiment shared overwhelmingly by a great majority of the volunteers was the desire to fight for the 'happiness, liberty, and prosperity [of] the Spanish nation'.[120]

Grounds for Action: The 'Spanish Cause'

Difficult collective undertakings often attract a shorthand phrase capable of summing up their reason and purpose. For the Patriots and their allies, that role was fulfilled by the 'Spanish cause' (*la causa española*). This was a set of views and ideals that both defined and sought to encourage participation in the war against Napoleon. As a concept, it would survive, *mutatis mutandis*, and within and beyond Iberian frontiers, well into the twentieth century.[1] Scarcely heard of before 1808, examples of the use of this expression during the 6-year struggle against Napoleon are too numerous to be included here,[2] which is remarkable considering that none of those who used it at the time appear to have ever tried to give it a definition. This chapter will not attempt to pin the butterfly and give it a name, but to describe what, it will be argued, was the multifaceted meaning of the Spanish cause encountered by the British volunteers.

A historiographical current of the last two decades has tended to doubt the very existence of a national cause. An influential argument put forward in Spain is that this concept belongs to the mythology created by moderate liberals during the reign of Isabel II (1833–68), as part of the invention of traditions that took place in most European nation states throughout the nineteenth century.[3] This included the term the 'War of Independence' (*la Guerra de Independencia*; in French, *La guerre d'indépendance espagnole*)[4] which, it is alleged, was invented to present what was an international conflict with aspects of civil war (French vs. British; pro-Napoleonic Spaniards vs. anti-Napoleonic Spaniards) as the people's fight for the freedom of their *patria*.[5] Napoleon's aim was not to convert the Spanish monarchy into a dependent territory of the French empire, but to substitute the ruling dynasty in what amounted to a replay of the War of Succession that a century earlier had forced the transition from Habsburg to Bourbon rule. Spanish liberals are accordingly described as collaborators of the anti-Napoleonic resistance.[6] From a different viewpoint, and distancing himself from earlier work,[7] Charles Esdaile contends that the risings against Napoleon 'were not the product of outraged patriotism'.[8] They should be seen as a collection of regional conspiracies and 'murky affairs'[9] by discontented office seekers, radicals in search of a political revolution, clerics horrified by Bourbon anti-clericalism and members of the aristocracy opposed to the creeping advance of royal authority.[10] As for the famous *guerrillas*, they were not the fruit of a great popular upsurge against the invaders, but the artificial creation of agents of the ruling authorities in league with groups of the Spanish elite whose self-interest happened to be bound up with the defence of the old regime.[11]

There is much to be said for many of these assertions, especially as they come from a generation of scholars committed to finding an antidote to the totalitarian and ultra-nationalistic miasma that pervaded all accounts of this period in Spanish textbooks, particularly during the dictatorships of Primo de Rivera and Francisco Franco.[12] The myth of a uniform, ever-bellicose resistance – the literal interpretation of the phrase 'the nation in arms' – founders on the facts. But there are also flaws in what a young Spanish historian has aptly named as 'an extreme current of revisionism'.[13] This is particularly the case with the theory of a post-conflict invention of a Spanish cause that presents problems when examined against written records relating to the experience of the British volunteers. The most basic objection occurs in regard to the term 'War of Independence', which appears, in literal and half-complete fashion ('independence' and/or *independencia*) in their writings as well as in those of many of their British and Spanish contemporaries.[14] For example, on 11 September 1808, in communication with the volunteer Charles Doyle, the British agent in Seville, Major William Cox, talked of the admiration he felt for the way 'Patriotick (sic) Men unite for the purpose of expelling a perfidious Enemy, of asserting the independence of their Country, of restoring their unfortunate Sovereign to his Throne, and re-establishing the National Form of Government'.[15] Thus described, the Spanish cause was a campaign of resistance and liberation carried out by people who voiced clearly defined and cogently presented demands. Although their interpretations could vary, as we shall see, the core of these demands remained unaltered. By the time the conflict was drawing to an end, the annual register *Guía política de las Españas para el año 1813* made a point of marking on its front page the year of publication as the fifth of the 'holy Spanish insurrection' and of the first sign of Spain's 'freedom and independence'.[16]

It would be easy to dismiss these examples as occasional flights of rhetoric if it were not the case that four years earlier a Catalan officer in the regiment *Guardias Walonas*, Francisco Xavier Cabanes, published a record of service precisely under the title *Historia de las operaciones del Exército de Cataluña en la Guerra de la Usurpación o sea de la Independencia de España* (*History of the Operations of the Army of Catalonia in the War of Usurpation viz the War of Spanish Independence*). This 15-chapter book enjoyed wide distribution, meriting a second edition, published in Mexico in 1810.[17] Cabanes was in Madrid at the time of the 1808 rising and, more by accident than design, found himself fighting with civilians in the streets of the capital. He alluded to the experience in the opening chapter of his book, providing testimony, not of a passive mob manipulated by selfish elites, but quite the contrary. He was startled by the way the multitude took the initiative and demanded action from the army and the political authorities who, he said rather euphemistically, had been left paralysed by embarking 'on a rational assessment of the risks' inherent in defying the intruders.[18] This account agrees with Ronald Fraser's empirical description of the events of 2 May as a plebeian-led revolt.[19] Being a professional military man, Cabanes was both elated and unsettled by this display of people's power. Popular patriotism drummed up resistance, but also had a propensity to favour knee-jerk reactions that resulted in unnecessary loss of lives.[20] When it came to analysing the conflict from a political perspective, by contrast, the Catalan officer had no doubts. While the war of 1701–14 had undeniably been a dynastic dispute, Bonaparte's appropriation of the Spanish throne was 'a felony' that had brought about the 'the rising of all Spaniards'.[21]

At the beginning of the conflict, the volunteers were equally persuaded that Spaniards were united in their zeal to liberate their country from Napoleonic rule. In correspondence with an English friend, in June 1808, the first volunteer to offer his services to the Spanish Patriots, Samuel Ford Whittingham, transmitted an encouraging picture of patriotism:

> I shall only observe that some of the most able Men in Spain are at the head of the new Government [probably the provincial *Junta* of Seville, his first official point of contact], and that the enthusiasm of the people is equal to what one should desire to see in England on a similar occasion.[22]

Although he soon began to question the capacity of the leadership, his opinion regarding the Spaniards' patriotic commitment remained unchanged. Even after the French entered the northern coastal town of Bilbao in preparation for a bigger assault on Madrid, he claimed that 'the enthusiasm of the Spaniards is worthy of their cause, and their bravery such as you would wish your best friends to possess'.[23] Eighteen months earlier, Whittingham had experienced defeat at the hands of Spaniards (American and *peninsulares*) who rose against the second British invasion of Buenos Aires.[24] He saw, therefore, no reason to doubt that his former enemies, now comrades-in-arms, could be nothing but solidly united by their 'worthy cause'. This was a popular war of self-determination, one that involved civilians as much as soldiers and generals. After all, he told his friends, the feature that distinguished this conflict from all others was that 'Bonaparte has now to fight a people'.[25]

It would be foolish to believe that every single Spaniard rose against the French, and even more to deny the existence of pro-French collaborators (*afrancesados*). Historians still debate if their number exceeded the 12,000 who emigrated at the time of the first Bourbon Restoration, although the growing consensus is that they constituted a minority within a disgruntled élite.[26] In any case, it cannot but appear striking that, in the very few instances that the *cause espagnole* surfaced in the pages of the French press, it was not to refer to the pro-French faction, but invariably to the Spanish insurgents.[27] The *afrancesados* failed to articulate their own all-inspiring Spanish cause, both abroad and at home. This was not for lack of trying. Under personal orders of the Emperor, the Spanish government of Joseph I unleashed a propaganda arsenal of 32 publications, added to the official *Gaceta de Madrid*.[28] The aim was to spread the promises of political and economic reform, modernization of the state administration and respect for Catholic religion enshrined in the Constitution of Bayonne (7 July 1808), as well as to counter any argument presented by the resistance.

From the seclusion of his palace in Madrid, Joseph was convinced that 'everybody will be here our friends if we talk about the independence of Spain, the liberty of the Nation, of its Constitution and of its *Cortes* (parliament)'.[29] The latter, however, was never convened. While the Patriotic government could do little to control the media, the press of the *afrancesados* was submitted to the censorship of the *Ministerio de Policia General* (General Ministry of Police), also in charge of confiscating any publication deemed sympathetic to the insurgency.[30] Yet, the Josephine administration drew little advantage from the information blackout. Dominated by a passion for rationalism and cultural regeneration,[31] the press of *el rey filósofo* (the philosopher king) deprived itself of recourse to three subjects that, anthropologists tell us, were hallmarks of Hispanic identity: the attachment to traditions and to a glorious past, the universality and pre-eminence of the Catholic religion and the safeguard of honour.[32] Popular religious festivities were thus treated with contempt or transformed into feasts of utilitarianism. In occupied Santander, for example, Saint Joseph's Day (19 March) ceased to provide the chance of a pious and joyful rest, to become instead an occasion to praise the eponymous monarch through the accomplishment of useful deeds such as opening a fish market, digging potatoes and planting trees.[33] No mention could be made to key events in Spanish history because, for the most part, they were related to the building of an overseas empire that dwarfed the French or to the resistance and eventual expulsion of invaders, no matter whether they were the Carthaginians or the Moors. Yet, these events appear to have been deeply ingrained in the Spanish psyche. Soon after the fall of Saragossa – and to the great annoyance of Napoleon who wrote from Paris to point out the blunder – the Minister of War, Gonzalo O'Farrill, committed twice the *bêtise* of alluding in proclamations to the siege of Sagunto (219–218 BC), the Valencian city that after 9 months of resistance turned itself into ashes before falling into the hands of Hannibal.[34]

Three years into his reign, Joseph desperately tried to win over the populace by attending Mass, and through the legalisation of bullfighting, that emblematic theatrical display of Spanish honour put to the test for the collective pleasure of witnessing an invariably triumphant outcome. The bloodletting spectacle had been banned in 1805 by the similarly enlightened, and despised, regime of Godoy, but the prohibition was hardly ever enforced until the French arrived. Now, Joseph offered free entry to the *corridas*, but with little avail. A few cheers shouted by grateful punters fell short of giving him the consensual support needed to consolidate his position as a legitimate Spanish king.[35] Napoleon had already reached the conclusion that the charm offensive would produce little, if any, positive result. Coercion, not persuasion, had to be the policy of preference towards Spaniards. In 1810, he decreed that the whole of northern Spain should be divided into a number of military districts whose governors would be responsible to Paris.[36] Once the illusion of respecting the integrity of the Spanish territory, guaranteed by the Constitution of Bayonne, was shattered, the whole dream of conjuring into life a Napoleonic Spanish cause just collapsed.

Such a failure perhaps serves to illustrate the perils of attempting to manufacture a national cause, particularly when the task is left in the hands of a fringe group lacking in credibility. In the eyes of the vast majority of the Spanish population, the *afrancesados* were not dissenters who offered an alternative model of governance. They were traitors who had forfeited their Spanishness through their betrayal and whose property, as the volunteer and British agent Charles Doyle once suggested, should be 'immediately confiscated and divided amongst the soldiers; their houses burned and they themselves hanged'.[37] In occupied areas, these measures became the weapon of choice of an insurgency that could easily turn into banditry, sometimes helping and on occasions hindering war efforts, yet at all times committed to the Spanish cause.[38] Anybody who subscribed to Napoleon's regime, no matter whether they collaborated from ideological affinity or as means of survival under foreign occupation, was a legitimate target, an aberration, a 'degenerate',[39] the exception that confirmed the rule of unanimity in the Spanish resistance against the French invader.

This view might seem at odds with the numerous examples of disagreements in the Patriots' ranks that have coloured much of the historiography. The volunteers themselves noticed that discord was rife, particularly within the Spanish military hierarchy. In August 1808, Doyle highlighted in a letter to Arthur Wellesley what he interpreted as personal rivalries between the leading Spanish generals:

> Think of General Cuesta refusing to send his Cavalry! [to the aid of Saragossa] and General Castaños allowing his army (. . .) particularly his cavalry to remain (. . .) in Andalusia, the Cavalry of Extremadura in the same way, and yet that army can be thus (. . .) wanted in either Province.[40]

If most Spaniards were united in their desire to repel the French advance, it was equally true that they found it almost impossible to agree on how to do it. Spain was in urgent need of a coordinated command structure to iron out internal differences and thus release the power of Spanish patriotism through a proper liberation effort. Doyle and his colleague Whittingham sought to foster such consensus with the organization of a Council of War, which took place near Madrid, in September 1808. Although the objective of a single command remained elusive, the meeting resulted in the first organization of the provincial armies into a national force.[41]

Many disputes were caused by inter-regional tensions. In the wake of the collapse of the central administration, civil *juntas* took control of the government in provincial capitals such as Oviedo, Valladolid, Badajoz, Seville, Valencia and Saragossa. These bodies – as well as those that appeared in the Spanish colonies – responded to an old Castilian tradition, the '*Ley de Partida*', that called in times of emergency for the formation of local governments by 'magistrates, priests, rich men and other good and honest men'.[42] In Catalonia, with Barcelona occupied by the French, *juntas* were organized in the towns of Lérida, Manresa, Tortosa, Villafranca del Panadés and Gerona. By the end of June 1808, all were united under a General *Junta* of the Principality. All these bodies claimed to exercise sovereign power on behalf of Ferdinand VII as the embodiment of the Hispanic monarchy. Almost all of these *juntas* raised their own armies. It was to them that many of the volunteers first became attached: in the Asturian army, *teniente de infanteria* James Arbuthnot and *coronel* Philippe Keating Roche; in the Galician, *teniente coronel* William Parker Carrol; in the Aragonese, *brigadier general* Charles Doyle; in the Extremadurian *teniente coronel* Patrick Campbell; and in the Andalusian, *coronel* Samuel Ford Whittingham.[43]

Claiming rights associated with its old status as the administrative hub of Spanish America, the *junta* of Seville attributed to itself the title of 'Supreme *Junta* of Spain and the Indies'.[44] This body happened to control the best and biggest Spanish force under the command of General Francisco Javier Castaños.[45] The overwhelming victory of Castaños's forces at Bailén (19 July 1808), Napoleon's first battle defeat, encouraged some in the Seville government to seek an increased sphere of influence. In a letter to his brother-in-law, on 11 August 1808, Whittingham described an incident caused by one member of the *junta*, Count de Tilly, who proposed that the region governed by the neighbouring *junta* of Granada, with which there had been some disputes, should be annexed by force.

> General Castaños then arose from his seat, and, striking the table with his hand, he said, "And who is the man that will dare to lead a division of my army, contrary to my orders? I do not consider the army I have the honour to command as the army of Andalusia, but as the army of Spain, and never will I stain the laurels which it has won by suffering it to become the vile instrument of civil discord. The affairs of Granada may be amicably and easily settled". As soon as the General had done speaking, Don Vicente Ori stood up, taking off his *banda* [sash], threw it upon the table, saying that he would never be a member of any body where such words as those which he had just heard from Count de Tilly were tolerated. The discussion ended by an apology on the part of the Count for what he had said, and a recantation of his ideas upon the subject of civil war.[46]

This episode has been singled out as an example of the *junta* of Seville's 'campaign of aggrandizement'.[47] On close examination, it rather appears a failed attempt by a minority to extend their power base. The unanimous support of the members of the *junta* to Castaños' retort, including the 'recantation' of Count de Tilly who Whittingham, at any rate, considered a troublemaker,[48] shows that the Spanish cause could neutralize disputes within the Patriots' ranks. There is no doubt that many Spaniards struggled, and even failed, to live up to patriotic expectations. Doyle called these people the 'clogs which need to be removed'.[49] Indeed, as it will become clearer in the following pages, a great deal of the work carried out by the British volunteers consisted of eliminating such obstacles, many resulting from pre-existing social tensions and rivalries heightened by the war. But meanness and selfishness were not the absolute norm. Most Patriots accepted, almost instinctively, that the priority was to fight for the survival of Spanish territorial integrity and cultural identity. All 'egoisms' – a term frequently used by Spaniards to refer to their numerous shortcomings both at local and personal level –[50] were to be left behind. The *Junta* of Catalonia, for example, made it a requirement for all its members to pledge to 'provide all possible assistance to the rest of the provinces [of Spain] that are fighting for the same cause'.[51] The fall of the *Junta Central* in January 1810 would lead many of the Latin American *juntas* to demand autonomy within the empire. A year later, some even called for secession from an Iberian regime that seemed doomed. None, however, ever sided with the French.[52]

In Aragon, the crisis caused by the French invasion led to the revival of old institutional structures alien to Castilian tradition. Proclaimed governor of Saragossa and captain general of Aragon (25 May 1808), the first political act of José Rebolledo de Palafox y Melci was to summon the Aragonese *Cortes*, which had been abolished with the rest of that kingdom's *fueros* by the *Nueva Planta* decrees of 1707–16.[53] The man who was to give volunteer Charles Doyle his rank of *mariscal de campo* in the Spanish army[54] called this *Cortes* not only to have his appointment confirmed and request counsel, but also to proclaim Ferdinand VII as the only legitimate monarch.[55] Unlike the War of Succession, there were no anti-Bourbon risings in Aragon and Catalonia.[56] A return to the model of multiple *regnum* of the Habsburgs did not entail the removal from the throne of the Bourbons, even less of its newest incumbent of whom Palafox was, at the time, a close friend. With his power legitimized by the Aragonese *Cortes* on 9 June 1808, Palafox launched a strong verbal attack against the Council of Castile for its inactivity during the French invasion. He implied that its pusillanimity was treacherous as well as confirmation that, in its hour of need, the Castilian-orientated model of government had failed to preserve the integrity of the Spanish monarchy. Palafox challenged the Council to immediately summon deputies from all the provinces with the double mission of naming the head of the Spanish army and constituting a new national government.[57] His antagonism towards the Council extended to its former president, the Duke of Infantado, who joined the Patriots after having been in the entourage that accompanied Ferdinand VII to Bayonne. Doyle attempted a reconciliation bid, offering himself to arbitrate between the 'two men who could save Spain',[58] but his efforts were obstructed by the second siege of Saragossa and Palafox's imprisonment in France.[59] At any rate, it was clear that for the leader of the Aragonese, the Spanish cause was a call to resist the French as well as an opportunity to restore a less centralized political system.

It would be certainly anachronistic to read in Palafox's actions even the mildest form of separatism. He stated this clearly to the interim president of the Council of Castile, Arias Mon y Velaverde:

> Because in the case I might be useful to my Motherland, of course I consider as
> such the whole of Spain, and although I had no little to do to preserve the capital
> of Aragon, considering it a place strategically important for the defence of the
> rest of the Nation, I assisted Navarre, La Rioja and Catalonia, and I found later
> that they reciprocated.[60]

The implication of his statement was clear: the Patriots' cause could be nothing but 'Spanish'. Similar was the view of the Patriots in Catalonia. During the second siege of Gerona, the longest of the war,[61] Irish volunteer Rudolf Marshal lost his life leading a mixed group of Catalan *guerrilleros* and local ad-hoc militias known as *somatents* and *miguelets*. On 23 September 1809, the *Diario de Gerona*, the four-page daily newspaper published (in Spanish, rather than Catalan) by the besieged, highlighted that the last words of the Irish volunteer were that he died happy to have defended 'the cause of so brave a Nation'.[62] Whether these words were ever pronounced it is hard to say; nonetheless, the meaning of the term 'Nation' can be fathomed from a letter that Marshal addressed to the British consul in Cadiz, James Duff, only a few weeks earlier:

> I hope the Nation is satisfied with poor Gerona. She has detained the whole
> French Army of Cataluña for now more than 17 weeks, the most important
> weeks of the year and has paid all the expenses of every kind herself having
> received from the Nation only 200,000 Reales (10,000 Dol.) altho her expenses
> are 2,000 dollars a day.[63]

Marshal's 'Nation' was not Catalonia, but the *Monarquía Hispana*, then represented by the *Junta Central*, which had, indeed, ordered the nearby *Junta* of Tarragona to dispatch 200,000 reales to the defenders of Gerona in May 1809.[64] The eventual fall of Gerona, followed by the French occupation of much of the principality's territory, encouraged a pre-existing distrust of the Catalans towards the Spanish central government. Volunteer Edwin Green attributed this attitude to their conviction that the *Junta Central* was Castilian prone, thus it could not have their interests at heart.[65] Yet, the Catalan Patriots never advocated a model of governance removed from the Spanish sphere. Perhaps reflecting what some historians consider as 'dual patriotism' (love for both the *patria chica*, Catalonia, and the *patria grande*, Spain),[66] they remained fully engaged in what they called *la guerra del Francès* (the war against the French) as well as in la *guerra de la independencia española* (the war of Spanish independence).[67]

The retreat and death of Sir John Moore in Galicia, the second fall of Madrid, Wellington's Pyrrhic victory at Talavera (27–8 July 1809) followed by a series of Spanish defeats contributed to seed doubts in Whitehall about the strength, unity and commitment of their ally. A British agent who was serving in the *Ejército de la Izquierda* (Army of the Left), William Parker Carrol, felt compelled to uphold the vision of a Spanish community of purpose in a letter to the British Foreign Secretary, Marquis Richard Wellesley:

> It has been a subject of painful regret to learn that I, as well as other officers employed in Spain, appeared to some individuals to have overrated, if not misrepresented the zeal and patriotism of the Spanish people. If there was no patriotism in Spain when the British army entered it, in the name of common sense what power has operated to continue the war under every disadvantage the armies had to encounter since that period and to afford us a well-grounded hope of a favourable termination of the contest? (. . .) I know I have been thought by some to have painted in too glowing colours the enthusiasm of the Patriots, all I can say is, that I painted agreeably to the impressions left on my mind. If my prism magnified, it was an error on the right side, and I should deem myself culpable had I thrown cold water on the flame, had I frozen the genial current of Patriotism (. . .) The Patriotic Cause, notwithstanding the challenges and reverses it has met with, bears a good appearance. I may be enthusiastic, but I cannot resign my firm and fixed opinion, that Spain will never be subjugated to the Tyrant of the Continent.[68]

Carrol's assessment was not the result of a first impression. At the time of penning this letter, he had already served 2 years in the Spanish army and witnessed many of the disasters that followed Moore's defeat at Corunna.[69] Yet, he was able to recognize in the Spaniards – particularly those in the lower classes – a steadfast resolution to defend their land and national identity, the latter simply defined by their determination not to be absorbed into the French political and cultural sphere. Moreover, such a 'genial current of Patriotism'[70] had the strange quality of turning every defeat into an opportunity to regenerate military might against the foreign invader. Carrol's views remained the same throughout and even after the war ended. In 1823, with Bourbon France preparing to invade Spain to remove the liberal government, *mariscal de campo* Carrol twice offered to abandon his position of lieutenant governor of Malta to 'immediately run in her (Spain's) defence as at the time of the (previous) invasion'.[71]

If the campaign of 1822–23 had strong political implications, the one that preceded it had a few as well. Writing from Gibraltar, on 5 June 1808, Whittingham mentioned something along those lines when he underscored that

> the spirit of the people is wound up to a pitch of enthusiasm almost beyond anything one can form an Idea of without seeing it, and by the absence of their weak monarchs, they have all the advantages of a revolution without its terrific consequences![72]

At this very early stage of the conflict, it seems that for Whittingham the Spanish cause had also the appearance of a bloodless revolution – an opportunity to introduce changes in the political structure of Spain without the 'terrific consequences' of a civil war. The years of the corrupt, pro-French Godoyist administration were to be left behind. Indeed, fellow volunteer Carrol described Spanish patriotism as a 'bud' of national renewal that had managed to show 'its head through the heap of rubbish and labyrinth of weeds with which this luxuriant Garden has been overrun for upwards of 20 years'.[73] If the crisis had created a chance for political reform, the restoration of Ferdinand VII to the throne was out of bounds of any change. Any implied criticism of *El Deseado* (the Desired one) was soon banished from the volunteers' correspondence as they acknowledged that Spaniards would never recognize any other cause than 'that one of Ferdinand VII, which is that of Spain'.[74]

British volunteers worked with all successive Patriotic governments and many welcomed the call of the *Cortes* in Cadiz, which they viewed as the chance to unite the country and legitimize the government after the catastrophic vacuum left by the imprisonment of the crowned heads of the Bourbon dynasty.[75] Although no evidence has been found to assert that they considered constitutional reform – the fundamental task of the *Cortes* – an indivisible part of the Spanish cause, what is undeniable is that the subject dominated the spirits of many in the Spanish élite. In April 1809, the rich merchant, Lorenzo Calvo de Rozas, who had been appointed by Palafox as secretary of the Aragonese *Cortes*, advanced the idea of a written Spanish Constitution as the best means to achieve 'the principal object, that is the defence of our independence, the expulsion of the enemy and the freedom of our captive monarch'.[76] These goals may recall those mentioned earlier by the British agent Major William Cox – but there was something subtly different in de Rozas' remarks. He told Spaniards that they were fighting 'not to place their restored independence under the free will of a capricious Court, of an ambitious favourite or of the personal qualities of a sovereign'.[77] If the invader had flattered Spaniards with the promise of a constitutional regime, he had to be opposed with a system 'with the same end'.[78] In this interpretation of events, the Spanish cause needed to embrace a thorough reform of the old regime as a way of counteracting Napoleon's Constitution of Bayonne. His idea was welcomed by some of his peers at the *Junta Central*, particularly the representatives of the provinces of Galicia, Catalonia, Castille, Murcia, Alava, Rioja and Leon led by the future liberal leader José María Queipo de Llano y Ruiz de Sarabia, Count de Toreno and the clergyman Guillermo Hualde. On 17 June 1810, they urged the Regency to convene the *Cortes* to keep the cause relevant to the people, so 'they will see that they are not only fighting to expel the enemy, but also to consolidate their future happiness'.[79]

Not all Patriots agreed. Conservatives found a powerful voice in Pedro Caro y Sureda, Third Marquess de La Romana. A hero of the War of the First Coalition against revolutionary France (1793–95) and former captain general of Catalonia, Romana had become a legend after he ingeniously brought back (with British assistance) 9,000 of the 14,000 men of his 'Division of the North' that Charles IV had dispatched to Denmark in aid to Napoleon. Coming from a family that held influence in the Bourbon court,[80] Romana was not ready to accept the notion of 'popular sovereignty' already implied in many of the communications of the *Junta Central* of which he was a member. In December 1809, he warned his colleagues that if they pursued that line, they would risk losing their legitimacy because, he argued, the Spanish Constitution was monarchical and the Spanish people 'had never pretended to rule as sovereign'.[81] If they had appointed and supported provincial *juntas* and the *Junta Central*, it was because they saw them 'as an Image of the King'.[82] Any constitutional innovation, he warned, would lead to anarchy, civil war and the end of the Spanish cause.[83]

Although such reform went ahead regardless, there was an element of truth in his gloomy prognosis: from that point, the cause acquired an additional, yet different meaning for those Patriots who saw it as a fight for political reform and those who saw it as a war against uninvited innovations brought about by the French invasion. Still, this conflicting addition did not change the fundamental premise of the Spanish cause as a national struggle for liberation. Neither questioned in any way the strength of what has been called 'ethno-patriotism',[84] an emotional attachment to a vaguely defined ethnic and cultural group and a political community built around the monarchy and the Church. This sense of Spanishness, traced back to the sixteenth century by historians such as Tamara Herzog and Mateo Ballester Rodriguez[85] and explored by Jorge Cañizares-Esguerra and Scott Eastman for this period,[86] was shared by all Patriots, no matter whether or not they celebrated the birth of a political nation proclaimed by the Constitution of 1812. It seems futile to deny that rather than unite Spaniards behind a single political nation, the *Cortes* of Cadiz would contribute to splitting them apart,[87] but as Brian Hamnett noticed some years ago, it is a testimony to the binding effect of the opposition to Napoleon's hegemony that this did not happen openly until the war was well and truly over.[88] The British volunteers who fought under Romana, such as William Parker Carrol and Reginald Macdonell,[89] were absolutely devoted to the general, but did not necessarily agree with his political opinions. Carrol, for example, was an early advocate of summoning a national *Cortes*,[90] he pledged his oath to the Constitution of 1812 and remained a staunch supporter of the Spanish constitutional government. Moreover, when it came to advancing the objective of liberation, his actions, as we shall see in Chapter 4, accorded little with his political convictions.[91] The cause of *liberalism* should not be confused with that of *liberation*. All Patriots rallied behind the latter regardless of their political opinions.

There was another point on which they also concurred: their cause was *justa* (just).[92] This conviction fitted within the modern interpretation of a just war as a collective act of self-defence and resistance to aggression[93] rather than within the traditional remit of a conflict fought for religious or political purposes.[94] There is no doubt that the Patriots' struggle implied the preservation of the Catholic faith from the perceived threat of French atheism as well as the defence of honour. So-called *cruzadas* were, indeed, organized in a few provinces,[95] but they were not intended to enforce the mass conversion of infidels or the annexation of new territories for Christendom. The idea was to evoke a past that conferred on Spaniards a reputation for snatching victory from the jaws of defeat by sheer fanatical determination in the expectation that this would rouse national pride in the ranks and instil terror in the invaders. On 14 February 1811, John Downie called the people living in French-occupied areas of the province of Cáceres to join his *Legión de Extremadura* in the defence of 'honour, law, religion and the captive Ferdinand VII'.[96] By then, he had already pledged to give his 'life, fortune, everything for Spain, everything for the just cause she defends'.[97] Spain had been wronged by its erstwhile French ally. Honour needed to be satisfied. As the war progressed into an ever-increasing cycle of indiscriminate violence, it became clear that this yearning could add a dark meaning to the Spanish cause.

> Look at your Province felled by the vandals of the Seine; look at your Religion mocked, and your temples ravaged by the destroyers of Europe; turn your eyes back to your old parents and to your tender children atrociously sacrificed by the fury of these barbarians; consider your wives and sweet daughters, victims of the licentiousness and brutality of these monsters . . . Revenge, revenge, shouts the honour of Spain, and your ears cannot be deafened to such an imperious voice.[98]

Downie's incitement to take revenge underscored an important question regarding the scope of the Spanish cause: was it a struggle to annihilate the enemy, thus a mission that could entail taking the fight to the other side of the Pyrenees in order to engage in a policy of regime change in France; or was it a campaign limited to pushing back the enemy to his own territory, forcing him to sign an armistice? The latter was the view favoured by Spaniards at the beginning of the conflict. Sent to negotiate the details of the Anglo-Spanish alliance, Major General Lord William Henry Cavendish Bentinck noticed during a meeting with Patriot generals in Madrid that Spaniards had little appetite for a fight outside their frontiers. He pressed the matter regardless, stating that 'no diversion could be more effectual and more formidable to Bonaparte than the march of a large combined British and Spanish army over the Pyrenees'. Crucially, he added that if Spaniards approved, Great Britain 'would be glad to send at once into Spain every disposable man at her command'.[99] General Castaños poured cold water on the idea, thanking Bentick for the offer while warning that if the British army was to join the fight in the Peninsula, it would be in the capacity of an 'auxiliary force' of the Spanish army.[100]

Bentinck's proposal, which tied British military participation to Spanish acceptance of an assault on French territory, had revealed a gap in the interpretation of the 'common cause'. On 4 July 1808, in a speech read by the Lord Chancellor in both houses of Parliament, George III had promised to make 'every exertion in His power for the support of the Spanish cause' with no other object than

> That of preserving, unimpaired, the integrity and independence of the Spanish Monarchy. But He trusts that the same efforts which are directed to that great object, may, under the blessing of Divine Providence, lead, in their efforts, and by their example, to the restoration of the Liberties and the Peace of Europe.[101]

The 'but' opening the last sentence was full of meaning. From a British perspective, the Spanish cause provided a chance to establish an Iberian bridgehead from which to turn the tide against Napoleon after a decade of confrontation. In pursuit of that far-reaching goal, British policy towards Spain waxed and waned, alternating from the exuberant project of an allied offensive on French territory to considering, at least once, in early 1810, a strategic disengagement, that is abandoning Spain to Napoleon.[102] It is no accident that the conflict is known in Britain as the 'Peninsular War' – a term that only began to be in vogue, at least in the British press, from late in that year.[103] Fighting in Spain was only a means to a much bigger objective. For Spaniards, by contrast, the war was one of self-determination, thus primarily confined to their territory. The British volunteers subscribed wholeheartedly to the emancipatory view. Yet, it was precisely for that reason that they also gave heed to the idea of chasing the enemy 'perhaps even up to Paris',[104] anticipating with that, the change of heart that would lead Spaniards to invade the south of France under Wellington's command in the summer of 1813.[105] Five years of waging a devastating war would lead Spaniards to the same conclusion: there was no other way to secure their independence.

So, it seems that the Spanish cause could present itself under different guises among those who fought against Napoleon. For the British volunteers, who never doubted its existence, it was permanently fixed on the fundamental mission of expelling the French invader, fighting with the Spanish people, no matter the fluctuations in official British policy. The introduction of political reforms, the defence of cultural heritage, mores and religion, and even the possibility of engaging in retaliation – if not necessarily regime change – on the other side of the Pyrenees could, at times, be embraced, but only as subsidiaries emanating from the basic goal of liberation. A feature in this evolving, and often conflicting concept also remained constant: its popular character. As the expression of a people's war, the Spanish cause marked a watershed in the European struggle against Napoleon. It was a cause to which foreigners could relate, feel emotionally attached and even subscribe. Within Iberian frontiers, this had other implications. One could ask, for example, whether liberal reformers would have ever dared to advance the principle of 'popular sovereignty' if they had not been riding on the wave of a people's revolt.[106] Indeed, questions might always be posed about the nature of the conflict for the purpose of academic analysis, but the evidence presented here suggests that contemporaries had no hesitation in considering it a struggle for independence initiated, and largely sustained, by common people. Even the enemy seems to have acknowledged this by associating the term '*la cause espagnole*' with the insurgency and by its ill-judged efforts to provide a persuasive competing discourse.

We should be weary, no doubt, of romanticising the concept of a 'people's war'. Two years into the conflict, General Castaños lamented that the 'populace who compose the greatest mass of the Nation' have had 'the first voice in our glorious revolution' because being 'full of enthusiasm and unacquainted with other principles, admitting of no other ideas than those of attack, they urge, induce and compel the execution of plans on generals against their own convictions'.[107] The flame of visceral patriotism, it turned out, could only be quenched in blood. If left to its own devices, a war driven by popular diktat would have driven the liberation enterprise onto a path of self-destruction. Castaños's preoccupation had little to do with imposing the use of regular over irregular forces. The victor of Bailén saw no such dichotomy: he favoured an integrated approach that would multiply the number of guerrilla forces, rather than subsuming them under the army. What troubled Castaños was the 'disconcerted system of improvident means' so far applied by the Patriots. The Spanish cause was in desperate need of leadership and coordination. He was not alone in that opinion, but among the British volunteers there were many who, for better or worse, would try to do something to change that situation.

4

An Ideology of Single-Mindedness

The imprisonment of the Bourbon kings and the all-too-visible fissures in the model that so far had allowed the functioning of the Spanish Monarchy turned the liberation of Spain into a campaign where military and political matters were often intertwined. This chapter aims to trace the volunteers' involvement in the political arena. Particular attention will be paid to their role in the reconfiguration of local and national institutions and to the way they navigated between frequently divergent positions held by the British and Spanish governments. The extent to which they became embroiled in partisan politics and, crucially, if they were driven by any specific ideology will also be assessed. This examination will be made by reference to some key episodes in their participation in the war that illustrate in some detail how they were quick to recognize the uneasy symbiosis in which the military and the political spheres operated in the Hispanic world.

This awareness can be easily observed in the case of those volunteers who were originally sent to Spain by the British government with the specific – and limited – mission of gathering information on military operations and of expressing only the 'desire'[1] of the British government to give assistance to the Spanish Patriots. Soon after arriving at Santander, on 1 August 1808, Major Philip Keating Roche informed the Secretary of War, Lord Castlereagh that, confronted with a war of words between the Cantabrian government and their counterparts in Asturias, he took the step of intervening 'to reconcile those differences and unite if possible at this critical moment all parties in the Common Cause of the Country'.[2] He claimed success in the undertaking, but warned that inter-provincial harmony remained fragile because disputes were the result 'of the want of a general Government'[3] and that 'until a *Cortes* or Regency is established the Spaniards can never be totally formidable to the French'.[4] The message was clear: without political unity, victory in the war could never be achieved. The problem was that arbitration between provincial governments was never in his brief. Uncharacteristically for a military agent – but less for a man who a fortnight later would be appointed *coronel* in the Asturian army[5] – Roche had no hesitation in earmarking the Duke of Infantado for the role of Regent.[6] An anti-Godoyist friend of Ferdinand VII who had him appointed head of the royal council (the Council of Castile), Pedro de Alcántara Toledo, Duke of Infantado had accompanied the new King on his ill-fated trip across the Pyrenees and appears to have rallied to Napoleon to the point of contributing to the draft of the Constitution of Bayonne. However, after the Patriots' victory at Bailén, he decided, like many others, to declare for the Spanish cause.[7] Perhaps due to his close association with the King, Roche was led to believe that Infantado was still 'greatly beloved' by the people and thus predicted that

> Such a man, *as Regent* would act like electricity upon the whole Nation and until something of this sort happens, it is in vain to hope for ultimate and permanent success.[8]

A week later, from the Asturian port of Gijon, Roche stressed the need for British political intervention stating that 'there will be *no Salvation* for this country' without 'the British government pressing the respective juntas'.[9] He suggested that Britain should make conditional the delivery of money and military supplies until they were formally requested by 'a general Assembly of the *Cortes*, at such place *as England shall point out*', for unless the British government took that decision, the provinces 'will be engaged in useless disputes & discussions upon the subject'.[10] The British government reacted unenthusiastically. Castlereagh praised Roche's efforts for conciliation and promised a promotion, yet at the same time summarily repeated the original terms of his brief by way of prelude to informing that he had just been placed under the orders of Major General Leith who was sent to Asturias 'to assist the (military) efforts of the Province'.[11] It was clear that Britain had no desire to be dragged into Spanish politics.

Roche's views were taken up by his fellow Irish colleague, Charles William Doyle. In his double role as British military agent and *brigadier general* in the Army of Aragon, Doyle organized with another British volunteer, Samuel Ford Whittingham, Captain in the British army and *coronel* in the Army of Andalusia, what they described to the British authorities as a 'Council of War' held in the Madrid home of the Duke of Infantado.[12] Attended by the leaders of the main provincial armies, the meeting on 5 September 1808 resulted in the amalgamation of their military resources into a national force organized in four armies: those of the Left (Galicia, Asturias and the army of the Marquess de la Romana in transit from Denmark), the Centre (Leon, Castile and Seville), the Right (Catalonia, and a few forces from Saragossa and Granada) and of Reserve (Aragon and Valencia).[13] But the reorganization of the Spanish forces was far from the only subject on the agenda. Doyle was convinced that this was the moment to advance the candidature of the Duke of Infantado as head of a Regency government. He thought that this grandee could 'very well assume a tone of authority which just now is so much wanting' because 'he may well be looked upon as the organ of King Ferdinand'.[14] He stated this to Castlereagh only four days before the Secretary of War had dismissed Roche's similar suggestion. By then, Doyle had already prevailed upon Infantado to travel to Madrid with precisely that objective in mind.[15] The meeting of representatives from all the provinces that would establish the first national government, the 35-member *Junta Central*, was scheduled for the end of the month at the nearby town of Aranjuez. Doyle 'sounded the officers of the Army'[16] and, he said, found them 'unanimous'[17] in their opinion that Infantado should be elected Regent.[18]

Doyle hoped that the King's friend, in association with an assembly composed of representatives from all the provinces, rather than the resulting *Junta Central* which blended executive and legislative authority, would have been able to curtail the 'great power' arrogated by provincial governments, particularly the one represented by the *Junta* of Seville.[19] Having adopted the name of 'Supreme *Junta* of Spain and the Indies', the Andalusians seemed determined to make the *Junta Central* stillborn by simply refusing to pay the upkeep of their provincial army when it was engaged in operations coordinated by the national government. The Army of Andalusia, under the command of the victor of Bailén, General Francisco Javier Castaños, was the strongest of the Spanish Patriotic forces.[20] Without it, there was little chance of mounting an effective counteroffensive against the French.

From the itinerant headquarters of the Spanish army in the northwest of the country, William Parker Carrol, captain in the British Army and *teniente coronel* of the Army of Galicia, had been encouraging Doyle to press ahead with his political plans because, he warned:

> If you leave it before the members from the different provincial juntas are met and *united* in a general Council of the Nation I dread the consequences. Indeed if you do not remain to reconcile their parting interests, and endeavour to amalgamate these hitherto unassimilating obscure (and in many instances [one word not clear] bodies) I have my fear. . . .[21]

Carrol counselled that all decisions should be made 'in the name of the Council *of the Nation*'[22] because he dreaded that 'the Duke of Infantado acting alone in the hands of the Council of Castile, only his most innocent intentions may be [one word unclear] and misrepresented'.[23] During the Madrid uprisings, the Council of Castile's fear of disorder made it side with the French invaders.[24] The majority of its members later recanted, but the shadow of collaboration with the French lingered over the institution. Although Infantado had not been in Madrid at the time of the revolt, he risked suffering a similar fate if he claimed to be entitled to lead the executive national government based solely on the restoration of the royal council.

These men knew perfectly well that by treading into the political arena they were going outside their role as British military agents. Carrol said as much to Doyle when he noted that as from now

> Your Mission remaining [sic] a separate one as far as relates to your acting entirely as you may deem expedient, which is your duty to the cause you have undertaken to assist.[25]

It was only as an afterthought that Carrol suggested that Doyle should request from Lord Castlereagh some 'freedom of action'.[26] He was sure that this would be granted because, as he told his Irish comrade, 'it only requires a statesman of the influence that you ordinarily possess over all ranks of people in this country' to induce Lord Castlereagh to confer 'you *card* [sic] *blanche*'.[27] Never was confidence more misplaced. Doyle's actions caused alarm in London. On 31 August 1808, the Under-Secretary of War, Edward Cooke, issued a letter expressing Lord Castlereagh's 'strong dissatisfaction'[28] with Doyle for exceeding his instructions when he accompanied the Duke of Infantado to Madrid and took 'measures to have him appointed Regent and to form a Council of Generals for determining upon future operations'.[29] This was an emphatic confirmation of London's lack of interest in Spanish political matters and a clear reminder that the British government expected their military agents to be nothing more than a pair of eyes and ears.

In the event, Doyle's political plans were hijacked by a crisis created by the scarcity of money to fund the operations of the recently reassembled Spanish army. This happened just as the French were gathering forces to launch an attack on Saragossa – an offensive that was to open the way to Madrid.[30] Doyle joined forces with Whittingham to have 200,000 pesos delivered by the British consul James Duff to the *Junta* of Seville redirected to cover the cost of a Spanish counteroffensive.[31] This was not an easy task. The Andalusian *junta* dragged its feet, demanding that the rest of the provinces should shoulder the financial burden and citing practical reasons, including that the money had been sent in bars of silver that needed to be coined.[32] After much arguing, Doyle managed to get the needed funding, which he delivered in person,[33] marking an important victory for the Spanish cause over the forces of self-centred regionalism.

In the emergency, the candidature of Infantado for the Regency was set aside, but this no longer seemed to matter. Infantado himself had decided instead to take control of the forces defending the capital. Although this proved to be an unlucky choice, the *Junta Central* gave him the command of the Army of the Centre. In 1811, after further military misfortunes, he was made ambassador to London. Yet, the Duke did eventually become not only Regent but also a member of the first constitutional Council of Regency, ruling from the period immediately before the proclamation of the Constitution of 1812 until March 1813.[34] Meanwhile, Doyle's achievements strengthened the conviction among the British volunteers that military and political activities could not be completely disassociated from each other.

The so-called Marquess de La Romana's coup

Such a view was to have important repercussions in Asturias, where William Parker Carrol took a leading role in an incident described by some historians as the founding moment of the period of military intervention in Spanish politics: the so-called *coup d'état* of Pedro Caro Sureda, Marquess de la Romana.[35] To fully grasp the implications of this episode, first it is necessary to describe the conditions and circumstances from which it developed, particularly as Asturias was – and in many ways still remains – one of the most distinctive regions of Spain. A landscape of rugged coastal cliffs and high mountains, cold and humid winters contribute to an exceptionality largely born out of being the only region of Spain never colonized by the Moors. As the cradle of the *Reconquista*, this region and its inhabitants gained a special status within the Spanish monarchy. Asturias was no mere province but a principality: from the fourteenth century all heirs apparent of the Spanish throne received the title of 'Prince of Asturias'. In common with many *foral* regions, by the late eighteenth century up to 70 per cent of the population could still claim the noble status of *hidalgos*, which originally exempted them from paying direct taxes and conferred on them some privileges when recruited in the army.[36]

Crucial to an understanding of the events of 1808, Asturias had a long experience of representative government through its *Junta General del Principado*. The members of this body were elected by local councils through a system of universal male suffrage normally expressed by shouting in favour of, or against, candidates during open parish assemblies.[37] Although there were no restrictions on nominees, candidates tended to be wealthy propertied men. The *Junta General* elected a standing commission of nine members (*Diputación*), including its president (*procurador general*), for a 3-year term to run affairs between sittings of the *Junta General*. Judicial matters remained in the hands of the provincial *Audiencia*, a body that was also the administrative representative of the national government. In 1717, the Bourbon regime granted to the *Audiencia* powers of supervision over all acts approved by the *junta* and over its accounts. The president of the *Audiencia* (*regidor*) was to preside over the *junta*'s proceedings. The *Audiencia*, in turn, depended on the *junta* for determining the level of their members' salaries, even when the same members were expected to be the enforcer of national laws at the provincial level.[38] This imposed interdependence created tensions that would come to the forefront in 1808–09.

News of the Madrid uprising against the French arrived in the principality's capital, Oviedo, on 9 May 1808 when the *Junta General* gathered in town for one of its triennial sessions. Two weeks of popular commotion followed during which the magistrates of the *Audiencia* tried to keep order while awaiting instructions from Madrid. This attitude was rooted in their traditional subservience to the central government, but in the new circumstances, rendered them suspicious in Patriotic eyes. In contrast, the 48-member *Junta General* declared itself immediately against the French invaders and backed popular enthusiasm to preserve the Bourbon monarchy. Yet, on the night of 24–5 May, a group of the Asturian élite headed by the recently appointed *procurador general*, the radical lawyer and economist Alvaro Florez Estrada, staged a *coup* within the *junta* with the intention of creating an opportunity for far-reaching political reform.[39] Amid serious agitation, it was decided that proceedings were no longer to be chaired by the *regidor*, but by a newly elected president. Instead of naming a *Diputación* to run the affairs, the new assembly decided that it would deal with all matters in the plenary session.[40] It also adopted a new name, the *Junta Suprema de Asturias* (Supreme *Junta* of Asturias), more befitting to the sovereign role it was now assuming over the rest of the country. In the name of 'el pueblo' (the people),[41] the new executive assembly took control of the provincial army, sent two envoys to London in search of aid, confiscated ecclesiastical property for military purposes and began appointing civil servants and other officials – including magistrates. This set the *junta* on direct collision course with the *Audiencia* whose members were already alarmed by a display of powers that so far had been a prerogative of the monarch. Aware of the dubious legality of the body he represented, *procurador* Florez Estrada, aided by a couple of colleagues, forged two letters purportedly sent directly to the *junta* by the imprisoned Ferdinand VII confirming the body's legitimate role as the King's representative.[42] The stratagem did little to convince the lower orders who, excluded from the political process, were also feeling the impact of the *junta*'s wartime fiscal policies and of its military recruitment programme. Popular insurrections against the *junta* broke out on 7 June and 19 June.[43] Although there is no evidence to back claims that the *Audiencia* and the high clergy masterminded these disturbances,[44] it was clear from the outset that the rebels sided with them, equally outraged by the *junta*'s decision to allow the recruitment of seminarists into the army (among them the Scottish volunteer James Arbuthnot)[45] and by the harsh punishment inflicted on conscientious objectors. Fearful of disorder, the *Junta Suprema* created the office of *Superintendencia de Policia* (Superintendency of Police) and placed gallows in Oviedo's main public square as a deterrance.[46]

On 31 August, the *Junta Suprema* was purged by a group headed by *procurador* Florez Estrada. Arguing that the body was too slow to react to events and needed to be reduced in size, the electoral map was redrawn to remove four districts and, with that, ten seats. Elections were called overnight to renew the mandate of the new 38-member *Junta Suprema*.[47] Among those who lost their seats was a deputy who had been elected twice to represent the *junta* at the national level in the soon-to-be created *Junta Central*: the Governor of the District of Grado, Ignacio Florez Arango. Little is known about Arango's political affiliation or career, except that he defeated Florez Estrada in the election for one of the two positions of Asturian representative[48] and that, as provisional president of the *junta*, he consented to a request made by the Oviedo populace to have a 'Representante del Pueblo' (Representative of the People)[49] attending the assembly's deliberations, albeit with no vote.[50] The unorthodox manner of Arango's removal threw a cloud over those who were later appointed as Asturian representatives to the *Junta Central*: Gaspar Melchor de Jovellanos and Marquess de Camposagrado, particularly as both had relatives and friends in the *Junta Suprema* – and Jovellanos had no seat in that assembly.[51]

Relations between the two main institutions of Asturias worsened when the *junta* decided to deprive the *Audiencia* of its role as court of first instance and took some steps that interfered with judicial matters.[52] Full-scale riots blew up again, this time fuelled by rumours that the *junta* was preparing to repeal a 1785 law that protected tenant farmers from having their rents linked to increases in property taxes.[53] It took the provincial government two days (25–26 September 1808) to restore order. On 29 September, the assembly issued a decree that banned all meetings of more than ten people, applied the death penalty for anybody who publicly criticized the authorities, made 'masters responsible for the excesses of their servants, artisans for those of their apprentices and fathers for those of their children'.[54] Crucially, in order to guarantee the enforcement of the restrictions, the *junta* ordered the provincial army to remain 'permanently in the capital'.[55]

The constraints placed on the Asturian army to move outside Oviedo seriously hampered war operations. To meet military and police commitments, the *Junta Suprema* planned to increase its army to 24,000 men, but recruitment became difficult after Asturian troops suffered crushing defeats assisting the Castilian army in Medina de Río Seco (14 July 1808) and fighting with the Army of the Left at Espina de los Monteros (10–11 November 1808).[56] Matters were not helped by the repeal of a Royal Order of 1807 that had limited all exemptions from military recruitment to titled nobles with incomes of over 12,000 ducados. The *Junta Suprema* argued that means testing was a 'violation of the privileges of the nobility designed to ruin the province'[57] and staunchly defended a concession granted in 1734 by Philip V that exempted the whole of the Asturian aristocracy from military enrolment.[58] As we have seen, up to 70 per cent of Asturians claimed *hidalgo* status, but a revision ordered by the Bourbon administration in 1797 registered 62,255 (around 17 per cent of the population). Of them, only 16 nobles possessed documentation to back their claims.[59] The exercise caused enormous resentment, and the Asturian authorities had challenged it since then. The problem was that by repealing the Royal Order of 1807, and while new legislation was being formulated, an earlier norm was inadvertently brought back into force. Dating from the previous conflict against France, the War of the First Coalition (1793–95), the old royal order called for the recruitment of all men from the age of 16 to 45, regardless of social rank.[60] Carrol found that many self-proclaimed *hidalgos* were enraged by the situation, but not necessarily because they wished to avoid taking arms.[61] As Colin Lucas found among the lower sections of the French élite who resented being mixed with commoners at the time of the doubling of the Third Estate, the Asturian *hidalgos* were revolting against a loss of status.[62] They feared that serving side by side with plebeians would undermine their claims of nobility. Unsympathetic to their dilemma, the lower orders saw no reason for privileges and argued that if the *hidalgos* refused to serve, they would not join the ranks either. Carrol claimed to have persuaded the *Junta Suprema* that the solution lay in the creation of a separate regiment 'composed of the young men of noble and distinguished birth'[63] who should be 'honoured by being sent to the advance of the Army under General Ballesteros' (the head of the Asturian army).[64] The Irish volunteer tried to address the anxieties of the lower orders with a proclamation calling Asturians 'to fight together until the last drop of blood'.[65] It was only after taking these measures that he cheerfully reported to London that

> those young men who before refused to enter the ranks as private soldiers are now most anxious to grasp the Musquet [sic] and enrol themselves into the Corps of Distinguished Asturians. The populace also are quiet, pacific and pleased at the example set by their superiors.[66]

The establishment of a *corps* of noblemen was not a new idea. The Asturian *Diputación* had suggested a similar scheme in 1794, but the war was over before enlistment was accomplished – perhaps unsurprisingly considering the difficulties of determining claims to nobility.[67] There are reasons to believe that Carrol's initiative eventually suffered a similar fate because no trace has been found of the Corps of Distinguished Asturians in the few surviving provincial military records. Successful or not, whether only a scheme on paper or a reality, the important thing to note here is that Carrol was prepared to back the derogation of a law passed *ante-bellum* by the legitimate government of Spain for no other reason than military expediency. More importantly, he claimed to have taken these steps in consultation with the Asturian authorities, but without reference to any immediate British military superior or diplomatic agent in Spain.[68] This was to become a recurrent pattern of behaviour.

Complaints against the *Junta Suprema*, meanwhile, multiplied, particularly when, unable to meet its own recruitment targets on time, the Asturian government refused military assistance to Patriots in neighbouring provinces. There were financial as well as political reasons behind the refusal. All high-ranking officers of the army served without pay while they remained in Asturias, but on crossing the provincial frontier, they had to be provided with funds according to their respective ranks on the rationale that they would not be able to demand from the locals the sort of hospitality their compatriots were expected to offer.[69] The Asturian government could not afford the expense. Although unable to account for money and supplies already received from the British government, the *Junta Suprema* requested more assistance. Unsurprisingly, accusations of mismanagement and corruption soon reached Carrol's ears.[70] In February 1809, the *junta* ordered a forced loan, further alienating the overburdened propertied classes. Discontent began to manifest itself in small acts of civil disobedience, which the *junta* tried to contain by force.[71] The British volunteer despaired when the complicated arrangements he made with the British navy to launch a combined attack with the Asturian army on French-occupied Santander had to be abandoned because General Ballesteros, who had been waiting 6 weeks for the *Junta Suprema*'s instructions, received

> the most peremptory order to send one of his best and strongest regiments immediately to Aviles (four leagues to the Westward of Gijon), the Junta thus answering his proposition of an attack upon the Montaña, and evincing their disinclination that the Army should pass the boundary of this Province.[72]

Rumours of treachery began to circulate, particularly after calls for assistance by the *junta* of Leon, historically associated with Asturias,[73] were ignored, leaving the principality vulnerable to an invasion from the South.[74]

Relations with the *Junta Central* were hardly better. On 1 October, the recently created national government told the Asturian authorities that it could no longer exercise sovereign power for civil and military appointments. Regardless of that warning, on 9 October, two days after the *Gaceta de Oviedo* published the *Junta Central*'s order,[75] the Asturian *Junta Suprema* appointed two new members in the *Audiencia* and ordered the arrest of whoever defended the *Central*'s prerogatives – including the head of the Gijon's customs office, Pedro Manuel Valdés Llanos, a close friend of Gaspar Melchor de Jovellanos.[76] On 18 December 1808, the Asturian *junta* received a copy of an order issued a month earlier by the *Junta Central*. The document granted the Marquess de la Romana not only the command of the armies of Old Castile, Asturias and Galicia, but also 'the most ample faculties' to exercise both 'military and political authority in those regions'.[77] The measure was probably designed to be applied against the Captain-General of Castile, General Gregorio de la Cuesta, who briefly exercised pro-consular powers in defiance of the civilian *juntas*. But this was never spelt out. The order simply urged the Marquess to take 'extraordinary and vigorous measures to ensure the salvation of the Motherland' and to punish 'those vile and degenerated men' who betray their country and their King 'usurping the title of their defender when in reality they are selling them like cowards'.[78] Carrol forwarded a copy of the *Junta Central*'s order to London expressing 'very great satisfaction' because, he said,

> such energetic orders are called for in this hitherto ungoverned, and in many parts, what is worse, ill-governed Country, and I ardently hope and trust that the intention of the Supreme Junta [for *Junta Central*] will be acted upon, up to the very spirit and letter of the Law.[79]

Since his arrival in Spain, and like his colleagues Philip Keating Roche and Charles Doyle, Carrol had urged the British government to intervene in Spanish politics to remove all obstacles placed in the road of liberation. In his first letter to the secretary of the Duke of York in August 1808, Carrol described Spain as 'a sleeping lion' whose claws had been clipped,

> [but] she is now awake and still professes strength amply sufficient to crush the snakes and vipers that infest her dominion and have been attempting to know [sic] her vitals. And if the British Lion rampant will afford a little nourishment and assistance to the Spanish lion, neither to couchant [word not clear], she will not only be perfectly able to resist the Hydra of France, but probably be the mediate cause of the destruction of this hitherto Gigantic Monster.[80]

The British government remained mute. Official silence did little to dissuade Carrol from acting on his views. He was thirsty for action – to such an extent that in September 1808 he begged the Spanish General Joachim Blake to give him 'something to do' because he was 'almost dead with *ennui*' and so 'lonely and somber' that if he was not allowed to join him at headquarters 'you will hear of my committing suicide'.[81] After visiting Blake, in October 1808, Carrol published a series of public addresses directed to the inhabitants of Biscay (which were also mentioned by the British press)[82] anticipating the success of Spanish arms. Charles Lefevre, a British Captain of Engineers who was in Bilbao at the time, reported with alarm to the British authorities that members of the Galician government had shown him 'a very long letter in Spanish signed by Lieut. Col. Carrol in which there appearing [sic] to be some promises'.[83] In a letter to the Duke of York, in December 1808, Carrol conceded that he was exceeding the limits of his duty 'as a soldier, whose province is solely to act in the field',[84] but he argued that he saw himself as 'being at present employed, in some measure, civilly to report the state of the country'.[85] This was quite an assumption. Not only was there an important gap between gathering information and meddling in Spanish politics, but also his immediate superior, General John Broderick, had reminded

him on more than one occasion that it was 'contrary to the instructions of Lord Castlereagh to enter into any discussions with the civilian authorities'.[86]

The embarkation of British troops on January 1809, after Moore's tragic retreat across Galicia, initiated a hiatus in communications. All letters sent to British headquarters were returned. By mid-February, Carrol reported that the *Junta Suprema* had received no news from the British Army or from La Romana since 3 December and that it was still in the dark regarding events in Galicia.[87] With General Broderick back in London and no other military superior in the vicinity,[88] Carrol saw in the information blackout an opportunity to shape events. On 2 February, he issued a proclamation belittling rumours of an allied disaster, asserting that the Galicians were successfully resisting the advance of Soult's troops and encouraging Asturians to fight on because, he said, 'while you remain loyal to your own interests, the soldiers of Great Britain will never abandon your cause'.[89] He forwarded a copy of the proclamation to London – but only after it was printed and circulated. A fortnight later, he told his British superiors that the Asturians had offered him the command of the Corps of Distinguished Asturians.[90] Although it is not clear that such *corps* ever existed, he claimed that he had declined the offer, but at the same time warned that it was his 'most ardent wish to fulfil the orders of my government by assisting in every way, as a Volunteer, in the Glorious cause of the Spanish Nation'.[91]

The British army had withdrawn completely from Spanish soil. London issued no new instructions on how to proceed. So Carrol decided to reinterpret his orders to keep the alliance alive. Far from contemplating a return to Britain, he openly declared that he had joined the Spaniards because he was committed to the 'Glorious cause of the Spanish Nation'.[92] This was to be the priority superseding all others, whether British or even Spanish officialdom was prepared to see the point or not. In pursuit of the ultimate goal of liberation, he was determined to play to the hilt his dual status as British military agent and British volunteer within the Spanish forces.[93] Confronted with the procrastination of the *Junta Suprema* regarding the transfer of Asturian troops to liberate Santander, for example, Carrol tried to break the deadlock, asserting first to the Asturian authorities that their neighbours 'freed from the oppressive yoke under which they now labour would flock to our standards'.[94] Then, he enticed the Asturians by suggesting that British merchants who had stored wool to the value of 72,000 reales in that city would 'cheerfully pay' for the recaptured property – 'an advantageous transaction in the present indigent state of the Principality'.[95] If this was not enough, he stressed that the 'British Government and the British Commercial Nation may expect such exertion'.[96]

Powerful as these arguments were, they had no effect. Unpopular, impoverished and badly informed, the Asturian government saw little advantage in lending troops to other provinces that could well be needed at home. When the man appointed by the *Junta Central* to oversee the Asturian army, the Marquess de La Romana, requested assistance, he too was refused. La Romana's ragtag army, composed mainly of the remnants of General Blake's forces, was in desperate need of food, clothing, arms, ammunition, and it demanded its pay. Romana's future actions could have been motivated partially by fear of not meeting his men's demands, considering that on 7 January 1809 the Spanish commander at the Battle of Somosierra, General Benito de San Juan, was executed by mutineers demanding food, and that a few months later, at Ferrol, another general, Jose Vargas, was murdered with a carpenter's compass for the inability to pay his men.[97] More to the point, ever since the British army's evacuation, Romana had been chased by the enemy from his headquarters in Leon into Galicia and, as Fugier noted, the French considered the seizure of Asturias to be of vital strategic importance. It did not take long for the imperial forces to mount a three-pronged invasion of the principality.[98] Time was running out for parochial considerations.

By mid-March, having lost all confidence in the ability of the *Junta Suprema* to take positive action, Carrol wrote letters to Lord Castlereagh and the Duke of York warning that he had taken upon himself the charge 'to adopt such Plans and measures as appear to me most necessary'[99] and that he trusted in their success because

> The influence which an officer Commissioned by the British Government possesses over all descriptions of People in this Country affords the greatest facilities for carrying into effect all such measures as are for the benefit of the common cause. I have the good fortune to possess this influence and enjoy the perfect confidence of the People and the Armies.[100]

He provided a few details of his plans, but a hint of events to come can be evinced from his criticism of the Asturian government. Carrol told London that among the 'nearly 30 members' of the *junta* there were some

> of moderate talent and most of them well meaning Patriots, but it is to be apprehended that among such a number there are also a few timid lukewarm say-disant [sic, for *soi-disant*, so called] Patriots who damp the energies of the rest, cause unnecessary delays and clog the wheels of Government: whether the conduct of such men arises from inability or worse motives matters little, the effects to the common cause in either case is the same. To a disinterested

observer of the proceedings of this Junta it would appear that they were afraid of
incurring the displeasure or draw the vengeance of the Enemy upon them were
they to adopt energetic measures. From the many favourable opportunities of
attacking the common foe which they have neglected to take advantage of the
most [un]favourable conclusions have been drawn by many Patriots.[101]

Carrol seemed to be implying that the Asturian government was laying the
ground for collaboration under an eventual French occupation. In a country
seized by an atmosphere of distrust which turned everyone into a potential
'enemy within', these were perilous words to spread about. Indeed, a number
of *afrancesados* would declare themselves ready to serve under the invaders,
including the Bishop of Oviedo, Gregorio de Hermida.[102] Addressed to members
of the British government, Carrol's statement could have inflicted a deadly wound
on the already ailing Anglo-Spanish alliance. Aware of this danger, Carrol tried
to defuse any suspicion of treachery by asserting that he deemed it

> but Justice to state that except in a very few instances I attribute the want of
> energy and the defects which exists more to the timidity and want of talents of
> the Governors in most of the departments than to any motives more derogatory
> to the character of Patriots.[103]

Having asserted the commitment of the majority of the Asturians to the Spanish
cause, Carrol declared that it was 'the universal wish of this Province' that a *junta*
'composed of seven or more members should be appointed in the room of, or
selected from, the present assembly' as the only chance to 'save the principality if
vigorously attacked'.[104] He did not specify who was to make such an appointment.
Crucially, however, he stated that the Patriots told him that

> I as appointed by the British Government have only to propose and sanction this
> salutary change to affect its being most easily and more promptly carried into
> execution. As I have no Instructions from your Lordship how to act upon such
> points as may occur I am diffident and apprehensive of taking upon me to follow
> the dictates of my own Judgement and feelings, least I should appear to outstep
> the line of my duty. I request your Instructions.[105]

Well before the letter could reach London, however, Carrol entered in
communication with the Marquess de la Romana. Desperate for succour, the
chief of the Army of the Left, who had just arrived in Asturias, declaring himself
ready to protect that 'Asylum of Spanish Liberty',[106] begged Carrol to request
more assistance from the British government to continue the struggle. Carrol's

reply was an unambiguous invitation to depose the provincial government and seize power. He began by enumerating all his frustrated efforts to have Ballesteros's troops moved out of the province, his addresses and proclamations to the army and to the people, whom, he said, had their 'greatest ardour and readiness to undertake any enterprise . . . damped by the manner in which they are governed'.[107] Carrol said he failed in prevailing upon the *junta* 'to abandon their system of inactivity and supineness'. Travelling throughout the principality, he had discovered that, while the 'peasantry are willing, zealous and obedient in the extreme', the 'Gigantic force' of 20,000 men that the *junta* had promised to create 'is at present formidable only on paper'. He added that several Patriots had offered the *junta* plans for the organization and discipline of a military network that would provide an early warning system of invasion, called a 'General Alarm', but that these plans were ignored 'for what reasons I cannot divine'. Significantly, he pointed out that the Asturian assembly had established

> their absolute Power (a power not acknowledged) suffice it to say, that by a combination and concatenation of strong measures and decrees, enforced only by Arms, decrees which I fear had not for their object the good of the General and Common cause, [thus] they have rendered themselves highly obnoxious to the People of the Province.

Carrol not only questioned the legitimacy of the *junta* but also asserted that it was 'entirely guided by the will and caprice of three or four individuals'. From his references to the system of 'General Alarm', there are reasons to believe that Carrol was in contact with Ignacio Florez Arango who had designed and provisionally set up an early warning system of invasion before his exclusion from the *junta*.[108] However, while Arango argued for a return to the *ante-bellum* order with the appointment of a nine-member *Diputación*,[109] Carrol stated that he was

> fully aware that in times like the Present it is advantageous that the Supreme Authority should be vested in a few, and if possible, in one individual (thus following the example of Rome, where in time of danger it was the custom to elect a Dictator. I am however sensible of the difference of the Present time and those Epochs).[110]

While presenting himself as 'unbiased by any private or interested motives' and admitting that he could not have been 'favoured with more Pointed Marks [sic] of distinction and stronger proof of civility from the *Junta* of Oviedo', Carrol delivered the most devastating blow to his hosts:

> I beg leave strongly to recommend your Excellency repairing to this City and
> adopting such plans and measures for the Better Government and defence of
> this Province and the Active Operations of its Armies as to your Excellency shall
> seem meet.[111]

Allowing for any hesitation on the part of Romana, Carrol stressed that the
province was the 'rallying Point of Spanish freedom' and at the time 'one of the
most important Channels of communication between the Peninsula and Great
Britain'. He argued that he was, therefore, persuaded that his government would
send the most ample supplies but only 'provided the interference and authority
of your Excellency ensures the Prompt and advantageous distribution thereof'.[112]
Carrol had left Romana little room for manoeuvre. If he failed to enter into the
provincial political arena, the Marquess risked being deprived of vital British aid
at a time when he could rely on little else. Carrol pressed this point during a first
meeting with the Spanish general on 29 March – a meeting he reported to the
British government only 13 days later.[113]

If there is anything surprising in these circumstances, it is how long it took
Romana to follow the interventionist route. The Marquess arrived in Oviedo on
4 April 1809.[114] Three days later, in a letter addressed in poor French to the British
Foreign Minister George Canning, he confirmed that one of the reasons bringing
him to the province was to ensure the support of the British government. He also
mentioned that while there were no immediate reasons to fear a French invasion
of the province,

> there is more to be feared from the disorder reigning within the Junta, which
> is composed of people detested by the Public, without opinion, without force,
> the object of Execration for the most valuable part of the Province: yet I do not
> attribute all faults to them, as I am expected to believe.[115]

As the representative of the *Junta Central* and commander of the northern armies,
including the Asturian forces, Romana's next step was to demand a report from
the *Junta Suprema* on its activities and war preparations. The assembly replied
two weeks later justifying all its actions on the exercise of sovereign power.[116]
Romana also consulted two of the members excluded from the *junta*, Arango
and Gregorio Jove Dasmarinas Valdés. They replied calling for a return to the
ante-bellum order with the election of a nine-member *Diputación*.[117]

On 24 April, Carrol published a proclamation designed to 'prepare the minds
of the People'[118] for a change of government. He congratulated the Asturians
on the good fortune of the arrival of the 'Heroe Romana',[119] depicted as a virile

demi-god, a military messiah who was the salvation of Spain, the commander that the *Junta Central* had already identified as 'the man needed to rule a very important portion of this Peninsula'.[120] He cautioned that 'only if you remain under his axis [sic] and follow his orders and dispositions blindly, I can guarantee the salvation of the Motherland'.[121] His proclamation ended with the most outrageous claim. Carrol pledged that 'por mi mano' (by my hand) Great Britain was to show the greatest generosity and that all kinds of relief were to arrive at any moment. He also promised Asturians that if they obeyed Romana, 'your grateful Prince and King will bestow on you a liberal and honest government'.[122]

On 2 May 1809, goaded by Carrol's propaganda, and after nearly a month of consultations, Romana ordered troops headed by Colonel José O'Donnell to enter the Cathedral Chapter where the *junta* was in session and expel its members from the building. The Marquess issued a proclamation announcing that, in virtue of the powers entrusted to him by the *Junta Central*, he had dissolved the *Junta Suprema* as unworthy of the authority Asturians conferred on it in May 1808 and because

> the present junta of Asturias, although highly favoured by British generosity expressed in all kinds of subsidies, is the one which co-operated the least in the great enterprise of expelling the enemy from its native soil.[123]

That body, he added, had illegally seized sovereign power and ruled in the most despotic fashion by armed force. It had suppressed laws and arbitrarily arrested many of its opponents on trumped-up charges of treachery. Significantly, Romana recalled that the Asturian *junta*, instead of

> ensuring the observance of the Laws of our Sovereign and the *Junta Central*, the respect of courts and judges, it has done the opposite . . . and protected by a force which should be assigned to the defence of the Nation, it took upon itself to exercise arbitrary power and absolute Sovereignty.[124]

Confronted by this, the Marquess claimed that he had no option but to intervene to uphold the rights of Ferdinand VII, to defend the interests of Spain and to prevent a bloodbath. Far from following Carrol's suggestion to seize personal power, Romana nominated a *Junta de Armamento y Observación* (*Junta* of Armament and Observation) of nine members – a figure similar to that of the old *Diputación* – composed entirely of former members of the *Junta General*, the traditional representative body of the province. Among them were two of the members displaced from the *Junta Suprema*, Arango and Dasmarinas, and two of the deputies first sent to England, Andrés Angel de la Vega and José María Queipo de Llano, Count de Toreno. The latter claimed to have relinquished the appointment because he considered Romana's actions as 'a petty and ridiculous imitation of Napoleon's 18 Brumaire'.[125] Toreno's view has been highly influential on subsequent historiography,[126] yet, in the light of the evidence presented here, it seems that Romana's actions deserve to be reassessed. Unlike Napoleon, the Marquess took no seat in the *junta*, showed little interest in interfering in its activities and restored the independence of the judiciary.[127] It seems difficult to agree with a historian who asserted that 'at Oviedo a leading general had decided unilaterally to overthrow the civil power and to reshape the political system in a form more congenial to himself'.[128] Romana may have not been prepared to accept the notion of 'popular sovereignty', but his intervention in Asturias was not an act of rebellion against the *Junta Central*. He had acted on behalf of the central government, which had conferred on him full powers to discipline and rule over the northern regions. This was even accepted by Jovellanos, who at least initially, as Lady Holland noted in her diary,

> [Jovellanos] does not disapprove of his proceedings against that Junta, where I believe he [Romana] acted in the capacity of delegate from the Supreme Junta [*Junta Central*]. The Junta was thwarting Romana in all his regulations about the army, which by robbery and secret intrigue they would soon have destroyed.[129]

Although privately Jovellanos doubted the legality of removing a body that was, in his view, 'constitutionally elected',[130] initially he did not speak out.

Lord Holland interpreted matters differently. He warned Jovellanos and his colleagues in the national government that Romana had set a bad example for other provinces and that the 'magic word *Central*' would not prevent them from suffering a similar fate.[131] On 20 May, Jovellanos and Camposagrado wrote to their colleagues, declaring themselves unable to participate in any discussion on the Romana affair because they had 'relatives among the members of the condemned *junta* to which we owe our appointment'.[132] It was not until 6 July (over a month after the French had occupied Asturias) that Jovellanos and Camposagrado raised the issue again, now to demand the reinstatement of the *Junta Suprema* as the clear heir of the *Junta General* because, otherwise, they reasoned, 'how can we consider legitimate our representation?'[133] On the following day, the *Junta Central* passed a resolution assuring the Asturian delegates that no challenge had ever been made to their status.[134] The complaints continued, but the Asturian *Junta Suprema* was never reinstated.[135]

By the end of the year, with much of the province liberated by Spanish forces and Romana back in Seville to participate in the deliberations of the *Central* (alongside Jovellanos and Camposagrado), the national government called for elections for a new *junta* in Asturias, which in May 1810 took the name of *Junta Superior de Armamento y Defensa* (Superior *Junta* of Armament and Defence).[136] Oviedo was to be taken and retaken by the French four times, and though imperial forces occupied most of the principality, they were never fully able to consolidate their hold. Just the same could be argued for the Superior *Junta* of Armament and Defence which, over 18 months of its existence, only managed to rule for 360 days, peregrinating from one place to another, chased first by the forces of Bonnet and later by those of Bessières.[137] The *Junta Superior Provincial* that replaced it in August 1811 reported directly to the national government in Cadiz, as also did the *Diputación* established on 1 March 1813 as part of the implementation of the Constitution of 1812. The old *Junta General* was reinstated in 1814 and ruled as the main body of provincial government until 1835, largely convinced that the Asturian *fueros* had been preserved. Yet, Asturias was not immune from the centralist efforts of both absolutist and liberal regimes, which successfully encroached on its traditional representative system of government and limited its competences. It was to take more than a century before the principality fully recovered its autonomy.[138]

Another aspect to bear in mind regarding this episode is that Romana's actions were taken following orders from the *Junta Central* and under the strain of a foreign invasion. His *junta* governed for little less than 3 weeks because, by the time it took power, it was too late to put in place effective measures to thwart the advance of the French. This sets Romana's case apart from the series of *pronunciamientos* that took place soon after Ferdinand VII's return to the throne (including the first successful of Major Rafael del Riego that resulted in the 1820–23 liberal government),[139] as well as from those military interventions in politics with which it has been associated, such as the events of 1936 and *El Tejerazo* of 23 February 1981.[140] Moreover, it could be argued that Romana might not have followed the route of regime change if Carrol had not first convinced him that such action was the only way to guarantee the British assistance he so desperately needed. Indeed, the most remarkable feature of this episode is Carrol's ability to shape events single-handedly towards the goal of liberation. He was so masterful in convincing Romana and the rest of the Patriots that he operated with the full knowledge and authority of the British government that historians have tended to take this for granted – one even had Carrol described as a 'British consul'.[141] After the events in Oviedo, the Irishman placed himself completely under Romana's orders and, while he continued reporting to London, he did so sporadically. On 29 July 1809, he asked leave of absence from the British service, informing Lord Castlereagh that the Marquess had granted him 'the rank of Colonel in the Spanish service and the command of the Regiment of Hibernia'.[142]

British interventionism

Ironically, a powerful reason behind British official silence regarding events in Asturias was that, after Moore's retreat, the government in London finally adopted a concrete policy regarding affairs in the Peninsula: one that concentrated British efforts on Portugal's liberation, reducing all strategic interest in Spain to those regions that were perceived as buffer zones capable of halting the advance of the enemy, as in the case of Galicia and Andalusia.[143] In 1809, the bulk of British military and financial resources was diverted to aid the Austrians in their first unsuccessful rising against Napoleon and also to prepare the equally disastrous Walcheren expedition. Unaccustomed to cooperating in the organization of large-scale military operations, the Foreign Office and the War Department ended up embroiled in a conflict of their own over the management of the military agents sent to Spain.[144] Political rivalry between their respective heads, George Canning and Lord Castlereagh, compounded the situation. After months of wrangling, Canning won the battle for complete control of British war policy and resources in Portugal and the Spanish world. Positioning himself for the premiership amid the disintegration of the Portland administration, Canning decided to leave the implementation of his policies in the Peninsula to the Wellesley brothers, in the expectation of their eventual support. He promoted Sir Arthur Wellesley to the command of the British forces in Portugal[145] and dispatched Sir Arthur's eldest brother, Marquess Richard Wellesley, as ambassador extraordinary and plenipotentiary to Spain.[146] Consequently, the War Department ordered all military agents to report exclusively to the British ambassador in Seville and, when necessary, to Canning himself.[147] All agents acknowledged receipt of these instructions but, as it will be shown, those who held a commission in the Spanish army complied, sometimes reluctantly, leaving other channels of communication open and addressing diplomats only when they considered it useful to further schemes which were designed to bring closer the complete liberation of Spain.

Before departure, Marquess Wellesley allowed the British press to hint that his stay in Spain would be short because he was to be replaced by his younger brother Henry in less than two months – time enough to enforce a change of government more congenial to British interests.[148] These rumours were largely in tune with Canning's instructions – a veritable charter of interventionism. Wellesley was told to 'not decline any occasion of offering a fair and unreserved opinion'[149] upon political questions, 'urging in the strongest manner'[150] such arrangements as may appear to him necessary for the effectual prosecution of the war on the part of Spain and 'for the administration of the internal affairs of the Government in the manner the most conducive to the welfare of the nation, and to the preservation of the monarchy'.[151] Indeed, Canning warned that 'the Alliance between His Majesty and Spain would be dissolved by any change which should abrogate the monarchical Constitution of Spain'.[152] Wellesley was also to make the establishment of a British garrison in Cadiz the '*sine qua non*'[153] of further British military assistance and to promote the idea of placing the overall command of the war in the Peninsula in the hands of a British officer – preferably Sir Arthur Wellesley.[154]

The Marquess arrived in Cadiz on 31 July 1809,[155] just in time to get involved in the bitter row between his brother Sir Arthur and the Spanish authorities that followed the Pyrrhic victory of Talavera (27–8 July 1809).[156] In this context, the Marquess of Wellesley's diplomatic mission soon became a constant battle to squeeze supplies out of London and to batter the troubled and impoverished Spanish *Junta Central* into political submission.[157] Perhaps because his stay was meant to be short, Marquess Wellesley preferred the company of the small British community in Seville to that of Spaniards.[158] Accordingly, in trying to press ahead with Canning's instructions, he became increasingly reliant on information provided by some of the British volunteers, whose high status within the Spanish army gave them privileged access to leading Spanish figures. In his first despatch to Canning, the Marquess reported that as he landed in Cadiz he received verbal intelligence of the action in Talavera from Lieutenant Colonel Charles Doyle, including 'the glorious success of his Majesty's troops under the command of Sir A. Wellesley on that memorable occasion'.[159] The messenger was the same Doyle, who, identified with his Spanish rank of *General* in the Marquess' dispatches, warned the ambassador that

> The situation of this Country after the battle of Talavera seems to be this: promulgate somewhere the glorious victory obtained by the British and not the follow up by the Spaniards because it [sic] wanted Provisions!!! This want also

applied to the Spanish Army, and this want continued to apply to both armies up to the hour at which the British Commander found it imperiously necessary to fall back upon his resources.[160]

In the same report, Doyle advised against a British retreat and suggested different possible scenarios for an Anglo-Spanish offensive.[161]

As detestation of the actions – and inactions – of the *Junta Central* became a national sport, the volunteers' correspondence could not fail to echo such criticism. From the headquarters of the Spanish army in Extremadura, Roche lamented that the enthusiasm of 'the entire Nation is so badly seconded by those to whom its resources are committed'.[162] But when news of Wellington's march towards Portugal became widespread, Roche advised against it:

> The evils and abuses in the Army and other consequent disasters and disgrace all owe their origin to the weakness, corruption and folly of the [Central] *Junta*. There is not a good Spaniard, my Lord, who is not penetrated with this truth – and who does not look up to your Lordship – to Lord Wellington & the British as their only salvation, from foreign as well, as domestic tyranny . . . Notwithstanding, My Lord, the melancholy and cheerless state of things, your Lordship may but [be]satisfied of one incountournable fact: which is that the same spirit of animosity and abhorrence for the French is unquenched and will not for many years to come be subdued whatever may be their fate in the mass of the people – and I would stake my existence upon the issue.[163]

Totally committed to the Spanish cause, Roche added that if, instead of withdrawing, a British force of 60,000 was to advance over Madrid, the Spaniards would 'manifest by some terrible effort their determination to get rid of the French and the *Junta*'.[164]

The idea of leaving the command of an Anglo-Spanish offensive in the hands of Wellington had already been discussed and accepted by the *Junta Central* less than a month after Talavera.[165] The Marquess, however, rejected this concession, considering it only as an opportunity to increase the pressure for political change. He bluntly delivered to the Spanish Foreign Minister Martin de Garay a list of precise measures to be adopted, which included the appointment of an Executive five-member Council of Regency, the immediate call of the *Cortes* and the thorough reform of the military department.[166] Wellesley delivered these 'suggestions' in his already well-known pro-consular style,[167] leaving the members of the *Junta Central* completely aghast. Complaints soon reached both the Spanish and British press about the petulant demands of the British ambassador. Wellesley reacted furiously, demanding to know the source of the leak.[168] For that, he turned to volunteer Whittingham. The Bristolian Captain of the 13th Light Dragoons and *brigadier general* in the Spanish Army was in Seville recuperating from a serious wound received in his jaw while leading two Spanish battalions in Talavera.[169] Wellesley offered Whittingham the care of a British surgeon and accommodation in his official residence. He felt flattered by these attentions, although he could not fail to mention to his brother-in-law, the independent MP and treasurer of the Bristol Dock Company, Richard Hart Davis, that

> living with Lord Wellesley is more like living with an amiable monarch than with a private person. His good breeding is perfect; and so nice is his sensibility on this point, that the slightest deviation shocks and offends him.[170]

Whittingham used his convalescence to socialize with leading Spanish families,[171] a situation that placed him in a favourable position to satisfy Wellesley's requests for confidential information.

On his first assignment, however, Whittingham declared himself unable to help. He said he just could 'not trace to its source'[172] the reports in the press of the demands made by Wellesley to the Spanish government, although he ventured that they arose from 'the house of one of the members of the *Junta*'.[173] He also warned the ambassador that it was the belief of public opinion that, if such demands

> were without foundation, the English ambassador would insist upon their being publicly contradicted by the Government! The silence to [sic] which has been observed upon the subject so interesting and important, leads every one to conclude that the reports are not without foundation.[174]

The British volunteer was calling Wellesley's bluff here. A week later, while Wellesley was still negotiating a British withdrawal with members of the *Junta*, Whittingham told the Marquess that he had received intelligence that it was already generally believed, not just among Spaniards, but 'in the French army', that the English had retired upon Lisbon, having given up the cause of Spain altogether'.[175] A few weeks later, stocks rose in the City of London amid rumours that the Marquess had received instructions to leave Seville and proceed to Madrid, Bayonne and eventually Paris to 'terminate a negotiation already commenced for the re-establishment of peace with France'.[176] British merchants in Gibraltar began lobbying for British troops to take control not just of Cadiz but also of Ceuta, Mallorca and Minorca.[177] It did not take long for these reports to reach Seville. Together, they pointed towards an abrupt end of the Anglo-Spanish alliance.

Such a prospect terrified both the Spanish government and the British volunteers. On 27 October, the *Junta Central* decided that, in order to avoid a public confrontation with the British ambassador, it was better not to issue an official reply to his demands. Instead, they dispatched Garay to inform Wellesley confidentially that, inspired by his suggestions, the *Junta* had appointed a six-member Executive Council composed of the Marquesses of la Romana and de Villel, Josef Garcia de la Torre, Francisco Xavier Caro, Sebastian de Tocano and Rodrigo Riquelme.[178] This was the closest they could get to Wellesley's Council of Regency.[179] On the following day, the *Junta Central* published a proclamation announcing that the idea of a Regency had been discarded because it was redolent of old laws and institutions that would prove useless in a situation that demanded 'principles and measures which are absolutely new'.[180] This hardly surprised Wellesley who was in close contact with the Marquess de La Romana and had already requested Whittingham to provide him with some background on potential candidates for the Executive Council and for the sole command of the Spanish army. The British volunteer accomplished this task with information that was largely in the public domain. In his report on the representative from Granada, Rodrigo Riquelme, for example, Whittingham warned that, although talented,

> by the Severity [sic] of his mind he would, it is thought, in a similar situation, make a worthy imitator of Robespierre. His vanity is excessive. His detestation of everything that is English extreme! He has, however, never been suspected of attachment to the French.[181]

Whittingham's assessment went little beyond that provided by the British press several months earlier when Riquelme was singled out as the member of 'a little cabal of provincial lawyers'[182] who detested the English, was bloodthirsty and backed press censorship and other measures designed to curtail personal liberties. Each report became an opportunity to promote the figure of General Javier Castaños, the victor of Bailén who recruited Whittingham into the Spanish army and who, after defeat in the Battle of Tudela, was in self-imposed internal exile in Algeciras. Hence, Riquelme was depicted as a troublemaker whose actions while at the provincial *junta* of Seville had been neutralized by 'the moderation and firmness of General Castaños'.[183] When reporting on the

Duke del Parque, rumoured about to receive the overall command of the Spanish army, Whittingham strenuously opposed the idea. He described the Duke as 'completely unfitted'[184] for that role because he was one of the Spanish grandees attached to the lifeguard of King Joseph Bonaparte who only joined the Patriots after the victory of Bailén. General Castaños, he said, wisely decided against giving him the command of a division when they entered Madrid because 'the people strongly opposed it believing him a traitor'.[185] Castaños, in contrast, could honestly claim to have been the first Spanish general to declare himself against the French intruders.

The 'Tilly Affair'

By the end of September, Wellesley had his eyes fixed on his future career in England, where a duel between Canning and Lord Castlereagh opened for him the route to the cabinet in the latest of Perceval's reshuffles.[186] The news of his appointment sent shivers down the spine of the British volunteers. A week before Wellesley's departure from Cadiz, Whittingham entreated the Marquess to consider that

> However the conduct of the Spanish Government may increase the difficulties of cooperation, alienate the spirit of the English from their cause, and would apparently justify a total separation of the interests of the two nations, yet it must never be forgotten that in fighting the cause of Spain, we are struggling for the last hope of continental Europe.[187]

Similar to the suggestions made by his colleagues Roche and Doyle, Whittingham calculated that a British force of 50,000 infantry in Portugal and a garrison of 10,000 in Gibraltar would enable England to enter into cooperation with the Spanish army and, 'very probably under the able direction of Lord Wellington, to decide the fate of the War in a few weeks!' Yet, he contemplated that, if the 'blindness of the Spanish Government, and the weakness of Austria' prevented such a scheme, Britain could secure the possession of Cadiz, Ceuta, Cartagena, Mallorca and Murcia, but only 'in trust for and in the name of Ferdinand the 7 [sic]'. By so doing, the veteran of the failed invasion of Buenos Aires reckoned that Britain would not only avoid accusations of self-interest but would also secure 'that influence over the public opinion in South America without which all our efforts would probably be of no avail'. He also strongly recommended that 'on no account, at no time, under no pretence' should the right of placing an English garrison in Cadiz be made a condition for providing Spain military assistance because

> It will never be granted till (sic) necessity makes it unavoidable and then no previous stipulations are necessary. The demand will be laid hold of by the French party [the *afrancesados*] to indispose the Nation with the English, and it is to be feared that the South Americans may also be affected by false and exaggerated statements of the interested pretentions of the English.[188]

Whittingham penned much of this letter while brooding over the result of a meeting he had at the time with a Spanish politician – a meeting he only reported to Wellesley several weeks later.[189] The man in question was one of the two representatives of Seville in the *Junta Central*, the Count de Tilly. There is much mystery surrounding this figure. The Andalusian historian Manuel Moreno Alonso asserts that he was 'Francisco de Guzmán Ortíz de Zúñiga Marabel Ponce de León, Señor de Gil de Olid y de la Margarita, y Conde de Tilly', an Extremadurian aristocrat educated in Paris who was completely unknown in Seville until he took a decisive role there in the uprising against the French in June 1808.[190] Moreno Alonso believes him to be the brother of Andrés María de Guzmán, known as 'Don Tocsinos', a Granada-born friend and collaborator of the French revolutionary Georges Jacques Danton with whom he was guillotined in April 1794.[191] This assertion follows reports provided by his contemporaries, Alcalá Galiano and the Count de Toreno,[192] and agrees with a bulletin issued on 12 December 1808 by the police in French-occupied Madrid stating that the Patriots' *Junta Central* was 'under the will of two men, one named Lorenzo Calvo, grocer at Saragossa (…) the other named Tilly, sentenced some time ago to prison for robbery, younger brother of a Guzmán who played a role under Robespierre during the Terror'.[193] In his dictionary of the Napoleonic Consulate and Empire, the French historian Alfred Fierro identified a Count de Tilly (*Comte* de Tilly) as Jacques-Louis-François Delaistre (Vernon, 2 February 1749; Paris, 10 January 1822).[194] This Count fought against the *Chouans* and commanded the French army over the Belgian nine departments. Crucially, after fighting against the Prussians and Russians, and by then a sexagenarian, he retired to Spain where he was made *Chevalier de l'Empire* (1809) and Baron (1812).[195] A 'general Tilly' also appears in the Spanish archives as the Josephine governor of Segovia from 1809 to 1813.[196] In any case, it remains difficult to assess if the Count de Tilly who sat at the *Junta Central* and represented the government of Seville in the Battle of Bailén was a relative or had contact with these namesakes.

Whispers of these connections probably reached the Patriots because by late 1808 Tilly became the target of dozens of anonymous letters accusing him of dishonesty and treachery.[197] A Spanish grandee, the Count de Montijo, formally requested his dismissal, throwing doubts over his aristocratic origins and accusing him of conspiring with general Castaños to reverse the victory of Bailén through the defeat at Tudela.[198] Rumours that agents of Bonaparte had infiltrated the Spanish national government circulated even in London. Now as a *coronel* in the Spanish army, Walter Savage Landor told fellow poet Southey that he saw confirmation of this in the *junta*'s slowlesness to summon the *Cortes* and the 'extreme absurdity' of inviting all Spaniards to give their views on the way the government and the Constitution should be shaped.

> To agitate minds both of the wise and of the ignorant, to make every man's vanity turn out against his neighbor's, to bid people choose their representatives yet exercise their judgment by giving their votes individually, coult not enter any sound head for any good purpose. The scheme was formed in the Tuileries, and is worthy of its author.[199]

While Castaños was removed from his command and virtually banished to Algeciras,[200] Tilly successfully defended his actions and had Montijo sent to prison by order of the *Junta Central*.[201] Rumours of his 'ill-gotten' fortune and profligate character persisted,[202] yet he was appointed a member of the War Committee in charge of the direction of war operations and military appointments. He was also dispatched to carry out delicate missions, including the purchase of horses from Muslim North Africa at a time when the Catholic Spanish army had almost no animals to furnish the cavalry.[203] Whatever his background and connections, it seems evident that Tilly was a talented man who exercised considerable influence over his colleagues in the *Junta Central,* so much so that Whittingham described him 'as the abbé Sieyes (sic, for Siéyès), the principle director of the Government'.[204] Some historians included Tilly among those who favoured political innovations in the *Junta Central*,[205] but the archival records point to erratic behaviour – on occasions, for example, he backed the calling of the *Cortes,* while on others he voted against measures directed to implement that project.[206]

Tilly's fatal mistake was to entrust Whittingham, whom he had befriended during the campaign of Andalusia, with an ambitious plan. According to the account of the British volunteer, Tilly approached him in Seville to confide that, as he considered it utterly impossible to save Spain, he had decided to secure himself a safe escape to South America.[207] He had a ship at his disposal to take

Figure 2   Samuel Ford 'Santiago' Whittingham (1772–1841), from an original miniature engraved by H. Adlard, reproduced in Ferdinand Whittingham (ed.), *A memoir of the services of sir Samuel Ford Whittingham* (London, 1868), frontispiece. Shelfmark: 210 e.214 © The Bodleian Libaries, University of Oxford.

him to Mexico where the local archbishop, who at the time was also the viceroy of Mexico ('a creature of my appointing, his will is subservient to mine')[208] was conniving with the 'English Americans'[209] to enter into an alliance, offensive and defensive. The American ambassador in Seville had made a similar offer to the *Junta Central* in case that body was forced to migrate to South America. Such an alliance, apparently stressed Tilly,

> would ultimately lead to a connection with France, destructive to the hopes of England in that part of the world. Buenos Aires *certainly* and probably Peru, will recognize the rights of the Princess of Brazil, and become provinces of the Portuguese Government, but the Superior resources of Mexico will ultimately give her an unlimited control over the general politics of South America, and the policy of England requires that Mexico should form no alliances which may lead to separate the interior (sic, the interest?) of the two countries. As it is natural to conclude that England can have no views of conquest when she will derive infinitely greater advantages from independence, her immediate and principal attention must of course, be directed to the saving of such ports in

European Spain as shall give her the command of the Mediterranean in spite of the continental requisitions of Buonaparte.[210]

Tilly's scheme was reminiscent of ideas publicly advocated in London by an English landowner who had resided in Sicily until 1807, Gould Francis Leckie: England should leave Peninsular Spain under France's area of influence and concentrate all efforts in controlling key ports in the Mediterranean and trade routes with an independent Spanish America.[211] Tilly offered to relinquish the alliance with the Americans and to put England in possession of Ceuta and Cadiz on the condition that he and General Castaños would be allowed to travel to Mexico with 5,000-armed troops as soon as the *Junta Central* and the last of remnants of the Spanish army abandon Seville.[212]

As a British agent, Whittingham should have transmitted Tilly's offer immediately to Wellesley or to his subordinate in Seville, Bartholomew Frere. Instead, he travelled to Algeciras to confer with General Castaños.[213] In correspondence with Wellington, who believing Whittingham to be in Seville, had asked him to consult General Venegas on preparations for the defence of Cadiz,[214] the British volunteer said nothing of the Tilly affair. He argued that he had to travel to Gibraltar for an operation on his injured jaw and apologized for transmitting in writing Wellington's queries to Venegas whom, he enigmatically said, needed to be warned of 'difficulties which will be thrown in his way (and) of which he has no idea'.[215]

Whittingham´s trip to Algeciras allowed him to plan a strategy with Castaños that would be consistent with the defence of the Spanish cause. With British troops withdrawn from Spanish soil and defeat at the Battle of Ocaña opening the road to the French conquest of Andalusia, hopes for the Spanish Patriots were at their lowest ebb. Yet, it was in this context that Castaños wrote a long letter to Wellesley disassociating himself from Tilly's plans and stating that 'Spain must be defended while there are still Spaniards there' because

To imagine that Spain can counteract the Power of Napoleon and shake off the Iron Yoke under the disconcerted system of improvident means, which are being adopted, would be temerity. But to suppose an attainment of that object impossible is an error or a malicious idea attempted to be spread about by those who are endeavouring to diminish the National Spirit in order that the Tyrant may thereby consummate his undertaking (. . .). Such is in my opinion the Count's objective. The singular victory of Bailén was a demonstration that the French armies are not invincible.[216]

The veteran general conceded, however, that victory was not to be achieved on battlefields, observing that 'so far the conflict has been carried forward by the enthusiasm and valour of the people in *masse*' and that this had strengthened his opinion that 'we must carry on a really national war'.[217] Accordingly, he recommended increasing the number of *guerrilla* units. He also requested the British to launch a naval expedition in the Cantabrian region to deliver weapons to the insurgents in San Sebastian. He vouched for the benefit of such an operation because, he was persuaded, 'Spain will return one day to its freedom and independence'.[218] In an enclosed letter, Whittingham completed the alternative scenario: if the French were to take control of continental Spain, the duke of Alburquerque could be put in charge of the organization of a 'Spanish Emigrant army' in England 'whose future views shall be directed to the recovery of the Peninsula'.[219] Castaños, meanwhile, would travel to Mexico at the head of 5,000 Spanish troops, with 10,000 extra muskets, because

> from his superior abilities and knowledge of the world, [he would] direct the politics of that country in great measure if not entirely, and he will be enabled to counteract the operations of French emissaries, in whatever shape they may present themselves.[220]

English vessels had already intercepted substantial correspondence from Napoleon's agents in Latin America, so Whittingham's precautions were not inappropriate.[221] To Wellesley, now in London, the British volunteer admitted that he had delayed in relaying the count's scheme and had kept matters secret because he thought it imperative first to consult Castaños, 'the only man in Spain in whom I should place unlimited confidence'.[222] He failed to mention, however, that while at Gibraltar, on 8 January 1810, he had married the daughter of an Intendant of the Spanish army and that General Castaños had not only made the short trip from Algeciras to be present at the ceremony, but that he had also given the bride away.[223]

Whittingham's close association with the victor of Bailén was to prove fruitful. In late January 1810, the provincial *junta* of Seville – where Tilly also held a seat – summoned Castaños to take the role of Captain-General of Andalusia. Castaños enrolled Whittingham as one of his generals of division and another British volunteer, *coronel* Patrick Campbell, as his *aide-de-camp*.[224] On 13 January 1810, with the Imperial army advancing over the Sierra Morena, the *Junta Central* announced it was to move to the Isla de Leon, Cadiz's immediate hinterland, allegedly to prepare for the *Cortes*' opening on 1 March. A fortnight later, however, in its new location, the *junta* declared itself dissolved and, as a last measure, appointed a five-man Council of Regency headed by General Castaños. The other members of the Executive were the Bishop of Orense; Francisco de Saavedra, secretary of the *junta* of Seville; Antonio Escaño, minister of the Navy in the *Junta Central*; and Miguel de Lardizábal y Uribe, a native of Mexico.[225] A few months earlier, Tilly had opposed the concentration of power in a council.[226] Now, he backed the idea and was among those present at the ceremony of transfer of power.[227] Soon after that, Castaños provided Tilly with a passport for Gibraltar. Unbeknownst to the Count, however, the new Regent had asked the governor of the British colony to arrest him as a 'Spanish State Prisoner'[228] accused of conspiring to sail for Mexico to establish himself as head of an independent government against the interests of the Spanish cause. Castaños directed the Governor of Ceuta to do likewise should the count escape to that garrison.[229] Tilly was arrested in Gibraltar, shipped back to Cadiz and imprisoned on orders of the Council of Regency on the basis of a testimony submitted by Whittingham.[230] The British volunteer was expected to provide the courts with written evidence of Tilly's alleged crime, but over a year passed without this ever being submitted.[231] Although there are no records pointing clearly to Tilly´s death, most historians agree that he died in prison without a trial.[232] In the meantime, the Regency elevated Whittingham to the rank of *mariscal de campo* and entrusted him with the establishment and management of a division and also of an innovative military academy in Mallorca destined to train many of the Spanish officers who contributed to the liberation of the Peninsula.[233] Castaños´s plan for strengthening the operations of the *guerrilla* with aid delivered by the British navy was also implemented, not just in the North, but also in the East, as the Spaniards managed to keep Suchet at bay for almost a year fighting with both regular and irregular forces.[234] Whittingham´s outmanoeuvring of Count de Tilly gave a new lease of life to the Spanish cause and demonstrated the high degree of dexterity the volunteers could display in political matters. In the short term, the ploy also placed the Bristolian in a position of considerable influence in the Anglo-Spanish alliance, to the extent that soon it was widely commented in England that he was 'the strongest link that unites the two nations in Spain'.[235]

British caudillos or liberators?

The east coast was the scene of an incident that further exemplifies the power those enjoying the double status of British envoys and volunteers in the Spanish army could exercise over military and political figures. During much of 1810, *brigadier* Roche facilitated communications between the Spanish forces and the British navy at Cartagena. By the end of that year, he managed to gather support in Cadiz for the creation of a Reserve Division for the defence of the Mediterranean coast.[236] The Regency also favoured him with the rank of *mariscal de campo*.[237] However, from the moment he arrived in Alicante, in early 1811, he found it difficult to get the full endorsement of the town authorities for the lodging and subsistence of his new force. The governor of Alicante, Antonio de la Cruz, complained of the manner in which Roche demanded material assistance from the local authorities, when he had authority to manage the aid delivered by the British navy. He also disliked the way in which Roche issued orders for strengthening fortifications and, particularly, that Roche dealt with *guerrilla* chiefs who had been banned from entering the town, having been accused of vandalism.[238] In September 1811, the governor sent an angry letter to the military commander of the region, General Joachim Blake, demanding Roche's dismissal and threatening resignation on the basis that his authority was being totally undermined by a man who operated in

> the unpleasant circumstances of being both a Spanish General and the man charged by his government [the British government] with the task of distributing the aid which is arriving from all corners to cover our needs (. . .) and he meddles in those areas that are of my sole authority, which he ignores, providing a bad example to the rest.[239]

De la Cruz received a prompt reply – but probably not the one he was expecting. Blake told him that he could not resign because he was needed in the emergency and advised him against challenging openly those 'persons who, for their connections and relations have a particular support'.[240] Accordingly, Blake suggested he should equip himself with endurance ('armese usted de sufrimiento') in order to proceed ahead 'in the daily sacrifice for the Motherland'.[241] What de la Cruz ignored was that among Roche's powerful connections was Blake himself. As head of the second Regency, a few months earlier, Blake had supported and signed Roche's promotion to *mariscal de campo*. Moreover, the British volunteer was at the time in charge of reinforcing the distressed army of Blake in Valencia.[242] Roche was also favoured by the support of many of his Spanish colleagues, the members of the Third Regency and the new British ambassador in Cadiz, Henry Wellesley.[243] De la Cruz took the warning on board and stoically followed Roche's suggestions – a change in attitude that kept him in his position for over a year, among the longest periods in office for a town that changed governor six times during the war.[244]

Yet, Roche never showed any intention of seating himself in the governor's chair. Indeed, although often powerfully influential, none of the British volunteers ever became fully fledged *caudillo*s. Their interventions in the political arena were short-lived, destined to influence events, rather than to control them by seizing power. Their instinct was to support the existing authorities and to look for established figures seen as capable of amalgamating national support, as in the case of the Duke of Infantado, promoted by Doyle, Roche and Carrol to head the proposed Regency in 1808.

Neither is there evidence that the volunteers' involvement responded to any specific partisan ideology. Carrol pressured the Marquess of La Romana into removing from power the *junta* of Asturias and even tried to convince him of the advantages of temporary dictatorship – yet he was a strong believer in political representation and became an ardent defender of the liberal administration of 1820, to which he offered his services.[245] Indeed, the majority of the volunteers strongly supported the Constitution of 1812 to which they pledged allegiance.[246] It could be argued that this was just a formality: it was mandatory for all regiments to take the oath.[247] Yet, there are other indications of the volunteers' support for constitutionalism. On 3 December 1810, Doyle published a proclamation calling the people of Valencia 'to start anew with complete trust in the *Cortes*, because they deserve it',[248] and he sent a copy of the text to his friend, the liberal José Canga Argüelles, then member of the provincial *junta* of Valencia and later deputy in Cadiz.[249] Troops recruited and trained by Doyle were popularly known as the 'Constitutional Army'.[250] It is believed that the First Lieutenant of the Royal Marines and *teniente coronel de los Reales Ejércitos*, Daniel Robinson,[251] writing under the pseudonym *Philos Hispaniae*, produced the first translation into English of the text of the Cadiz Constitution: *The Political Constitution of the Spanish Monarchy Proclaimed in Cadiz, 19 March, 1812* (London, 1813).[252] Little is known of the circumstances surrounding the production of this work, but reading the preface is enough to be convinced of the passionate support of the author for the achievements of a congress 'without parallel in history'.[253] After the war, Robinson became a vocal advocate of Spanish liberalism, joined the forces of the constitutional government in Cadiz in 1822–23 and those of Queen Isabel during the First Carlist war.[254] But during the conflict, all the British volunteers, without exception, fought for the return of Ferdinand VII. Even the erstwhile republican poet Walter Savage Landor supported the restoration of the monarch. It was only after Ferdinand VII reinstated the Inquisition and annulled the Constitution of 1812 that the writer returned his military commission to the Spanish government arguing that he had served 'in the cause of Spanish liberty against Napoleon' which included 'the restoration of the legitimate government', but that he would have 'nothing to do with a perjurer and traitor'.[255] Among all the volunteers, Whittingham was probably the only one who evinced a tendency towards absolutism, considering the role he was to play escorting Ferdinand VII on his way back to Madrid, soon after the *Cortes* was dissolved and most of the liberal leaders arrested.[256] Four years earlier, he thwarted the plans of the Count de Tilly and contributed to his downfall, yet there are no reasons to believe that he did so in order to oppose any progressive programme of government. His deeds were diverted towards a more far-reaching objective: the defence of the Spanish cause.

Lack of participation in partisan politics during the war should not prompt the conclusion that the volunteers' actions were completely devoid of ideology. They did follow a systematic scheme of ideas – one that could perhaps be considered as an ideology of liberation. It was its implementation rather than any motivation expressed for volunteering – which, as we have seen could be numerous and various – what turned this men into liberators. The volunteers' main objective was the recovery and preservation of the territorial integrity and sovereignty of the Spanish monarchy – the *Monarquía Hispana* – embracing the European, American and Asian dominions, no matter if before their arrival in the Peninsula a few showed themselves partial to South American emancipation.[257] To achieve this goal, they adopted a flexible, yet specific pattern of behaviour. First came collaboration with existing political institutions. As we have seen, the vast majority of the volunteers received their first Spanish military ranks from provincial *juntas* and accordingly sought to operate within their remits. Yet, they had no hesitation in masterminding the demise of a *junta* if it proved – as in the case of the *junta* of Asturias – incapable of fusing policy, resources and personnel into a single project reaching beyond their boundaries. Thus, in search of a political force capable of galvanizing popular enthusiasm for the fight against the 'French tyrant', they tended to favour the concentration of political power in few hands. War demanded quick decisions and models of centralized government seemed more effective in delivering them. Thus, when the national government represented by the 35 members of the *Junta Central* proved as feeble in the coordination of military efforts as those of the provincial *juntas*, it also met with their criticism.'The heads of nations must often be stirred, and occasionally be removed', advised Landor, because 'the water that one year is covered with lilies and lotuses, in another may contract a film, and in a few after may have nothing but weeds above and mud below.'[258]

The volunteers believed that full British official involvement in Spanish political and military life could speed the process of liberation. Consequently, they advocated British interventionism well before that policy was embraced by politicians in London. They were also united in advising against Wellington's retreat to Portugal, calling instead for an Anglo-Spanish offensive. Those volunteers who had been sent originally as British military agents regularly exceeded their brief and often exercised the considerable power conferred by their double status of Spanish generals and British envoys over local and national politicians. While loyal to their country of birth, they occasionally neglected their duties towards British politicians and worked in association with Spanish figures to deflect interest from any scheme, such as Tilly's, which threatened to turn the liberation project into one of British permanent disengagement. This was the case even when such a scheme promised a much-desired peace, providing Britain with the control of key ports in the Mediterranean and privileged access to Latin American markets, at the expense of surrendering peninsular Spain, and with that the bulk of the European continent, to France. The British volunteers' primary allegiance was to the cause of Spanish liberation. They were not fighting to enact political change within Spain or to advance British interests, although these objectives could be served along the way if they proved conducive to the victory of the Spanish cause. Theirs was a reductionist ideology, one that relegated all priorities behind the supreme objective of achieving the outright liberation of Spain from the French yoke.

Interpreters and Disseminators of Culture

'Men make history, but history also makes men',[1] the thought-provoking axiom of Fernand Braudel applies to many of the actions and attitudes of the British volunteers in the difficult years of the war in Spain. While Chapter 2 explored the underlying reasons behind their decision to join the Spanish forces, now is the time to examine some of their activities within the context of the cultures and mentalities in which they operated and of which they would become, often inadvertently, interpreters and disseminators. This appears particularly relevant considering that these men operated in the so-called 'Romantic' period, an era when one of the most common and deeply rooted beliefs, in the words of a historian, was that 'reason could never hope to be more than the messenger-boy of turbulent passions'.[2] Evidence will be presented here that tends to confirm this tenet, but only for as long as it remains firmly tied to the realm of public convictions. In the British volunteers' case, reality often encouraged a role reversal in the relationship between reason and sensibilities. Strong emotions, spontaneous acts of personal heroism and other elements considered as integral parts of the Romantic experience,[3] including recourse to folkloric particularisms,[4] appear to have responded to utterly rational and reasonable motives.

It is widely accepted that for much of the eighteenth and early nineteenth centuries, the Spanish monarchy played in Britain the role of the traditional enemy capable of joining forces with American rebels against British interests and siding more often than not with the antagonistic French. From 1760s' onwards, however, a shift in British perceptions can also be noticed through an increased and positive interest on everything Hispanic.[5] Fiction writers, preachers and historians began to idealize Spain – or to be more precise, Old Spain, because the Hispanic world they found so fascinating was firmly set in the past. One of these admirers was William Robertson, author of a biography of Charles V, first published in 1769, but that remained popular until the end of the nineteenth century.[6] For the Scottish scholar, it was under Charles V's rule in the sixteenth century that Spain had attained its highest level of development and

> the powers of Europe were formed into one great political system, in which each took a station, wherein it has since remained with less variation, than could have been expected after the shocks occasioned by so many internal revolutions, and so many foreign wars.[7]

Early nineteenth-century readers could perhaps reasonably infer that Spain, as the cradle of a proven European order, was worth defending against the destabilizing forces of Napoleonic France. It is also during this period when Enlightenment rationalism focused on the future began to be countered by a revival of interest in the past as a source of inspiration and guidance, a variety of historicism exemplified by the popularity of Macpherson's *Ossian* and evocations of ancient heroes, such as Charlemagne and, to a lesser extent, El Cid known in Britain as 'the Spanish Hercules'.[8] As the birth place of *Don Quijote*, a figure who somehow managed to find his way into British popular culture ever since Cervantes' work was first translated into English in 1612,[9] Spain was also perceived as pre-eminently a 'land of honour',[10] or in the words of one of the British volunteers, as 'the most honourable country on Earth'.[11]

This happened at a time when there was a surge in Britain of what might be described as an obsession with the upholding of honour, a phenomenon perhaps part of what James Chandler has called 'the age of sentimental probability',[12] lasting until the 1840s. Social anthropologists warn us that honour is a social construct that mirrors a particular culture, therefore it should not be considered as static but as an ever-changing conceptual field.[13] The transformation of the concept of 'virtue' – which often implied that of honour – in long eighteenth-century British society has been discussed by many scholars.[14] The study of duelling has also attracted a plethora of authors, but the majority seem preoccupied with the ritual – the thrown glove, the appointment of seconds, the encounter at dawn, etc.[15] In an effort to provide a more insightful view of this practice, Stephen Banks has attempted to define the concept of honour as something that was only noticeable when it was wounded and as the means for some men to feel appropriately masculine by prevailing over others through aggressive action.[16] It is difficult to know whether these definitions could also be applied to other activities rather than duelling. So far, no study specifically on the subject of honour has been carried out for this period in a British context. Andrew and Banks offer scant references to attitudes in Ireland and Scotland, as the titles of their respective works rightly indicate.[17] Nonetheless, many of their observations are useful. We know, for example, that among the English military, honour could open a route towards respectability in a society that, strongly disapproving of standing armies, was reluctant to consider soldiers as gentlemen.[18] It was also believed that the best way to develop a corps of fighting men capable of holding back their desire for self-preservation was to inspire them with a passion stronger than fear – and the concept of honour appears to have fitted that role.[19]

In an Iberian context, honour had wider implications. Anthropologists have suggested that this concept, long prevalent among Mediterranean societies, began to be inextricably associated with notions of Spanishness during the Golden Age. It was not enough to be born in any Spanish dominion to be a Spaniard – only those whose honour was untarnished could really claim this nationality.[20] Indeed, in the middle of the war, in 1811, the Cadiz newspaper *El Redactor General* dedicated a front-page article to the subject, considering it as 'the true distinctive characteristic of the Spanish people'.[21]

Although acquired at birth, this virtue required a life-long, conscious effort of preservation. The Golden-Age writer Lope de Vega described honour as something a person 'does not possess, but that is conferred by others'.[22] Safeguarding it was of paramount importance in preserving status and reputation in the community. Loss of honour was equated to loss of life.[23] But this concept could also serve as a measure of social standing, ranking on top of an imaginary vertical line those persons with much honour (usually, the nobility and high clergy) and differentiating them from those with a lower degree of honour, known as *honrados*, and those who lived in the margins of society for having almost no honour at all.[24] This convention remained so strong in societal terms that by the mid-to-late eighteenth century, the politician and director of the Royal Academy of History Pedro Rodríguez de Campomanes (1723–1802) and the philosopher Antonio Xavier Pérez y López (1736–1792) became convinced that artisans were migrating to Portugal, not in search of better economic opportunities, but weary of seeing their activities considered utterly devoid of honour, ranking them alongside executioners and slaughter-men.[25] In a military context, the Bourbons habitually manipulated the levers of the system of honour to maintain the loyalty of the officer corps of their underfunded army. In the first decade of the Bourbon regime, the Marquess de Santa Cruz de Marcenado, considered among the most influential military writers in eighteenth-century Europe,[26] recommended that, to avoid mutiny in the army, it was necessary to

Núm.º 20.º   {10 qtos.}   67

EL REDACTOR GENERAL.

Cadiz jueves 4 de julio de 1811.

ORDEN DE LA PLAZA. = Gefe de dia el coronel D. Agustin Fernandez de la Somera, comandante del 1.ᵉʳ batallon de Cazadores distinguidos. Parada: los cuerpos de la guarnicion. Ronda : Voluntarios distinguidos.

VARIEDADES.
El honor.

El hombre social necesita de la estimacion de los demas: esta es para èl un bien de primera necesidad, y el desprecio le hace un ser miserable. De aquí ha nacido el sentimiento del honor que dirige al bien todas las acciones humanas por el temor del desprecio, y el deseo de la estimacion.

El honor es un suplemento necesario de la lei, cuya influencia no puede extenderse à todas nuestras acciones : en donde acaba la autoridad de aquella, alli empieza el imperio del honor ; imperio mas poderoso que el de la lei misma; pues cuando se hallan en contradiccion estos dos principios, el honor es el que vence.

Despues del patriotismo, manantial de las virtudes antiguas, el honor es el sentimiento que eleva mas la naturaleza ¿ Què efectos tan poderosos no ha producido aun en los siglos bàrbaros que siguieron à la destruccion del imperio romano? ¿Què grandeza no diò à unos hombres medio salvages? El creò aquella caballeria tan valiente y generosa para proteger à los dèbiles en medio de la anarquia de las leyes y de la atrocidad de las costumbres, y en cuyo seno pareciò haberse refugiado todas las virtudes ahuyentadas del resto de la tierra.

Hablando del honor podemos proponer estas dos cuestiones 1.ª ¿ tiene mas influencia en el caràcter del español, que en el de otros pueblos? 2.ª ¿Cualès seràn las causas de su mayor influencia ? Dexamos por ahora su resolucion para excitar la curiosidad de los ilustrados, contentàndonos con decir, que si comparamos los rasgos de heroismo y de grandeza de alma que presentan los anales de cada una de las naciones modernas, decidiremos que la España excede à todas: podemos añadir, que

los mismos extrangeros convienen unànimemente en que el honor es el verdadero distintivo del pueblo español.

¡ Nacion valiente y generosa, cuyo reconocimiento y amor son entre nosotros la mas preciosa, y algunas veces la ùnica rècompensa del hombre grande, no te limites à rendir homenage al mérito ; es preciso que sepas tambien indignarte contra el delito ! ¡Afrenta ; desprecia à aquellos hombres que te deshonran, haciendo estèril tu celo, tu valor, y todas tus virtudes : y cubre de oprobio al delincuente astuto, ò poderoso, que tan frecuentemente se acoge à tu seno para evitar el golpe de la espada de la lei!

Cuando es tan raro el amor de la patria, el honor es el resorte mas poderoso que puede tocar un legislador para llegar al grande objeto que se propone ; pero sobre todo en la profesion militar es el que empleado hàbilmente debe producir maravillosos efectos. No olviden nuestros politicos modernos, que los antiguos, sin embargo de ser conducidos al heroismo por el amor de la patria, procuraron mover el sentimiento del honor con brillantes distinciones y pomposos homenages concedidos al mèrito militar; y hallaràn la causa de la diferencia entre sus virtudes y las nuestras.

IMPRESOS

Manifiesto que la junta de Cadiz dirige el pueblo que la instaló, acerca de lo ocurrido en ella de resultas del reglamento de provincias. En consecuencia de las òrdenes recibidas por la junta para que su constitucion se variase, conforme à aquel reglamento, representó al consejo de Regencia en 9 de mayo de este año: que „ desde su instalación habria ceñido sus funcio„ nes à la defensa de esta plaza, si la triste suerte „ del erario no la hubiese estimulado à propo-

Figure 3 Article 'El Honor' (The Honour), published in the front page of the Cadiz newspaper, *El Redactor General*, 4 July 1811, by courtesy of *Ministerio de Cultura de España*.

ensure that soldiers were paid what they were owed and that officers should receive the promotion they merited promptly because, he argued, 'the former acts for utilitarian reasons, while the latter serves on the basis of honour'.[27] This rationale engendered some abuses. Not only many officers took to gambling to make up for insufficient funds, but honour at times was confused with an exaggerated *amour propre* that undermined discipline by interpreting all reprimands from superiors as insults that could only be avenged by duelling.[28] Yet, even after the failure of the campaigns of 1794, the military expert Clemente Peñalosa y Zuñiga predicated the notion that in Spain 'military tactics shape soldiers, honour creates heroes'.[29]

In Britain, the outbreak of the Spanish War of Independence would have the effect of turning Spain into a field of honour in its fullest sense. As we have seen, many British artists contemplated the idea of engaging directly in the conflict to test their mettle. Yet, only one followed that call: Walter Savage Landor.[30] Unlike other British volunteers, Landor lacked military experience, spoke little Spanish and was even deficient in French, the language of the enemy and *lingua franca* of Spanish polite society, but he had the advantage of easy access to substantial funds, thanks to a family bequest. Using this personal wealth, he was able to donate 10,000 reales (about £110 of the time)[31] to the government of Galicia and finance the cost of transferring troops, which he led in person on a 300-kilometre march to the headquarters of the Spanish general Blake in Astorga.[32] He then linked up with other Spanish forces advancing across the north of the country. Apart from close encounters with marauding French groups, he experienced no direct combat – something that deeply mortified him because he wished to be in the middle of a battle. He told his friend Southey that

> In this expectation, I remained nearly three months in the neighbourhood of the Galician army, sometimes at Reynosa, sometimes at Aguilar. I returned to Bilbao after the French had entered. I had the satisfaction of serving three launches with powder and muskets.[33]

For the poet, however, his highest act of heroism consisted in carrying on his shoulders for 6 or 7 miles a child too heavy for an exhausted mother after a battle in Bilbao. 'These are things' – he said – 'without difficulty and without danger, yet they please, independently of gratitude or applause'.[34] Heroism, he discovered, could also be found in humanitarian aid.

Landor's exploits in Spain were short-lived: having arrived in Corunna in early August, he was back in Britain by late October.[35] But, however brief his time in Spain, his exposure to Spanish sensitivities made a lasting impression and provided much material for his next work, the tragedy *Count Julian*.[36] Traditional Spanish concepts of honour form the central theme of the play, based on a Spanish legend. The hero, Count Julian, seeks revenge on his monarch, Roderic, the last Visigoth king of Spain, who deflowered his daughter. In doing so, he betrays Roderic to the Moors, an act that leads to the Muslim conquest of Hispania. What is significantly novel in Landor's treatment of the legend is the stress he laid on the argument that, by placing the defence of personal honour over that owed to his homeland, Count Julian lost in the process his entitlement to be considered truly Spanish. This would have been interpreted at the time as an allusion to the *afrancesados* – those Spaniards who supported the puppet government of Joseph Bonaparte in Madrid. In the mouth of Count Julian, Landor set the requirements for being a true Spaniard:

> All are not Spaniards who draw breath in Spain,
> Those are, who live for her, who die for her,
> Who love her glory and lament her fall.
> O may I too –
>
> (Act 2, Scene 1)[37]

By betraying Spain, Count Julian was aware that he would not only be considered as a traitor to his King, but he was to become stateless as well. Thus, the tragedy is a long declaration of repentance for dishonouring his homeland in the quest for avenging the honour of his daughter. Spanish readers would have understood from the very beginning of the play that there was no possibility of a positive outcome: Count Julian was damned if he did not avenge his daughter, but he would also be damned by so doing. Landor tried to make this clear to British readers by opening his tragedy with Count Julian lamenting

> I have avenged me, Opas,
> More than enough: I sought but to have hurled
> The brands of war on one detested head,
> And died upon his ruin. O my country!
> O lost to honour, to thyself, to me,
> Why on barbarian hands devolves thy cause,
> Spoilers, blasphemers!
>
> (Act 1, Scene 1)[38]

In the same way that Count Julian opened the gates of Hispania to the blasphemous Moors, the *afrancesados* were seen as collaborating dishonourably with the atheist French for the sake of deposing the corrupted Bourbon administration. Many served the new regime only as a means of survival under foreign occupation, but this short-term strategy of subsistence would, it was predicted, result in long-term social exclusion.[39] It is possible that Landor took the figure of José de Mazarredo (1745–1812), one of the defeated admirals of

Trafalgar who became a minister in the Josephine administration, as a prototype for his dramatic hero. Landor mentioned Mazarredo in a letter addressed to Southey in November 1809. Opening with joyful news of a Spanish victory ('May the spirit of prophecy never forsake you, and never be less propitious to the cause of freedom!'),[40] Landor immediately lamented to learn that 'a most excelent man and most experienced officer' such as Mazarredo had made the error of judgement of joining the French because 'he thought it less disgraceful, as perhaps some others do, to writhe for a moment under superior strength than to slumber out all his days in a sty of his own littering'.[41]

Landor's tragedy also provides the reader with some hints of an autobiographical nature, as reflected in the following extract where it is clear that he changed the original locations of the legend – Ceuta and Toledo – to fit those he had personally visited

> If strength be wanted for security,
> Mountains the guard, forbidding all approach
> With iron-pointed and uplifted gates,
> Thou wilt be welcome too in Aguilar –
> Impenetrable, marble-turreted,
> Surveying from aloft the limpid ford,
> The massive fane, the sylvan avenue –
> Whose hospitality I proved myself,
> A willing leader in no impious war
> When fame and freedom urged me – or mayst dwell
> In Reynosas dry and thriftless dale,
> Unharvested beneath October moons,
> Amongst those frank and cordial villagers.
>
> (Act 2, Scene 2)[42]

Likely urged on by 'fame and freedom' to travel to Spain himself, Landor conveyed effectively here the deceptive impression of impenetrability of the mountainous Spanish Northern regions, particularly the area surrounding Aguilar,[43] which the French eventually captured. The dreadful implications of war for a rural society are easily inferred through his depiction of the 'frank and cordial villagers' of Reynosa living with 'unharvested' fields (probably resulting from the recruitment of their youths in the army) and 'beneath October moons', that is, with winter approaching.

The poet's poor command of French lay at the root of a bitter dispute with the British envoy Charles Stuart that fits squarely within Banks' definition of honour as something only noticeable when it is wounded.[44] In Corunna, shortly after his arrival, Landor had understood Stuart to be telling their Spanish hosts that he – Landor – was 'fou' (mad) and that he 'n' a pas l' argent' (doesn't have the money). Landor brooded over this slight for 10 days as he trekked through the mountains to Astorga. On his return to Britain, he made it his business to print and distribute copies of a letter composed in the course of that march. Addressed to Stuart's secretary, Charles Vaughan, the letter complained that he had been portrayed by Stuart as a 'prepostrous impostor'.[45] He demanded a retraction in order to restore his standing in the estimation of the 'brave and generous' Spanish people.[46] Though mollified by the British envoy, who persuaded the Spanish authorities to accord him the rank of *coronel* in the Spanish Army,[47] Landor declared himself disgusted with his fellow countrymen – a judgement reinforced, in his view, by the national disgrace of the Cintra Convention, which permitted captured French forces to return home fully armed on the strength of disingenuous promises that they would play no further part in the war. Landor did not return to the Peninsula, but he never abandoned his commitment to the Spanish cause.

The first edition of *Count Julian* was published – anonymously – in 1812, when the war was still raging.[48] At the time, many readers attributed it to Byron. In a letter to Lady Melbourne, dated 5 April 1813, the future martyr in the cause of Greek emancipation complained of 'a Mr. Landor's tragedy, the reputation of which I was obliged to bear this winter'.[49] Byron disliked Landor and the feeling was reciprocal. Landor always felt that the man famously branded by Lady Caroline Lamb as 'mad, bad and dangerous to know' had stolen his thunder and enjoyed an unmerited celebrity.[50] Although *Count Julian* had a very limited print run and never reached the stage, Landor's view of Spain was widely discussed in intellectual cricles and inspired other Romantic writers of his period, particularly his friend Southey, author of the first popular history of the Peninsular War.[51] His Spanish experience had a lasting influence on his writings[52] and they, in turn, proved influential to future generations, including the artists of the pre-Raphaelite movement, equally attracted to a past that was a mix of legend and historical reality.[53]

Some of the volunteers, while they were not necessarily writers,[54] were no less attuned to Spanish historicism. Long before Joseph Bonaparte usurped the throne, popular resistance to the modernizing influences of the Bourbons – often imported from France – had found expression in cultural forms. Spaniards remained deeply attached to the authors and playwrights of the sixteenth and seventeenth centuries, such as Lope de Vega and Calderón de la Barca, and they idealized the heroes of the Reconquest of Spain from Moorish occupation.[55] Historicism permeated all social classes and political opinions. At the time of the Peninsular War, Spanish intellectuals, such as the head of the Royal Academy of History, Canon Martinez Marina, predicated all constitutional reform on the case for a return to the medieval Castilian *Cortes*.[56] Many key figures of the so-called 'Fernandist party' who sided with the Patriots, such as the Count de Montijo and the Duke of San Carlos, supported a traditionalism that, built on opposition to the absolutism represented by the Godoy regime, purportedly defended the 'ancient constitution' and the old 'fundamental laws'. They attributed much of Spain's decline to the gradual demolition of Spain's medieval past of corporate and regional distinctions.[57] In disturbing and menacing circumstances, recourse to an idealized past went beyond the remit of a mere reaction against innovations. Historicism became a source of validating authority – through the strength of allegedly effective deeds – as well as the source of much-needed moral courage and hope. It was in this context that the sieges of Saragossa and Gerona fostered comparisons with earlier Iberian feats such as the martydom of Sagunto (219–218 BC).[58] During the 7th week of the 7-month-long siege of Gerona, for example, the Irish volunteer Rudolf Marshal told the British consul in Cadiz:

> How long we shall be able to fight it out against the 3 plagues of war, pestilence and famine I can not foresee, but this is certain that while we have a Bit to eat and a charge of powder left we will fight it out and when we can no longer maintain the Post we will not capitulate, but sword in Hand march out and cut our way thro the Enemy or die gloriously like the Saguntines.[59]

In Asturias, the Patriots took inspiration from the figure of Don Pelayo, the first Asturian monarch whose victory at Covadonga over the Moors in 722 assured the survival of a Christian stronghold in northern Iberia and opened the way for the *Reconquista*. At the time of Moore's defeat in Galicia and the second fall of Madrid, when everything appeared to be lost, the Irish volunteer William Parker Carrol sought to rally the Asturians with a proclamation that contained an analogy between past and present: 'Remember Covadonga, remember that you were the first to proclaim the National Independence and the freedom of your Prince-King'.[60] The Asturian provincial government had been the first to refuse allegiance to the French regime and to dispatch envoys to London in search of aid to build up the resistance. Recent and distant past provided good examples for keeping up the fight, particulary in the context of regional historical continuity.

Among the volunteers, the most fervently attached to historicism was a Scot weaned on Robertson's biography of Charles V and on Macpherson's stories of Gaelic heroism. In 1810, John Downie proposed the raising of a corps of 3,000 men to Marquess de la Romana, head of the Army of the Left. Under the name of the *Leal Legión Extremeña* (Loyal Legion of Extremadura), or simply *Legión de Extremadura* (Legion of Extremadura), this regiment would adopt both the attire and tactics of the late sixteenth century.[61] Downie was well acquainted with the frontier region of Extremadura, since he had been engaged in several unauthorised *reconnoitre* expeditions from the Portuguese headquarters of the British Army in Castelo Branco[62] before relinquishing his Commissariat post to join the Spanish *guerrillas* in early 1810.[63] Governing one of the poorest provinces of Spain, further devastated by the passing of French, Spanish and British armies, the authorities of Extremadura had already turned to the past to organize the resistance. On 20 April 1809, the Supreme *Junta* of Extremadura declared a 'Holy War' against the French and raised a 'Crusade' of peasants and clergy identified by the black flag with a red cross used during the *Reconquista*.[64] The national *Junta Central* applauded the measure and even went to the extreme of ordering the chief of the regional army, General Gregorio de la Cuesta, to ensure that all Extremadurian soldiers should wear the Crusaders' cross on their chests.[65] If Downie wanted to distinguish his troops from these so far unsuccessful forces, then he did not need to look far for inspiration. A British visitor noticed at the time that the cathedral choir of Seville – a city Downie visited a few days before launching his project – was still attired 'in the Spanish garb of the sixteenth century, with slashed doublets, shoes adorned with roses and hats with plumes of feathers'.[66]

Based on La Romana's recommendations, Downie was made *coronel* in the Extremadurian army, a rank that was soon recognized by the Spanish army as well.[67] Although considered as a provincial regiment, Downie promised that the *Leal Legión de Extremadura* would be ready to be dispatched wherever the Spanish national authorities decided.[68] It was to be a force in the service of Spanish liberation, not the instrument of local interests. Yet, the Scot adroitly exploited regional attachments by recalling in his proclamations that the two most famous Spanish Conquistadors, Francisco de Pizarro and Hernán Cortés, were natives of Extremadura. His first recruitment call, on 28 July 1810, was accordingly addressed to the 'Descendants of Cortés and Pizarro' who were summoned to 'revive in your deeds the valour and the virtues of such illustrious ancestors'.[69] Henceforth, the memory of the Conquistadors, and particularly that of the native of Trujillo, Pizarro, was to be invoked frequently by both

Figure 4 Juan (John) Downie (1777–1826), unknown artist, *circa* 1812, by courtesy of *Museo de las Cortes de Cádiz, Excmo. Ayuntamiento de Cádiz.*

provincial and national authorities in their communications to the people of Extremadura.[70] Proof, not just that imitation is the sincerest form of flattery, but that Downie had successfully identified a lever with which to open Spanish collective memories of daring feats, linking the provincial to the national effort.

The image of the Conqueror of Peru also had strong connotations for a British audience due in part to the extraordinary success of *Pizarro*, Sheridan's adaptation of August von Kotzebue's *Die Spanier in Peru oder Rollas Tod*, the most popular play of the 1790s in London and the second most popular of the entire eighteenth century.[71] For some reason so far unexplained, it was particularly appreciated in military circles. The British agent and volunteer George Landmann remembered it being performed by an all-male cast in the officers' mess of the garrison in Gibraltar in the early 1800s.[72] Although originally the piece allegorized the Conquistador as Napoleon, the Spaniards as French and the peace-loving Native Americans as Britons, it was enough to introduce British audiences to one of the most emblematic figures of Spanish history. It is possible that such a presentation, added to the widely accepted belief that Scottish warriors drew pride and courage from wearing ancient tartan belted plaids, sporrans and *sgian dubhs* (ceremonial knives), proved helpful to the Scot when he decided to exploit connections with British politicians and supply officers to procure materials for the manufacture of red and white tights, padded doublets, short cloaks and wide-brimmed caps reminiscent of those worn by Pizarro's men.[73] He was initially successful, to the extent that he was even authorized to take arms and ammunition from Wellington's stores.[74] But that authorisation was withdrawn as soon as the Duke realized the material and potential political implications of his original endorsement of the project. Since Talavera and his retreat into Portugal, Wellington was locked in a power struggle with the Spanish authorities for the control of war of operations in the Peninsula. He had asked them to refrain from granting commissions to British officers in their army without his prior consent, which he conditioned to the implementation of wide reforms in the Spanish military system. He was furious because the Spaniards ignored his demands and also feared that British officers and soldiers would quit the Portuguese service to serve in Spain.[75] With Wellington's opposition, British assistance became minimal and sporadic.[76] Consequently, the manufacture of the uniforms and the organization and running of the force had to be financed largely from Downie's own pocket and that of his elder brother Charles, whom he enrolled in the legion.[77] Charles Downie was a relatively prosperous sheep importer in Paisley, Scotland, and it appears that he used some of the profits collected from the sale of Merino sheep formerly belonging to the deposed Prime Minister Godoy to fund his brother's project.[78]

In Spain, Downie's request to the *Cortes* for 3,000 men had been favourably received.[79] His most ardent supporter was Francisco Fernández Golfin, deputy for Extremadura and *coronel* in the Army of the Left.[80] Golfin was a leading figure among Spanish utopian liberals who believed that heroic acts carried out by a small group of men, even if unsuccessful, were needed to encourage and stimulate the efforts of others. It was on that premise that he became a recruiting agent for Downie's legion.[81] He was not alone. The Scot's initiative merited the support of a far-ranging group of deputies. The Fernandist diplomat Evaristo Pérez de Castro, representative of Valladolid, and the moderate liberal José Castelló (Valencia) claimed – as did Golfin – to be acquainted with Downie and as such vouched for his patriotism and the veracity of his promises.[82] The ultra-conservative Alonso María Vera y Pantoja (Mérida),[83] the reformist priest Joaquín Lorenzo Villanueva (Valencia)[84] and the man considered as the 'father of Spanish constitutionalism' Agustín Argüelles Alvarez (Asturias),[85] all applauded Downie's determination.[86] Although parliamentary records of the debate are too brief to allow us to discern the variety of reasons that most likely were behind such overwhelming support, what is important is that nobody considered Downie's scheme outlandish. A motion introduced by Golfin and Argüelles recommending the Regency to speed the implementation of the Scot's project – which was mainly meant to facilitate the supply of soldiers – was passed without a single objection.[87]

However, not all Spaniards showed such enthusiasm. On 19 August 1811, as the recently appointed commander of the Army of Extremadura, General Javier Castaños, the former regent who as head of the Executive had approved Downie's plans almost a year earlier, warned Secretary of War José Heredia that 'theory was failing to turn into practice'[88] because recruitment for the legion was proving slow. He attributed this shortcoming to the sixteenth-century-style uniforms which 'for Soldiers and Peasants little versed in history, instead of recalling the feats of their forbearers, they think it is something ridiculous because it is no longer in use.'[89] That may well have been the case, but there were more pressing reasons behind the shortage of recruits, which serve to qualify Castaños's assessment. The war in Extremadura had not only devastated the province's economy, but also exacerbated a population crisis which, since the turn of the century, had plagued the region.[90] In demographic terms, Extremadura was a desert. Moreover, Downie had already warned the *Cortes* that the occupation of almost a third of the province by French troops was not only making enlistment difficult, but also eliminating any chance of requisitioning horses in sufficient numbers for a cavalry regiment.[91] Based on the original arrangement, the responsibility for providing men rested with the provincial authorities.[92] Nevertheless, Downie issued three proclamations in over a month in an effort to increase the number of both recruits and horses.[93] He targeted not just Extremenians, but all Spaniards living in both free and occupied areas, as well as *guerrillas* fighting in neighbouring La Mancha.[94] He faced competition from officers in the Spanish army in search of recruits for their own regiments, including the Chief of Staff of the Army of the Left (now 'Fifth Army'), Martín la Carrera.[95] Castaños thought that with his limited knowledge of Spanish military practice, Downie would find it advantageous to accept the command of one of the many existing battalions put together from the defeated armies of the Centre and the Left. As Downie rejected the offer, Castaños suggested that the fabrics brought from England should be used to manufacture modern uniforms and that the legion, which so far had recruited 560 men out of the 3,000 originally proposed, should be divided into four battalions (Tiradores de Badajoz, Mérida, Truxillo, Plasencia) each with 500 men.[96] Encouraged by the idea that this would allow the first battalion of the legion to take the field attached to the Fifth Army, Downie accepted the bulk of Castaños's suggestions[97] – bar the one regarding outfit – because he stated that among the men he had already recruited, the ancient uniforms served to awaken memories of past glories, the desire to be free and, crucially, 'there is not one who does not wish to dress as his Grandparents'.[98]

In later years, much satire would be derived – notably by the novelist Benito Pérez Galdós – from recollections of Downie's men not only attired in garb dating from the time of Philip II, but also armed with swords, slings and crossbows.[99] Yet, at the time there were compelling practical reasons for this. Patriotic Spain had lost access to armament factories – all unfortunately located close to the French frontier, thus now under occupation or out of reach – and had to accept anything procurable at inflated black market prices. Assistance was sought from London, but Whitehall, fearful that foreign demand for weapons would drive up prices at home, reacted by prohibiting exports of firearms. Spain would receive British weapons, but only by way of 'grant-in-aid', which would be used to influence the conduct of the war and to bargain for commercial privileges regarding Spanish America.[100] Downie was well aware of this situation. As early as in June 1810, he had written to his former chief Francisco de Miranda to acknowledge gratefully that the Venezuelan liberator had been the first one to mention the idea of using lances to overcome the scarcity of weapons.[101] It was not that Downie was blind to the advantages of modern weaponry. As we have seen, he did his outmost to recruit men armed with rifles and pistols.[102] Nevertheless, almost two decades later, Robert Blakeney, a young British soldier who claimed to have seen the Legion of Extremadura in action, scorned Downie's efforts describing him as 'a person once rational, but now bent on charging with his motley crew the hardy and steadily disciplined cavalry of France' and the legion itself as an 'equestrian Spanish band, clothed like harlequins' whose members were 'intractable as swine, obstinate as mules and unmanageable as bullocks'.[103] Blakeney penned these impressions in 1828 and they remained unpublished until 1899.[104]

The judgement passed at the time was strikingly different. The first engagement of the legion took place on 7 March 1811, around the village of Don Benito, near Medellin and proved to be successful, resulting in the capture of seven Frenchmen and over 20 horses – an outcome that merited the admiration of officers in the Fifth Army.[105] On 23 June 1811, transmitting information published by the *Gaceta de Extremadura*, the newspaper *El Conciso* reported in Cadiz the arrival in the hills of Yelves, in route from Medellin to Badajoz, of

> one squadron and two battalions of the Legion of Extremadura, formed by Colonel Downie. His suit in the old Spanish style brings to mind the glorious times of the Cordobas, Cortes, Pizarros, & c. whose successors have not denied nor will deny that are worthy of such ancestors. Soon these brave Extremadurians will take the fields of glory, and will familiarise the French with these names because, if they had heard of them with veneration in past centuries, with no

less respect they will hear of their heroic grandchildren, irreconcilable enemies of the tyrant of France and of Europe.[106]

On 28 August 1811, the legion's cavalry, now attached to the army commanded by the Spanish general Count de Penne Villemur, had a brief encounter with a small detachment of the forces of the General Maximilien Foy on the outskirts of the ancient village of Arroyo del Puerco (today known as Arroyo de la Luz). After fierce fighting, the French escaped and took refuge in the nearby town of Cáceres from where they were also expelled, after heavy losses were registered in both sides.[107] This action served as a prelude to the Battle of Arroyo Molinos, on 28 October 1811. A combined force of British, Portuguese and Spanish troops surprised a French division under General Jean-Baptiste Girard. The result was the capture of 1 general (André-François Bron de Bailly), 1 colonel (the Prince d' Arenberg), 35 lieutenant colonels and inferior officers and other 1,400 prisoners, 200 of whom were apprehended by Downie's men,[108] who now included the recently arrived British volunteer Edmond Temple.[109] Contrary to Blakeney's later testimony, the British commander Lieutenant-General Rowland Hill told Lord Wellington that the legion had conducted itself 'in a manner to excite my entire approbation',[110] thus contributing to a victory crucial in halting the French advance into Portugal. To the Spanish authorities, the British commander talked of his admiration for the 'zeal, good conduct and gallantry' of the Spanish troops, including those of Colonel Downie.[111] From January to early April 1812, the infantry and cavalry of the legion accompanied General Pablo Morillo in a series of raids over French-occupied areas of Extremadura and Andalusia. This included a spectacular dash to Seville when the legion managed to arrive at its very gates, culminating in a skirmish at Espartinas (5 April 1812), as a result of which Downie was promoted to the rank of *brigadier* and the legion as a whole received the highest order of Patriot Spain – the *Gran Cruz de San Fernando*.[112] Downie was soon granted the personal honour of the *Orden de Carlos III* as well.[113] Far from resting on their laurels, the legion volunteered to join a similar expedition under the orders of the *mariscal de campo* Juan de la Cruz Mourgeon in the area surrounding Seville known as Condado de Niebla. With Downie as second in command, they succeeded in displacing the French from the village of Sanlúcar la Mayor, a strategic point in the French line of defence of that city.[114]

All these victories, albeit small, demonstrated, at least to the Spanish themselves, that they could carry the day by sheer valour, notwithstanding the scarcity of fighting men, horses and the rudimentary weaponry. The powerful impact on Spanish spirits is clear from the poems dedicated to Downie that intertwined

British and Spanish Romantic traditions. One entitled *El heroísmo* (Heroism)[115] invokes 'Osián divino' (Divine Ossian) to celebrate 'Downie, el osado' (Downie, the daring). McPherson's *Ossian* had been translated into Spanish in 1788 and enjoyed wide circulation as from 1800.[116] In another poem, *La voz del patriota en Extremadura* (The Patriot's voice in Extremadura),[117] the poet suggested that the Scot had resurrected the conquistador phantoms of Pizarro and Cortés in making 'el loco francés' (the mad Frenchman) run away. The author of these verses was Cristóbal de Beña, a young poet who was among the first to join the legion and became Downie's military secretary.[118] His work, however, should not be considered part of a campaign to fabricate a hero as the poems were not published in London until 1813,[119] after Downie's feats had already taken place and been honoured by the Spanish authorities. A similar trend can be found in the work of a recognized leader of the Spanish Romantic movement, Ángel María de Saavedra y Ramírez de Baquedano, Duke of Rivas.[120] This is evident in the following sonnet entitled '*Al bizarro escocés Don Juan Downie*' (To the brave Scot Don Juan Downie):

¡Oh, de Fingal heroico descendiente	Oh, descendant of heroic Fingal
que de las selvas de la Escocia fría	that of the cold forests of Scotland
volaste a defender la patria mía	flew to defend my homeland
con duro brazo y corazón ardiente!	with hard arm and fiery heart!
tú que del manso Betis la corriente	you, that the current of tame Betis
con tu sangre teñiste el claro día,	dyed with your blood in clear day,
que Híspalis admiró la valentía,	that Hispalis admired the courage,
con que libraste a su oprimida gente:	with which you liberated his oppressed people:
tu merecida gloria eterna sea,	be your deserved glory eternal,
por donde quier que esgrimas el acero,	wherever you wield the steel,
victoria grata tus esfuerzos vea.	victory granted gracefully to your efforts
Y sigue siempre el estandarte ibero,	And always follow the Iberian standard,
pues España se jacta y se recrea	because Spain boasts and rejoices
de contar en sus huestes tal guerrero.	from having such a warrior in her army.[121]

The communion of Spanish and British literary traditions reflected the binational dimension of Downie's fame. During a brief trip back home in 1813, accompanied by fellow volunteer James Duff, fourth Earl of Fife, Downie was fêted from the very moment the pair landed in Portsmouth and all the way to Scotland.[122] While in London, the Earl of Glasgow, Lord Lieutenant of Renfrewshire, the county of Downie's family, presided at a banquet in his honour and presented him with a commemorative sword.[123] In Glasgow, Downie received the honour of the freedom of that city from the Chief Magistrate and local MP Kirkman Finlay.[124] On 19 May 1813, the Prince Regent knighted him.[125] Sir John Downie's reputation encouraged other Britons to volunteer with the Spanish forces such as Neil MacDougall[126] and Robert Steele who joined the legion in August 1813.[127] The new recruits appeared to have been attracted by the idea that, among the many testimonies of recognition conferred upon Downie in Spain, he had received the sword of Pizarro from the conquistador's descendant, Jacinto de Orellana y Pizarro, Marquess de la Conquista, who, too old to fight for the Spanish cause himself, asked the Scot to promise him that the weapon would never fall into the hands of the French.[128] Captain Edmund Temple, in the legion since August 1811, ended his semi-biographical satirical work *The Life of Pill Garlick; Rather a Whimsical Sort of Fellow*, published in Dublin and in London in 1813,[129] with the tale of how the main character had decided to join the Spaniards

> under the banner of Patriotism, and the motto of 'In ferrum pro Libertate ruimus' (sic). How there he thrashed the French on two or three occasions by the side of the heroic and truly meritorious possessor of the conquering sword of Pizarro.[130]

That sword had already featured in an episode that serves to illustrate the sensitivity felt by some of the British volunteers in matters of honour. Two days after removing the French from Sanlúcar la Mayor, on 27 August 1812, the Spanish forces under Cruz Mourgeon, including the *Legión de Extremadura*, and a brigade of British troops headed by Lt. Col. John Byrne Skerret resolved to storm Seville. They chose to do it through the western suburb of Triana with the intention of crossing a bridge over the river Guadalquivir that led directly into the city. The French, however, had barricaded the structure, cut ditches in the roadway and defended the entrance with a number of cannon. Two assaults on the enemy position failed, and rumours soon had it that a third would not be attempted. It was then that Downie spurred his way to the front, galloped along the bridge brandishing the sword of Pizarro, and, though struck by a ball from a round of canister that left a great gouge in his right cheek, blinded him in his right eye and tore off his right ear, jumped his horse clean over the enemy entrenchments. The infantry following him had been unable to cross the ditch, so he found himself there alone. He was quickly bayoneted and dragged from his mount. Severely wounded and close to being captured, Downie threw the precious weapon back to his companions on the other side of the river.[131] According to the diary of a British officer, Colonel Sir Augustus Simon Frazer,[132] Downie was 'loaded with every opprobrious abuse' by his captor, the French general Eugène-Casimir Villatte who ordered Downie to be tied to a gun '. . . which was literally done, and Sir John remained on it for some distance, till he fainted with fatigue, anger, and vexation.'[133] Although eventually released to the Allies on parole by order of Marshal Soult and formally exchanged for, it was claimed, over 150 French prisoners,[134] the British diarist added that since that encounter

> He [Downie] has never ceased to upbraid Vilatte (sic) with his ungenerous conduct; writing to him to demand either an apology, or a duel, all of which, he told us yesterday, he was about to repeat, as he commanded at one of our outposts [in northern Spain, almost a year later], and Villatte (sic) at the posts opposite. Altogether to convey more the idea of a Quixote to one's mind than any man I ever saw.[135]

We do not know if Villatte ever apologized. From the viewpoint of this British diarist, Downie's challenge to a duel was in keeping with contemporary English attitudes regarding the safeguarding of a man's reputation,[136] even if the way the challenge was offered was somewhat unusual. This behaviour accorded precisely with Spanish ideas of how a man should behave with honour. Downie could not allow Villatte to tarnish his reputation in the eyes of his British, but particularly, his Spanish comrades. Honour had not only to be defended, but had to be *seen* to be defended as well. The fact that the duel did not take place is not really important. What mattered was that Downie was prepared to stride out into no-man's-land in order to issue the challenge. Moreover, he had to perform this ritual under the eyes of impartial witnesses, in this case the massed ranks of the two opposing armies. Only through such bravado could honour be reacquired. This was not irrational behaviour. In both the British and the Spanish army, a man who failed to defend his honour could no longer maintain his standing as an officer.[137] In a Spanish context, the stakes were even higher. He was as good as dead. Retirement, resignation or suicide were often the only options.[138] As the sole volunteer to request the granting of Spanish nationality,[139] Downie might also have feared that a dent in his honour would undermine his claim to Spanishness.

Recently, it has been attributed to Spanish historiography of the late nineteenth century the belief that Spaniards were innately and uniquely honour-driven and dauntless, thus making them naturally apt for a war of resistance. The argument is that authors such as José Gómez de Arteche y Moro, Angel Ganivet and Enrique Rodríguez-Solis established this assumption as foundation for the myth of the unconquerable *guerrillero* to satisfy the political agenda of Spain during her last imperialistic struggle in Cuba.[140] Whereas there might be reasons to doubt these historians' account of a nation of *guerrilleros*, the volunteers' correspondence suggests that the conviction that Spaniards were naturally inclined to fierce resistance was already widely held at the time of the War of Independence. In his moving account of Moore's retreat from Corunna penned on 1 March 1809, the volunteer surgeon, Henry Milburne, made a passionate plea to persevere in supporting the Spaniards because, notwithstanding the checks and disasters they had sustained,

> their real character is [distinct], they are faithful to their engagements, constant in their pursuits, and possessing a sense of honour bordering on romantic.[141]

In March 1810, William Parker Carrol told the British Foreign Secretary, Lord Wellesley that Spain was never to be 'subjugated to the Tyrant of the Continent [because] there is something in the Spanish Character that will never assimilate or amalgamate with that of France'.[142] On 13 September 1811, hearing that Duff was planning to return home on becoming the fourth Earl of Fife, Whittingham rejoiced because he thought his fellow volunteer would have opportunities to lobby in favour of Spain by communicating to his friends – particularly the Prince Regent – 'the singular character of its inhabitants'.[143] Spaniards differed from other Europeans and needed to be understood in terms of their own peculiar culture.

The volunteers harnessed the belief in such distinctiveness to encourage the production of powerful instruments of propaganda in favour of the Spanish cause as well as other more enduring examples of material culture. In the early stages of the war, it was thanks to volunteer Charles Doyle that a single book contributed to promulgate Europe-wide sympathy for the Spanish cause.[144] While in Galicia, in 1808, Doyle met Charles Vaughan, the travelling academic who acted as Charles Stuart's secretary, and persuaded him to travel to Saragossa shortly after the first of its two epic sieges (June–August 1808).[145] Doyle introduced Vaughan to four figures who came to symbolize the Spanish character during the war: Agustina Domenech, the 22-year-old who took the place of an injured artilleryman in operating a gun against advancing French forces while vowing 'never to quit it [the gun] alive until *Zaragosa* was free'[146]; the fighting priest *Padre* Santiago Sasso[147]; the Countess Burita, an aristocratic Florence Nightingale type who dedicated time and money to caring for the injured, and the 'perfectly wellbred' though 'lacking in military experience'[148] local leader, General José de Palafox (1775–1847), who, when asked by the French to capitulate, sent three words as reply: 'guerra al cuchillo' (war even to the knife).[149]

The Convention of Cintra and the disaster of Moore's expeditionary force had brought about a sharp reduction of enthusiasm for Spanish liberation in Britain.[150] When the French mounted a second siege in December 1808, Doyle wrote to Vaughan – now back at Oxford – imploring him to seek public support for a relief operation, which the British government deemed futile.[151] Vaughan responded by producing his seminal wor*k*, *Narrative of the Siege of Zaragosa,* which was an instant success. As the book ran to five editions within its first year,[152] Doyle supplied Vaughan with further material to update his text, conveying images of cadaverous soldiers and civilians devastated by hunger and epidemics, forced to see their homes obliterated, their women raped and their clergy murdered by the enemy.[153] Though Vaughan's work had been overtaken by events – Saragossa fell to the French in February 1809 – the book provided ammunition for those in Britain who still supported the Spanish struggle.[154] The profits generated from the sale of the book and the publication of extracts in newspapers (500 dollars) were delivered by Vaughan (appointed in 1810 secretary of the British legation in Spain) to the Countess Burita for the aid of Aragonese refugees in Cadiz.[155] More importantly, his account of the siege – the first to appear in book form – inspired a generation of Romantic authors. Agustina is considered the model for Adosinda in Southey's *Roderick* and of the fighting women in Felicia Hemans's works ranging from *The Siege of Valencia* (1823) to the lyric *Woman on the Field of Battle* (1830).[156] In *Childe Harold's Pilgrimage* (1812), Byron referred to her as the 'Spanish maid', but tradition has it that he named her the 'maid of Saragossa'.[157] He certainly claimed to have heard her story during his brief visit to Spain in 1809, when Agustina was pointed out to him as they passed on a street in Seville.[158] Yet, his stanzas were published 3 years after Vaughan's book and by then Agustina's credentials as the epitome of the Spanish Amazon were well established.[159]

Volunteer James Duff similarly helped to bring about a wave of interest in a Spanish culture fixed on the idea of a passionate and indomitable national character that was rooted in the past. While fighting with the forces of Generals Cuesta and Areizaga, Duff befriended a Neapolitan officer, Federico Moretti,[160] a gifted musician now credited with bringing modern music notation to the guitar, particularly by annotating Andalusian dances, including sixteenth-century *seguidillas*.[161] Spaniards recognized the morale-boosting power of music to such an extent that in the Spanish army to be a musician was considered an honourable occupation, often leading to promotion.[162] Nursing a wound suffered during the defence of Matagorda, Duff postponed his homecoming in 1811, yet, when he did return to England, in May 1813, he brought the celebrated dancer Maria Mercandotti.[163] The young 'Andalusian Venus' introduced the exotic *bolero* to London audiences thirsting for excitement.[164] Years later, still under Duff's patronage, her dance, to music composed by Moretti's friend, the *afrancesado* Fernando Sor, caught the imagination of post-war Europe and, in the words of the music historian Brian Jeffery, became part of the Spanish aura of Romanticism, 'an aura that produced such works as Hugo's *Hernani* and Bizet's *Carmen*. Its popularity culminated in the most famous bolero of all, Ravel's *Bolero for orchestra* (1928)'.[165]

Obviously, it would be rash to attribute to the volunteers the whole construction of the archetypal image of the Spaniards' national culture, yet their role, while modest, deserves to be acknowledged. This is of particular importance because, by relaying back home their conviction of the existence of a singular Spanish character – full of inner strength and valour – the volunteers helped to keep the British public emotionally attached to the fate of the Spanish cause. They hoped with that to increase the chances of obtaining material assistance for the war effort – an undertaking that resulted in more successes than failures. The volunteers were sensitive to the distinctive meaning the concept of honour had in Hispanic society, particularly concerning its association with the notion of Spanishness. They also recognized that, with its echoes of the Moorish occupation, resistance to the occupying French had encouraged a prevalent historicism. They applied this knowledge to drum up support for their military schemes in both Britain and Spain, and to discourage Spaniards from surrendering to the French foe, whether by calling them to resist in Asturias against all odds, like Don Pelayo, or by facing the guns of the French army brandishing the sword of Pizarro. Even when their initiatives remained susceptible to occasional bursts of scepticism, as in the case of General Castaños' second thoughts regarding Downie's Legion of Extremadura, contemporaries were far from labelling them lunatics. On the contrary, they merited the overwhelming applause of both British and Spanish societies, which seems to suggest that at that time they were more receptive to examples of heroic historicism than, perhaps, later in the century. There is no denying that Spain – that idealized 'land of honour' – could at times serve as a testing ground for the volunteers' personal honour. Yet, this was never their sole concern. Even the poet Landor, who shed very little blood during his short sojourn, assimilated the way honour operated within a Spanish context in order to convey it to British readers. He did it in his tragedy *Count Julian* through the description of the agonizing dilemmas posed by collaboration in a country under foreign occupation. At a time when it was increasingly expected that artists should get closer to – and even experience at first hand – the full horrors of human conflict, Landor's Spanish adventure not only fulfilled that demand, but also contributed to shape future generations' perceptions of Spain as the last bastion of ancient moral values. The poet's involvement, as that of other British volunteers, served to demonstrate that Romanticism, seen here as the cultural force of the age, could be harnessed to serve very rational purposes, all geared in the short term to the furtherance of Spanish liberation.

Accidental Agents of Social Change

When, on 7 October 1808, the *Junta Central* called 400,000 men to arms,[1] many regiments faced a throng of unprepared recruits. At times, the British volunteer officers placed in charge of coordinating operations on the ground had to cope with up to 3,000 peasants arriving overnight, expecting to be fed, dressed and prepared for battle, in a matter of days.[2] By combining these conscripts with the remnants of defeated Spanish units, volunteer Charles Doyle did his utmost to turn into a fully fledged battalion the *Tiradores de Doyle* (Doyle's Snipers), a small force the Aragonese Captain General José de Palafox had created in his honour on 10 August 1808.[3] But only a few officers survived the battalion's baptism of fire in the second siege of Saragossa.[4] British surgeon Henry Milburne made a difficult journey from England to the dusty plains of Castile only to discover that after a skirmish with the French near El Escorial, the 800-men *Regimiento de Infanteria Voluntarios de España*, the Spanish volunteer force he was due to join, had been taken prisoner *en masse*.[5] Those captured were to be among the 14,196 Spanish prisoners of war who became a nightmare for the French authorities as they not only constituted the highest number of foreign nationals in French prisons, but also the least prone to cooperate with their captors.[6] Doyle managed to recompose his battalion – an effort he had to repeat twice during the conflict.[7] But it was clear that too many lives had been lost and with them, much of the public's good will and enthusiasm for the Spanish cause. There were numerous reasons for this, starting with the absence of political unity and of a single military command – two issues that some of the volunteers had urged the Spanish authorities to address on more than one occasion, as discussed above.[8] In a war characterized by the high involvement of civilians, popular enthusiasm tended to express itself in improvised, localized actions that failed to properly channel the energies of all members of the community, thus ending in defeat. The volunteers sought to put an end to this drain on morale and human resources through the introduction of a series of innovations that often unwittingly fostered social change.

Military training was to become one of their main concerns – something that had long ceased to be a priority for the Spanish army. Many of the small military academies created by Charles III were closed by his successor in 1790 under suspicion of being cradles of revolutionary thought. Due to financial problems, those opened in the 1790s by Godoy in Alcalá de Henares, Valladolid and Granada were closed in 1805, alongside the 109-year-old *Real Academia Militar de Matemáticas de Barcelona*, with its branches in Oran and Ceuta. All of these establishments were amalgamated into a single academy in Zamora with capacity for only 60 students, of whom many were officers sent on secondment by their regiments, rather than new recruits.[9] For the vast majority of Spanish officers, theoretical training was almost non-existent. Only those in the corps of engineers and artillery had access to scientific knowledge and the latest innovations in battlefield tactics, perhaps because they were considered technicians more than warriors.[10] It is true that officers who attended the *Seminario de Nobles* (the school for the Spanish élite founded in 1727) were often versed in geography, theology, literature and music. But for military training, they had to rely on the patchy instruction provided by the regiments they joined. Cadets were placed in the charge of a senior officer who was expected to impart the basics of military science (*principios de la guerra*), while the rest of the learning process consisted of emulation and surviving first-hand experience.[11] The rank and file fared worse. Regular soldiers were taught how to operate weapons, march and parade, but in such a short period of time (often far less than the average 24 days provided by the British militia)[12] that there was little chance of instilling in them the principles of discipline and subordination.[13]

The general conscription of 1808 introduced *de facto* a degree of social diversity into the army when the *Junta Central* removed all exceptions to the draft, no longer recognizing difference between nobles, plebeians, rich and poor recruits.[14] The transformation in the social configuration of the army was speeded by the numerous promotions granted to soldiers of all social origins, a practice adopted to reward bravery and encourage loyalty after a succession of defeats.[15] This policy, however, created its own problems. National illiteracy levels were as high as 75 per cent.[16] Byron, like many other travellers, noticed with some amusement that passports were demanded and checked by illiterate officers.[17] Even conceding that some might have been able to read,[18] there is little doubt that only a few of the new officers could write and that some could do neither, let alone formulate and discuss tactics.[19]

On 22 August 1809, Doyle proposed to the *Junta Central* the opening of depots in Galicia, Seville and Valencia with the sole mission of training an Army of Reserve.[20] He had shown an early interest in the subject as the author of two pamphlets published in 1804 for the instruction of junior officers, but addressed to the general public because, he explained in the preface, Britain was going through a period in which 'every man is a soldier'.[21] This view suited the situation in Spain. After a series of defeats in La Mancha, on 26 November 1809, Doyle pressed the idea of establishing training depots to the Marquess de la Romana, suggesting at the same time the adoption of the tactics of a partisan war because

> Experience has shown us that we are not capable of resisting the Enemy in the field, where the movements of large bodies are required, because we have not had time to organize and discipline our troops or because our officers are incapable![22]

The only way to remedy the situation, he argued, was to 'make the nation truly warlike' by schooling officers and regular soldiers alike.[23] Doyle's proposals were well received, yet little was done, apart from the *Junta Central*'s opening of the Military Academy at Seville on 14 October 1809. Access to this institution, however, was restricted to 'well-born' young men with a minimum 3-years study at university level.[24] These requirements were relaxed in a few cases, but it was clear that many still considered military training, and education in general, to be a privilege of the upper classes.[25]

Not that egalitarianism was a goal for the British volunteers. They had not taken up arms to create an alternative democratic society, as many of their more numerous successors in the International Brigades would certainly attempt over a century later.[26] It could be assumed, perhaps, that Whittingham, as the son of a merchant who knew how difficult it was to progress in the British army without an aristocratic background, might have been tempted to follow such a path. He entered the groundbreaking Military Academy of High Wycombe, directed by the French *émigré* General Gaspar Le Marchand, only because he received a scholarship. When he graduated with honours (after studying 16 hours a day, sustained on a diet of vegetables, due to lack of resources), he found that the only route available to him to join the officer corps was to purchase the rank of lieutenant in the 1st Life Guards.[27] Yet, when he was asked to propose a man for the role of his second-in-command in the Spanish army, Whittingham suggested the Marquess de Vivot on the sole rationale that he was 'the head of the nobility in Mallorca and has considerable estates'.[28]

The volunteers' overwhelming preoccupation was to prepare troops capable of confronting disciplined Napoleonic forces,[29] even when that meant, as we shall see, offering for the first time in Spanish history, basic state education to thousands of the lower classes. The shift towards such a scenario was slow. While nursing a wound in Cadiz, in September 1809, Whittingham translated Dundas' cavalry tactics into Spanish, intending to apply them to a new regiment. His work was more an act of homage than a literal translation as the manoeuvres he prescribed were proclaimed to be 'half English-half French and often neither'.[30] Dedicated to his Spanish *compañeros de armas* (comrades in arms), the book was written with officers and regular soldiers equally in mind because Whittingham's objective was to prepare 'each individual to know what to do as soon as he hears the voice of his general'.[31] Under the patronage of the regent, General Castaños, the British volunteer was granted the chance to put theory into practice. On 16 November 1810, after 6 months of heavy training and induction, for which, unfortunately, we have no details, the *Cortes* went briefly into recess in order to admire the 'innovative manoeuvres' performed by Whittingham's new cavalry regiment, formally attached to the Army of the Centre, in a parade through the tree-lined boulevards of Cadiz.[32]

It was during this period that Whittingham and fellow volunteer Philip Keating Roche obtained the full support of the new British ambassador, Henry Wellesley, for a more ambitious scheme. This consisted of raising and training two Spanish divisions to be clothed, armed and equipped by the British government. Based in Mallorca and Cartagena, respectively, these divisions were considered an innovation in the Spanish military system because they represented the first serious attempt to organize a professional Spanish Army of Reserve.[33] Unlike other regiments, they were not to be attached to any of the main field armies,[34] but were to be ready to provide assistance to whomever and wherever the Spanish authorities stipulated.[35] Initially, their operations were to be focused on the defence of territory in the Eastern provinces while contributing to distracting the enemy's attention from the rest of the Peninsula.[36] Whittingham and Roche's projects fitted well into the traditional British foreign policy of providing material aid to continental allies without intervening directly in the fighting. At the time, Britain also seemed keen on other projects presented by British volunteers, particularly John Downie's Legion of Extremadura and William Parker Carrol's efforts to unite the Spanish Irish regiments of Hibernia, Irlanda and Ultonia under a single command in Galicia.[37] However, while assistance to Downie's enterprise was withdrawn[38] and Carrol's Irish Brigade was never implemented,[39]

Whittingham and Roche's plans went ahead with full British and Spanish support.[40] Moreover, in a highly unusual step, Whittingham was appointed both commander and inspector general of his division. Expected gradually to reach 30,000 men, his division's infantry and cavalry regiments were to be drawn from the remnants of defeated units and from the 80,000 men decreed by the *Cortes* to be conscripted in the provinces bordering the Mediterranean. Whittingham's main task was to prepare these men to be ready for dispatch, in groups of up to 10,000 each 6 months, to the armies of Catalonia, Valencia and Murcia.[41] Volunteers Patrick Campbell, Neil Macdougall, Carlos Silvertop, Arthur Goodal Wavell and the surgeon Henry Milburne joined him in the project.[42] Although the extent of his prerogatives was to be contested repeatedly by both Spanish and British authorities (particularly Wellington),[43] the double status of commander and inspector general conferred on Whittingham unprecedented powers to select, organize, train and audit the quality of his subalterns' performance.[44]

Roche's brief was far more limited. Over the course of the war, his 5,000 man force was attached *de facto* for over a year to the Third Army under General Blake in Valencia.[45] This left Roche in charge of what might be described as an enormous military 'revolving door' in Alicante. Under his supervision, thousands of conscripts, survivors of defeated regiments and Spanish deserters, were dressed, fed and instructed along traditional lines, either to be sent immediately to halt the advance of the French or to be dispatched for further instruction to Whittingham in Mallorca or later, to Doyle in Cadiz.[46] In line with British eighteenth-century practice, Austrian, German, Polish, Swiss, Italian and even a few French deserters were conveyed to Gibraltar to join the British army.[47]

Educating for liberation

The breakthrough for a socially inclusive military education came on 18 August 1811, when the *Cortes* removed the test of nobility as a prerequisite for access to formal military instruction, following wider political reforms that included the abolition of feudal privileges and the introduction of the principle of compulsory public education, which would be enshrined in the Constitution of 1812.[48] This cleared the way for the volunteers to persuade the Regency and the British ambassador to extend their support to new educational projects.[49] On 12 October 1811, Doyle was authorized to open and direct a training depot in the Isla de Leon (the *Depósito Militar de Instrucción de San Fernando*) for the instruction of both junior officers and regular soldiers.[50] Contemporaries considered it 'the first experiment of the kind ever made in the Spanish Army.'[51] On 15 February 1812, Whittingham received official backing to open a National Military Academy in Palma (*Academia Nacional Militar de Palma*) for middle- to lower-ranking officers.[52] Other military academies were established within each of the six Spanish field armies, but they were all short-lived.[53] By contrast, those under the guidance of the British volunteers remained open until after the end of the war.[54] While Whittingham's establishment was attended by up to 77 officers at a time, normally in rotas of 72-days training,[55] the depot in Cadiz could accommodate up to 3,000 students.[56] Although a few complaints were raised regarding the lack of recruits,[57] more than 8,000 men received basic education and military training in just the first 9 months of the depot's operations.[58]

Unlike other Spanish academies, those of the volunteers were allowed to employ a good number of British officers on their staff.[59] This was a considerable concession at a time when the Anglo-Spanish alliance was at its lowest ebb. Much of the antagonism was caused by a plan put forward by the British ambassador, under which his brother, the Duke of Wellington, was to be given the command of the Spanish army and British officers posted to its ranks. In exchange, Britain was to grant a substantial loan to Spain to carry the war effort. This proposal was followed up by the more alarming suggestion that all provinces bordering on Portugal should be placed under British authority.[60] Rumours also circulated that Britain was supporting rebellions in Spanish America; that she planned to seize Cadiz as she had Gibraltar; and that she would replace all Spanish officers with British ones in order to subject Spanish soldiers to corporal punishment,[61] a practice banned in Spain since 1770.[62] In this climate, the British volunteers could well have been perceived as Trojan horses in a British take over. The Cadiz depot had been granted vacancies for six British senior officers and twenty sergeants,[63] yet from the surviving records, it seems that not even half of these vacancies were ever filled. Doyle brought to Spain a few Irish compatriots: two captains in the Royal Marines, Francis 'Francisco' Lee and Robert Steele;[64] Captain Jeremy 'Gerónimo' Robinson,[65] Sergeant John Mealican,[66] and the ensigns John O'Hara,[67] Paul Palmer[68] and 'Jorge Coppy' (George? Samuel Bloss Copping?).[69] The latter four came from the 87th regiment in Guernsey, headed by Doyle's uncle, Sir John Doyle.[70] Steele left the depot after a few weeks of service to join Downie's Legion of Extremadura.[71] Nonetheless, the prospect of an increased British presence in Cadiz created some unease. On 11 November 1811, the liberal newspaper *El Redactor General* praised Doyle for instructing men who

Figure 5 Charles William Doyle (1770/1782?–1842), engraving by Thomas Hodgetts after Margaret Sarah Carpenter, *circa* 1828, © National Portrait Gallery, London.

'without military background and often disarmed tend to produce or increase turmoil'.[72] Little over a month later, however, the same newspaper reproduced an article originally published by a lesser-known periodical, the *Revisor Político*, casting doubts on the advantages of receiving military education from nationals of a country so guided by mercantilist principles as to consider the purchase of military ranks acceptable.[73]

> Is science also for sale? But what will these English officers achieve? What progress will the rigour of their discipline make on Spanish recruits? It will exasperate them, undoubtedly; war will become so abhorrent that they will be driven to give up the enterprise that, for love of national independence, they have attempted so far.[74]

There were no reasons for such fears. Not only was the number of British officers involved relatively small, but the Spanish government had also made it a condition of the academies' creation that, while Britain would bear the bulk of the expense, they were to be run by a majority of Spanish nationals and follow Spanish guidelines.[75] Whittingham and Doyle could appoint the staff, select and veto students; they also had a say on the subjects taught, as long as the principles of tactics adopted by the national army were included.[76] But the day-to-day running of the schools was left in the hands of Spanish officers: in Mallorca, *coronel* Ramón Senseve, a commander of Whittingham's Mallorcan division;[77] in

Cadiz, *capitán* Mariano Perez de Guzman, replaced in July 1813 by *coronel* Juan Bazan.[78] José María de Torrijos y Uriarte, future leader of the Spanish utopian liberals, was a prominent member of the depot's staff.[79] This was far from a case of simply applying alleged British order and method on unruly Spaniards.

The syllabuses in Mallorca and Cadiz were relatively similar. Reading and writing were the highest priorities because, as a report on the activities of the academy in Palma clearly stated:

> Lacking instruction there is no freedom and equality among men (...) Because, how could we consider as a free man someone who does not know how to read, when we see that he depends and remains subjected to others who have that basic knowledge, and that we could even call him a slave in that respect? How could we call free a captain who does not know how to manage a company when we see (shameful thing) that he depends for everything on the skills of a Sergeant? And how?!!!![80]

Education was not only the *sine qua non* of freedom and equality, two terms that had ceased to be the exclusive domain of the enemy's public discourse and now appeared in newspapers and in many of the *Cortes* debates.[81] Education was also the most basic requisite to legitimize authority. Defeat after defeat had demonstrated that mass conscription and sheer brute force were not enough to win the war. It was time for those who had been admitted recently to the officer corps to acquire the knowledge necessary to justify such a status.[82] In both Mallorca and Cadiz, students learnt drill, tactics and manoeuvres, rifle practice and how to conduct ambushes, as well as arithmetic, grammar and orthography.[83] In Cadiz, lessons were mandatory for all, including the 180 boys, between the ages of 13 and 14, who were recruited as drummers, fife and cornet players.[84] Elementary education of the regular soldiery was an innovation even from a British perspective. Signature literacy rates in the British army often amounted to no more than 41 per cent.[85]

Both establishments adopted the practice of dividing classes in two, separating the more advanced students from those who required more attention.[86] Regardless of their educational level, social origin and military background, all students wore a distinctive outfit and received a modest salary. In Palma, the uniform consisted of a turquoise jacket with white buttons, blue trousers and a hat decorated with silver ribbon and a cockade. In Cadiz, students wore pale blue jackets with golden buttons, white waistcoats and pale blue trousers. On 12 December 1811, their attire was adopted as the basic pattern for the uniforms of the whole Spanish infantry on the rationale that many of their members were expected to be alumni of the Cadiz depot.[87] Chaplains were included on both staffs, and in Palma, where the academy occupied the building of the seminary appropriately known as *Sapiencia* (Wisdom), at least two clergymen gave lessons.[88] No reference, however, has been found to the teaching of religion and *historia sagrada* (sacred history) that was mandatory in other Spanish military academies.[89] In Palma, the curriculum for junior officers was 'fortified' with some principles of logic (among the 80 questions set in the exams were 'What is a consequence?' and 'What is a thesis and a hypothesis? State the relationship or dependence that one has over the other').[90] In Cadiz, the plan of studies included military law, cleanliness and hygiene (a subject considered crucial for 'the economy of the Treasury, the health and proper discipline of the soldiers')[91] and the geography of Spain, including the names of the principal rivers, the limits of the provinces, the 'character of their inhabitants' and 'events that happened in their territories during this war'.[92]

Doyle considered knowledge of some basic geography vital for the success of the liberation campaign. In February 1812, he published in Spanish a 30-page pamphlet imparting rudimentary principles for the recognition of natural geographical formations and man-made features in the landscape such as towers and fortresses.[93] Aided by a few graphics, he explained, for example, how to differentiate the slope of a hill from that of a mountain.[94] This was something of a revelation for many soldiers who had never strayed beyond the plains of southern Spain and now were expected to be ready to fight in the rocky landscapes of Aragon and the Pyrenees. Under the motto *Fortuna belli artem victos quoque docet* (Fortune also teaches the vanquished the art of war), Doyle encouraged students not only to consider the correct interpretation of the terrain as 'the best military guide',[95] but also to risk capture while in search of truthful information rather than 'follow blindly the vague or tendentious data transmitted by unknown persons'.[96] His pamphlet was distributed among the students of the depot and publicized in the local press.[97]

Little is known of the students who attended the military schools in Cadiz and Palma. So far, no matriculation lists have been found for either establishment, and until all the files at the Military Archive of Segovia are digitalized and compiled, it will remain difficult to trace their enrolment and subsequent careers. We know that in Cadiz the vast majority were conscripts from eastern and southern Spain. There were also a few young Spanish Americans who, after being taken prisoner by the enemy, joined the French forces only to be captured by the British, who in turn dispatched them from Malta to Doyle's depot for their instruction and rehabilitation under the banner of the Spanish cause.[98] After graduation, many filled the ranks of the battalions *Tiradores de Doyle, Jaen, Africa, Málaga, Zamora, España* and *Guardias Reales*[99] as well as Downie's Legion of Extremadura.[100] In Palma, almost all of the students were junior officers of the operational units *Guardias de Corps, Primero de Córdoba, Segundo de Burgos, Segundo de Mallorca, Batallón de Granada, Segunda Legión Catalana, Batallón de Cazadores de Mallorca, Dragones de Almansa, Dragones de Olivencia, Regimento de Suizos, Segundo de Tarragona, Quinto de Granaderos* and *Batallón de América*.[101] All of these forces participated in the campaigns that led to the complete liberation of Spain, and some continued the fight against Napoleon well outside Spanish territory.[102] An alumnus of the Cadiz depot, *capitán* of the *Tiradores de Doyle* Nicolás de Mimussir was one of only two Spaniards who fought at Waterloo.[103]

In the land of Amazons and orphans

Behind the pedagogic efforts of the volunteers lay a profound and unshakeable belief in the capabilities of the common Spaniard, who they singled out as the backbone of the liberation campaign.[104] Women were not excluded from this view. Charles Doyle, Edwin Green and Philip Keating Roche had no qualms in pressing into service hundreds of 'amazonas benditas' (blessed Amazons)[105] for the defence of Tortosa, Tarragona and Alicante.[106] Although not completely improbable in exceptional circumstances, it was difficult to find women in similar roles even in revolutionary France.[107] This made Spanish women a powerful force of deterrence, as sometimes it was enough for them to just make an appearance on the barricades to petrify the enemy.[108] Necessity made female participation in the defence operations acceptable for the Patriots. They considered it an expedient and transitory phenomenon that posed no threat to traditional female domesticity.[109]

The situation was different for the Spanish women who wore military dress and carried weapons, something completely unheard of before the Napoleonic invasion.[110] Charles Doyle played a crucial role in guaranteeing the international celebrity as well as the respectability of the most famous of these female combatants, Agustina of Saragossa.[111] He was the author of the letter that persuaded the *Junta Central* to grant her full membership of the army, an unprecedented status for a woman. On 20 July 1809, Doyle wrote to the Secretary of War, Antonio Cornel, calling for national recognition of the two medals, rank and salary of *sargento primero* that General José de Palafox had bestowed on

Agustina for her services during the two sieges in Saragossa. He asserted that this was well deserved

> because, not only did she fulfill the duties of a valiant soldier, but her example also encouraged the heroism of others of her sex, as has been verified during the first and second sieges [of Saragossa] when those admirable Heroines endured hardships, braved the risks and showed themselves ready to perish at the hands of the Enemy.[112]

For the British volunteer, Agustina was no mere soldier; she was the mould from which all Spanish heroines would be cast. Based on such glowing references, she was awarded the rank of *alferez* in the Spanish infantry (three grades higher than *sargento primero*, but far below the rank of *capitán* she had requested) with full salary and a pension.[113] In that capacity, Agustina served in the defence of Teruel and Tortosa, fought with two *guerrilla* bands and took part in the Battle of Vitoria in 1813. At the end of the war, Ferdinand VII awarded her the rank of *subteniente* in the artillery (barely higher than *alferez* in the infantry). But she remained in active service for the rest of her life, wearing her uniform and medals until her death in 1857, at the age of 71.[114] More significantly, she became an icon of national unity and an example for the advancement of women's rights well into the twentieth century.[115]

There is no denying that Doyle's regard for Agustina was unconventional. Although a married man, he allowed himself to be seen in the streets of Seville walking with Agustina – she dressed in petticoats and a military loose coat with one gold epaulet, in open defiance of those who whispered that her actions were leading women to take to the battlefield instead of attending to their domestic concerns.[116] He also introduced the young woman to many of his British acquaintances, including the travel writers William Jacob[117] and Sir John Carr,[118] as well as Admiral Purvis who gave a banquet on board his flagship, to which she was welcomed with full military honours.[119] Fellow volunteer and British agent George Landmann also feted her during a brief trip to Gibraltar.[120] This evidence, nonetheless, is not strong enough to allow for the argument that Doyle, or indeed any of his colleagues, were in favour of turning 'the world upside down'[121] by conferring military ranks to all women. Agustina was so much an exception to the rule that she served to illustrate the extremes to which Spanish patriotism could go.

On a personal level, Doyle was moved to intervene in Agustina's favour, not by her manly actions, but by her vulnerability. He related to his friend Charles

Vaughan, author of the first published account of the siege of Saragossa, the way she had managed to escape from the French, only to see her 5-year-old son die from a fever a few days later. She joined the army of General Blake and saw victory in the Battle of Alcañiz, but her situation was highly precarious.

> She then came to Seville and (*between you and I*) was dependent *upon me* for her subsistence poor creature, at last I gave in a memorial for her and with the *greatest difficulty* – shame to report – succeeded in getting her 12 reales a day which added to the 6 that she got for the siege in her pension, now with the rank of ensign.[122]

Agustina was as much a victim of the war as she was a heroine. She was among thousands who shed blood, lost relatives, friends and belongings in the whirlpool of the Spanish conflict.

As the French advanced south, many flocked to Cadiz in search of safe haven. In a matter of months, the port city that was the main gate to trade with Spanish America doubled its population, from 50,000 to 100,000 inhabitants.[123] Even in normal circumstances, such an increase would have put a tremendous strain on the resources of the wealthiest of economies, let alone on one upset by years of financial misfortunes, crowned by foreign invasion and war. Since 1761, some members of the Spanish military had recourse to a system of financial assistance known as the *Montepio Militar* funded by deductions from the salaries of potential beneficiaries and donations from the Spanish Crown. The scheme was available to some regiments to the exclusion of others and tended to benefit only the highest-ranking officers. A month before its dissolution, the *Junta Central* established a system of retirement for all officers with the avowed intention of encouraging recruitment. In reality, however, only those who were injured or 'exhausted' by the war could draw any payment – and they had to have a minimum of 15 years of continuous service.[124] The rest of the soldiery, including their widows and parents (not to mention any extended family) had to rely on traditional networks of assistance represented by the Church, relatives and friends, all similarly affected by the conflict.[125] Hundreds of children orphaned by the war were seen wandering the streets, to the alarm of the *Junta* of Cadiz, which eventually reopened an old Jesuit primary school just to keep them away from muggers and prostitutes.[126] Social tension had the potential to erode the popular support necessary to keep up the struggle against Napoleon. Many of the British volunteers reached into their pockets to assist their troops.[127] Doyle donated a *duro* per day (about 20 *reales*, less than one pound sterling) and his salaries of *mariscal de campo* and *teniente general* for the upkeep of seven civilian refugees from Saragossa, Tortosa, Gerona and Tarragona for the complete duration of the war.[128] Yet, gestures such as these were nothing but a drop in an ocean of despair. Something on a much larger scale needed to be done if a human catastrophe was to be avoided in a city that, at times, was the Spanish government's last remaining refuge in the Peninsula.

Volunteer James Duff came up with such a scheme. Soon after the French began besieging the town, in February 1810, the *mariscal de campo*, now known as Viscount Macduff,[129] joined forces with a London merchant, Frederick Grellet, to promote the establishment of a *Fondo Patriótico* (Patriotic Fund). Grellet was a partner of Kuhff, Grellet and Co., a City of London firm that had traded with Spain since at least the 1790s.[130] He had already provided, through his mercantile contacts in Corunna, 45,176 *reales* (about 500 pounds at that time) to the Spanish cause.[131] Together, they persuaded the editors of *El Diario Mercantil* to publish and distribute a four-page free supplement to the newspaper edition of 4 June 1810 announcing, in Spanish and English, that on the British monarch's birthday, 24 May 1810, they had decided to open a general subscription

> for a fund which may prove not only an encouragement to the personal exertions of the Spanish soldier; but likewise a most desirable, as it must be a most acceptable relief and assistance to the wounded and the widows, orphans or nearest relatives of those who may fall in defence of their country and their King.[132]

The Spanish version of the text urged all Patriots and their sympathizers to contribute, while the English version was addressed specifically to 'all British subjects, especially those who have or may visit Spain'.[133] It was claimed that the idea followed 'an institution similar to that in England, from which the most happy (sic) results have been experienced'.[134] Grellet was a member of Lloyd's list,[135] so there are reasons to believe that the scheme was based on Lloyd's Patriotic Fund, a charity that since 1803 had supported – and continues to support – active and retired British soldiers and their families.[136]

Considering the dire circumstances, the response to Macduff and Grellet's initiative was overwhelming. Such was the number of donations received that the first meeting of subscribers had to be postponed twice in order to allow for the publication of two lists with their names.[137] Among them were leading members of the British diplomatic and consular legation (unsurprisingly, perhaps, as the latter was headed by Macduff's namesake and cousin James Duff) as well as representatives of British, Portuguese, Spanish *peninsulares* and Spanish American merchant families.[138] In little over a month, the fund collected

SUPLEMENTO
AL DIARIO MERCANTIL DE CADIZ

DEL LUNES 4 DE JUNIO DE 1810.

*Se nos ha remitido el siguiente escrito para insertar en
nuestro diario de hoi, dia en que se celebra el cum-
pleaños del Señor Don Jorge Tercero (Q. D. G.) dig-
no rei de la nacion britanica, intima y generosa aliada
de la España. ¡Gratitud eterna al magnánimo pueblo
que ha respondido á los gritos de nuestra independencia,
y en cuya fraternal union lograremos lanzar de la penín-
sula á los viles que la están profanando!....*

FONDO PATRIOTICO.

Desde el momento en que se presentaron en la Isla
de Leon los beneméritos y esforzados defensores de
la patria que componian el exército del Excmo Sr.
Duque de Alburquerque, que llegó en ocasion tan opor-
tuna para hacer incontrastable la resistencia á toda
irrupcion del enemigo, nació en los corazones de una
porcion de fieles aliados de la España, que residen
actualmente en Cadiz, afectos á la justa causa que
tan gloriosamente sostiene, la idea de que en tales cir-
cunstancias convendria una suscripcion para socorro
de los hospitales militares, ayuda de vestuario y otros
objetos conducentes al bien de las tropas, como efec-
tivamente la entablaron, ascendiendo á mas de cin-
cuenta mil rs. las cantidades que se han juntado hasta
hoi Pero en vista del esmero con que el Gobierno
ha atendido y atiende á estos ramos, se ha propuesto
y determinado dar otro destino no ménos noble y útil
á dicha suscripcion, aplicando el actual fondo acre-

can su vida á la patria: aprecia el buen espíritu de
los individuos que concurran á ella, y particularmente
de V. que lo promueve. Por lo mismo lo autoriza para
dicho objeto, como igualmente para que haga el anun-
cio al público, segun lo desea, en los periódicos de esta
ciudad = Dios guarde á V. muchos años. Cadiz 20 de
mayo de 1810. = Andres Lopez = Sr. D. Federico
Grellet.

PATRIOTIC FUND.

Scarcely had the brave Spaniards under the command of the Duke of Alburquerque reached the Isla
de Leon and so opportunely and effectually checked
the views of the ennemy upon Cadix in february last,
when a few natives of Great Britain at present here,
friends to Spain and her noble cause, conceived that
it would be desirable to set on foot a subscription in
aid of the comforts of the Spanish soldiery, either in
their hospitals, cloathing or other military necessaries;
and accordingly a sum exceeding fifty thousand rials
has already been collected But as these objects have
and continue to be so earnestly attended to by the
government, it is now proposed to apply the sum
already collected towards the establishment by general subscription of a fund which may prove not only
an encouragement to the personal exertions of the
Spanish soldier; but likewise a most desirable, as it
must be a most acceptable relief and assistance to the
wounded and the widows, orphans or nearest relatives of those who may fall in defence of their country and their King

The advantages that must attend the cooperation
of the British nation in raising a fund of this nature
in support of the common cause, are too obvious to

Figure 6 'Fondo Patriotico' – 'Patriotic Fund', front page and page three of special bilingual edition of *El Diario Mercantil de Cadiz*, 4 June 1810, by courtesy of *Ministerio de Cultura de España*.

150,019 *reales de vellón* (about 1,667 pounds) of which 44,250 (491 pounds) had been pledged to be renewed annually. When the subscribers finally met, on 28 June 1810, they confirmed in the statutes of the organization that

> under no pretext are these funds to be applied to any other end than that stipulated by the subscribers which is to assist, as circumstances require, the widows and children of sergeants, corporals and soldiers of the army and the navy who die, are disabled or unable to acquire their necessary subsistence.[139]

Joaquín de Villanueva,[140] an officer deputed to attend the meeting by the military governor of Cadiz, Andres López y Sagastizabal, was elected president of the fund.[141] Duncan Shaw, a wealthy Irish-Scot banker with strong links to the Americas,[142] was appointed treasurer. No further details have been found regarding the institution's internal structure and the identity of its beneficiaries, but it seems that the fund remained active until the end of the war and that it served as a template for the *Don Patriótico* (Patriotic Donation) established later that year to finance the activities of the *guerrillas*, particularly those led by Juan Martín, *el Empecinado*.[143]

No riots or great mass disturbances took place in Cadiz during its 30-month-long siege, a situation that could partially be attributed to the efforts made to address the needs of those most vulnerable in society. When it came to securing social cohesion, and with that the necessary consent to build up and present a united front against the French, the situation of widows and orphans could be as important as that of soldiers and generals. The British volunteers' initiatives in this area as well as in military education and in the recognition of female talent outside a domestic setting were designed to respond to short-term challenges presented by the war. Victory in the liberation campaign remained their main priority. Nonetheless, by placing the common Spaniard at the heart of all concerns, they often swam against the current in a social environment still imbued with discrimination and elitism. This made the British volunteers, albeit unintentionally, agents of social change.

'Half Spanish, Half English, and Wholly Patriot'

An important, if not the most crucial, role played by the British volunteers was that of intermediaries in the Anglo-Spanish alliance – a far from easy task. The object of this chapter is twofold: to describe the unstable tightrope the volunteers had to tread when liaising between Spanish colleagues and their compatriots and to assess the impact that their dual status of British subjects and volunteers in the Spanish forces might have had in terms of national loyalties and identities. In order to get a full picture of what was at stake regarding the latter point it is necessary first to establish the place the volunteers occupied in Spanish society.

A multitude of shared experiences on battlefields, sieges and skirmishes brought the volunteers closer to their Spanish brothers-in-arms with whom they had the chance of making life-long friendships. That of 'Carlos' and 'Pepe' – Charles Doyle and José de Palafox – was particularly close. When Doyle's youngest son, Percy William visited Madrid in 1831, the hero of the siege of Saragossa – who carried Doyle's miniature portrait with him everywhere, including during his five-year imprisonment in France – was his first port of call. The former grandee had been stripped of all his honours by the King for taking the side of the Constitution during the *trienio liberal* (the Liberal Triennium of 1820–23) and was in economic difficulties which Doyle tried to assuage by settling some of his debts.[1] The intimacy and strength of their relations were the natural outcome of having their fate intertwined in both victory and defeat. Looking back on his experience of surviving French artillery fire during the disorganized flight that followed the Battle of Ocaña, *mariscal de campo* viscount Macduff, now fourth Earl of Fife, could years later remark jokingly:

> So long as the Spaniards would face the enemy, I was always to be found in the front, and when they were determined to run, why, I was obliged to run, too. But I was in the rear at every retreat . . .[2]

The vicissitudes of war placed the volunteers in close proximity with people of all social ranks. In 1810, the travel writer William Jacob recorded meeting General Doyle, accompanied by his Spanish *aide de camp* and Spanish servants, on his way to Catalonia, 'after sleeping the preceding night among the horses and mules at a gypsy hut on the plain below'.[3] Close cohabitation with Spaniards in filthy and cramped conditions became almost inevitable for those volunteers who spent a good part of the conflict as prisoners of war. The French tended to separate prisoners by nationality, but the majority of those captured in Cantabria and other northern areas were dispatched *en masse* to Bordeaux where they could remain for weeks, sometimes even months, before they were segregated and dispatched to detention camps allocated to their nationals.[4] Transit conditions were often atrocious; hunger, beatings and sleep depravation a common occurance.[5] Irish volunteer John Clarke was long enough in Bourdeaux to have time to contact relatives living there who, not only provided food and medical assistance for him and his Spanish cellmates, but also opened a subscription among foreign merchants for the relief of all Spanish PoWs.[6] Representing by 1810 the highest number of foreigners in French prisons (over 30,000 that increased to 65,000 by 1812),[7] the French eventually found it difficult to segregate the Spaniards. In the camps of Mâcon and Valenciennes, British and Spanish prisoners shared the same cells.[8] These were the places of detainment of volunteers John Kearney, James Arbuthnot and Clarke. Kearney was jailed in Mâcon from January 1810 until a failed escape attempt led to his transfer to Montpellier in early 1811, where he remained until the end of 1813.[9] Arbuthnot was imprisoned in Valenciennes from 1811 to the end of the war[10] while Clarke was transferred from Bordeaux to Paris and then to Valenciennes from where he escaped in April 1811.[11] All of these men returned to Spain as soon as they gained their freedom and continued their careers in the Spanish army, in the case of Arbuthnot until his death in 1863.[12]

The volunteers amassed a vast capital of goodwill with Spaniards for their staunch commitment to the Patriot cause. As their battle scars demonstrated, they were not 'war tourists', *à la* Byron. Downie's right cheek bone was shattered by grapeshot during the final assault on Seville[13]; *teniente coronel* Arthur Goodall Wavell lost the use of his right arm after a fall in the Battle of Chiclana[14]; the Earl of Fife covered with a tartan scarf a scar made by a sabre blow on his neck and suffered a permanent limp from a piece of shrapnel in his right leg while defending the Fort of Matagorda.[15] In Talavera, a musket ball struck Whittingham's mouth, carried away a large portion of his teeth, broke the jawbone and came out behind his ear. An inexperienced surgeon bound up his fractured jaw with a wooden splint, thereby driving all the splinters of the jawbone together with the pieces of the ball and teeth into the lacerated flesh. For 6 months afterwards, he was unable to take nothing but tea and soaked bread.[16] While trying to prevent the French capture of the Catalan fortress of Begur, Doyle received a shot in the chest from which he miraculously survived.[17]

Many of these injuries required long periods of convalescence in Seville and, after the fall of that city, in Cadiz. Here they were often accommodated in the homes of respectable families. For example, in mid-1810, Duff quit the residence of his cousin, the consul, to take lodgings in the house of José Pérez de la Fuente, the Basque owner of a brush factory.[18] The volunteers' *entrée* into Cadiz society was a privilege not necessarily shared with regular British soldiery, who were not permitted to enter the town for a long time, and then they were confined to cantonments beyond the city walls, for fear that their presence would amount to a *de facto* occupation of what, at certain periods, represented the Spanish patriotic government's last refuge in the Peninsula.[19] Only from late 1811 did the authorities allow a complete block (20 Calle de la Carne) to be exclusively 'occupied by the English'.[20] In contrast, British volunteer officers could attend *tertulias*,[21] such as those organized by María 'Mariquita' Strange, wife of the Irish merchant Pedro Strange, which attracted guests of all political persuasions and from all corners of the Spanish world.[22] They also patronized the theatre and even found time to organize their own private sessions of *bolero*, *fandango* and other popular Spanish dances where they socialized with *peninsulares* and Spanish Americans, rich and humble members of society alike.[23] At some stage during the war, Doyle listed in a notebook the names of all his Spanish acquaintances. Some pages are missing, but those that survive contain more than fifty names, including pillars of society (the families Aranda, Ulloa, Hermida, the Spanish Americans Alvear and Goyeneche, among others) as well as some less eminent, often nameless, but probably equally valuable contacts, such as 'el portero y su mujer' (the doorman and his wife) and the 'canónigo enfermero' (a canon priest who served as a nurse).[24]

By immersing themselves in the Spanish public sphere, the volunteers grasped quickly the pivotal role played by friendship and family connections in Hispanic society.[25] Romantic entanglements could offer a speedy introduction into the Spanish community,[26] but only in one instance, that of Whittingham, they were consecrated at the altar during the war.[27] His entrance into the Balearic family of his wife, Magdalena, daughter of Pedro de Creus y Ximenes, an importer of

Figure 7 Juan (John) Downie (1777–1826), painting by José María Halcón y Mendoza (1819), member of the Royal Academy of San Fernando, reproduced by courtesy of *Museo de la Real Academia de Bellas Artes de San Fernando*. Notice his right cheek and eye injuries.

tobacco, former magistrate at Seville and Intendant of the Spanish royal armies with properties in Mallorca, Minorca and Andalusia,[28] conferred Whittingham privileged access to the Andalusian and Balearic elites. This proved to be useful, particularly at the time of setting up his division and military academy in Palma.[29] Family links were also the *sine qua non* of the network of British and Irish merchants resident in Spain. Related by blood, trade and friendship, the families of the Irish merchants Patricio Wiseman, Pedro Strange, Duncan Shaw and the brothers Bartolomé, Miguel and Eduardo Costello offered the volunteers personal loans, credit and donations for many of their schemes, and perhaps more important, access to their web of leading friends and business correspondents in all corners of Spain and Gibraltar.[30] For example, in Tarragona, a note of introduction from Pedro Strange was enough to give Doyle the backing he needed to raise money from a local banker of Irish descent, William Gorman, for the risky business of persuading officers in Napoleon's army, including many French nationals, to join the allied forces during the hard winter of 1811 – a mission contrary to instructions of the British government, which had counselled against the recruitment of French deserters.[31]

An indication of the esteem in which Spaniards held the volunteers, as well as of the reasons why such respect was deserved, can be evinced from some of the delicate missions to which they were assigned. In September 1808, John Kearney, a mere *subteniente* in the army of Galicia, was commissioned by the Marquess de la Romana to act as Spanish liaison officer at the headquarters of the army of Sir John Moore. After the disaster of Corunna, he was forced to embark with the British expeditionary force, but he made his way back from England and joined the *Regimiento de Málaga* where he was immediately promoted to the rank of *teniente*.[32] In 1811, General Castaños assigned two of his colleagues Diego (James) Corrigan and Enrique (Henry) Wilson to represent Spanish interests at the headquarters of the British Commissariat. This was a thorny task because scarcity fostered tensions within the Anglo-Spanish alliance. Nonetheless, they fulfilled it until the end of the war, with the full approbation of their superiors.[33]

A reputation for probity and ability was believed to have conferred on some of the volunteers a high degree of influence over the Spanish authorities. On 6 April 1809, General Joachim Blake wrote to Doyle looking for a way to get a pension for the widow of a common friend who died of a fever, instead of in battle – a requisite for accessing that benefit. He said he was convinced that Doyle's recommendation 'will accelerate, no doubt, her inclusion in the *Montepío*' (the army contributory pension fund).[34] Four years later, fearing that he was to be relegated to a desk job, Ceuta-born *brigadier* Pedro Patricio Sarsfield y Waters asked Doyle to 'interpose your influence with Government' to procure him 'a pass for the Army of Catalonia, as Chief of Staff, an employment which would suit my fancy wonderfully'.[35] We do not know if Doyle attended to any of these requests, but the fact that they were made is testimony to the important place he had earned among the Spaniards.

Tensions among friends

Such a standing was not easily won. It resulted from overcoming reservations and serious hostilities. The volunteers' status as subjects of a country considered one of Spain's traditional enemies, added to the harsh realities of war, occasionally generated antagonism. As early as September 1808, Whittingham told a friend that the opinion of 'the best informed amongst the Spaniards is that England knows she may favour them with pecuniary, [but] will never risk a man in their defence!'[36] This apprehension, reinforced by the demoralizing withdrawal of British troops after the Battle of Corunna, could sometimes cast a shadow over the volunteers' commitment. During the defence of Tortosa, in February 1809, Doyle had to restrain a fellow volunteer, *coronel* Edwin Green, from publishing a proclamation condemning a few Spaniards who had vilified British members of the Spanish army for avoiding a head-on confrontation with the enemy:

> For God sake do not let one of your proclamations see day light!!! What a hand the Enemy will make of the English being suspected by the Spaniards!!! For Heavens (sic) burn any copies [one word unclear] of it..!!! What does it signify if they say we are French disguised as English or not? Our deeds will speak for themselves.[37]

Green complied with Doyle's request, but he found it increasingly difficult to work under Spanish terms. In the summer of 1809, the 32-year-old *coronel* took leave and travelled to England to recover from an illness and marry a childhood sweetheart.[38] On 1 September 1809, he approached a civil servant at the War Office to offer his services as British agent in Catalonia.[39] Three months later, Green was duly appointed to that commission on the strength of two factors: First, his rank in the Spanish Army and his experience fighting in that region[40]; second, because Doyle, Whittingham, Roche and Carrol were by then considered as 'belonging to the Spanish Service, and actually employed in the command of Spanish Corps'.[41] Although Green remained completely devoted to the Spanish cause for which he fought as head of an Anglo-Catalan battalion until the war ended,[42] it would seem from the absence of records tracing his service in Spanish military archives that he had no desire to make a career in the Spanish army.

Volunteers' initiatives, such as the organization and professionalization of an Army of Reserve,[43] were warmly applauded by the Spanish authorities, yet tensions could arise during their implementation. Whittingham's position as commander and Inspector of his 30,000 man division in Mallorca led him into a tug of war with the Captain-General of the island, Gregorio de la Cuesta. The 69-year-old veteran general, scarred by the experience of working with Wellington in a troublesome alliance at the Battle of Talavera, felt that his position was now being reduced to that of a mere civil administrator. He was also alarmed by the steady arrival of British volunteers to join Whittingham's staff, and by his direct contacts with Spanish national authorities, local and Cadiz merchants in search of means to feed and dress his soldiers at a time when the island was trying to cope with a swarm of refugees coming from the mainland. A long succession of quarrels and petty disputes only ended with Cuesta's death from natural causes on 26 November 1811.[44]

A couple of months earlier, Henry Milburne was working as Inspector of the Spanish Royal hospitals in the Balearic Islands when the local health authorities ordered two Royal Navy vessels, HMS Invincible and HMS Temeraire, to go into quarantine in the port of Mahon, capital of the island of Minorca, because they had been seen in the vicinity of Cartagena where an epidemic of yellow fever had just been declared.[45] For much of the war, the Patriots could only operate freely in the south and eastern coastal areas of the country which were notorious for suffering from what at the time were known as 'intermitting and remitting fevers'.[46] There were at least two outbreaks of yellow fever in Cadiz in 1810 and 1813, others suspected as such in Cartagena and Gibraltar in 1810 and 1811. Malaria was endemic to the region of Valencia, mainly because its vast rice plantations constituted an ideal habitat for mosquitoes carrying the parasite that caused the disease. Because of their imperial policies both Spaniards and Britons had encountered fevers in the West Indies, but they had arrived to different conclusions. The Spanish medical community believed these illnesses to be contagious and caused by a noxious bad air (*miasma*). This interpretation had a strong impact on the execution of the war. The Spanish authorities applied stringent *cordon sanitaires* which could last from 14 days to 6 months. Troops were barred from crossing areas declared contaminated; this also had a negative impact on ship movements, particularly on the British fleet that was effectively the only means of transport of the allies. The prevalent view among physicians of the Royal Navy (as opposed to those of the British army where the issue was still under debate) was that these were not humanly transmitted diseases – and they were right.[47]

After visiting the vessels, Milburne asked the authorities to remove the restrictions because there was no danger of contagion. He argued in a letter published by the regional daily *Diario de Palma* that none of the doctors and sailors who had been in close contact with the patients had contracted what he diagnosed as one of the 'fevers of the hot countries' to which 'English sailors were particularly susceptible'.[48] A scornful anonymous rebuke from a Spanish doctor soon claimed in the local weekly *Semanario de Menorca* that the British surgeon was placing the interests of his compatriots ahead of those of the island's population. Milburne replied through the press that, unlike his Spanish colleagues who, adamant not to break the quarantine, had never been on board the ships, he had witnessed the autopsies of some of the casualties and gathered enough information from the crew and the Royal Navy doctors to be able to give absolute assurances of the absence of risk. He did so, he said, 'not as the friend of a particular society, but of the entire human race'.[49] The Spanish medical community would remain attached to contagion theories for many years to come, but HMS Invincible was allowed to leave port 6 days after Milburne's first letter reached the authorities, and HMS Temeraire, where health conditions were comparatively worse, followed suit a few weeks later.[50]

Growing dissension in the political arena following the adoption of the Constitution of 1812, coupled with the blow to national pride caused by Wellington's appointment as commander-in-chief of the Spanish Army, somewhat darkened the atmosphere around the volunteers' activities. On 25 March 1813, the battalion *Tiradores de Doyle* was targeted for criticism. At a public session of the *Cortes*, a letter was read coming from a liberal military commentator, General Luis de Landaburu y Villanueva who, after professing deepest gratitude to Doyle for his work to assist the Spanish cause, requested a change in the name of the force, and the removal of Doyle's family coat of arms from its standard, arguing that Article 373 of the Constitution stated that 'the Spanish nation does not belong to any particular person or family'.[51] The *Tiradores de Doyle* was, indeed, an oddity. No other Spanish battalion bore the name of a living person, let alone that of a foreigner. But Doyle had never claimed the battalion as his personal property and so far, nobody had made such a connection. Ironically, the proposal was adopted, not by the *Cortes*, but later, by the Bourbon Restoration regime. Ferdinand VII placed the name of the extinct *Regimiento de Balbastro* over that of Doyle, erasing in the process all trace of its existence by dating back its creation to 1794, the date of formation of the old Barbastro regiment.[52] The rebranded force was dispatched to Montevideo to fight Spanish American rebels in November 1814, scarcely a few months after Landaburu's imprisonment for supporting the constitutional regime.[53]

Doubts about the necessity of appointing Wellington – a foreigner – as head of the Spanish army were publicly expressed in 1812 by General Francisco Ballesteros, under whom volunteers John Clarke, Reginald Macdonnell and James Arbuthnot had been happy to serve.[54] Ballesteros' remarks might have never been xenophobic, but they were used by a vociferous minority to spread unfounded rumours that the British and Portuguese allies were basking in the sunshine of unmerited glory and had plans to replace the French as occupiers.[55] Doyle became embroiled in an incident that highlights both this jingoism and the beginning of the process of fragmentation of the pro-constitutional factions, labelled since 1811 as *liberal*.[56] This rupture would result in the emergence of antagonistic political cultures and parties ('moderates' vs. 'progressives'), a phenomenon so far traced back by historians to the *trienio liberal*.[57] On 4 November 1813, the liberal newspaper *El Conciso*[58] ran a two-line story announcing the appointment of Chief-of-Staff General Luis Wimpffen as Minister of War.[59] This implied the removal of the incumbent, radical Juan O'Donojú from his post,[60] yet the information remained unchallenged for three days.[61] Doyle made the *faux pas* of trying to confirm with officials at the ministry of War what it turned out to be inaccurate news and in the process seems to have expressed some delight on the prospect of a ministerial reshuffle. This soon reached the ears of the editor of the 'Jacobin' newspaper *El Duende de los Cafés*, Juan Jacinto López, himself an employee at that ministry.[62] Writing under a pseudonym, López published a story suggesting that Doyle had violated Article 223 of the Constitution which established that no foreigner (including those who had been granted citizenship) could take a seat in the Spanish government.[63] Doyle, it was alleged, had backed the appointment of a foreigner in place of O'Donojú, 'the enemy of all Tyrants and saviour of the Constitution'.[64] O'Donojú was a first-generation Irish Spaniard believed to have republican leanings and to dislike the British.[65] Wimpffen was a Swiss national, albeit with a 20-year career in the Spanish army and many friends among future moderate liberals with whom he had worked in drafting legislation for the organization of urban militias.[66] Enraged by an accusation that opened the door for sanctions from the *Cortes*,[67] Doyle demanded a rectification. He argued that he had never advanced Wimpffen's candidature, but admitted to have 'smiled with some pleasure' at the prospect of O'Donojú's relegation.[68] López published Doyle's comments almost verbatim in his paper's next edition[69] and distributed an anonymous free pamphlet calling for Doyle's execution for meddling in Spanish affairs. Entitled *Errores del señor Doyle, ligeramente advertidos por un español que siente los insultos de su patria* (Mistakes of Mr. Doyle, swiftly noticed by a Spaniard who feels the insults received by his motherland) the text proclaimed that

> if somebody, as a Spanish general, was to appoint himself a tyrant and dictate laws or undermine existing legislation, the Government has executioners and gallows, and the Spanish nation has many courageous sons who will preserve her liberty, laws and government; and, if abandoning the character of Spanish general anybody would attempt to do the same as a foreigner, he would learn at the cost of his blood how much Spaniards love the independence and glory of

their motherland (. . .) (therefore) all Spaniards must feel themselves authorised to persecute Mr. Doyle as they would a beast.[70]

This incitement to murder was circulated at a time of increasing, politically targetted street violence in Cadiz.[71] To Doyle's great astonishment, not only did López ignore a second request for rectification,[72] but also the *Junta de Censura* of Cadiz, the body that since the abolition of the Inquisition decided on matters of censorship at local level on behalf of the *Cortes*,[73] intervened, muddying the waters even further. On 8 December 1813, the *junta* ruled that both the free pamphlet and the edition of 18 November of *El Duende de los Cafés*, containing Doyle's comments, were 'subversive'.[74] Although Doyle launched an immediate appeal, criminal proceedings were brought against him in the local courts. For 3 months, the censors refused to re-examine the case. But the departure of a member from the *Junta de Censura*'s board (about whom, unfortunately, we have no information) triggered a *volte-face*. On 29 March 1814, the censors ruled in Doyle's favour.[75] On the same day, the liberal magistrate Joaquín Aguilar,[76] who had been assigned the cause in the Cadiz courts, sent Doyle a friendly note congratulating him on his victory.[77]

Relations with Moore and Wellington

If the pre-eminence and British origin of the volunteers could ruffle a few feathers among Spaniards, their attachment to the Spanish cause had a similar effect with some leading compatriots. Well back in 1808, the Oxford academic traveller and future British envoy at Seville and Cadiz, Charles Vaughan, warned Doyle that General Sir John Moore 'displayed much asperity against all employed with Spanish armies, calling them the Partizans (sic) of the Spaniards'.[78] Moore had just arrived to Salamanca and was believed to have been given authority over British military agents. Doyle had asked Vaughan to intercede with Moore to enable him to remain with hard-pressed Spanish forces in Saragossa. Aragon's capital was preparing itself for a second siege that was to end with 54,000 dead,[79] the worst war tragedy in the history of Spain before that of Guernica in 1937.[80] A few days earlier, he had received an order from the British War Minister Lord Castlereagh to abandon Aragon, travel immediately to Catalonia and to remain there. This was an order that Doyle felt could not obey. He wrote to his British superior expressing his 'most heartfelt regret at being ordered from this Province into another' and warning that 'General Palafox seems to feel my being ordered away very sensibly and in truth to turn my back upon him at this momentous crisis does deeply wound me'.[81]

Time soon ran out for a reply from London. Considering that 'the public good will be better promoted by you staying where you are', Vaughan promised his friend: 'If I am permitted to talk with this tyger (sic, for Moore) I shall feel my way about (concerning) you'.[82] But he tempered any hint of success in his mission with the remark that he would rather stay in Spain as Doyle's *aide-de-camp* 'than feeding upon the dull prejudices of our own countrymen at home'.[83] In the event, Vaughan had no chance to intercede with Moore. So Doyle chose to ignore his orders for two weeks during which he helped to build up defences at Saragossa, called for assistance from the *Junta Central* and gathered together a regiment from dispersed troops under his own command.[84] On 27 November 1808, he wrote to Palafox from Lerida to reassure him that as envoy in Catalonia he would make sure that Saragossa would be well provided with artillery and ammunition.[85] A week later, from Tarragona, *mariscal de campo* Doyle confirmed the dispatch of weapons and provisions, but warned his friend that resources were running out: 'I don't have even a *peseta*, poor boy!!!'.[86] A further two months of desperate efforts to coordinate a rescue mission ended in failure.[87] On 21 February 1809, Saragossa surrendered. In a letter to Palafox's older brother, Francisco, the Irish volunteer could hardly contain his emotion: 'Ah! Saragossa, Saragossa, you have killed me! This is a blow I shall never forget in my life!!'[88]

Doyle maintained his correspondence with British representatives, but this became increasingly sporadic. For the Irish envoy who only a few months earlier had been instructed to rouse in the Spaniards 'the inclination of aiding and taking an active part in the noble struggle in which they are engaged',[89] the official British view of the Spanish cause had become too cold and detached. In Catalonia, far from simply gathering intelligence, Doyle organized and led the task of fortifying the strategically important towns of Lerida, Tortosa and Tudela in an effort to keep open the Patriots' access to Aragon.[90] Doyle – and the same applied to his fellow volunteers – had not travelled to Spain to be a mere witness of events. When Roche warned him in November 1810 that this was attracting criticism in British diplomatic circles, Doyle replied angrily from Valencia:

I thought I was allowed to work away in this corner of the Nation without giving rise to private debates as to the necessity of representing to Mr. Wellesley (Marquess Wellesley, then British ambassador in Cadiz) my exertions and activity (. . .) I am afraid Roche that all of us who have been employed in this Country will have (three words struck out) but I do also assure you that I should feel perfectly satisfied in the consciousness of having done all in my power to be useful, and altho it would seem that some of my own Countrymen ignorant of my conduct and (sic, are) not satisfied with it, yet believe me Roche, the people of this part of the Country give me sufficient proofs of their approbation and gratitude. I am therefore perfectly contented.[91]

Spain's liberation was the volunteers' primary concern. For those with the dual status of volunteers and British agents, this often entailed responding to events as they unfolded, regardless of instructions drafted weeks earlier by superiors with little knowledge of the country and even less of the evolving circumstances. In this respect, they appeared to have adopted an old Spanish formula, that of 'obedezco, pero no cumplo' (I obey but do not implement) that allowed generations of Spanish bureaucrats, particularly in Latin America, to delay the application and sometimes completely circumvent royal directives for the local good.[92] By exercising their own discretion, they became free agents – and this was a position that they saw no reason to abandon for as long as it benefited the 'common cause'.[93]

Perhaps unsurprisingly, relations became particularly difficult with Wellington, a man unaccustomed to delegate responsibility or to assimilate other people's ideas.[94] After the Battle of Talavera, Anglo-Spanish co-operation foundered: the commander of the British forces blamed the poor results of the campaign on the perceived pusillanimity of the Spanish army led by Cuesta, while the Spaniards considered Wellington's persistent demands for supplies, accompanied by threats of immediate retreat to Portugal, as signs of prevarication. Antipathy peaked when Wellington made his co-operation with the Spanish army conditional upon the removal of Cuesta, the establishment of a reliable system of supply, the admission of a British garrison in Cadiz and his appointment as commander-in-chief of the allied forces.[95] Roche and Macduff, who acted as liaison officers during and after the battle, were often caught in the verbal crossfire. In a letter to his brother, Marquis Wellesley, dated 21 September 1809, for example, Wellington sardonically referred to an encounter with 'Lord Macduff, who has taken the Spanish cause under his protection'.[96] The Scottish volunteer had arrived at his camp with a letter from General Francisco de Eguía quoting correspondence with the British ambassador (none other than Wellesley himself) instructing the commander to take up a particular defensive position. The Spaniards proposed acting in concert with the British in this deployment. Wellington refused outright. When Macduff exclaimed 'What? Will you not carry into execution an arrangement settled by the British ambassador?',[97] the

British commander sent him back to Spanish headquarters with the message that his brother knew perfectly well that any of his suggestions would only be executed if Wellington's terms for remaining in Spain were met. As Wellington judged that they had not, 'the proposal must be considered as never having been made'.[98] Such a reaction left the British volunteers in the Spanish army in an unenviable position because to the Spaniards it seemed to confirm the duplicity of their ally. Roche had already warned the British ambassador that 'nothing can exceed the degree of irritation of General Eguía and all his army' at the hinted withdrawal of British troops from Spanish soil.[99] 'Your Lordship will therefore easily imagine', Roche told Wellesley, 'that my situation here is not of the most agreeable nature. . .'[100]

Somehow, the volunteers managed to tame the wrath of their Spanish colleagues. Matters with Wellington, however, hardly improved when he was appointed *generalísimo* of the Spanish Army on 22 September 1812. Whittingham, Doyle and Roche were at times authorized to draw money from the British treasury to fund military operations and the activities of their military training establishments.[101] As funds from Spanish sources dried up, due to the effects of war and the *de facto* loss of control of the Spanish Latin American colonies after 1810, English subsidies became the only official lifeline. The British volunteers used their contacts with merchants in Gibraltar, Cadiz, Catalonia and Valencia as well as the fortunes of family and friends to supplement resources, but even these efforts were often insufficient.[102] In February 1812, known as the 'famine year',[103] Whittingham's troops in Mallorca began to show clear signs of starvation; some officers even fainted for want of food.[104] Supplies received from the mainland offered short-term relief, but the drama was compounded by letters from Wellington (8 January 1813) addressed to Roche in Valencia, and to Whittingham in Mallorca, instructing that British funds should not be used for hospitals, food provisions, means of transport or salaries, but limited to cover costs of 'clothing, arms and accoutrements for your corps'.[105] In a further letter, 28 January 1813, Wellington told Roche that if he could not find subsistence, he should remove himself with a detachment to Mallorca and leave the rest of his troops under the command of the British-Sicilian army in Alicante.[106] The situation facing Roche was dire: some officers of his division were accused in the *Cortes* of taking hostage the authorities of four Valencian towns (Elche, Gijona, Novelda and Aspe) in search of supplies.[107] Perhaps fearing mutiny, Roche protested. Wellington tersely replied that if he disliked the situation or should he 'make any further difficulties' he must resign his command.[108]

That is precisely what Whittingham did on 6 August 1813.[109] He had been deeply hurt by Wellington's earlier attempt to remove him from the position of Inspector General of his division, a move that Whittingham felt had undermined his standing in the Spanish army.[110] He thought his fears had been confirmed when the Spanish government ignored his calls for the promotion of some officers of his division and decided to separate the regiment of Burgos, which he had formed, from his command.[111] On 22 August 1813, Whittingham told his brother-in-law that Wellington's insistence that British money should not be used to acquire provisions had been the last straw.[112] Whittingham's resignation took Wellington by surprise and seems to have opened his eyes to something his brothers Richard and Henry, as diplomatic envoys, had already realized: the British volunteers had a unique understanding of Spanish attitudes and mentalities and they knew how to operate within that context. To undermine their position in the Spanish army offered no benefit to the prosecution of the war. More importantly, their services were needed. Wellington, therefore, relented. On 20 September 1813, he asked Whittingham to withdraw his resignation, in return for authorization to access British stores to feed his troops.[113] On these terms, the Spanish divisions of Whittingham (reduced now to 5,399 men)[114] and Roche (3,314 men)[115] played a crucial role in the liberation of the Eastern provinces and in the Pyrenean campaign.[116]

A question of identity

At this point, we must enquire whether the problematic duality of the volunteers as British subjects fighting for Spanish forces in the context of the turbulent Anglo-Spanish alliance gave rise to any issues regarding national loyalties and identities. In terms of nationality, none of the volunteers who provided information for the *hojas de servicios* (Spanish military records) ever referred to themselves as 'British'. They declared to be Irish,[117] Scottish[118] or English.[119] In original sources, both in English and Spanish, the label 'British' tends to appear associated with institutions, such as in the 'British government' (*gobierno británico*)[120] and the 'British army' (*ejército británico*).[121] There was also the added complication that for Spaniards the preferred noun of nationality to refer to any person who spoke the language of Shakespeare was *inglés* (English), no matter where they were born. This could sometimes even apply to Americans who for much of the nineteenth century were still known as *ingleses americanos* (English Americans).[122] Therefore, it was not unusual that for expediency in communications with Spaniards, Scottish and Irish volunteers would identify themselves as being *inglés* (English).[123] From this perspective, Linda Colley's claim that war and contact with 'the other' promoted a sense of Britishness[124] could only hold true if we consider that the term 'English' played the unifying role attributed to that of Briton.[125]

There is evidence that some of the volunteers were not completely at ease with the idea of being considered as 'English'. On 16 November 1809, Doyle drafted a letter to fellow Irishman Lord Castlereagh venting frustration at the little recognition received for his exertions, stating that the British did not recognize his work while the Spaniards saw him as an Englishman. The latter, he found particularly annoying: '(. . .) your Lordship may suppose how it will have affected me to be told that I did my duty as an Englishman!!!'[126] Whereas he had no problem in alluding to British officials as 'English', he clearly hated to be considered as an 'Englishman' himself. Left in draft form, the letter appears never to have been posted. We can only speculate whether this was because Doyle realized that invoking his Irishness would have little impact on Castlereagh, a leading member of the Anglo-Irish community who had steered the Acts of Union in both houses of Parliament[127] or because he decided to content himself with the expressions of recognition received from Spaniards, even when these were professed to an outsider. Whatever the reason, no evidence has been found pointing to any incompatibility between the Irish and Scottish self-awareness of the volunteers and their status as subjects of the British monarchy. Irish volunteers tended to favour contacts with fellow Irishmen,[128] and Scots found it easier to socialize with Scots,[129] but this did not preclude relationships with members of other communities of the British Isles. In correspondence with Spaniards, Stirling-born John Downie often referred to Doyle as his 'paysano' (compatriot),[130] the same expression used by Englishman Charles Silvertop concerning fellow volunteers John Clarke, an Irishman, and Reynaldo Macdonell, a Scot,[131] and by Irishman Edmund Temple in reference to Downie.[132] In the aftermath of the Battle of Talavera, the Scotish *brigadier* James Duff nursed Whittingham, who had suffered a jaw injury, to the extent of feeding him by hand, while the Irish coronel Roche busied himself writing to Whittingham's family to assure them that the Bristolian had survived.[133]

All that remains to be explored in this context is the impact of the volunteers' unique standing in Spanish society. This appears relevant in light of a remark made by Doyle to his friend, the Aragonese leader José de Palafox, after only a few months of service in the Spanish army: 'It is true, by God, it is true. My friend Villahermosa [a relative of Palafox] is right when he says that I am more

Spanish than English.'[134] On first consideration, this could be interpreted as Doyle's sudden recognition of a transformation in his national self. From reading other correspondence with Spanish colleagues during the crisis that ended with the fall of Saragossa, it becomes clear that the comment had little to do with his national identity. It was an indication of a subtle shift in his commitment to the struggle which was to bring him closer to the Spaniards' basic interpretation of the 'common cause' as a war of national liberation.[135] In terms of nationality, only one of the British volunteers, John Downie, made a formal request to be considered a Spanish subject.[136] He made it on 29 April 1812, a few weeks after leading a spectacular incursion on French-occupied Seville with his sixteenth-century-attired *Legión de Extremadura,* an act of bravado that the Spaniards warmly and gratefully rewarded.[137] The extent to which Downie had found a deep personal affinity with Spanish culture and society had attracted comment in the *Cortes* a year earlier. Backing Downie's project of raising a legion, the deputy for Extremadura, Francisco Fernández Golfin recounted a dinner-table exchange he had witnessed during which Wellington teased Downie that he had become Spanish 'down to the shirt' and Downie responded: 'It goes much deeper than that, my Lord.'[138]

Although backed by the *Cortes* at committee level, it remains unclear whether Downie's nationality application was ever granted. Questions had been raised regarding his adoption of the Catholic religion (a requisite set by the *Cortes* before naturalization), and we ignore whether this issue was settled or not.[139] That Downie had an overriding desire to be accepted by Spaniards as 'one of us' cannot be doubted. He made it abundantly clear on several occasions. The most dramatic was during the exhumation and transfer to the church of San Isidro of the remains of Luis Daoiz and Pedro Velarde, the artillery heroes of 2 May 1808, a spectacular pageant decreed by the *Cortes* to commemorate the sixth anniversary of the Madrid rising and to celebrate the liberation of the capital. At the pinnacle of the ceremony, surrounded by political, military and ecclesiastical dignitaries, Downie asked – and was allowed – to open the coffins in order to remove two buttons from the uniform of Daoiz and a tooth from Velarde's skull to keep them as talismans of Spanish heroism,[140] a gesture that gave *pathos* and impulse to a national cult of these martyrs of the liberation campaign that persists to this day.[141]

The Scot's newly adopted Spanishness posed no threat to his existing national identity. It was an addition to, not a replacement for, allegiance to his country of birth. The majority of the subjects in this study, including Downie, remained deeply attached to their motherland, that 'land of freedom' represented by the British monarchy,[142] which they often held out as a positive influence and an example for Spain to follow. On 14 January 1814, the moderate liberal newspaper *El Universal* published in four columns a letter from Downie urging the *Cortes* to attend to the needs of the armed forces because the struggle against Napoleon was not yet over, and stressing that the rest of Europe expected no less from Spain, 'a nation that illuminated by the radiant sun of Great Britain, held alone the flame (of freedom) in the continent long before another powerful nation (Russia) decided to come to learn the sacrilegious plans of the proscribed Corsican.'[143] Matthew Brown found that in the Latin American wars of independence volunteers repeatedly stressed the British nature of their enterprise, which they saw as continuing the struggle against tyranny fought against Napoleon, and to which all free-born Briton was duty-bound to join.[144] Britain's role as a declared or tacit ally, as it was the case in Latin American, reinforced this attitude, but it was far from giving it substance. For that it may be helpful noticing that long before the Glorious Revolution, a notion that liberty was in the blood of anybody brought to the world under the Union Jack took firm hold in British popular culture. The country of the Magna Carta, constitutional monarchy and free trade was believed to produce individuals naturally inclined to be always ready to fight on the side of liberty. In that context, it was common for Britons to expect that they would be recognized as innate liberators.[145]

In Spain, the volunteers remained anxious to promote British interests and practices because they saw no incompatibility between them and those of their host country.[146] For example, on 26 May 1810, Whittingham told his brother-in-law, the wool-merchant MP for the market town of Colchester, Richard Hart Davis that nothing would enable him

> to do the Spanish cavalry so much good as clothing, arming, and equipping one corps in the English style (. . .). This corps would serve as a model for clothing, arms and furniture, and would, I am convinced induce the Spanish Government to make further contracts in England for the future clothing and arming of their troops.[147]

At least in this respect, no trace has been found of what Murray Pittock calls 'fratriotism', that is the adoption of foreign causes and cultures as a means of expressing reservations concerning economic and socio political developments in the country of birth.[148] Even when some of the volunteers might had been motivated to join the Spaniards because of lack of opportunities at home

(Silvertop's frozen military career due to his Catholicism comes here to mind),[149] it cannot really be said that their commitment to the Spanish cause was ever a disguise for a battle by proxy against British injustices. In spite of all the difficulties arising from the duality of their situation, the British volunteers remained focused in pursuing to the end their mission to free Spain. In so doing, as Doyle once told the Spanish Minister of War Eusebio Bardaxi, they considered themselves 'half Spanish, half English, and wholly Patriot'.[150] National loyalties and identities were accommodated to coexist in harmony behind the volunteers' distinctive objective of securing Spain's outright liberation.

The Aftermath

In the early hours of the evening of 31 July 1812, on hearing the news of the allied victory at Salamanca (22 July 1812), a large crowd in the besieged city of Cadiz gathered under the balcony of the house of volunteer James Duff, fourth Earl of Fife. They remained there until shortly after midnight, dancing on a makeshift *tablado*, cheering and hand-clapping songs composed on the spur of the moment to honour three men: the brother of the 'medio-dios' (semi-God)[1] Wellington, Ambassador Henry Wellesley, the commander of the Royal Navy Rear-Admiral Arthur Kaye Legge and the *mariscal de campo* Fife.[2] It was a defining moment. In a matter of weeks, the French lifted the siege and abandoned Andalusia for good. The celebrations in Cadiz marked the beginning of the end of the war. But the fighting was to continue for much longer. Indeed, it was only on 19 May 1814, with Ferdinand VII back on the throne, 5 months after signing the peace treaty of Valençay (11 December 1813), that General Baron Pierre-Michel Rouelle surrendered his 12,000-men garrison of Sagunto. He laid down arms to the Spanish forces of volunteer Roche that had laid siege to that strategically important fortress for 7 months.[3] Since the liberation of Andalusia, however, most Spaniards were under the impression that it was no longer a matter of if, but when the French would abandon the Peninsula, and that such a *dénouement* was imminent. Based on this assumption, attitudes and decisions were adopted that would have far-reaching consequences.

In the political arena, this mindset had the effect of displacing much attention and energies from the goal of liberation to that of implementing – or undermining, depending on each individual's views – the Constitution that had been proclaimed a few months earlier (19 March 1812). In many ways, that was a revolutionary text. With one stroke, it abolished seigniorialism and the Inquisition, substantially restricted the authority of the King, asserted the state's control of the Church, introduced modern ideas of national sovereignty and political representation, and enfranchised all men, except those of African ancestry, without requiring property qualifications. Advocates of fast and uncompromising enforcement of the 'Liberal Codex' within the government, described by the British *attaché* Charles Vaughan as 'Jacobins',[4] threw themselves into a race to monopolize all positions of power in reaction to the arrival of deputies from liberated areas with little inclination to support radical views. Under the rule of 'Jacobin' Juan O'Donojú, the War Department of the Fourth Regency (8 March 1813 to 10 May 1814) placed 'Jacobin' officers in key positions and gave them priority for the scarce resources available to the Spanish Treasury. Those soldiers admitted to the officialdom during the war were particularly favoured by the ministry because they were expected to be grateful for the political reforms that had allowed them to take a first step up the promotion ladder. Those with ranks acquired *antebellum* or those not belonging to O'Donojú's wide circle of friends were considered as potential political opponents and, consequently, often had requests for supplies and promotions refused. Some were relegated to administrative jobs regardless of their battlefield record. This had a detrimental effect on the morale of the Spanish army as a whole and worsened the relationship with its British commander-in-chief, with whom the Regency (the body vested with executive powers since the fall of the *Junta Central* on 30 January 1810) was already engaged in a power struggle.[5] Roche never disclosed his political sympathies; nonetheless, as a confidant of Tomas O'Donojú, Inspector General of the Army and brother of the War Minister, he saw all his recommendations for promotion of men in his division endorsed by the government.[6] Some of his colleagues had no such luck. As a *protégée* of General Castaños, Whittingham found himself among those relegated by the 'Jacobins' who wrestled for complete control over the constitutional regime. Castaños had publicly pledged his support to the Constitution[7] and was believed to sympathize with liberal ideals,[8] but he was an old professional officer prepared to serve under governments of all political persuasions.[9] This made him suspect in the eyes of a ministry that demanded exclusive loyalty. Whittingham despaired of this state of affairs, which he attributed to a 'Republican party'.[10] In a letter to his brother-in-law, in July 1813, he vented his frustration:

> No man has considered the Spanish Revolution with greater impartiality than myself. When we were reduced to Cadiz and the Balearic Islands, my spirits were high (. . .) Lord Wellington's memorable battle of Salamanca put the Spaniards in possession of the best part of their country, and gave them the means of forming great and powerful armies! Have they taken advantage of these circumstances? Have they done anything for their own salvation? Their whole time has been

occupied in the forming (sic) of a cursed Constitution, and their army has been forgotten and neglected! We have not, I again repeat, increased our army 20,000 men in the last year, nor is there in my opinion any hope of amendment.[11]

Whittingham's prognosis was correct, at least regarding recruitment for the war in the Peninsula, as the Spanish government showed signs of increasingly relying on the manpower added by the presence of British and Portuguese troops on Spanish territory. The number of recruits in Doyle's training depot in Cadiz, for example, dwindled to a few hundred during the last 2 years of the conflict.[12] At the same time, General Francisco Javier Abadía was recalled from active service to establish a 3,000-man Army of Reserve with the exclusive mission of enforcing the concept of a single, homogeneous 'Spanish nation', enshrined in the Constitution of 1812, on Latin America.[13] It rather appears that the British volunteers could help the Spaniards to liberate themselves from the French, but they could do little to help them to exorcise their own demons.

Nonetheless, with all these disappointments, liberation was achieved. A year after the cessation of hostilities in May 1814, 26 out of the 42 volunteers remained registered on active service in the records of the Spanish army.[14] This figure seems to suggest that over half of the British volunteers tried to continue their careers in Spain – something not altogether surprising in light of the considerable personal investment they had made in the future of that country. Within a decade, however, the numbers dwindled to only seven.[15] The majority left Spain during the first 5 years of the Bourbon Restoration. At first sight, there is no reason to believe that this resulted from lack of recognition. At least 17 of the volunteers were awarded the highest accolade of the Spanish monarchy, the order of Charles III.[16] However, nine of them only received this distinction during the period 1817–19,[17] a move perhaps associated with efforts by the Spanish government to deter British veterans of the Napoleonic wars from joining the ranks of the Spanish American rebels.[18] By then, a few had already seen their courage recognized at home. Towards the end of 1817, knighthoods had been granted to John Downie,[19] Whittingham,[20] William Parker Carrol, Roche,[21] Charles Doyle[22] and Robert Steele,[23] although in the latter's case this honour did little to prevent him from falling into a debtor's prison for expenses incurred while in the Spanish service.[24]

None of the volunteers ended their activities under the Spanish flag in sudden or acrimonious circumstances. It is true that Landor resigned his rank of *coronel* in disgust at Ferdinand VII's reinstatement of the Jesuits and the Inquisition,[25] but this was a rhetorical gesture performed at long distance and several years after his return home.[26] The situation was different for Roche who, in 1815, was made commander of a division of the Army of Aragon.[27] Soon after that, however, he began taking periods of short-term leave on health grounds, often to travel back to London,[28] where he finally died in 1829.[29] He left all his possessions to a married sister and two nieces still living in Valencia.[30] During the two decades that Charles Silvertop remained enrolled in the *Regimiento de la Princesa*, he also took leave frequently, not only to visit his Catholic family in Northumberland, but also to undertake mineralogical research in Granada.[31] The latter resulted in a series of academic papers that he presented at the Geological Society of London soon after retiring from the Spanish army in 1831. His work was later compiled into a book, to which scientists still refer.[32] In its preface, the former British volunteer lamented the 'many obstacles to detailed examination' in the Spain of the dying days of Ferdinand VII's reign,[33] such as the inaccuracies of maps, the lack of good roads and the Spaniards' reluctance to adopt the locomotive. Still, as it had become a habit for the British volunteers during the war, he could not avoid trumpeting the inner qualities of the inhabitants of what, for him, was still an exotic land:

> Spain, in a geological sense, as in many others, remains to be deciphered. It is full of interest in every point of view, moral and physical, but the *delicta majorum immeritus lues* (for the sins of the fathers undeservedly suffers) hand upon it (sic), and until the ordeal be passed, it will continue an enigma to the great loss of all civilized Europe. The country teems with genius and latent energy, and when the incubus, which for so many centuries has pressed them down, shall be fully removed, it will be one of the brightest stars in the European constellation of nations.[34]

Charles Doyle had been among the most fervent advocates of the Spanish potential for greatness. In early 1816, there were rumours that he was to be offered the captain generalcy of Murcia,[35] but this never happened. A few months earlier, Ballesteros, then War Minister, had ordered the closure of his innovative training depot at Cadiz, arguing that it 'no longer offered any advantage'[36] because the Infantry was to return to the 'system that it has always followed'.[37] But the idea of imparting elementary education to the soldiery irrespective of their social origin was to live on. Whether this was the case at Whittingham's academy for junior officers in Mallorca remains unclear because the reintroduction of the requisite of noble status to join the Spanish officer corps, on 17 June 1814, probably changed the social profile of the student body.[38] The British volunteers' legacy in this field was to endure through the intervention of the Duke of Infantado. A staunch supporter of Doyle's depot,[39] Infantado paid for volunteer John Kearney to travel to London to learn the Lancaster method of mutual instruction which he successfully introduced, not only in the lowest echelons of the Spanish army, but also in dozens of new primary and secondary schools around the country. Kearney undertook this with the full support of both the absolutist regime of Ferdinand VII and the *trienio liberal*.[40] The Protestant origin of the method and its association with British radicalism was to discredit it during the years of conservative reaction that followed the liberals' downfall in 1823.[41] Kearney's career also suffered, even though he was a Catholic with little interest in politics.[42] Nonetheless, it is believed that his efforts served as an inspiration for the first national plan for elementary education (*Plan y reglamento de estudios de primeras letras del reino*) of 1825 that would eventually lead to the Moyano Law of 1857, which made primary education compulsory.[43] As for Doyle, seeing plans he had submitted for a spa for convalescent soldiers in Murcia dogged by bureaucracy,[44] he headed homewards. He promised to return after dealing with family affairs, but his Spanish friends knew better. On 24 April 1816, the *intendente* (chief administrator) of the army in Murcia, Antonio de Elola,[45] wrote him a poignant letter regretting his departure. He rightly predicted that it would mean the end of the thermal bath project and of other public works proposed by the Irish volunteer, but conceded that

> it is not fair that you give up your interests, personal relations and wellbeing for a foreign country that does not even pay you a salary. I do not trust that I shall see you on Spanish soil again, let us hope that God proves me wrong.[46]

Indeed, Doyle never came back, although he remained technically 'on leave' from the Spanish army until at least 1835, the year of his last surviving correspondence with the Spanish authorities.[47] On 8 October 1837, the French liberal government of King Louis-Philippe awarded Doyle the *legion d'honneur* in his double capacity of lieutenant general in the Service of His Catholic (Spanish) Majesty and lieutenant general in the British army.[48] Leaving aside the reasons for the award, which remain unclear,[49] the acknowledgement of his double status – two decades after he left Spain and only 5 years before his death – seems to confirm that he never formally retired from the Spanish service.[50]

Some of the volunteers who remained in Spain could not avoid being dragged into the political and economic turmoil of Bourbon Restoration. On 20 March 1814, Whittingham's frustration with the political manoeuvrings of the 'Jacobins' in the *Cortes* and the Regency had reached such a pitch that he contemplated leaving the country, convinced that 'the Republican party is every day gaining ground; and civil war must ultimately decide the contest'.[51] A few days later, however, he met the King and his brother, the *Infante* Don Carlos, on their progress south from the French frontier. The British volunteer was impressed by the warm popular welcome the two royals received. This contrasted, he said, with the contempt regular Spaniards had for the constitutional government who, 'in the fury of their republican zeal',[52] had 'attacked, openly and in the most violent manner, the nobility, the clergy, and the army' and 'in the plenitude of their financial ignorance' had done away with all the old duties to establish, instead, a uniform income tax.[53] Whittingham's escort of Ferdinand VII to Madrid in April 1814 following the violent closure of the *Cortes* (an incident in which he denied participation) caused unfavourable comments from radical Whigs in the opposition at Westminster.[54] It did not help matters that he was almost immediately promoted to the rank of *teniente coronel*.[55] Some of the criticism was well founded as there can be little doubt that Whittingham favoured a return to the old regime. During the royal progress to Madrid, he had recommended adopting this course of action to General José Zaya whom, he believed, had been dispatched by the King to ascertain his opinion.[56] Although he was against the persecution of liberals, the British volunteer justified subsequent events on the basis that 'there was no longer doubt from the republican papers that have been seized, and the secret correspondence with France, that had the King sworn to the Constitution, he would have gone to the scaffold in less than six months'.[57]

For 5 years, Whittingham led the life of a member of the Spanish establishment, combining supervision of his Mallorcan academy with court duties in Madrid, such as sitting on the board that reformed the statutes of the military *Orden de San Fernando* to fit the post-war scenario.[58] While in the capital, he used his influence to lobby successfully against the slave trade (the great cause of his family friend William Wilberforce) which Spain abolished in 1817.[59] Yet, none of his responsibilities, which entailed onerous travel and protocol expenses, was ever matched by remuneration. In 1819, with five children to feed and his salary seriously in arrears, Whittingham had no choice but to take the British lieutenant governorship of Dominica, procured for him through the political influence of his brother-in-law, now an avowed Tory MP.[60] In a last plea to the King, addressed in the third person as it was the form, Whittingham hinted that he could still give up his plans because

> having fought in Spain, built his military reputation in Spain, being married to a Spaniard and with Spanish children, Spain is his *Patria* and it is only the desire to sustain his family which reduces him to accept a position under another sovereign.[61]

But there was no last-minute royal intervention. In the grim state of the nation's finances, Ferdinand VII could only confer that which the Bourbons had always offered to their generals: honorific rewards.[62] Whittingham thus became a victim of the policy of turning back the clock that he had himself advocated 5 years earlier.

John Downie was similarly lavished with honours, including the prestigious command of the Alcazar of Seville, the King's fortified residence in Andalusia,[63] for which he received an annual salary that barely covered one month of food expenses.[64] It was only by ceaselessly nagging the King for more provisions that the Scot managed to carry on with his duties. Downie had been an outspoken supporter of constitutionalism, to the extent that the first published English translation of the Constitution of 1812, attributed to fellow volunteer Daniel Robinson, had been effusively dedicated to him.[65] But he grew weary of the disputes within the liberal ranks and of the republican rhetoric adopted by the most extremist newspapers after the revolution of 1820.[66] In a public address to the *Cortes*, on 24 May 1821, Downie warned against discarding the monarchical system because

> it is important not to lose sight of the love you owe to the Constitution and to the Constitutional King, whose ideas are so bound together, that it is not possible to offend one without discrediting the other who has declared him inviolable.[67]

Two years later, on 11 June 1823, the *Cortes* pronounced Ferdinand VII 'temporally insane',[68] and forced him to abandon Seville, where he had been residing for 3 months against his will. Downie and his nephew Benjamin Barrie attempted to smuggle the King out of the country. Later, Downie explained to a friend that his intention was 'not to draw the sword against the *Cortes*', but to defend the King, who 'had always treated him with friendship'.[69] The conspiracy was discovered and both he and his nephew were imprisoned in Cadiz.[70]

Without the original 'Spanish cause' to fight for, the British volunteers lost the element that had bound them together. They were no longer driven by an ideology of liberation, but by partisan politics. The events of 1820–23, therefore, pulled them in different directions. The *tenientes coroneles* Francis Lee and Daniel Robinson fought with the liberal armies of Enrique O'Donnell and Rafael Riego;[71] William Parker Carrol offered to relinquish a prestigious appointment in Malta to follow suit.[72] Even John Downie's brother and co-founder of the *Legión de Extremadura*, Charles Downie, paid for his role of *aide-de-camp* to General Riego with 2 years in jail. He was only released after the King relented to his brother's pleas for clemency.[73] Circumstances had changed dramatically since 1814. Although it cannot be denied that, as from 7 April 1823, Spain had to deal with another French invasion, this was not a repeat of the incidents of 1807–08. Unlike Napoleon's forces, the 'One Hundred Thousand Sons of St. Louis' dispatched with the blessing of the Holy Alliance met with very little popular resistance.[74] Moreover, the aim of the army led by the Duke of Angoulême was not conquest, but to restore a still relatively popular King to his full absolutist powers. This was not a national war of independence, but a case of foreign intervention in favour of one side in a domestic dispute that was believed to cast a shadow over Europe's balance of power.[75]

This distinction is important because it helps explain why there is little to be found in common between the experience of the British volunteers during the Peninsular War and that of their compatriots who volunteered to fight in the corps of Sir Robert Wilson (1823) and the British Auxiliary Legion of Evans in the first Carlist war (1835–38). The terms of engagement already distanced these men from their predecessors. The new wave of British volunteers was recruited in regiments organized *a priori* in Britain and under contracts carefully negotiated, agreed and signed with the Spanish government. Salary, bounty and time limit of their service were crucial considerations and clearly defined.[76] These were business-like arrangements subscribed with men considered to be professional soldiers. But what is more important is that their mission was to assist the ruling Spanish authorities in their fight against supporters of a domestic 'tyrant' (Ferdinand VII) and of a Spanish usurper-to-be (the *Infante* Don Carlos). These British volunteers could be strong supporters of liberal regimes, but they were not national liberators.

An international network of liberation

Outside the Iberian Peninsula, yet still within the bounds of the Hispanic world, it is possible to find traces of continuity as well as some affinity between the British volunteers' experience in the Peninsular War and that of other liberators. The foiled expedition of the former *guerrillero* Martín Xavier Mina to Mexico (1817) and the adventures of Giuseppe Garibaldi in Brazil and Uruguay (1835–48) are often cited as examples of Europeans' personal involvement in wars of liberation overseas.[77] They may well have fitted that criteria (although Mina's attachment to the principle of a single Spanish nation cast a few doubts),[78] but similar patterns of behaviour would have to be drawn on abstract considerations because no concrete links have been found connecting the Spanish liberal martyr and the Italian national hero with the British volunteers in Spain. Ample evidence of other contacts, however, exists. We have seen that at least four prominent volunteers acquired some first-hand knowledge of the *Monarquía Hispana* before ever setting foot in the Peninsula. Whittingham, Roche and William Parker Carrol were veterans of the second British attempt to capture Buenos Aires in 1807.[79] John Downie had been second-in-command of the army of Colombia. He joined the Spanish campaign with the blessing of the Venezuelan liberator Francisco de Miranda, who saw the Peninsular conflict as a chance to establish a precedent for self-determination.[80] Downie and Miranda remained in contact until at least August 1810.[81] Two of the most trusted *aides-de-camp* of Charles Doyle during the war were the Buenos Aires-born Justo Rufino de San Martín (younger brother of General José Francisco de San Martín, liberator of Argentina, Chile and Peru)[82] and José María de Torrijos y Uriarte.[83] The latter was to become the leader of the Spanish utopian liberals[84] whose tragic death in 1831, depicted by Antonio Gisbert in his celebrated painting *Fusilamiento de Torrijos y sus compañeros en las playas de Málaga* (1888), was hailed by the Spanish poet Antonio Machado as the event that marked the birth of the Spanish Romantic movement.[85] In 1815, Torrijos refused to join the expeditionary force to 'pacify' the Latin American colonies because, he said, 'did not desire to enslave our Latin American brothers'.[86] This was at the time when one of the regiments trained under his supervision in Cadiz and of which he had been commander, the *Tiradores de Doyle*, was dispatched to Montevideo.[87] In 1829, while in exile in London (living with aid provided by Doyle and other British friends), Torrijos translated into Spanish the first biographical account of General San Martín produced by William Miller, one of San Martín's best officers in the army of Peru and a British veteran of the Peninsular War.[88]

The Earl of Fife had an even closer relationship with the future liberator of the Southern Cone. The two men probably met while fighting under the orders of General Antoine de Coupigny, a French émigré in charge of the second division of the Andalusian army. It seems that a shared love of music, theatre and cigars also contributed to bring them together.[89] San Martín was then a *capitán* in the Spanish army.[90] During a period of convalescence in Cadiz, Fife (then known under the subsidiary title of viscount Macduff) befriended several members of what was loosely called the 'American party',[91] including the deputy for Nueva Granada (Colombia) José Mexía Lequerica,[92] the Alvear family and the banker Duncan Shaw.[93] In 1811, San Martín decided to travel to London, recognizing

Figure 8 James Duff, Lord Macduff, fourth Earl of Fife (1776–1857), detail of copy by
F. R. Pickersgill (1820–1900) of oil-on-canvas by Sir Henry Raeburn (1756–1823), *circa*
1815, currently at the Earl's ancestral home, Duff House, Banff, Scotland. Reproduced
by permission of Aberdeenshire Museums Service.

that the British capital was the most important hub in Europe for the cause of
Latin American independence. He found, however, that the Spanish government
was not eager to allow a skilful soldier with 22 years of experience to leave the
Peninsula, even when he managed to get from his military superiors a licence to
travel to Lima.[94] It remains unclear whether Macduff was privy to San Martín's
ulterior motives, but the fact is that he obtained for his friend a ticket to England,
several letters of introduction and even letters of credit, which, according to
Miller's biography, San Martín did not need to resort.[95] It was because of this help
that San Martín was able to arrive in London. From there, in the first months of
1812, he made the trip to Buenos Aires, which would turn him into the hero of
three nations (Argentina, Chile and Peru).

The two friends kept up correspondence all through the years of the liberation
campaign.[96] Having fulfilled his duty in America, San Martín headed back to
England after being refused entry by the Bourbon regime in France, where he
had hoped to join his brother Justo Rufino, then living in Paris. He arrived at
Southampton in May 1824 and spent a few months making arrangements for
the education of his only daughter Merceditas in a girl's college in Hampstead,
London, and having a series of meetings with Peruvian envoys and Latin

American friends. Then, he travelled to Scotland to meet the Earl. With the British press eagerly following each of his movements,[97] San Martín tried to keep a low profile, travelling only as a tall, swarthy man in foreign dress amid a contingent of tourists. Not even announced his visit to his friend, whom he surprised at his home in Banff, 90 km north of Aberdeen, on Fife's return from a week of hunting on property that today constitutes the Royal Estate of Balmoral. 'When I arrived here on Sunday I found General San Martín who came on Friday. If you wish to see him you must be here tomorrow as he goes away Friday (. . .). He is an extraordinary man', the Earl told his brother-in-law Richard Wharton Duff in a scribbled note dated 18 August 1824.[98] Fife' residence, Duff House, had been designed by the architect William Adam in 1735 with only one aim: to impress. The founder of the dynasty, William Duff, a lawyer who made his fortune as a landowner, wanted to convince the world that he was a descendant of Lord Macduff, the mythical friend of the Shakespearean Macbeth, so he commissioned Adam to construct the grandest mansion in Scotland. San Martín spent only a week within its ornamented walls, time sufficient for his status of hero to be acknowledged by the local authorities whom, no doubt at the Earl's suggestion, decided to grant him the title of 'Freeman of the Royal Burgh of Banff' on 19 August.[99] That was the only recognition San Martín received in the Old Continent. It was bestowed 6 months before Foreign Minister George Canning – an acquaintance of Fife – obtained parliamentary approval for a treaty of commerce and friendship with the Buenos Aires government, the first step towards international acceptance of Latin American independence.[100] Thereafter, the two men would follow their different ways. After a thwarted attempt to return to Buenos Aires, San Martín lived in Belgium and France, where he died in 1850. Fife left a life at court and a seat in Parliament to put down roots in his own country where he spent a good deal of his fortune establishing new villages, such as Dufftown, now known as the capital of Scotland's malt whisky distilling, and in the restoration of Pluscarden Abbey, the religious house founded in 1230 by the Scottish king Alexander II, all with the social aim of giving employment to veterans of the Napoleonic wars.[101]

At least three of the British volunteers were personally involved in the Latin American struggle.[102] For a long time, nobody knew exactly the political shape that emancipation would take in that continent. Various schemes were discussed, including one that envisaged the creation of a sort of Hispanic Commonwealth led by a prince of the Spanish branch of the Bourbons.[103] This uncertainty may have eased the transition of the British volunteers from fighting under the Spanish flag to that of the American nations. By late 1818, Charles Morgan

Carrol and his cousin Michael Carrol had joined the Argentine-Chilean army of the Andes led by San Martín. Made commander of the third battalion of the *Escuadrón de Dragones de la Patria*, the former *teniente coronel* of the Spanish army Carlos Morgan Carrol,[104] now known as Carlos María O'Carrol, became a martyr of the Latin American cause. He met a horrendous death at the hands of pro-Spanish *guerrilla*, near the southern Chilean village of Los Angeles on 23 September 1820.[105] Several streets and avenues today bear his name in the city of Rancagua and other urban areas of the Chilean region of Biobío.[106] His cousin, an *aide-de-camp* of the liberator Bernardo O'Higgins, continued in the service of the Chilean army until at least January 1830.[107] Arthur Goodall Wavell, by now a retired *teniente coronel* of the Spanish Ultonia regiment,[108] also joined the Chilean army with the rank of *coronel* on 6 July 1820. In January 1822, Wavell arrived in Mexico as an official envoy of the Chilean government to transmit that country's recognition of Mexico's independence.[109] He gained the confidence of the Emperor Agustín de Iturbide who conferred him the rank of *brigadier general* in the Mexican army and later dispatched him as secret emissary to persuade the British government to recognize his country's independence and to attract British investment. While in Mexico, he met his fellow volunteer Daniel Robinson, who, after the failure of the *Liberal Trienium*, took a job as surveyor for a British mining company. That would not last long, but before returning to Europe he had a daughter there whom he named Maria de Guadalupe Ana Antonia Robinson, probably drawing inspiration from 'Our Lady of Guadalupe', a symbol of mestizo culture associated with the Mexican emancipation movement.[110] Wavell remained in the service of the Mexican army until 1833,[111] mainly occupied in the production of textbooks on infantry and cavalry tactics and pamphlets on the defence of various regions of the country[112] – all very reminiscent of the initiatives taken by fellow volunteers Whittingham and Doyle in Spain.[113] Wavell was particularly interested in the defence of Texas where he was involved in an unsuccessful colonization scheme ('The Old Three Hundred') with the businessmen Moses and Stephen Austin, the latter known as the Father of Texas.[114]

Non-combatant activities took other British volunteers to Spanish America. The Irishman Edmond Temple, *capitán* in the *Legión de Extremadura*,[115] joined as working partner the 'Potosi, La Paz and Peruvian Mining Association' set up in the 1820s by General San Martín's army surgeon, James Paraoissien.[116] He travelled much of the continent and related his experiences in a two-volume book,[117] now considered as essential reading for the history of travel writing in Latin America.[118] On the cover, he still identified himself as 'knight of the Royal and Distinguished [Spanish] Order of Charles III'.[119] Nine years earlier, on 3 April 1821, fellow volunteer Patrick Campbell had been forced at gunpoint to leave Spain, accused by Catalan liberal insurgents of not adhering to the constitutional regime. The Scot refuted the charge vigorously, arguing – as was common among the volunteers – that, 'being an Englishman (sic), he could hardly imagine anybody could doubt his support for liberal and constitutional principles that were the distinctive characteristics of his nation of birth'.[120] Without admitting error, the Spanish government granted Campbell a year's paid leave to remain in London.[121] But after two years without a commission, the Scot decided to join the British diplomatic service. In October 1823, he was appointed British representative at Cartagena de Indias, in the newly established Republic of Colombia.[122] While in that service, Campbell became a close friend of the liberator Simon Bolivar.[123] It was to him that Bolivar penned that famous letter where he stated that the United States 'seems destined by Providence to plague America with miseries in the name of Freedom'.[124]

These examples of British volunteers' involvement in Latin American affairs serve to underpin the importance of keeping a transatlantic perspective on the history of this period. They do little, however, to further the long-held, but never well-substantiated view that Latin American independence was somehow the result of a skilful British conspiracy or that San Martín was recruited to the independentist cause by the Earl of Fife or any other British subject.[125] No evidence has been found to back such a straightforward explanation. This is not to deny that some of the British volunteers and many of their Spanish *peninsulares* and American colleagues appear to have been part of what could be described as an informal international network of liberation, one that went beyond that occupational fraternity that Stephen Conway has recently called 'Military Europe'.[126] The terms 'informal' and 'network' need to be underlined because there is nothing revealing a common mission or political programme, but rather a casual community of shared opinions and aspirations. Indeed, it cannot even be said that all Britons supported the emancipation of Spanish America. Volunteer James Arbuthnot fought against Latin American 'rebels' in Venezuela, Panama and Colombia for 9 years (1814–23) before returning to Spain, where he had a long military career leading to the positions of captain general of Catalonia (1843) and military governor of Lerida (1847) and Galicia (1854 and 1863).[127] While in London in 1816, Roche served as intermediary and sponsor of a plan to 'pacify America', offered with little success to the Spanish government by Rear

Admiral Sir Home Riggs Popham, the man in charge a decade earlier of the first British invasion of Buenos Aires.[128] Even John Downie, erstwhile *coronel* of the army of Colombia, made a show of loyalty to the Spanish Crown by offering to lead the remnants of his *Legión de Extremadura* on one of the expeditions 'to quiet down Your Majesty's colonies in Americas'.[129] The argument here is not that the British volunteers masterminded the emancipation of Latin America, but that there are significant points of convergence between their experience in Spain and that of the liberators on the other side of the Atlantic – a concurrence that might have been enhanced by the cross-fertilization of ideas resulting from direct personal contacts.[130]

A full comparative study that could result in an outline of the process of liberation goes beyond the scope of this book, and it may well be a precarious route to take because the British volunteers could be considered as little-known 'outsiders' in charge of relatively small forces, while most of the Latin American liberators attained fame, leading vast armies in a continent that had given them birth. Nonetheless, a few elements of what appears to constitute a common pattern will be mentioned here by way of a postscript. The most important common denominator is that all these men embraced a cause of emancipation, no matter that this was not necessarily the same one. In so doing, they were driven by the same ideology – one that made all considerations, both of a personal and political nature, subservient to the attainment of liberation. As we have seen, many British volunteers subscribed to liberal views, but in the years of the Peninsular War, they fought not to enact political change, but to release Spaniards from French tyranny. For their Latin American counterparts, the situation was similar. In San Martín's words, he had crossed the Atlantic in 1812 'to work for the independence of his native land. As for the form of its government, it will get what it requires in exercise of this same independence'.[131] The message was clear: liberation came first; political organization was to emanate as a consequence of the achievement of the main priority. Just as the British volunteers had in their minds an *a priori* ideal vision of a united Spain,[132] the Latin American liberators spoke of their homeland as a thirsty-for-freedom 'America' (not Colombia, Argentina, Chile, etc.).[133] There are also striking similarities in their attitudes and mentalities, particularly their unrelenting determination and self-confidence, which often implied the belief that it was up to individuals to alter the course of history. This is clearly articulated in the following statement written by the Earl of Fife on 3 June 1817, after San Martín's victory at the Battle of Chacabuco (12 February 1817):

You cannot, my friend San Martín, imagine how the news of your good conduct fills me with satisfaction. I have always had a great friendship for you and since my arrival from Spain, I have been telling my compatriots: "Patience: a man over there will surprise everybody". I was convinced that a blow would be struck by your arm. I will not become involved in the political history of your affairs, nor in your motives – you can only count on me as your good friend, and one who is extremely interested in the welfare of San Martín – and I hope that the time will arrive in which we shall have the opportunity to embrace and talk about the extraordinary things that have happened since Cadiz.[134]

It may seem odd that Fife deliberately disassociated his trust in San Martín's capabilities from the reasons that might have spurred his friend into action, but this was the language used by one liberator to speak to another with whom he did not necessarily share the same cause. Although he was proud of his friend's achievements, Fife never abjured his status of Spanish *mariscal de campo* and knight of the *Orden de San Fernando*.[135] His comment should be interpreted as an inner appreciation of the value of courage and decisiveness in any liberation campaign. These qualities were considered of paramount importance in order to overcome all obstacles, be it by sheer daring, as in the case of Downie galloping towards French guns brandishing Pizarro's sword,[136] by outmanoeuvring those who hindered or conspired against the cause[137] or by the introduction of social and cultural innovations.[138] San Martín, the man who seven times crossed the Andes to accomplish his emancipatory mission, once attributed his decision to join the Spanish American struggle to the knowledge that 'se había de empeñar' (it was to be quite a challenge).[139] For the British volunteers, leaving aside all vexation, misunderstandings and frustrations, it was the Peninsular experience that would remain the adventure of a lifetime. So much so that, almost a decade later, Whittingham, now quartermaster general of the British troops in India, after describing in a letter the beauties and dangers of the subcontinent, encouraged Fife to visit him with the simple remark: 'Does not all this tempt you in some degree? We should almost fancy ourselves again in Spain!'[140]

Conclusion

On the strength of this work, it seems now justified to assert that there was significant – and hitherto unrecognized – British involvement in the Peninsular war beyond the ambit of the military operations exclusively sanctioned by the British government. Spanish resistance to Napoleon galvanized British public opinion to a degree perhaps not fully appreciated until now, leading men from widely different backgrounds to go in aid of a community that, as a political entity, had been hostile to their country of birth, and of which the majority knew almost nothing. What they found was bewildering: an embattled society trying to come to terms with a sudden vacuum of legitimate authority and also one determined not to succumb to the diktat of a French world order. The British volunteers' desire to help Spaniards to preserve their liberty fitted well within the scope of the 'Spanish cause', a term that had at its core the defence of Spanish freedom from foreign intervention along with multiple, often contrasting, subsidiary meanings, such as the attainment of substantial political reforms and the exertion of revenge on the enemy. Top of the list of priorities was the restoration of Ferdinand VII to the throne and the recovery and preservation of the territorial integrity and sovereignty of the *Monarquía Hispana*. At times, tensions and disagreements within Patriot ranks gave all the appearance that the conflict could turn into a civil war. But this did not happen. Internal dissent was debilitating and caused much frustration, but never managed to completely quash Spanish insurgency against the French. The volunteers' trust in the will and capability of common Spaniards – as opposed to that of many of their leaders – proved to be well placed. No other nation in Europe resisted French invasion so consistently, for so long. While they were conscious of that danger – and yes, there were times when a reminder from their British friends was called for – Spaniards somehow knew when to step back from the brink.

Between 200,000 and 310,000 French troops, that is to say three-fifths of the Empire's total armed strength (and almost four times the force that Napoleon originally had designated for this duty) were tied down in Spain over a period of 6 years, draining as a result the French Treasury. Napoleon only withdrew

27,000 troops for the Russian campaign. Over 50,000 died in battle, killed by the *guerrilla* or by illnesses partly caused by the awful conditions in which they had to subsist.[1] The regular versus irregular fighters' dichotomy and other historiographical debates that revolve around arguments that pit British involvement against Spanish dogged tenacity are not useful in explaining such outcome. This is because, ultimately, victory arose from the fusion of all these elements. Whitehall's approach to the conflict could fluctuate from inertia to direct intervention; yet all its policies were predicated on establishing an Iberian base from which to launch an offensive against Napoleon's Empire or, at worst, contain its advance. The latter prompted the consideration of abandoning Spain to Napoleon at least once, in 1810. The withdrawal of British troops in the aftermath of Moore's disaster, repeated by Wellington after his troubling experience in Talavera appeared to point in that direction. During those dark years, the majority of the British volunteers remained in Spanish soil. A few even chose that period as the moment to offer their services.[2] Although small in numbers, their continuous presence implicitly sent the message that Spaniards were not alone.

But it was not by virtue of being on the spot or voicing support that they became liberators. They assumed that role by fitting all their principles and actions to the requirements of the 'Spanish cause'. In that endeavour, they could be cunning and ruthless in equal measure. Those volunteers who were also British military agents often disregarded orders emanating from London and exerted considerable influence on political authorities by exercising to the full their double status of Spanish generals and British envoys. As tends to be the case with people who, deliberately or fortuitously, have been neglected by history, the recognition of the role played by the British volunteers in the Peninsular War should give cause to re-examine the overall picture of the conflict, including some key episodes such as what now it appears unjustifiable to call, the 'Marquess de La Romana's coup' in Asturias.

Findings in this book point to the merits of anchoring any future research in the culture and mentalities of the time. Contemporary attitudes to the historical past in both Britain and Spain and the safeguard of honour – particularly in a Spanish context where the concept was deemed integral to national self-awareness – informed many of the actions and attitudes of the volunteers and their contemporaries. Against this background, it becomes clear why undertakings, such as John Downie's sixteenth-century-attired *Legión de Extremadura*, merited a high degree of both notoriety and recognition at the time. Some authors have dismissed Downie as a self-important fool, but during the period of the Spanish War of Independence his courage, charisma, ingenuity and unquestioned loyalty to his superiors established him as a binational hero. On this point, this study has attended the call Javier Fernández Sebastián made to fellow historians to avoid prompting scandal and moral indignation in their readers by making value judgements on the events and processes that today we may consider unwise or mistaken, and instead engage in an effort to understand 'the actors in their own terms'.[3] Sensitive to traditions and mores, the volunteers bridged the cultural divide with actions designed to buttress and boost Spanish resistance, as well as keeping the British public attached to the fate of a fundamentally distinctive European nation. From an exploration of their deeds and stances it has now become clear, for example, that the belief that Spaniards possessed an indomitable and passionate character naturally suited to fierce resistance was not a product of post-war nineteenth-century historiography, but a conviction already widely held in the early 1800s.

As officers of an army with which Britain had recently been at war, the volunteers often suffered offhand treatment by the British military command, while the duality of their status at times made them equally suspect in Spanish eyes. These tensions cast a shadow over their activities, but had little impact on their national loyalties and identities. No evidence has emerged pointing to any nationalist sentiment of a political nature among the Irish and Scottish volunteers, as opposed to a sense of cultural self-awareness, which was, indeed, present. Similarly, affinity with the Spanish way of life did not diminish their attachment to their country of birth and to the British monarchy, which they often presented as an example for Spain to follow. It was common for them, just as for most Britons, to assume that their native attachment to the 'land of freedom' would be considered God-given proof of their commitment and suitability to all missions of emancipation from tyranny. They were not just war volunteers but British liberators. Foreigners usually interpreted this moral self-belief as arrogance, but perhaps it could be said that in the same way that honour was the structural value of Spaniards, freedom may have been that of Britons.

Altering the existing social structures and mores was not integral to their plans, yet they could not avoid sowing a few seeds of equality through a series of innovative measures designed to build up morale and better prepare the Spanish society to engage in a war characterized by the high involvement of civilians. This included the creation and running – in close partnership with Spaniards – of two pioneering training establishments where elementary education was offered, in addition to military instruction, for first time to recruits from all backgrounds. Women were elevated to the status of national heroines, particularly the emblematic Agustina of Aragon who owed her full membership of the Spanish army – an unprecedented status for a woman – to the intervention of one of the British volunteers. The first 'Patriotic Fund', a non-governmental association, was established to assist those ignored by the precarious Spanish military welfare system. From the perspective of those who see war as a succession of battles and victories, the volunteers' contribution may look modest; still, there is little doubt that without their far-sightedness and determination, things might have turned out very differently. If many of their initiatives suffered in the unsettled period that followed Ferdinand VII's restoration, part of the blame could be imputed to the fact that they had not been conceived to last but to respond to the contingency of the emancipatory campaign. Perhaps this was part and parcel of the experience of being a liberator. The man to whom the epithet was first attached, Simon Bolivar, once said that he preferred the 'the title of Citizen to that of Liberator, because whereas the latter derives from war (circumstances), the former derives from the Laws'.[4] Notwithstanding differences in context and transcendence of their personal careers, similarities in the ethos, discourse and *modus operandi* of the British volunteers can be found among liberators that operated in Latin America, particularly those with whom they had direct contact. The implications of these relationships merit further investigation, independently from the case that they may open – as it is to be hoped – a new avenue of research into the phenomenon of national liberation in nineteenth-century Euroamerican Atlantic history.

Appendices

Glossary

Afrancesado: literally, 'frenchified one'; Spanish supporter of French culture and politics in general, but specifically of the Napoleonic regime during the war.

Bodega: a cellar and/or shop for the sale of wines or sherry only.

Cortes: representative assembly at national or regional level.

Chouans: French Royalist rebels, particularly active in the western departments of France.

Foral: appertaining to the 'fueros'.

Fueros: local traditional rights, privileges, codes of justice and institutions of self-government, many popularly based, dating back to the Middle Ages.

Generalísimo: supreme military commander.

Guerrilla: literally, the 'little war'; bands of irregular warriors.

Hojas de servicio: the record of service of an individual in the Spanish military.

Ilustrados: literally, 'enlightened one'; intellectuals (men of letters, economists, philosophers, etc.).

Junta: committee of government or administration, often elected.

Majos and *majas*: colloquial term used to describe flamboyant young men and women, mainly of the lower classes in Madrid.

Miguelets: Catalan militia; in the Basque provinces, an irregular local homeguard.

Peninsulares: European Spaniards.

Pronunciamiento: literally, 'pronouncements'; occasionally, indirect statements by army officers intended to influence government's policy, but more frequently armed revolts by one section of the army destined to put pressure on the government, rarely leading to a *coup d'état*.

Regencia: (Regency) the body that exercised executive power on behalf of the absent King after the dissolution of the first Patriot government, the *Junta Central*, on 30 January 1810. There were four Regency councils, commonly known as *Regencias*, during this period: the First Regency (30 January 1810 to 28 October 1810) comprising General Francisco Javier Castaños, Antonio

Escaños, Esteban Fernández de León, Miguel Lardizábal Uribe and Pedro Quevedo Quintano, bishop of Orense; the Second Regency (28 October 1810 to 22 January 1812) with Pedro Agar, General Joachim Blake, Gabriel Císcar, Domingo Mariano Traggia, Marquess de Palacio, José María Puig, Ramón Rufino Patiño Osorio, Marquess de Castelar; the Third Regency (22 January 1812 to 8 March 1813) with Juan María Villavicencio, Pedro de Alcántara Toledo, Duke of Infantado, Joaquín Mosquera y Figueroa, General Enrique José O´Donnell, Ignacio Rodríguez de Rivas, Juan Pérez Villamil; and the Fourth Regency (8 March 1813 to 10 May 1814) presided by Luis de Borbón y Villabriga, cardinal of Toledo.

Señoríos: feudal fief.

Somatens: Catalan homeguard.

Sorteo: ballot for military service.

Tablado: a platform normally used to stage *flamenco* and other Andalusian dances.

Tertulias: gatherings held at private homes and considered as the first and foremost example of modern sociability in Spain.

Table 1 The volunteers' place of birth, age at time of joining the Spaniards, social and military background, place and year of engagement

Source	Name	Place of birth	Age	Propertied and/or educated	Military background	Place and year of engagement in the Spanish forces
1	James Arbuthnot (*Jaime Arbuthnot y Arbuthnot*)	Scotland	17	Yes	No	Asturias, 1808
2	Benjamin Barrie	Scotland	16	Yes	No	Cadiz, 1811
3	Patrick (*Patricio*) Campbell	Scotland	28	Yes	Yes	Headquarters Army of Extremadura in La Mancha, 1809
4	Charles (*Carlos*) Morgan Carrol	Ireland	32	Yes	Yes	Galicia, offered services in 1810, joined in 1812
5	Michael (*Miguel*) Carrol	Ireland	23	Yes	Yes	Galicia, 1812
6	William (*Guillermo*) Parker Carrol	Ireland	32	Yes	Yes	Galicia, 1808
7	Richard Parker Carrol	Ireland	29	Yes	Yes	Galicia(?), 1810
8	John Clarke (*Juan Clarke or Clark*)	Ireland	21	n/a	Yes	Leon, 1808
9	George or Samuel Bloss Copping? (*Jorge Coppy*)	Ireland (?)	n/a	n/a	Yes	Cadiz, 1812
10	James (*Diego*) Corrigan	Ireland	23	n/a	n/a	Cadiz, 1811
11	Charles (*Carlos*) Downie	Scotland	33	Yes	No	Extremadura, 1811
12	John (*Juan*) Downie	Scotland	31	Yes	Yes	Spanish–Portuguese frontier near Badajoz, 1810

(*Continued*)

Table 1 (Continued)

Source	Name	Place of birth	Age	Propertied and/or educated	Military background	Place and year of engagement in the Spanish forces
13	Carlo Doyle	Ireland (born in Warsaw)	21	Yes	Yes	Galicia, 1808
14	Charles William Doyle (*Carlos Guillermo Doile*)	Ireland	38 (26?)	Yes	Yes	Galicia, 1808
15	James Duff, Viscount Macduff, fourth Earl of Fife (*Diego, vizconde Macduff, conde de Fife*)	Scotland	32	Yes	Yes	Seville, 1809
16	Edwin Rowlandson Green	England	31	Yes	Yes	Catalonia, 1808
17	John Kearney (*Juan Quearney Donnelan*)	Ireland	25	n/a	No	Galicia, 1808
18	George (*Jorge*) Landmann	England	29	Yes	Yes	Seville, 1809
19	Walter Savage Landor	England	33	Yes	No	Galicia, 1808
20	Francis (*Francisco*) Lee	Ireland	28	n/a	Yes	Cadiz, 1812
21	Reginald (*Reynaldo*) Macdonnell	Scotland	29	n/a	Yes	Galicia, 1810
22	Neil Macdougall	Scotland	23	n/a	Yes	Mallorca, 1811
23	William (*Guillermo*) Mac Veagh	Ireland	n/a	n/a	Yes	Seville, 1809
24	W. McMahon	Ireland (?)	n/a	n/a	Yes	Cadiz, 1811

#	Name	Country	Age			Service
25	Rudolf (*Radulfo*) Marshal	Ireland	n/a	Yes	n/a	Catalonia, 1808
26	John Mealican (*Juan Méelican*)	Ireland	18	n/a	Yes	Cadiz, 1812
27	Thimoteo (*Timoteo*) Meagher	Ireland	n/a	n/a	Yes	Galicia, 1812
28	Henry (*Enrique*) Milburne	England?	n/a	Yes	Non-combatant	Galicia,1808 (frustrated; re-engaged at Mallorca, 1810)
29	John (*Juan*) O'Hara	Ireland	n/a	n/a	Yes	Cadiz, 1812
30	Paul Palmer (*Pablo Palmes*)	Ireland	n/a	n/a	Yes	Cadiz, 1812
31	Manuel Poe	Ireland	n/a	n/a	Yes	Cadiz, 1812
32	Charles Reed	England	n/a	Yes	n/a	Catalonia, 1809 (first recorded service)
33	James O'Ryan (*Jayme O Rian*)	Ireland	18	n/a	n/a	Cadiz, 1812
34	Daniel Robinson	England	19	Yes	Yes	Catalonia, 1810
35	Jeremy (*Gerónimo*) Robinson	Ireland	n/a	n/a	n/a	Cadiz, 1813
36	Philip Keating Roche (*Felipe Qeating Roche or de la Roche*)	Ireland	36	Yes	Yes	Asturias, 1808
37	Charles (*Carlos*) Silvertop	England	26	Yes	Yes	Seville, 1809
38	Robert Steele (*Roberto Steile*)	England	25	Yes	Yes	Cadiz, 1813

(*Continued*)

Table 1 (Continued)

Source	Name	Place of birth	Age	Propertied and/or educated	Military background	Place and year of engagement in the Spanish forces
39	Edmond (*Edmundo*) Temple	Ireland	n/a	Yes	Yes	Cadiz, 1811
40	Arthur (*Arturo*) Goodall Wavell	Scotland	25	Yes	Yes	Cadiz, 1810
41	Henry (*Enrique*) Wilson	Ireland	n/a	n/a	n/a	Galicia, 1811
42	Samuel Ford Whittingham (*Santiago Whittigham or Witinga or Güttinghan*)	England	36	Yes	Yes	Cadiz, 1808

Sources (unless stated, full references are given in Notes):   **(1)** AGMS, A-2104 *Expediente* Jaime Arbuthnot; **(2)** AGMS, B-933 *Expediente* Benjamin Barrie; **(3)** AGMS, E-688 *Expediente* Patricio Campbell; **(4)** AGMS, C-1704 *Expediente* Carlos Morgan Carrol; **(5)** AGMS, C-1704 *Expediente* Miguel Carrol; **(6)** AGMS, P-541 *Expediente* Guillermo Parker Carrol; **(7)** Ibid; Robertson, *Long way from Tipperary*, p. 31; NA FO, 72/116, ff. 174–5: William Parker Carrol to Marquis of Wellesley, 18 February 1811; 'Richard Carrol', in *FamilySearch* Ancestral File, at http://www.familysearch.org accessed 21 January 2008; **(8)** AGMS, C-2843 *Expediente* Juan Clarke; **(9)** AGMS, C-3283 *Expediente* Jorge Coppy (sic, for Copping?); BOD North, c. 16, ff. 390, 391, 395, 418; **(10)** AGMS, C-3476 *Expediente* Diego (James) Corrigan; **(11)** AGMS, D-1176 *Expediente* Carlos Downie; **(12)** AGMS, D-1177 *Expediente* Juan Downie; **(13)** Doyle, *A Hundred Years of Conflict*, pp. 140–86; BL, Add. 49486, f.128: Carlo Doyle, Santander, 12 September 1808; **(14)** Stephens, 'Doyle, Sir (Charles) William (1770–1842)', DBN; but a manuscript report at the ANF backing his candidature to the *Legion d'honneur* stated that he was born in Dublin, 16 April 1782, see ANF, LH/801/030: 'Charles Guillaume Doyle né en Dublin, le 16 avril 1782, Lieutenant General dans le Service du SMC'; three obituaries (*The Examiner*, 5 November 1842, p. 14; *John Bull*, 5 November, 1842, p. 540; *The Age*, 6 November, p. 8) stated he died at 62 years of age (born on 1780); AGMS, D-877 Carlos Guillermo Doile (described only as Irish, no exact place or date of birth mentioned); **(15)** AGMS, M-8 *Expediente* 72 Vizconde Macduff; Tayler, *Book of the Duffs*, I, pp. 203–10; **(16)** 'Edwin Rowland Joseph Green', in *FamilySearch* Ancestral File, at http://www.familysearch. org accessed 20 March 2007; *The London Kalender or Court and City Register for England, Scotland, Ireland, and the Colonies* (London, 1808), p. 212; NA WO, 1/227, f. 237: Doyle re. Green, 17 September 1808; **(17)** AGMS, Q-1 *Expediente* Juan Quearney Donnelan; **(18)** AGMS, L-228 *Expediente* Jorge Landmann; Federic Boase (ed.), *Modern English Biography Containing Many Thousand Concise Memoirs of Persons Who Have Died between the Years 1851–1900 with an Index of the Most Interesting Matter* (6 vols, London, 1965), II, p. 290; **(19)** ASL, Vaughan Papers, C: Landor to Vaughan, Villafranca, 15 September 1808; Super, *Landor – A Biography*, pp. 2, 85; Elwin, *A Peplevin*, p. 119; Wise and Wheeler, *A Bibliography of the Writings*, pp. 33–4; **(20)** AGMS, L-700 *Expediente* Francisco Lee; **(21)** AGMS, M-8 *Expediente* 69 Reynaldo Macdonnell; **(22)** NA WO, 1/1123, ff. 315–16: Patrick Campbell re. MacDougall, 7 May 1811; 'Neil Macdougall'; in *FamilySearch* Ancestral File, at http://www.familysearch.org accessed 5 March 2008; **(23)** AGMS, M-8 *Expediente* 60 Guillermo MacVeagh; **(24)** BOD North, c. 16, f. 393: Doyle re. W. McMahon, 13 April 1813; **(25)** AGM, *Fondo Blake*, Microfiche 2, Caja 2, No. 7: Marshal to Blake, 9 June 1809; **(26)** AGMS, M-2581 *Expediente* Juan Meélican (Mealican); **(27)** AGMS, M-2409 *Expediente* Timoteo Meagher; **(28)** Johnston, *Roll of Commissioned officers in the Medical Service of the British Army*, pp. 159, 191; Milburne, *Narrative*, p. 103; **(29)** BOD North, c. 16, f. 389: Palmer to Doyle, 27 March 1813; Ibid., c. 16, f. 390: Copping to Doyle, 25 March 1813; **(30)** AGMS, P-267

Expediente Pablo Palmés (sic, for Palmer); BOD North, c. 16, ff. 389–91: Palmer to Doyle, 27–8 March 1813; (**31**) AGMS, P-541 *Expediente* Guillermo Parker Carrol: Testimony of Manuel Poe, 27 May 1812; AHN, *Estado* 7368, *Orden de Carlos III*, No. 215, Extract Decree: Manuel Poe, *capitán agregado al Regimiento infantería de Hibernia*; (**32**) *The Edinburgh Annual Register* (Edinburgh, 1811), pp. 552–3; *Felix Farley's Bristol Journal*, 15 April 1809, p. 2; (**33**) AGMS, O-548 *Expediente* Jayme O Rian; (**34**) AGMS,R-1365, *Expediente* Daniel Robinson; 'Obituary Captain Charles Robinson', *The Gentleman's Magazine* (London, 1853), p. 439; *Notes and Queries*, 187/10 (1944), p. 167; (**35**) AGMS, R-1365 *Expediente* Gerónimo Robinson; (**36**) AGMS, Q-1 *Expediente* Felipe Qeating (sic, for Keating) Roche and R-1496 Felipe de la (sic) Roche; (**37**) Henry Blackburne Hamilton, *Historical Record of the 14th (King's) Hussars 1715–1900* (London 1901), p. 528; AGMS, S-2807 *Expediente* Carlos Silvertop; (**38**) AGMS, E-1594 *Expediente* Roberto Steile (sic, for Steele) and E-1596 Roberto Steele; Steele, *The Marine Officer*, pp. 2–14; (**39**) AGMS, T-314 *Expediente* Edmundo Temple; (**40**) AGMS, U-6 *Expediente* Arturo Wavell; (**41**) AGMS, U-34 *Expediente* Enrique Wilson; (**42**) Whittingham, *A Memoir*, pp. 561–62; BCL, Rl Pr 2pb Biog.U-Z-B 4120; AGMS, V-43 *Expediente* Santiago Whittingham.

Biographical Notes

These notes are intended only to provide details of the British volunteers' war record under the Spanish flag and other information relevant to topics covered by this book.

1. **James Arbuthnot** (*Jaime Arbuthnot y Arbuthnot*): born in Edinburgh, Scotland, 24 December 1791, son of William and Mary Ann Arbuthnot. Seminarist at the *Real Colegio de Escoceses de Valladolid* (Royal Scots College of Valladolid) from 1803. *War record*: at Battle of San Vicente de la Barquera (19/11/1808); several actions in Santander until captured (26/08/1809), escaped; defence of bridge Colloto, captured again (14/02/1810). Prisoner in France from mid-1811 to 29/04/1814. *Ranks in the Spanish Army*: *teniente* (04/10/1808), *capitán* (02/09/1814), *teniente coronel* (26/02/1820), *coronel* (28/12/1833), *teniente coronel mayor* (08/09/1835), *brigadier* (04/04/1840), *mariscal de campo* (30/06/1843). Fought against Latin American 'rebels' in Venezuela, Panama and Colombia (1814–1823) before returning to Spain. Captain-General of Catalonia (1843), military governor of Lerida (1847) and of Galicia from 1854 to his death on 16 June 1863.

2. **Benjamin Barrie:** born in Paisley, Renfrew, Scotland, 5 April 1795. *War record*: joined the Legion of Extremadura founded by his uncle John Downie on 18 September 1811; at some stage was allowed to travel back to Scotland to continue his education; returned to Spain in 1815. *Ranks in the Spanish Army*: *subteniente* (18/09/1811), *coronel* (1837). British consul in Alicante (1846–1879). Retired from the Spanish army on 30 March 1880.

3. **Patrick** (*Patricio*) **Campbell:** born in Inverchaolain, Argyllshire, Scotland, 1 January 1780. Major Royal Artillery at Gibraltar (1808). *War record*: at skirmishes in Medellin (early 1809), around Talavera (22/07/1809) and Alcabón (26/07/09); Battle of Talavera (27–28/07/1809); siege of Cadiz (05/02–11/1810); travelled to England to gather supplies for Whittingham's division at Mallorca (mid-1811); actions in Alicante (10/08/1812); defence of Alcoy (09–15/11/1812); second Battle of Castalla (13/04/1813); siege of Tarragona (03–11/06/1813); blockade of Barcelona (Feb-April 1814, ending 16/04/1814). At Roussillon (France) then at Catalonia with Spanish army of General Castaños as paymaster (role shared with W. Parker Carrol July–December 1815). *Ranks in the Spanish Army*: *teniente coronel* (04/02/1809), *coronel* (12/08/1809), *brigadier* (26/06/1815). *Orden de Carlos III* (1819). In Barcelona until he was expulsed from the country

by radical liberals on 3 April 1821. Last recorded salary paid at Spanish embassy in London, May 1822. Appointed British representative in the newly established Republic of Colombia (October 1823 till end of 1830), in Egypt and Syria (1833–1840); Colonel in the British army (1840). Died on 25 June 1859.

4. **Charles** (*Carlos*) **Morgan Carrol:** born in Tulla, Tipperary, Ireland, 1780. Ensign 87th Regiment in the British army. *War record*: 18 actions mainly with the Hibernia regiment including at Brecha de Tarifa (07/10/1812), Pamplona (30/06/1813), Bayonne (April 1814). *Ranks in the Spanish Army*: *teniente coronel* (01/11/1812) in the Hibernia regiment. In service with regiment commanded by Carlos O'Donnell in October 1815. *Orden de Carlos III* (granted in *absentia* 1819). By the end of 1818 he had joined the Argentine-Chilean army of the Andes and made commander of the third battalion of the *Escuadrón de Dragones de la Patria*; killed by pro-Spanish *guerrilla*, near the southern Chilean village of Los Angeles, on 23 September 1820.

5. **Michael** (*Miguel*) **Carrol:** born in Tulla, Tipperary, Ireland, 1789. Lieutenant in local militia. *War record*: at skirmishes in Lequito, San Juan Somorrostro (Biscay); two incursions into Bilbao; entry into France (29/12/1813); supporting *guerrillas* in road to Bayonne (23/12/1813 –27/02/1814); fought in France with Spanish forces, returning to Spain on 04/06/1814. *Ranks in the Spanish Army*: *capitán* (25/11/1812) in the *Regimiento Infantería de la Princesa*. Licenced to travel to England on 16 January 1817. By the end of 1818 he had joined with his cousin Charles Morgan Carrol the Argentine-Chilean army of the Andes; an *aide-de-camp* of the liberator Bernardo O'Higgins, continued in the service of the Chilean army until at least January 1830.

6. **William** (*Guillermo*) **Parker Carrol:** born in Tulla, Tipperary, Ireland, 27 January 1776. Studied at Trinity College; Captain 88th Regiment Connaught Rangers; hostage during invasion of Buenos Aires (1807), back in England in January 1808. *War record*: actions at Bilbao, Durango, Espinosa de los Monteros (10–14/11/1808), Oviedo (12/1808), Corunna (01/1809), Burgos (03/1809), Oviedo (05/1809), passage of river at Cornellana and defence of bridge of Peñaflor in Asturias (18/05/1809), defence of Vigo and bridge of San Payo (04–08/06/1809). As commander of Hibernia Regiment: at Tamames (18/10/1809), Alba de Tormes (19/10/1809), Carpio (23/11/1809), Medina de Campo (24/11/1809); first siege of Badajoz (01–03/1811); Battle of Albuera (16/05/1811); coordinator of joint operations of 7th Army and British navy by order of General Castaños (1812); chief of 3rd Division of 5th Army and of 1st Brigade (Pamplona and Bayonne). At Roussillon (France) and Catalonia

with army of General Castaños as paymaster (role shared with Campbell, until January 1816). *Ranks in the Spanish Army*: *teniente coronel* (28/07/1808), *coronel* (01/08/1809), *brigadier* (01/12/1810), *mariscal de campo* (13/10/1814). *Orden de Carlos III* (1814). In service until February 1816; requested prorogation of leave of absence to marry in England (March 1817). In Britain: knighted (1816), Colonel (1820); Lieutenant Governor of Malta (1822) and of Corfu (1829); Major General (1830); commander of the western district of Ireland (1839–1842). Died in Tulla House, Nenagh, Ireland, 2 July 1842.

7. **Richard** (*Ricardo*) **Parker Carrol**: born in Tulla Tipperary, Ireland, 1782. Captain 98th Regiment, brother of William and Charles Parker Carrol. *War record*: joined the Hibernia Regiment in 1810; several actions in the Spanish–Portuguese frontier; *Rank in the Spanish Army*: *teniente coronel* (1811).

8. **John Clarke** (*Juan Clarke* or *Clark*): born in Ireland, 1787. Some service in the British army. *War record*: actions at Leon and Galicia (1808–1809), Albuera (16/05/1811), Usagre (25/05/1811), Antequera (04/09/1812), Guadelete (01/06/1812), Loja (05/09/1812). Captured in mid-1809. Sent to Bordeaux, then Paris and Valenciennes; escaped and returned to Cadiz (04/1811). *Ranks in the Spanish Army*: *teniente coronel* (25/08/1811), *coronel* (19/08/1814). *Orden de Carlos III* (1813). Retired on 14 January 1820.

9. **George or Samuel Bloss Copping?** (*Jorge Coppy*): born in Ireland, date unknown; Ensign 87th Regiment. *War record*: at Doyle's depot in Cadiz 1812–1814. *Rank in the Spanish Army*: *subteniente* (1812). Requested letter of reference to join the British Army on 1 March 1814.

10. **James** (*Diego*) **Corrigan**: born in Ireland, 1787. *War record*: at Badajoz (07/02/1811); Gebosa (09/2/1811); captured in Santa Engracia (19/02/11); enroute to France, managed to escape when at Toledo 03/1811. Appointed Spanish liaison officer at British commisariat in Portugal and later in Britain (05/1811 till end of war). *Ranks in the Spanish Army*: *subteniente* (19/03/1810) *teniente* (17/09/1812). In service with the *Infantería Ligera Segundo de Cataluña* (light infantry) on 1 April 1821.

11. **Charles** (*Carlos*) **Downie**: born in Kippen, Stirling, Scotland, 24 May 1775; importer of Merino sheep, elder brother of John Downie. *War record*: actions with Legion of Extremadura (1811–1813). *Ranks in the Spanish Army*: *capitán* (17/12/1812), *coronel* (1832). *Orden de Carlos III* (1819). In licence from *Regimiento de Caballería de la Albuera* (cavalry) at time of death in Madrid, 4 June 1843.

12. **John** (*Juan*) **Downie:** born in Kippen, Stirling, Scotland, 28 December 1777. Merchant in the West Indies; Colonel in the 'Colombian army' of Francisco de Miranda (1806–1808); Assistant Commissary in the British Army (1808–1810). *War record*: with *guerrilla* in the Spanish–Portuguese frontier and at Badajoz (March to June 1810). As founder of the Legion of Extremadura (July 1810): actions of Don Benito and Medellin (07/03/1811), skirmishes of Arroyo del Puerco (28/08/1811), Arroyo Molino (28/10/1811), Battle of Espartinas (05/05/1812), capture of Sanlúcar la Mayor (25/08/1812), storming of Seville (27/08/1812), Battles of the Pyrenees (25/07/1813–02/08/1813) Bidassoa and Vera (7/10/1813), Nivelle (10/11/1813), passage of river Nive (09/12/1813). *Ranks in the Spanish Army*: *coronel* (22/07/1810), *mariscal de campo* (27/07/1815). *Gran Cruz de San Fernando* and *Orden de Carlos III* (1812). In Britain: knighted (1813). Commander of the *Alcazar*, the royal palace and military fortress of Seville, from 1814 until his death, 5 June 1826.

13. **Carlo Doyle:** born in 1787, in Warsaw, Poland, where his father, Welbore Ellis Doyle was British military envoy. Baptized as Carlo on his mother's wishes. Ensign Coldstream Guards (1803); in expeditions to Bremen and Hanover; *aide-de-camp* to the Lord Lieutenant of Ireland, the Duke of Bedford; Captain in the 87th Prince's Own Regiment (1807). *War record*: attached to the Spanish *guerillas* in the north of Spain in 1808, fought with them in the Battle of Espinosa de los Monteros (10–11/11/1808); followed the Marquess de la Romana into the Asturian Mountains, but was cut off on a *reconnaissance* by the French cavalry. Finding it impossible to get back to the Spaniards, joined the British army at the Battle of Corunna. **Rank in the Spanish Army**: no formal rank (*guerrilla*). Returned to England with the British forces in 1809; joined the 87th Regiment in Portugal where he was appointed Deputy-Assistant Quartermaster-General; Major (1812), Colonel (1815); Governor of Grenada (1840–45); Major-General (1846). Died in London in 1848.

14. **Charles William Doyle** (*Carlos Guillermo Doile*)**:** born in Bramblestown, Kilkenny, Ireland, in 1770 or on 16 April 1782 (?). Ensign 105th Regiment (1783?), Lieutenant 14th Regt. (1793?), Lieutenant 91st (1794?), Captain 87th Regiment, in the West Indies, Puerto Rico (1796), expedition against Cadiz, Minorca and Malta (1800), in Egypt (1801), promoted to Major (1803) and Lieutenant-Coronel (1805). *War record*: coordinator of first summit of Spanish generals (Madrid, 05/09/1808); assisted in the defence of Saragossa (October–February 1809); establishment in Peñíscola of biscuit factory to supply Catalonian forces (1809); various actions during sieges of Mequinenza (15/05/1810–18/06/1810),

Tortosa (16/12/1810–02/01/1811); fortification of Sagunto (01–05/1811); sieges of Tarragona (05/06/1811), Valencia (late 1811), Cadiz (at various times in 1810 to end of siege 24/08/1812); founder and head of training depot (*Depósito Militar de Instrucción de San Fernando*) until 1816. ***Ranks in the Spanish Army***: *brigadier* (14/08/1808), *mariscal de campo* (25/09/1808), *teniente general* (10/10/1811). *Orden de Carlos III* (1814). Took leave of absence in 1816 renewed periodically until 1835 (last record). In Britain: knighted (1816), Major-General (1819); commander of the south-western district of Ireland (1825–1830), Lieutenant-general (1837). In France: *legion d'honneur* (1837). Died in Paris, 25 October 1842.

15. **James Duff, Viscount Macduff, fourth Earl of Fife** (*Diego, vizconde Macduff, conde de Fife*)**:** born in Housedale, Dunecht, Scotland, 6 October 1776. Lieutenant-Colonel Invernesshire militia from 1803. ***War record***: at Battles of Talavera (27–28/07/1809), Ocaña (19/11/1809); siege of Cadiz, particularly in the defence of Matagorda (22/02/1813). ***Ranks in the Spanish Army***: *brigadier* (03/1809), *mariscal de campo* (03/11/1810). *Gran Cruz de San Fernando* (1812). Returned to Scotland in May 1813 to take responsibility of earldom of Fife inherited from his father, the third Earl of Fife. Grand Master of the Scottish Freemasons (1813–1816) and of the Provincial Lodge of Banff (1813–1821). MP for Banffshire from 1818 to 1827; Lord of the Bedchamber (1819–1821, dismissed for opposing a malt tax prejudicial to his constituents; reinstated from 1827 to 1835). Created a peer of the United Kingdom as Lord Fife at Canning's premiership (27 April 1827). Died in Duff House, Banff, Scotland, 9 March 1857.

16. **Edwin Rowlandson Green:** born in Birmingham, England, 27 June 1777. Major 10th Foot Regiment. ***War record***: several skirmishes in Catalonia, organization of defence of Peñiscola, siege of Tarragona, actions near Barcelona as head of Anglo-Catalan force (September 1808 till end of 1813). ***Rank in the Spanish Army***: *coronel* (29/01/1809). Never formally retired from the Spanish service, but began to operate as British agent from December 1810. Captured (27/07/1812) and taken to Barcelona; believed to have been released or that escaped. *Orden de Carlos III* awarded on 16 April 1816.

17. **John Kearney** (*Juan Quearney Donnelan*)**:** born in Ireland, 1783. ***War record***: several actions in Galicia, Spanish liaison officer in Moore´s army (14/10/1808–02/1809), at Battles of Ciudad Real (27/03/1809), Almonacid (11/08/1809), Ocaña (19/11/1809); action at Arquillos (21/01/1810). Captured (21/01/1810), sent to Mâcon, France; escaped, but recaptured and consigned to Montpellier

until April 1814. ***Ranks in the Spanish Army***: *cadete* (23/09/1808), *subteniente* (12/12/1808), *teniente* (14/02/1809), *capitán* (30/05/1815), *teniente coronel* (07/07/1819). Introduced the Lancaster method of mutual instruction in Spain (1818–1823). Requested, but failed to get a position of accountant in the army while in service in Lérida, May 1838.

18. **George** (*Jorge*) **Landmann:** born in Woolwich, Kent, England, 11 April 1780. Cadet at the Royal Military Academy (1793); Second lieutenant Royal Engineers (1795); First lieutenant (1797), sent to Canada; Captain-lieutenant (1802) back in England; Second captain (1804), joined garrison in Gibraltar (1806–1808); sent to Portugal as commander engineer (1808–1809) and in special *reconnaissance* mission to Cadiz responding directly back to London (1810). ***War record***: assistance in establishing defences in Cadiz and participation in several actions, including Matagorda (February 1809 till end of 1810); joined the division of General Francisco Ballesteros in the Battle of Villanueva de los Castillejos (07/01/1811) where his horse fell under him and sustained an injury to his left eye. Returned to England due to bad health (March 1812). ***Ranks in the Spanish Army***: *teniente coronel* (22/02/1809), *coronel* (25/03/1810). In Britain: Major (1813); Lieutenant-colonel (1814); commanding royal engineer in Thames district (1815) and Hull (1817); retired from the corps in 1824; chief engineer of the London and Greenwich Railway (1830s). Authored two books on his experiences, *Historical, Military and Picturesque Observations on Portugal, Illustrated by Seventy-Five Coloured Plates, Including Authentic Plans of the Sieges and Battles Fought in the Peninsula during the Late War* (2 vols, London, 1818) and *Recollections of My Military life* (2 vols, London, 1854). Died in London, 27 August 1854.

19. **Walter Savage Landor:** born in Warwick, England, 30 January 1775. Poet and prose writer. No military experience. ***War record***: paid and escorted troops from Corunna to Astorga; assisted gunners at Bilbao and provided humanitarian aid (early August to late November 1808). ***Rank in the Spanish Army***: *coronel* (14/11/1808). Returned to Britain, late November 1808. The Spanish experience inspired his tragedy *Count Julian*; best remembered for his *Imaginary Conversations* (1824–53), consisting of nearly 150 dialogues between notables both ancient and modern, including many Spaniards. Died in Florence, Italy, 17 September 1864.

20. **Francis** (*Francisco*) **Lee:** born in Ireland, 1784. Captain in the Royal Marines under Admiral Charles Fleming in the British fleet that defended Cadiz (1809–1812). ***War record***: at Doyle's training depot (10/10/1812 till 1814). ***Rank in***

the Spanish Army: *teniente coronel* (10/10/1812). *Orden de Carlos III* (1816). *Aide-de camp* of Captain-General José de Palafox (1815–1817); sick leave (1817); with the liberal army of O'Donnell and Riego in Andalusia and Catalonia (10/03/1820–08/09/1823).

21. **Reginald** (*Reynaldo*) **Macdonnell:** born in Scotland, 1781. Officer in the British army (regiment and rank unknown). *War record*: several actions under Marquess de la Romana in Galicia and later General Carlos O'Donnell (1810); skirmishes at Fuentes de Cantos, Azuaga, Olivenza, siege of Badajoz (07–10/02/1811), inside Badajoz (19/02/11); *aide-de-camp* of generals Ballesteros and Castaños in Extremadura (1811–1813); capture of village of Sorauven and check of French advance over Pamplona (29–31/07/1813 and 01–02/08/1813); Battle of Vera (07/10/13); entered France with Spanish army of General Castaños in 1815. *Ranks in the Spanish Army*: *teniente coronel* (18/09/1810), *coronel* (12/04/1811), *brigadier* (13/10/1814). *Orden de Carlos III* (1819). In service in Cadiz until January 1822. Rumours that he deserted to Latin America in April 1822 constitute the last entry in his Spanish service record. But he does not seem to be the 'Donald MacDonald' that the historian Eric Lambert identified as 'an *aide-de-camp* of general Ballesteros' who raised the First Venezuelan Lancers, because that man was killed by Indians four years earlier (1818).

22. **Neil Macdougall:** Argyllshire, Scotland, 1787. Lieutenant 75th Regiment. *War record*: joined Whittingham's forces in Mallorca (1811); several actions with *guerrilla* in Catalonia (early 1813), second Battle of Castalla (13/04/1813). *Rank in the Spanish Army*: no recorded formal rank (*guerrilla*). Killed at Castalla (13/04/1813).

23. **William** (*Guillermo*) **Mac Veagh:** Lieutenant in British army. *War record*: fought with Hibernia Regiment in Galicia from January to April 1810. *Rank in the Spanish Army*: *subteniente* (03/01/1810).

24. **W. McMahon:** born in Ireland, date unknown. Ensign 87th Regiment. *War record*: at Doyle's training depot in Cadiz (1812–1814). *Rank in the Spanish Army*: *sargento* (1812). Believed to have returned to Britain at the end of 1814.

25. **Rudolf** (*Radulfo*) **Marshal:** born in Ireland, date unknown, from a 'good family'; believed to be married in the UK. *War record*: commander of *somatens* and *miguelets* during the siege of Gerona (09/06–19/09/1809). *Rank in the Spanish Army*: *teniente coronel* (12/1808). Killed in Gerona, 19 September 1809.

26. **John Mealican** (*Juan Méelican*)**:** born in Ireland, 1794. First Sergeant 87th Regiment. *War record*: at Doyle's training depot in Cadiz (1812–1814). *Rank in the Spanish Army*: *subteniente* (24/4/1812). Seriously ill in Cadiz hospice from

February 1814; records find him teaching Spanish in Newfoundland (January 1817) where he died, 20 March 1832.

27. **Thimoteo** (*Timoteo*) **Meagher:** born in Ireland, date unknown. In the Irish militia. *War record*: fought with Hibernia regiment from May 1812. ***Rank in the Spanish Army***: *teniente* (30/06/1812).

28. **Henry** (*Enrique*) **Milburne:** unknown place (England?) and date of birth. Hospital-Mate 52th Royal Battalion promoted to Assistant Surgeon in York Rangers (1804–1808). ***War record***: arrived in Galicia (10/12/1808) to join the *Regimiento de Infanteria Voluntarios de España* but this was frustrated; provided medical assistance to Spanish civilians and French PoWs after Battle of Benavente (29/12/1808) and to British and Spanish soldiers at Corunna early January 1809; published *A narrative of circumstances attending the retreat of the British army under the command of the late Lieut. Gen. Sir John Moore, K.B., with a concise account of the Battle of Corunna; in a letter addressed to the Right Honourable Lord Viscount Castlereagh, one of His Majesty's Principal Secretaries of State* (London,1809); medical officer in Whittingham's division in Mallorca from November 1810 and in Minorca (1811). ***Rank in the Spanish Army***: *Inspector de los Reales Hospitales de España* (Inspector of the Spanish Royal hospitals) in the Balearic Islands (1811). No further records.

29. **John** (*Juan*) **O'Hara:** born in Ireland, date unknown. Ensign 87th Regiment. *War record*: at Doyle's training depot in Cadiz (1812–1814). ***Rank in the Spanish Army***: *subteniente* (early 1812). Transferred to the British Army at the end of 1814.

30. **Paul Palmer** (*Pablo Palmes*)**:** born in Ireland, date unknown. Ensign 87th Regiment. *War record*: joined Doyle's training depot in Cadiz (24/04/1812) and served there until the end of the war. ***Rank in the Spanish Army***: *subteniente* (04/1812). Transferred to the British Army at the end of 1814.

31. **Manuel Poe:** born in Ireland, date unknown. Some experience in the British service. *War record*: fought with Hibernia Regiment from May 1812. ***Rank in the Spanish Army***: *capitán* (1812), served with that rank until at least January 1815. *Orden de Carlos III* (1819).

32. **Charles Reed:** born in England, date unknown, son of a 'Mr. W. Reed of the house of Reed & Bell, in the City of London'. ***War record***: *aide-de-camp* of General Teodoro Reding, whom he tried to save by covering his retreat in the outskirts of Tarragona; captured by the French (25/02/1809). ***Rank in the Spanish Army:*** unknown.

33. **James O'Ryan** (*Jayme O Rian*)**:** born in Ireland, 1794. *War record*: at siege of Pamplona (22/06/1813–01/11/1813) and actions around Bayonne (02/02/1814–

02/04/1814). **Rank in the Spanish Army**: *teniente* (17/12/1812). Retired on health grounds as *teniente* in the Regiment Bailén, Barcelona, 23 September 1830.

34. **Daniel Robinson:** born in Hampshire, England, 1791. First Lt. Col. Royal Marines. **War record**: actions in coastal areas near Sagunto and Pálamos (10–14/09/1810); identified as author of the first full English version of the Constitution of 1812. **Rank in the Spanish Army**: *teniente coronel* (end 1810). In service under General Enrique José O'Donnell, in headquarters at Vitoria (1815); joined the forces of the constitutional government in Cadiz (1822–23); civilian job in Mexico (1824–1827); fought with the liberals in the first Carlist war (1836). Remained attached to the Royal navy until his death in London, 6 March 1849.

35. **Jeremy** (*Gerónimo*) **Robinson:** born in Ireland, date unknown. **War record**: at Doyle's training depot in Cadiz (1813–1815). **Rank in the Spanish Army**: *capitán*. Transferred from Cadiz to Vitoria to serve under General Enrique José O'Donnell (1815).

36. **Philip Keating Roche** (*Felipe Qeating Roche* or *de la Roche*): Ireland 1772. Major 4th Regiment, in charge of a brigade in the expeditionary force to Cape of Good Hope, Montevideo and Buenos Aires (1806–1807). **War record**: actions in Asturias and Leon (07–12/1808), Battle of Talavera (27–28/07/1809), combat in Castile (08–10/1809), Battle of Ocaña (19/11/1809); actions in Valencia, Alicante, Cartagena and Murcia with his own division (12/1810–04/1813); second Battle of Castalla (13/04/1813), action at Carcagente, Valencia (13/07/1813), siege of Fortress of Sagunto (10/10/1813–18/05/1814). **Ranks in the Spanish Army**: *coronel* (17/08/1808) *brigadier* (12/08/1809), *mariscal de campo* (31/12/1810), *teniente general,* (01/11/1814). *Orden de Carlos III* (1819). Serving at Alcalá de Henares in July 1820. In Britain: knighted (1816), Colonel (1820). Died in London, 15 February 1829.

37. **Charles** (*Carlos*) **Silvertop:** born into a leading Catholic family, Northumberland, England, 1784. Captain 14th Hussars. **War record**: actions around Cadiz during siege including with Whittingham´s cavalry (04/1810–04/1811); Battle of Albuera (16/05/1811); actions in Alicante and siege of Valencia (01/07/1813–18/12/1813); with General Morillo in the Pyrenees until the end of 1814. **Ranks in the Spanish Army**: *teniente coronel* (18/01/1810) *coronel* (26/05/1811) *brigadier* (honorific rank granted on retirement, 09/10/1831). *Orden de Carlos III* (1819). Retired after 21 years of service to return to England in 1831. Died in Rennes, France, 10 June 1839.

38. **Robert Steele** (*Roberto Steile*): born in Winchester, England, 1788. Second Lieutenant Royal Marines. *War record*: at Doyle's training depot in Cadiz (1812), Battles of Bidassoa and Vera (07–09/10/1813), Nivelle (10/11/1813), with General Morillo in the Pyrenees until end of 1814. *Ranks in the Spanish Army*: *capitán* (1813) *teniente coronel* (1815). *Orden de Carlos III* (1819). With *Regimiento suizo de Kayse* in Salamanca (19/01/1819). In Britain: knighted (1816), imprisoned for debts (1817); carried message of British ambassador in Paris to Madrid (1818); Colonel (1824); imprisoned for libel (1828); member of London committee of support to Spanish liberals in first Carlist war (1835); Deputy Lieutenant of Dorset (1838–40). Died in Paris, 17 January 1840.

39. **Edmond** (*Edmundo*) **Temple:** born in Ireland, unknown date. Some experience with Royal Marines and Irish militia. *War record*: with Downie's Legion of Extremadura from August 1811 to the end of 1814. *Rank in the Spanish Army*: *capitán* (08/1811). Retired from Spanish service on 18 October 1814. *Orden de Carlos III* (1816). Author of satirical work *The life of Pill Garlick; rather a whimsical sort of fellow* (Dublin and London, 1813) and *Travels in Various Parts of Peru, including a Year's Residence in Potosi* (2 vols, Philadelphia, 1830).

40. **Arthur** (*Arturo*) **Goodall Wavell:** born in Edinburgh, Scotland, 20 March 1785. Winchester College; Major 8th Regiment East Indies. *War record*: skirmishes at Casas Viejas (with *guerrilla*, 02/03/1811), Battles of Barroca (as *aide-de-camp* of *mariscal de campo* Pedro Sarsfield, 4/03/1811), Chiclana (05/03/1811); defence of Tarragona (03–04/1811), with Whittingham's division at Mallorca (1811–1813); siege of Tarragona (03–11/06/1813). *Ranks in the Spanish Army*: *capitán* (10/6/1811), *teniente coronel* (28/6/1811), *coronel* (28/12/1817). *Orden de Carlos III* (1817). Retired from the Spanish Ultonia regiment on 28 December 1817. Joined the Chilean army (1820); official envoy of Chilean government to Mexico (1822); *brigadier general* in Mexican army (1822–1833); investor in colonization scheme in Texas ('The Old Three Hundred', 1823–1853). Died in London, 10 July 1860. Grandfather of Field Marshal Sir Archibald Wavell, hero of the World War II and penultimate Viceroy of India (1943–1947).

41. **Henry** (*Enrique*) **Wilson:** born in Ireland, unknown date. *War record*: appointed Spanish liaison officer at British Commisariat in Portugal; liaison officer of Spanish Commisariat in Britain (05/1811 till end of war). *Rank in the Spanish Army*: *subteniente* (1811). In service with Regiment *Irlanda* on 20 April 1817.

42. **Samuel Ford Whittingham** (*Santiago Whittigham or Witinga or Güitinghan*): born in Bristol, England, 29 January 1772. Mounted Bristol Volunteers (1797); employed in the wool trade in Spain (around 1798–1801). Military Academy of High Wycombe, Ensign and Lieutenant First Life Guards (1803); secret mission to Portugal (1804); Captain 13th Light Dragoons (1805); Deputy Assistant Quartermaster-General in expedition force to Cape of Good Hope, Montevideo and Buenos Aires (1806–1807). *War record*: *reconnaissance* prior to Battle of Bailén (18/07/08), at Battles of Medellin (28/03/1809), Talavera (28/07/1809); organization of a cavalry regiment, the division of Mallorca and the *Academia Nacional Militar de Palma* (1810–1811); Battle of Barrosa (05/3/11); action at Alicante (07/08/12); second Battle of Castalla (13/04/1813); siege of Tarragona (03–11/06/1813); combat of Amposta (19/08/1813); in different actions in Pyrenees, Catalonia and Aragon (09/1813–03/1814) escorted Ferdinand VII from Saragossa to Valencia (12–18/03/1814) and during his entrance to Madrid (13/05/1814). *Ranks in the Spanish Army*: *coronel* (20/07/1808), *brigadier* (02/03/1809), *mariscal de campo* (12/08/1809), *teniente general* (16/06/1814). *Orden de Carlos III* and *Gran Cruz de San Fernando* (1812). King's counsellor and member of the Statutory Board of the Order of San Fernando. Retired from the Spanish service on 19 December 1819. In Britain: Colonel (1814); knighted (1815); governor of Dominica (1819–21); Quartermaster-General of British forces in India (1822–1827); as Major-General (1825) participated in the capture of Bharatpur (1826); military secretary to Governor-General in India, Lord William Bentick (1833–35); commander of forces in Windward and Leeward islands as Lieutenant-General (1836); commander of Madras army (1840). Died in Fort George, Madras, India, 19 January 1841.

Sources (unless stated, full references are given in Notes):

(**1**) AGMS, A-2104 *Expediente* Jaime Arbuthnot; Taylor, *The Scots College*, p. 326; (**2**) AGMS, B-933 *Expediente* Benjamin Barrie; (**3**) AGMS, E-688 *Expediente* Patricio Campbell; 'Patrick Campbell', in *FamilySearch* Campbell Branches of Ardkinglass – microfilm of MS at Inverary Castle, Argyll, Scotland, accessed 12 March 2008; (**4**) AGMS, C-1704 *Expediente* Carlos Morgan Carrol; Sutcliffe, *Sixteen years in Chile*, p. 235; (**5**) Ibid., AGMS, C-1704 *Expediente* Miguel Carrol; (**6**) AGMS, P-541 *Expediente* Guillermo Parker Carrol; (**7**) Robertson, *Long way from Tipperary*, p. 31; NA FO, 72/116, ff. 174–5: William Parker Carrol to Marquis of Wellesley, 18 February 1811; (**8**) AGMS, C-2843 *Expediente* Juan Clarke; (**9**) BOD North, c. 16, ff. 390, 391, 395, 418; (**10**) AGMS, C-3476 *Expediente* Diego (James) Corrigan; (**11**) AGMS, D-1176 *Expediente* Carlos Downie;

(12) AGMS, D-1177 *Expediente* Juan Downie; (13) Doyle, *A hundred years of conflict,* pp. 140–86; BL, Add. 49486, f. 128: Carlo Doyle, Santander, 12 September 1808; (14) Stephens, 'Doyle, Sir (Charles) William (1770–1842)', DBN; AGMS, D-877 Carlos Guillermo Doile (sic, for Doyle); (15) AGMS, M-8 *Expediente* 72 Vizconde Macduff; Tayler, *Book of the Duffs,* I, pp. 203–10, AB MS 3175 Duff Family Papers; (16) BOD North, c. 14, ff. 65–6: Doyle to Sir John Stuart re. Green's colonelcy in the Spanish Army, Tarragona, 8 February 1809; NA WO, 1/241, f. 121: Doyle to Castlereagh, Tortosa, 4 February 1809; *Archivo de la Corona de Aragón,* Diversos, *Junta Suprema de Cataluña, Caja* 16, No. LIII: Green to Vicepresident of *Junta de Cataluña,* Arenys de Mon, 21 August 1811; *Cobbett's Weekly Political Register,* 12 September 1812, pp. 336–7; AHN, Estado 7368, *Legajo* 7369, Extract No. 13, Order of Charles III; 'Edwin Rowland Joseph Green', in *FamilySearch;* (17) AGMS, Q-1 *Expediente* Juan Quearney (sic, for Kearney) Donnelan; (18) AGMS, L-228 *Expediente* Jorge Landmann, R. H. Vetch, 'Landmann, George Thomas (1780–1854)', rev. John Sweetman, DNB [http://www.oxforddnb.com/view/article/15976, accessed 23 February 2011]; (19) ASL, Vaughan Papers, C: Landor to Vaughan, Villafranca, 15 September 1808; Super, *Landor – A Biography,* pp. 2, 85; Elwin, *A replevin,* p. 119; Wise and Wheeler, *A Bibliography of the Writings,* pp. 33–4; (20) AGMS, L-700 *Expediente* Francisco Lee; (21) AGMS, M-8 *Expediente* 69 Reynaldo Macdonnell; (22) NA WO, 1/1123 ff. 315–16: Patrick Campbell re. MacDougall, 7 May 1811; (23) AGMS, M-8 *Expediente* 60 Guillermo Mac Veagh; (24) BOD North, c. 16, f. 393: Doyle re. W. McMahon, 13 April 1813; (25) AGM, *Fondo Blake,* Microfiche 2, *Caja* 2, No. 7: Marshal to Blake, 9 June 1809; (26) AGMS, M-2581 *Expediente* Juan Meélican (Mealican); *The Newfoundland Mercantile Journal,* 14 January 1817, p. 3; Ibid., 7 August 1818, p. 4; *The Newfoundlander,* 22 March 1832, p. 3; (27) AGMS, M-2409 *Expediente* Timoteo Meagher; P-541 *Expediente* Guillermo Parker Carrol: Testimony Thimoty Meagher, 27 May 1812; (28) Milburne, *Narrative,* pp. 11–26; *Diario de Palma,* 23 October 1811, pp. 190–2; (29) BOD North, c. 16, f. 389: Palmer to Doyle, 27 March 1813; Ibid., f. 390: Copping to Doyle, 25 March 1813; (30) AGMS, P-267 *Expediente* Pablo Palmés (sic, for Palmer); BOD North, c. 16 ff. 389–91 Palmer to Doyle, 27–8 March 1813; (31) AGMS, P-541: Testimony Manuel Poe, 27 May 1812; AHN, Estado 7368, *Orden de Carlos III,* No. 215: Extract Decree Manuel Poe; (32) *The Edinburgh annual register* (Edinburgh, 1811), pp. 552–3; *Felix Farley's Bristol Journal,* 15 April 1809, p. 2; (33) AGMS, O-548 *Expediente* Jayme O Rian; (34) AGMS, R-1365, *Expediente* Daniel Robinson; 'Obituary Captain Charles Robinson', *The Gentleman's Magazine* (London, 1853), p. 439; *Notes and queries,* 187/10 (1944), p. 167, NA (Prob) 1/2090 Will and Testament of Daniel Robinson; (35) AGMS, R-1365 *Expediente* Gerónimo Robinson; (36) AGMS, Q-1 *Expediente* Felipe Qeating (sic) Roche and R-1496 Felipe de la (sic) Roche; (37) AGMS, S-2807 *Expediente* Carlos Silvertop; (38) AGMS, E-1594 *Expediente* Roberto Steile (sic) and E-1596 Roberto Steele; Steele, *The Marine Officer,* pp. 2–14; BL, Add. 38366, ff. 121–9: *Documentos que acreditan los servicios hechos en España por el Teniente coronel de los Reales Exércitos D. Roberto Steele,* 1816; *The Morning Post,* 5 September 1818, p. 3; Ibid., 22 March 1828, p. 3;

North Wales Chronicle, 7 July 1835, p. 3; *The Morning Chronicle*, 25 February 1840, p. 3; **(39)** AGMS, T-314 *Expediente* Edmundo Temple; **(40)** AGMS, U-6 *Expediente* Arturo Wavell; McKenzie Johnson, *Missions to Mexico*, pp. 38–9; **(41)** AGMS, U-34 *Expediente* Enrique Wilson; **(42)** Whittingham, *A Memoir*, pp. 1–313, 561; BCL, Rl Pr 2pb Biog. U-Z-B 4120; AGMS, V-43 *Expediente* Santiago Whittingham.

Notes

Introduction

1   Emmanuel-Auguste-Dieudonne, Count de Las Cases, *Journal of the Private Life and Conversations of the Emperor Napoleon at Saint Helena* (4 vols., London, 1823), II, p. 220.

2   Geoffrey Best, *War and Society in Revolutionary Europe, 1770–1870* (Oxford, 1986), pp. 178–9; David Bell, *The First Total War: Napoleon's Europe and the Birth of Modern Warfare* (London, 2008), pp. 203–301. His view of this conflict as a 'Total War' has been challenged by John Lawrence Tone, see his 'Partisan warfare in Spain and Total War', in Stig Förster and Roger Chickering (eds), *War in an Age of Revolution, 1775–1815* (Cambridge, 2010), pp. 243–59.

3   Such is the extent of the material available that a simple search of the term 'Peninsular War' in the internet engine Google Books performed in 2011 resulted in over 1,890 entries mainly dealing with military activities including the classic works of Charles William Chadwick Oman, *A History of the Peninsular War* (9 vols., London, 1922) and José Gómez-Arteche y Moro, *Guerra de la Independencia. Historia militar de España de 1808 a 1814* (14 vols., Madrid, 1895), the more recent studies of David Gates, *The Spanish Ulcer: A History of the Peninsular War* (London, 2002); Charles Esdaile [from his *The Spanish Army in the Peninsular War* (Manchester, 1988) to *Fighting Napoleon: Guerrillas, Bandits, and Adventurers in Spain, 1808–1814* (London, 2004)]; John Lawrence Tone, *The Fatal Knot: The Guerrilla War in Navarre and the Defeat of Napoleon in Spain* (London, 1994); Antonio Moliner Prada, *La guerrilla en la Guerra de la Independencia* (Madrid, 2004).

4   Among the best examples, Miguel Artola, *Los orígenes de la España contemporánea* (2 vols., Madrid, 1959); Brian R. Hamnett, *La política española en una época revolucionaria, 1790–1820* (Mexico, 1985); Manuel Moreno Alonso, *La generación española de 1808* (Madrid, 1989); José María Portillo Valdés, *Crisis atlántica: autonomía e independencia en la crisis de la monarquía hispana* (Madrid, 2006).

5   Miguel Artola, *Los afrancesados* (Madrid, 1953); Hans Juretschke, *Los afrancesados en la guerra de la Independencia: su genesis, desarrollo y consecuencias históricas* (Madrid, 1962); Jean-Marc Lafon, *L'Andalousie et Napoléon: contre-insurrection, collaboration et résistances dans le midi de l'Espagne, 1808–1812* (Paris, 2007), among others.

6   For example, Jean René Aymes, *La guerre d'indépendance espagnole (1808–1814)* (Paris, 1973); Ronald Fraser, *Napoleon's Cursed War: Spanish Popular Resistance in the Peninsular War, 1808–1814* (London, 2008); Joaquín Alvárez Barrientos (ed.), La Guerra de la Independencia en la cultura española (Madrid, 2008).

7   Such as Elena Fernández, *Mujeres en la Guerra de la Independencia* (Madrid, 2009); José Gómez Arteche, *La mujer en la Guerra de la Independencia* (Madrid, 1906); John Lawrence Tone, 'A dangerous Amazon: Agustina Zaragoza and the Spanish Revolutionary War, 1808–1814', *European History Quarterly*, 37/4 (2007), pp. 548–61; María Antonia Fernández Jiménez, 'La mujer en la guerra', in Sociedad Estatal de Conmemoraciones Culturales (ed.), *España 1808–1814 La Nación en Armas* (Madrid, 2008), pp. 299–312.

8   In September 1808, Sir Robert Wilson, a veteran of the British Expedition to Egypt, took command of the Loyal Lusitanian Legion created that year under the auspices of the Foreign Office, the Portuguese embassy in London and the Bishop of Oporto. The force was raised from Portuguese refugees in England, but operated under orders of British volunteer officers who, unlike their peers in Spain, were always under British command, see John Scott Lillie, *A Narrative of the Campaigns of the Loyal Lusitanian Legion under Sir Robert Wilson* (London, 1812); [William Mayne], *A Narrative of the Campaigns of the Loyal Lusitanian Legion under Brigadier General Sir Robert Wilson, aide-de-camp to his Majesty, and Knight of the Order of Maria Theresa, and of the Tower and Sword with some Accounts of the Military Operations in Spain and Portugal during the Years 1809, 1810 & 1811* (London, 1812); Sir Robert Thomas Wilson, *Private Diary of Travels, Personal Services, & Public Events* (2 vols., London, 1861); Michael Glover, *A Very Slippery Fellow – The Life of Sir Robert Wilson 1777–1849* (Oxford, 1978); *idem, A Gentleman Volunteer: George Hennell* (London, 1979).

9   There are numerous studies on this subject starting from the classic by Stuart Joseph Woolf, *Napoleon's Integration of Europe* (London, 1991); Michael Broers, 'Napoleon, Charlemagne, and Lotharingia: Acculturation and the boundaries of Napoleonic Europe', *Historical Journal*, 44 (2001), pp. 135–54 and his 'Cultural imperialism in a European context? Political culture and cultural politics in Napoleonic Italy', *Past & Present*, 170 (2001), pp. 152–80; Katherine Aaslestad,

'Paying for war: Experiences of Napoleonic rule in the Hanseatic Cities', *Central European History*, 39/4 (2006), pp. 641–75, to mention just a few.

10 See Table 1.

11 Samuel Ford Whittingham (King's counsellor and member of the Statutory Board of the Order of San Fernando), James Arbuthnot (Captain-General of Catalonia, military governor of Lerida and Galicia) and John Downie (commander of the *Alcazar* of Seville, the King's fortified residence in Andalusia), see *Archivo General Militar de Segovia* (AGMS), V-43 *Expediente* Santiago Whittingham; Ana María Berazaluce (ed.), *Pedro Agustin Giron, Marques de las Amarillas – Recuerdos (1778–1837)* (3 vols., Pamplona, 1978), pp. 42–3; Isabel Sánchez (ed.), *Caballeros de la Real y Militar Orden de San Fernando*, I, pp. 14–16; AGMS, A-2104 *Expediente* Jaime Arbuthnot y Arbuthnot; AGMS, D-1177 *Expediente* Juan Downie: Notification of Royal appointment of Downie as commander of Alcazar of Seville signed by Duke of San Carlos, 17 June 1814.

12 Leopoldo Stampa Piñeiro, 'El General Whittingham: la lucha olvidada (1808–1814)', *Revista de Historia Militar*, 69 (1990), pp. 115–48; Mariano de Pano y Ruata, *El inglés Sir Carlos Guillermo Doyle y su plan de socorro a Zaragosa* (Madrid, 1909–10); Alicia Laspra Rodríguez, 'William Parker Carrol and the frustrated re-establishment of the Irish Brigade in Spain (1809–11)', *The Irish Sword*, XXVI, 104 (2008), pp. 151–70; Charles Esdaile, 'Guerrilleros, bandidos, aventureros y comisarios: la historia de Juan Downie', *Alcores*, 5 (2088), pp. 109–32.

13 *El Diario Mercantil*, 16 March 1810, p. 4.

14 Ibid., 30 March 1810, pp. 3–4; Ibid., 20 May 1810, p. 4.

15 *Diario de Sesiones y Actas de las Cortes Generales y Extraordinarias* (23 vols., Cadiz, 1810–13), III, p. 307.

16 AGMS, P-267 *Expediente* Pablo Palmés (sic, for Palmer).

17 AGMS, Q-1 *Expediente* Felipe Qeating (sic, for Keating) Roche.

18 AGMS, R-1496 *Expediente* Felipe de la Roche.

19 King's College, Special Collections, Aberdeen University (AB), MS 3175/ F54-2 Dispatch of General Cuesta on the Battle of Talavera published in the *Suplemento a la Gazeta de Gobierno*, 7 September 1809, p. 2.

20 Joaquín Lorenzo Villanueva, 'Mi viaje a las Cortes', in Miguel Artola (ed.), *Memorias de tiempos de Fernando VII* (2 vols., Madrid, 1957), II, p. 48.

21 Entry in diary of Carlos Maria Alvear, Cadiz, *circa* 1810, reproduced in Gregorio F. Rodríguez (ed.), *Historia de Alvear* (2 vols., Buenos Aires, 1913), I, p. 63.

22 AGMS, V-43 *Expediente* Santiago Whittingham; AGMS, U-6 *Expediente* Arturo Wavell.

23 AGMS, Q-1 *Expediente* Juan *Quearney* Donnelan.

24 Federico Heredero y Roura, Marqués de Desio and Vicente de Cadenas y Vicent (eds), *Archivo General Militar de Segovia – Indice de Expedientes Personales* (9 vols., Madrid, 1959).

25 Harman Murtagh, 'Irish soldiers abroad, 1600–1800', in Thomas Bartlett and Keith Jeffery (eds), *A Military History of Ireland* (Cambridge, 1996), pp. 297–312.

26 René Chartrand, *Spanish Army of the Napoleonic Wars* (London, 1998), p. 17.

27 Charles Esdaile, *The Duke of Wellington and the Command of the Spanish Army, 1812–14* (Basingstoke, 1990), p. 4; Charles D. Esdaile, 'The Wellington papers', *The Army Quarterly and Defence Journal*, 117 (1987), p. 60. Numerous books mention these British agents with no reference to their full status within the Spanish army, such as John William Fortescue, *A History of the British Army* (13 vols., London, 1910), VI, pp. 257–61; William Francis Patrick Napier, *History of the War in the Peninsula and in the South of France, from the Year 1807 to the Year 1814* (4 vols., Philadelphia, 1842), I, pp. 146–9, 182, to mention just a few.

28 Professor Charles Esdaile deserves all credit for voicing concern regarding this approach, even when he has not escaped the charge of Anglocentrism, see Charles J. Esdaile, 'Recent works of note on the Peninsular War (1808–1815)', *The Journal of Military History*, 74 (2010), pp. 1243–52 (esp. p. 1251); *idem*, *Napoleon's Wars – An International History, 1803–1815* (London, 2007), p. 358. On this subject, see also John Laurence Tone, 'Partisan warfare in Spain and Total War', in Stig Förster and Roger Chickering (eds), *War in an Age of Revolution, 1775–1815* (Cambridge, 2010), p. 246.

29 Akira Iriye and Pierre-Yves Saunier (eds), *The Palgrave Dictionary of Transnational History* (London, 2009), p. 18; J. H. Elliott, 'Atlantic history: A circumnavigation', in Michael J. Braddick and David Armitage (eds), *The British Atlantic World, 1500–1800* (Basingstoke, 2002), pp. 233–50.

30 See Christine G. Krueger and Sonja Levsen (eds), *War Volunteering in Modern Times: From the French Revolution to the Second World War* (Basingstoke, 2010) and Nir Arielli and Bruce Collins (eds), *Transnational Soldiers: Foreign Military Enlistment in the Modern Era* (forthcoming, 2012).

31 The subject has merited some interest in a national and transatlantic context and from a biographical perspective, see, for example, Austin Gee, *The British Volunteer Movement 1794–1814* (Oxford, 2003); Kevin Barry Linch, 'A citizen and not a soldier': The British volunteer movement and the war against Napoleon', in Alan Forrest, Karen Hagemann and Jane Rendall (eds), *Soldiers,*

Citizens and Civilians: Experiences and Perceptions of the Revolutionary and Napoleonic Wars, 1790–1820 (London, 2009), pp. 205–21; *idem*, 'The recruitment of the British Army 1807–1815' (University of Leeds, PhD thesis, 2001); Arnold Whitridge, 'Washington's French volunteers', *History Today*, 24/9 (1974), pp. 593–603; Lloyd Kramer, *Lafayette in Two Worlds: Public Cultures and Personal Identities in an Age of Revolutions* (London, 1996), pp. 17–30; James R. Gaines, *For Liberty and Glory: Washington, Lafayette, and their Revolutions* (London, 2007), p. 37; David A. Clary, *Adopted Son: Washington, Lafayette, and the Friendship That Saved the Revolution* (New York, 2007), pp. 75–85; Eric Lambert, *Voluntarios británicos e irlandeses en la gesta bolivariana* (2 vols., Caracas, 1980); Moises Enrique Rodriguez, *Freedom's Mercenaries – British Volunteers in the Wars of Independence of Latin America* (Oxford, 2006); Matthew Brown, *Adventuring through Spanish Colonies: Simón Bolivar, Foreign Mercenaries and the Birth of New Nations* (Liverpool, 2006); Carlo Jean, 'Garibaldi e il volontariato nel Risorgimento', *Rassegna Storica del Risorgimento*, 69/4 (1982), pp. 399–419; Lucy Riall, *Garibaldi: Invention of a Hero* (London, 2007), p. 45.

32 Krueger and Levsen (eds), *War Volunteering in Modern Times*, pp. viii, 1.

33 Krueger and Levsen (eds), *War Volunteering in Modern Times*, pp. 9–12; Graciela Iglesias Rogers, 'War volunteering in the 19th and 20th centuries. Heinrich-Fabri-Institut, Blaubeuren, 6–8 September 2007', *Militärgeschichtliche Zeitschrift*, 67/1 (2008), p. 148. The issue was addressed again without reaching a conclusion during a three-day conference organized by the *École Normal Supérieure*, the *Institut Remarque* (New York University) and the *Musée de l'Armée* (Paris, 12–14 April 2012). Despite its title, ('Se Battre a l'étranger pour des idées: Les volontaires armés internationaux et la politique – *XVIIIe-XXIe siècles*'), none of the papers presented during that meeting covered the eighteenth century or the Napoleonic period.

34 Krueger and Levsen (eds), *War Volunteering in Modern Times*, p. 2.

35 *Archivo General Militar de Madrid* (AGM), *Colección Cuartel General del Ejército del Norte*, f. 7343.49 and f. 7343.96: Intercepted French Reports, 12 June 1812 and 24 August 1812, respectively.

36 Bodleian Library, North Collection (BOD North), c. 15, f. 41: Letter of Charles Doyle to 'young Shelley', San Mateo, 30 July 1810.

37 'Copia de los partes dados por el general D. Carlos Doyle', *Gazeta de la Regencia de España y de las Indias*, 30 October 1810, pp. 852–4.

38 AGMS, C-2843 *Expediente* Juan Clarke: Report of services of Juan Clarke, Madrid, 31 May 1819.

39 Wenceslado Ramirez de Villa-Urrutia, Relaciones entre España e Inglaterra durante la Guerra de la Independencia – Apuntes para la Historia diplomática de España de 1808 a 1814 (3 vols., Madrid, 1911), I, pp. 146–7.

40 National Archives of the United Kingdom, War Office Papers (NA WO), 1/231, ff. 264–5: Copy of letter of Major William Cox, 61st Regiment, to Lord Castlereagh, Seville, 18 June 1808.

41 AGMS, C-3713 *Expediente* Guillermo Cox: Duque del Parque to Antonio Cornel, War Minister at the *Junta Central*, Headquarters, Felices de los Gallegos, 22 September 1809 and copy of letter of *Junta Central* to *coronel* Guillermo Cox granting him the rank of *brigadier* in the Spanish Army, Seville, 30 September 1809.

42 Ibid.: Cox to Spanish Ministry of War, Madrid, 8 January 1817.

43 Ibid.: Report of *Cámara de Guerra* (War committee), 29 June 1817.

44 José Alvarez Junco, 'La invención de la Guerra de la Independencia', *Studia Historica-Historia Contemporánea*, 12 (1994), pp. 75–99; Esdaile, *The Duke of Wellington*, p. 3; *idem*, *Napoleon's Wars*, pp. 347–8.

45 John Lynch, *Simón Bolívar: A Life* (London, 2006), pp. 75–6; Jay Kinsbruner, *Independence in Spanish America: Civil Wars, Revolutions, and Underdevelopment* (Albuquerque, 2000), p. 54. See the *Oxford English Dictionary* entry for that word: point 2.a: '(An epithet of) Simón Bolívar (1783–1830), Venezuelan statesman who led the campaign to liberate South America from Spanish rule. First recorded in 1818: *Caledonian Mercury* 15 June' and point 1.a 'A person who or (occas.) a thing which liberates; a deliverer. First recorded in 1615: E. Grimeston tr. P. d'Avity *Estates* 964 The image of Iupiter Elutherius, or liberator [Fr. liberateur], was erected in the place where the battaile was fought'. The entry is available online [www.oed.com/view/Entry/107881?redirected From=liberator#eid, accessed 20 December 2011].

46 William Wordsworth, 'Preface to lyrical ballads', in Stephen Gill (ed.), *William Wordsworth: The Major Works* (Oxford, 2000), pp. 598, 611.

47 On the high incidence of civilian involvement, see Moreno Alonso, *La generación*, p. 170; Fraser, *Napoleon's Cursed War*, pp. xi–xiv.

48 For the records assembled by John Downie's grandnephew and Samuel Ford Whittingham's son, see Enrique Barrie, *Biografía del mariscal de campo de los Exercitos Españoles Don Juan Downie* (Madrid, 1887) and C. B. Major-General Ferdinand Whittingham (ed.), *A Memoir of the Services of Lieutenant-General Sir Samuel Ford Whittingham, K.C.B., K.C.H., G.C.F., Colonel of the 71st Highland Light Infantry, Derived Chiefly from His Own Letters and from those of Distinguished Contemporaries* (London, 1868). Those by William Parker Carrol's

great-great-granddaughter are in June O'Carroll Robertson, *A Long Way from Tipperary* (Upton-upon-Severn, 1994).

49 Brown, *Adventuring through Spanish Colonies*, p. 6.

50 Esdaile, *The Spanish Army*, pp. 35, 87; *idem, The Peninsular War: A New History* (London, 2003), p. 512; *idem, Fighting Napoleon*, p. 242.

51 These discrepancies have been the subject of much debate among military *aficionados*, see discussions in the online forum of the Spanish *Asociación de Voluntarios de Bailen* [www.voluntariosdebailen.mforos.com/1249589/6546093-escala-de-rangos, accessed 18 May 2010].

52 In 1813, the Spanish Ministry of War published the following hierarchical scale for wages and rations in the Spanish Army: *capitán general, teniente general, mariscal de campo, brigadier, coronel, teniente coronel, sargento mayor, capitán, cabo batallón, teniente, subteniente, capellán* (chaplain), *cirujano* (surgeon) and *armero* (gunsmith). Yet, differences were still in evidence for the lower echelons: for example, a *sargento primero* in regiments of fusiliers had pre-eminence over a *sargento primero* in regiments of grenadiers, see BOD North, c. 16, f. 267: *Relación de haber que disfrutan por razon de su sueldo y raciones de campaña los oficiales generales y demás clases del Ejército Nacional*, Cadiz, 8 April 1813.

Chapter 1

1 See Table 1.

2 Boyd Hilton, *A Mad, Bad and Dangerous People? 1783–1848* (Oxford, 2006), p. 3.

3 Paul Langford, *A Polite and Commercial People – England 1727–1783* (Oxford, 1989).

4 Margaret Hunt, *The Middling Sort: Commerce, Gender, and the Family in England, 1680–1780* (London, 1996), p. 17.

5 John Brewer, *The Sinews of Power: War, Money and the English State, 1688–1783* (London, 1989), pp. 21–51. See also Stephen Conway, *War, State, and Society in Mid-Eighteenth-Century Britain and Ireland* (Oxford, 2006); John E. Cookson, *The British Armed Nation, 1793–1815* (Oxford, 1997).

6 Hilton, *A Mad*, pp. 114–19; Linda Colley, *Britons: Forging the Nation, 1707–1837* (London, 2003), p. 287; Cookson, *The British Armed Nation*, p. 5.

7 Alexandra Franklin, Mark Philp and Katrina Navickas, *Napoleon and the Invasion of Britain* (Oxford, 2003), pp. 8–9; Mark Philp (ed.), *Resisting Napoleon: The British Response to the Threat of Invasion, 1797–1815* (Aldershot, 2006), p. 1.

8   Gee, *The British Volunteer Movement*, pp. 1–11.

9   Colley, *Britons*, pp. 185–7.

10 See Table 1.

11 Laurence Brockliss and David Eastwood (eds), *A Union of Multiple Identities: The British Isles c.1750–c.1850* (Manchester, 1997), pp. 1–9; Patrick Fagan, *Catholics in a Protestant Country – The Papist Constituency in Eighteenth-Century Dublin* (Dublin, 1998), p. 8.

12 Brockliss and Eastwood, *A Union*, p. 4.

13 Fagan, *Catholics in a Protestant Country*, pp. 1–53.

14 María Begoña Villar García (ed.), *La emigración irlandesa en el siglo XVIII* (Malaga, 2000), p. 247.

15 In 1810, the parents of Nicholas Wiseman, future archbishop of Westminster, married in London while *en route* from Cadiz to Ireland, see Wilfrid Philip Ward, *The Life and Times of Cardinal Wiseman* (2 vols., London, 1897), I, pp. 23–8.

16 Murtagh, 'Irish soldiers abroad, 1600–1800', pp. 308–10.

17 Bartlett and Jeffery (eds), 'An Irish military tradition?', in *A Military History*, pp. 10–12.

18 Murtagh, 'Irish soldiers abroad, 1600–1800', p. 311.

19 See AGM, *Fondo Blake*, Microfiche 1, *Cajas* 2, 21–4, 34, 36, 39, Microfiche 2, *Cajas* 2, 21; BOD North, c. 16, f. 381: General Sarsfield to General Doyle, Calatayud, 6 February 1813.

20 AGMS, P-541 *Expediente* Guillermo Parker Carrol: Report on Carrol's proclamation calling Irish soldiers to desert the French forces, undated.

21 Murtagh, 'Irish soldiers abroad, 1600–1800', pp. 297, 310.

22 V. J. L. Fontana, 'The political and religious significance of the British/Irish militias interchange, 1811–1816', *Journal of the Society for Army Historical Research*, 84/338 (2006), pp. 132–8.

23 Edward M. Spiers, 'Army organization and society in the nineteenth century', in Bartlett and Jeffery (eds), *A Military History*, pp. 336–9.

24 BOD North, b. 3.4: Papers of William 'Guillermo' North y Gray.

25 Colonel Arthur Doyle, *A Hundred Years of Conflict – Being Some Records of the Services of Six Generals of the Doyle Family 1756–1856* (London, 1911), p. 2.

26 Birth and death dates in Robertson, *A Long Way*, p. 129.

27 Ibid., p. 15.

28 Ibid., p. 129; Edward H. Sheehan, *Nenagh and its Neighbourhood* (Tipperary, 1949), p. 45.

29 Colin Kidd, *Subverting Scotland's Past: Scottish Whig Historians and the Creation of an Anglo-British Identity, 1689–c. 1830* (Cambridge, 1993), pp. 205–9; Thomas Martin Devine, *Scotland's Empire 1600–1815* (London, 2003), p. 347.

30 Devine, *Scotland's Empire*, pp. 294–319.

31 James Duff (1776–1857) known as Lord Macduff from 1809 and fourth Earl of Fife from 1811, see 'James Duff, fourth Earl of Fife', in Henry Colin Grade Matthew and Brian Harrison (eds.), *Oxford Dictionary of National Biography* (60 vols., Oxford, 2004), XVII, p. 129; Table 1.

32 Alistair Norwich Tayler and Henrietta Tayler, *The Book of the Duffs* (2 vols., Edinburgh, 1914), I, p. 234, II, p. 422; *Records of Sandpits Cemetery in Gibraltar*, in Malta Family History website [www.lineone.net/~stephaniebidmead/gibralter.htm, accessed 20 January 2007].

33 Barrie, *Biografía del mariscal*, pp. 1, 12.

34 AGMS, A-2104 *Expediente* Jaime Arbuthnot y Arbuthnot; Maurice Taylor, *The Scots College in Spain* (Valladolid, 1971), p. 326.

35 Devine, *Scotland's Empire*, p. 296.

36 National Archives of the United Kingdom (NA) Home Office Papers (HO) 50/59: Military Correspondence, Internal Defence (Militia and Volunteers) Banffshire, second Earl of Fife to Secretary of State, 14 March 1803.

37 AB, MS 3175/1408/2: Correspondence, second Earl of Fife and James Duff on militia matters 1799–1805; John Malcolm Bulloch, *Territorial Soldiering in the North-East of Scotland during 1759–1814* (Aberdeen, 1914), p. 352.

38 Colin Kidd, 'Sentiment, race and revival: Scottish identities in the aftermath of enlightenment', in Brockliss and Eastwood, *A Union*, pp. 110–13.

39 National Library of Scotland (NLS), MS 4042, f. 287: fourth Earl of Fife to Barry O'Meara, no day or month, 1836. See Figure 1, an image of the fourth Earl of Fife in tartan regalia, *circa* 1830.

40 Gordon Wood, *The Radicalism of the American Revolution* (New York, 1993), p. 233.

41 Michael Rapport, *Nationality and Citizenship in Revolutionary France – The Treatment of Foreigners 1789–1799* (Oxford, 2000), pp. 25–8, 88, 138.

42 Simon Bainbridge, *Napoleon and English Romanticism* (Cambridge, 1995), pp. 1–133.

43 Letter of Walter Savage Landor to Henry Savage Landor, 13 August 1802, in Stephen Wheeler (ed.), *Letters of Walter Savage Landor, Private and Public* (London, 1899), p. 230.

44 Diego Saglia, "'O My Mother Spain!' The Peninsular War, family matters, and the practice of Romantic nation-writing', *ELH*, 65/2 (1998), pp. 363–93.

45 Ibid.

46 The Earl of Ilchester (ed.), *The Spanish Journal of Elizabeth Lady Holland* (London, 1910), pp. 1–200; Manuel Moreno Alonso, *La forja del liberalismo en España: los amigos españoles de Lord Holland (1793–1840)* (Madrid, 1997), pp. 23–37, 99–121.

47 Leslie Mitchell, *Holland House* (London, 1980), p. 220.

48 Charles William Doyle, James Duff (then known as Viscount MacDuff) and Samuel Ford Whittingham, see Ilchester (ed.), *The Spanish Journal*, pp. 230, 266, 271, 395.

49 Teresa Tortella, *A Guide to Sources of Information on Foreign Investment in Spain 1780–1850* (Amsterdam, 2000), p. 10.

50 Villar García, *La emigración irlandesa*, p. 256.

51 Such as the University of Dublin Centre for Irish-Scottish and Comparative Studies' project on Irish mercantile networks in Spain in association with the University of Malaga; see also Rafael Uriarte Ayo, 'Anglo-Spanish trade through the port of Bilbao during the second half of the eighteenth century: Preliminary findings', *International Journal of Maritime History*, IV, no. 2 (1992), pp. 193–217; Xabier Lamikiz, *Trade and Trust in the Eighteenth-Century Atlantic World: Spanish Merchants and their Overseas Networks* (London, 2010).

52 *Archivo del Ayuntamiento de Cádiz* (AAC), Census 1805–1813: *Padrones* 1032, 1034, 1055; Julian B. Ruiz Rivera, *El consulado de Cádiz. Mátricula de Comerciantes 1730–1823* (Cadiz, 1988), pp. 21, 25, 33. See Chapter 7.

53 Whittingham (ed.), *A Memoir*, p. 4; Ayo, 'Anglo-Spanish trade', pp. 193–217; John Lynch, *Bourbon Spain 1700–1808* (Oxford, 1989), pp. 356–7.

54 Bristol Central Library (BCL), Rl Pr 2pb Biog. U-Z – B 4120: Extract of biographical notes of Samford Whittingham published by the *Bristol Mercury*, 15 January 1870, with handwritten notes; Whittingham (ed.), *A Memoir*, p. 4.

55 Rory Muir, *Britain and the Defeat of Napoleon 1807–1815* (London, 1996), pp. 35–7; Karen Racine, 'Miranda, Francisco de (1750–1816)', *Oxford Dictionary of National Biography* (DNB), online edn, May 2006 [www.oxforddnb.com/view/article/89 687, accessed 28 August 2008].

56 Vincent Harlow, *The Founding of the Second British Empire 1763–1793* (2 vols., London, 1964), II, pp. 626–32; Muir, *Britain and the Defeat*, p. 35.

57 Jennifer Mori, *Britain in the Age of the French Revolution, 1785–1820* (Harlow, 2000), pp. 196–8.

58 John Lynch, 'British policy and Spanish America, 1783–1808', *Journal of Latin American Studies*, 1/1 (1969), pp. 1–30.

59 William Parker Carrol, Philip Keating Roche and Samuel Ford Whittingham, see *Trial of Lieutenant-General John Whitelocke, Commander-in-Chief of the Expedition Against Buenos Aires, Taken Verbatim by a Student of Middle Temple* (London, 1808), pp. 80–1, 86–8, 159–61; Whittingham (ed.), *A Memoir*, pp. 10–28; *The Times* 16 March 1808, p. 1.

60 Muir, *Britain and the Defeat*, pp. 35–7; Peter Spence, *The Birth of Romantic Radicalism* (Aldershot, 1996), pp. 56–8.

61 Muir, *Britain and the Defeat*, pp. 34–5.

62 James Sack, 'Lord Grenville and the Peninsular War', in Ronald Caldwell (ed.), *The Consortium on Revolutionary Europe 1750–1850* (Florida, 1994), pp. 146–52.

63 Muir, *Britain and the Defeat*, p. 39.

64 Ibid., pp. 37–42.

65 Landor to Robert Southey, 8 August 1808, in John Forster (ed.), *The Works and Life of Walter Savage Landor* (8 vols., London, 1876), I, pp. 115–16 and *idem* (ed.), *Walter Savage Landor – A Biography* (2 vols., London, 1869), I, pp. 220–1; Robert Henry Super, *Walter Savage Landor – A Biography* (London, 1957), p. 85.

66 Ibid.

67 Portillo Valdés, *Crisis atlántica*, pp. 14–53.

68 See, for example, British Library (BL), Spanish Tracts Nr. 18: Carlos IV's *Real Cédula de S. M. y Señores del Consejo por la Qual se Manda observar el Real Decreto Inserto, en que se extingue enteramente y para siempre la contribución del Servicio ordinario y extraordinario, y su quince al millar, en los términos que en él se expresan* (Madrid, 1795) and Ferdinand VII's *Real Provision del Consejo por la que se conceda facultad a los pueblos donde debe celebrarse la Proclamación del Señor Don Fernando VII, a fin de que puedan valerse para los gastos de ella de los efectos Propios, o qualesquiera otros; y se prescribe el modo en que ha de usarse el papel sellado* (Madrid, 1808).

69 Ibid., *Decretos Reales de José I, rey de las Españas y de las Indias*; see also 'Preamble of the *Constitución de Bayona*', in Horst Dippel (ed.), *Constitutions of the World: From Late 18th Century to the Middle of the 19th Century Europe, Spain* (13 vols, Berlin, 2010), pp. 195–236.

70 Moreno Alonso, *La generación*, p. 21; Xavier Ruben de Ventós, *El laberinto de la hispanidad* (Barcelona, 1987), p. 126; Vicente Palacio Atard (ed.), *De Hispania a España – el Nombre y el Concepto a través de los siglos* (Madrid, 2005), p. 22;

Manuel Lucena-Giraldo, 'The limits of reform in Spanish America', in Gabriel Paquette (ed.), *Enlightened Reform in Southern Europe and its Atlantic Colonies, c.1750–1830* (Farnham, 2009), pp. 307–20.

71 'Royal Decree, 29 June 1707', in William Norman Hargreaves-Mawdsley (ed.), *Spain under the Bourbons, 1700–1833 – A Selection of Documents* (London, 1973), p. 36.

72 Agustín González Enciso, Luis Miguel Enciso Recio, Teófanes Egido López, Maximiliano Barrio Gozalo and Rafael Torres Sánchez, *Los Borbones en el Siglo XVIII, 1700–1800* (Madrid, 1991), p. 396.

73 Raymond Carr, *Spain 1808–1975* (Oxford, 1982), pp. 62–3.

74 Renato Barahona, *Vizcaya on the Eve of Carlism, Politics and Society 1800–1833* (Nevada, 1989), pp. 18–19.

75 Esdaile, *The Spanish Army*, pp. 46–8.

76 Isabel Burdiel, 'Liberalism and nationalism in recent Spanish historiography: Failure as shared identity', in Isabel Burdiel and James Casey (eds), *Identities: Nations, Provinces and Regions 1550–1900* (Norwich, 1999), pp. 61–4.

77 González Enciso et al., *Los Borbones*, p. 396.

78 Richard Herr, *The Eighteenth-Century Revolution in Spain* (London, 1958), pp. 20, 76–9, 228–30.

79 Francisco Sánchez Blanco, *La mentalidad ilustrada* (Madrid, 1999), p. 331.

80 Gabriel Paquette, 'Empire, enlightenment and regalism: New directions in eighteenth-century Spanish history', *European History Quarterly*, 35/1 (2005), 109–10; Luis Sanchez Agesta, *El pensamiento político del despotismo ilustrado* (Madrid, 1953), p. 286; Charles C. Noel, 'In the house of reform: The Bourbon court of eighteenth-century Spain', in Paquette (ed.), *Enlightened Reform in Southern Europe*, pp. 156–65.

81 Herr, *The Eighteenth-Century Revolution*, p. 151.

82 NA WO, 1/1123, f. 413: Statement by William Parker Carrol of items lost in the Battle of Espinosa de los Montes, 11 November 1809; AB, MS 3175/F41/2/3: Bills for Spanish cloak and uniform of *coronel* James Duff, 1809.

83 González Enciso et al., *Los Borbones*, p. 421; Carlos Corona Baratech, *Revolución y reacción en el reinado de Carlos IV* (Madrid, 1957), pp. 48–9.

84 González Enciso et al., *Los Borbones*, pp. 423–4.

85 Esdaile, *The Spanish Army*, p. 7.

86 I. A. A. Thompson, *Guerra y decadencia. Gobierno y administración en la España de los Austrias, 1560–1620* (Barcelona, 1981), pp. 10–31.

87 Esdaile, *The Spanish Army*, p. 1.

88 Francisco Andújar Castillo, *Los Militares en la España del siglo XVIII – Un estudio social* (Granada, 1991), pp. 28–9.

89 Esdaile, *The Spanish Army*, p. 25.

90 Lynch, *Bourbon Spain*, p. 325.

91 Andújar Castillo, *Los Militares*, p. 94.

92 Carrie Douglass, '*Toro muerto, vaca es*: An interpretation of the Spanish bullfight', *American Ethnologist*, 11/2 (May 1984), p. 242. For more on this subject, see Chapter 5.

93 Andújar Castillo, *Los Militares*, p. 162.

94 Marques de Villareal de Alava, 'Prólogo', in Enrique Ocerin (ed.), *Indice de los expedientes matrimoniales de militares y marinos que se conservan en el Archivo General Militar, 1761–1865* (Madrid, 1959), pp. xx–xi.

95 Andújar Castillo, *Los Militares*, pp. 162, 251–8.

96 Alan Forrest, *The Soldiers of the French Revolution* (Durham, 2003), p. 36.

97 Andújar Castillo, *Los Militares*, p. 157.

98 José Juan Cadalso, *El buen militar a la Violeta – lección póstuma del autor del Tratado de los Eruditos* (Sevilla, 1790).

99 AGMS, M-8 *Expediente* 72 Vizconde Macduff: Bardaxi to Secretary of the *Junta Central*, 3 November 1810.

100 Charles Doyle was often addressed, wrongly, as Lord and *Milord* (My Lord), see BOD North, c. 16, ff. 9–10: Sebastiens de Torres and Josef Navarro, from the *Consejo de Castilla*, to *Milord* Doyle, Madrid, 30 August 1808; *Archivo Histórico Nacional* (AHN), *Estado* 43[1], *Legajo* 186, Nr. 7: *Junta de Gobierno de Cerbera* to Lord Doyle, 15 January 1809.

101 Gabriel Laffaille, *Mémoires sur la campagne du corps d'armée des Pyrénées-Orientales, commandé par le général Duhesme, en 1808: suivis d'un Précis des campagnes de Catalogne de 1808 à 1814, et de notes historiques sur les sièges de Barcelone et de Gérone, sur l'expédition des anglais contre Tarragone, en 1813, sur les généraux Duhesme et Lacy, etc.* (Paris, 1826), p. 312.

102 Jean René Aymes, Claude Morange, Gérard Brey, Annie Lacour and Albert Dérozier, *La Révolution française: ses conséquences et les réactions du 'public' en Espagne entre 1808 et 1814* (Paris, 1989), p. 29; Juan Pérez de Guzmán y Gallo, *El Dos de Mayo de 1808 en Madrid* (Madrid, 1908), pp. 227–8, 277–83, 613–14; Emilio de Diego García, 'El problema de los abastecimientos durante la guerra', in José Luis Martínez Sanz and Emilio de Diego García (eds), *El comienzo de la Guerra de la Independencia – Congreso Internacional del Bicentenario* (Madrid, 2009), pp. 297–8.

103   Paul-Charles-François Thiébault, *Relation de l'expédition du Portugal: faite en 1807 et 1808, par le 1er corps d'observation de la Gironde, devenu armée de Portugal* (Paris, 1817), p. 9; Aphonse Grasset, *La guerre d'Espagne (1807–1813)* (Paris, 1914), pp. 125, 314, 378, 398, 408.

104   Thiébault, *Relation de l'expédition du Portugal*, p. 11.

105   James [Joseph] Donaldson, *Recollections of an Eventful Life Chiefly Passed in the Army* (Glasgow, 1825), pp. 118–19.

106   Charles Esdaile, 'The Duke of Wellington and the Spanish Revolution', *Wellington Archive Exhibition* (University of Southampton, 2001) [www. archives.lib.soton. ac.uk/wellington/peninsularwar/essays/ess_esdaile.htm, accessed 20 June 2007].

107   María Gil Muñoz, 'Revolución en las instituciones militares de enseñanza durante la guerra de la Independencia: nuevos centros y pruebas de nobleza', in Jose Armillas Vicente (ed.), *La guerra de la independencia – Estudios* (2 vols., Saragossa, 2001), II, p. 849; Eric Christiansen, *The Origins of Military Power in Spain 1800–1854* (Oxford, 1967), pp. 7–9.

108   John Lynch, 'The origins of Spanish American Independence', in Leslie Bethell (ed.), *The Cambridge History of Latin America* (11 vols., Cambridge, 1984), III, pp. 20–1.

109   Esdaile, 'Wellington and Spanish Revolution', p. 6.

Chapter 2

1   Diego Saglia, '"O My Mother Spain!" The Peninsular War, family matters, and the practice of Romantic nation-writing', *ELH*, 65/2 (1998), 363–93.

2   Krueger and Levsen (eds), *War Volunteering in Modern Times*, pp. 11–13.

3   *Felix Farley's Bristol Journal*, 4 June 1808, p. 3.

4   *Felix Farley's Bristol Journal*, 11 June 1808, p. 3.

5   James Gillray, 'The Valley of the Shadow of Death', published by Hannah Humphrey, 24 September 1808, colour etching, part of the art collection of New College, University of Oxford.

6   'The Spanish cause', *The Ordeal: A Critical Journal of Politicks and Literature* (Boston, 1809) I, issue 9, p. 129; Ibid., issue 10, p. 151; Ibid., issue 16, p. 253; 'Spain: The Spanish cause', *The Christian Observer* (Boston, 1808) VII, issue 79, p. 478; 'Middlesex Meeting', *Bombay Courier*, 18 February 1809, p. 2.

7   Edward Michael Pakenham to his mother, London, 22 August 1808 in Thomas
    Pakenham, fifth Earl of Longford (ed.), *Pakenham Letters, 1800 to 1815*
    (London, 1914), p. 46.

8   Pakenham to his mother, Badajoz, 26 October and 20 December 1809, in Ibid.,
    pp. 47–8, 51.

9   Matthew Craske, *Art in Europe 1700–1830: A History of the Visual Arts in an Era
    of Unprecedented Urban Economic Growth* (Oxford, 1997), pp. 53–60.

10 Willard Bissell Pope (ed.), *The Diary of Benjamin Robert Haydon* (5 vols.,
    Cambridge, Massachusetts, 1963), I, pp. 51–2.

11 Ibid., pp. 58–9.

12 For Byron as prototype of the artist freedom fighter abroad see, among other
    works, Richard A. Cardwell (ed.), *The Reception of Byron in Europe* (2 vols.,
    London, 2004), I, p. 191, II, pp. 269, 363, 399; Ghislaine McDayter, *Byromania
    and the Birth of Celebrity Culture* (Albany, 2009), pp. 75, 80, 172; Geoffrey Bond,
    'Byron Memorabilia', in Christine Kenyon-Jones (ed.), *Byron: The Image of the
    Poet* (Cranbury, 2008), p. 80; Hilton, *A Mad*, p. 2.

13 Leslie A. Marchand (ed.), *Byron's Letters and Journals* (12 vols., London, 1973),
    I, p. 221.

14 Stephen Minta, 'Byron and Mesolongi', *Literature Compass*, 4/4 (2007),
    pp. 1092–108.

15 R. Woudhuysen, 'Sidney, Sir Philip (1554–1586)', DNB; online edn, May 2005
    [www.oxforddnb.com/view/article/25522, accessed 15 December 2010].

16 Walter Savage Landor, *The Works of Walter Savage Landor* (2 vols., London,
    1846), I, p. 6. I am grateful to Dr David Hopkin (Hertford College, University
    of Oxford) for drawing my attention to Sidney's reputation and to the reference
    made by Landor in his *Imaginary Conversations*.

17 Stephen Wheeler (ed.), *The Poetical Works of Walter Savage Landor* (3 vols.,
    Oxford, 1937), I, c. VI, p. 193.

18 Robert Southey, *History of the Peninsular War* (3 vols., London, 1823).

19 Landor to Southey, Falmouth, postmark 8 August 1808, in John Forster (ed.), *The
    Works and Life of Walter Savage Landor* (8 vols., London, 1876), I, pp. 115–16.

20 Bodleian Library, North Collection (BOD North), c. 13, f. 15: Charles Doyle to
    Junta de Galicia, circa November 1808.

21 Biblioteca Nacional de España (BNE), R/60246 (3) *Colección de documentos
    interesantes que pueden servir de apuntes para la historia de la revolución de
    España* (Valencia, 1809): Proclamation of the *Junta* of Vich, 18 June 1808;

Ronald Fraser, *La Maldita Guerra de España: Historia Social de la Guerra de la Independencia 1808–1814* (Barcelona, 2006), p. 199.

22 Henry Milburne, *A Narrative of Circumstances Attending the Retreat of the British Army under the Command of the Late Lieut. Gen. Sir John Moore, K.B., with a Concise Account of the Battle of Corunna; in a Letter Addressed to the Right Honourable Lord Viscount Castlereagh, one of His Majesty's Principal Secretaries of State* (London, 1809), p. ii.

23 Ibid., p. iv.

24 Colonel William Johnston, *Roll of Commissioned Officers in the Medical Service of the British Army Who Served on Full Pay Within the Period between the Accession of George II and the Formation of the Royal Army Medical Corps 20 June to 23 June 1898* (London, 1917), pp. 159, 191.

25 R. G. Thorne (ed.), *The House of Commons, 1790–1820* (6 vols., London, 1986), pp. 39–40.

26 Milburne, *Narrative*, pp. vi–viii; AGMS, M-5080 *Expediente* Juan Murphy.

27 Adrian John Pearce, *British Trade with Spanish America, 1763–1808* (Liverpool, 2007), pp. 208–14, 236–7, 244–6; Estela Guadalupe Jiménez Codinach, *La Gran Bretaña y la independencia de México, 1808–1821* (México, 1991), pp. 238–59.

28 (AGMS), M-5080 *Expediente* Juan Murphy; José María Massons, *Historia de la Sanidad Militar Española* (4 vols., Barcelona, 1994), II, pp. 50–6.

29 Milburne, *Narrative*, p. 103.

30 Robertson, *A Long Way from Tipperary*, pp. 32–6.

31 *Trial of Lieutenant-General John Whitelocke*, pp. 80–1, 86–8, 159–61; Whittingham (ed.), *A Memoir*, pp. 23–8; *The Times*, 16 March 1808, p. 1.

32 H. M. Stephens, 'Doyle, Sir (Charles) William (1770–1842)', rev. Charles Esdaile, DNB, September 2004 [www.oxforddnb.com/view/article/7997, accessed accessed 11 February 2012].

33 BOD North, c. 19, f. 14: Doyle to Lieut.-Col. Gordon, 18 June 1808.

34 BOD North, c. 19, f. 15: Doyle to Sir Charles Stewart, 18 June 1808.

35 National Archives of the United Kingdom, War Office Papers (NA WO), 1/227, f. 1: Instructions of Lord Castlereagh to Lt. Col. Doyle, 2 July 1808.

36 BOD North, c. 13, ff. 66–8: Doyle to E. Cooke at War Office, Madrid, 17 September 1808; Ibid., f. 78 Doyle to General José de Palafox accepting rank of *mariscal de campo*, Madrid, 28 September 1808.

37 BOD North, c. 13, f. 264: Doyle to *Junta Suprema de Aragón*, 27 December 1808.

38 Doyle, *A Hundred Years of Conflict*, pp. 140–86; British Library, Additional Manuscripts (BL, Add.) 49486, f. 128: Captain Carlo Joseph Doyle to Major General Leith, Santander, 12 September 1808.

39 Simon Bainbridge, 'The historical context', in Nicolas Roe (ed.), *Romanticism – An Oxford Guide* (Oxford, 2005), p. 21.

40 Landor to Robert Southey, 3 August 1808 in Stephen Wheeler (ed.), *Letters of Walter Savage Landor, Private and Public* (London, 1899) p. 233; Forster (ed.), *The Works and Life*, I, p. 118. The two Irishmen mentioned by Landor, O'Hara and Fitzgerald, have not been added to the overall lists of volunteers in this study as no evidence has been found of their engagement with the Spanish army. They were, however, also cited at the time in an article published by *The Aberdeen Journal* as two 'Irish gentlemen of family' who, travelling with Landor, were now 'desirous of proceeding to the army of General Blake', *The Aberdeen Journal*, 12 October 1808, p. 2.

41 Geoffrey Carnall, 'Landor, Walter Savage (1775–1864)', DNB, online edn, September 2004 [www.oxforddnb.com /view /article/15980, accessed 28 August 2009].

42 Landor to Government of Galicia, October 1808, in Forster (ed.), *The Works and Life*, I, p. 119.

43 As in those that emanated from the *Declaración de Guerra Santa* (Declaration of Holy War) proclaimed by the *Junta Suprema de Extremadura*, 20 April 1809, reproduced in Ramón Gomez Villafranca (ed.), *Extremadura en la Guerra de la Independencia, memoria histórica y colección diplomática* (Badajoz, 1908), pp. 184–5, and from the Edict of the *Junta de Badajoz*, 29 April 1809, supporting the *partidas de cruzadas* (crusades) organized by priests and monks in that province and in Saragossa, see Helminio Lafoz Rabaza, *El Aragón Resistente – La Junta Superior de Aragón y parte de Castilla 1809–1813* (Saragossa, 2007), pp. 150–1.

44 AGMS, A-2104 *Expediente* Jaime Arbuthnot y Arbuthnot; Maurice Taylor, *The Scots College in Spain* (Valladolid, 1971), p. 326.

45 Taylor, *The Scots College*, pp. 314–26.

46 AGMS, M-8 *Expediente* 69 Reynaldo Macdonnell.

47 AGMS, Q-1 *Expediente* Juan Quearney (sic, for Kearney).

48 AGMS, P-541 *Expediente* Guillermo Parker Carrol: Thimoteo Meagher to General Francisco Castaños, Santiago, 27 May 1812.

49 AGMS, S-2807 *Expediente* Carlos Silvertop.

50 Murtagh, 'Irish soldiers abroad, 1600–1800', pp. 308–10; Patrick Fagan, *Catholics in a Protestant Country – The Papist Constituency in Eighteenth-Century Dublin* (Dublin, 1998), pp. 4–40; María Begoña Villar García (ed.), *La emigración irlandesa en el siglo XVIII* (Malaga, 2000), p. 247.

51 See Introduction.

52 Agustín Guimerá Ravina, *Burguesía Extranjera y Comercio Atlántico: La Empresa Comercial Irlandesa en Canarias (1703–1771)* (Santa Cruz de Tenerife, 1985), pp. 45, 114. I am grateful to Professor Guimerá Ravina, vice-director of the *Instituto de Historia* of the National Research Council of Spain, for allowing me to read his research on Irish immigrants in the Canary Islands and for his opinion on my findings.

53 AGMS, P-541 *Expediente* Guillermo Parker Carrol.

54 Ibid.; Robert Dunlop, 'Hutchinson, Christopher Hely (1767–1826)', rev. Thomas Bartlett, DNB, September 2004; online edn, January 2008 [www.oxforddnb. com/ view/article/12881, accessed 20 January 2008].

55 Stephens, 'Doyle, Sir (Charles) William (1770–1842)', DNB; Alastair W. Massie, 'Doyle, Sir John, baronet (1756–1834)', DNB, September 2004; online edn, May 2006 [www.oxforddnb.com/view/article/8002, accessed 3 February 2008].

56 V. J. L. Fontana, 'The political and religious significance of the British/Irish militias Interchange, 1811–1816', *Journal of the Society for Army Historical Research*, 84/338 (2006), pp. 132–8.

57 BOD North, c. 13, f. 78: (Doyle's translation into English) Charles Doyle's reply to General José de Palafox's offer of rank of *mariscal de campo* in the Aragon army, Madrid, 28 September 1808; Ibid., f. 87 original letter in Spanish.

58 AGMS, S-2807 *Expediente* Carlos Silvertop: Carlos (Charles) Silvertop to *Junta Central*, Seville, 28 December 1809.

59 'Silvertop, of Minster-Acres', in John Burke (ed.), *A Genealogical and Heraldic History of The Commoners of Great Britain and Ireland Enjoying Territorial Possessions or High Official Rank; But Uninvested with Heritable Honours* (4 vols., London, 1836) III, pp. 301–2; Mark Bence-Jones, *The Catholic Families* (London, 1992), p. 112; Maurice R. O'Connell (ed.), The Correspondence of Daniel O'Connell (8 vols., Dublin, 1977), II, pp. 190–3.

60 AGMS, S-2807 *Expediente* Carlos Silvertop: Carlos (Charles) Silvertop to *Junta Central*, Seville, 28 December 1809.

61 This figure relates to the whole 6-year duration of the war, see Juan López Tabar, *Los famosos traidores: los afrancesados durante la crisis del Antiguo Régimen (1808–1833)* (Madrid, 2001), pp. 80–6.

62 Esdaile, *The Spanish Army*, pp. 35–87.

63 Colley, *Britons*, p. 287.

64 Whittingham (ed.), *A Memoir*, p. 561.

65   Bristol Central Library (BCL), Rl Pr 2pb Biog. U-Z – B 4120 Extract of biographical notes of Samford Whittingham published by the *Bristol Mercury*, 15 January 1870, with handwritten notes; Whittingham (ed.), *A Memoir*, p. 4.

66   Bristol Record Office, Richard Hart Davis Papers 41593/Co/154/66 Lord St. German to R. H. Davis, 14 August 1835.

67   Whittingham (ed.), *A Memoir*, p. 33.

68   BL, Add. 49490, f. 119: Whittingham to Lieut-Col. Gordon, 4 June 1808.

69   Archivo General Militar de Madrid (AGM), *Fondo Blake*, Microfiche 2, *Caja* 2, Nr. 7: Rudolfo Marshal to Blake, San Feliu de Guixols, 9 June 1809.

70   Ibid.

71   AGM, *Historiales de Regimientos*, *Rollo* 47, *Legajo* 8 'Ultonia', p. 79.

72   AGMS, S-2807 *Expediente* Carlos Silvertop: (translation) Silvertop to Spanish Minister of War, 28 December 1809.

73   Ibid.

74   AGMS, M-8 Exp-60, *Expediente* Guillermo Mac Veagh: a margin note signed by two officials of the Council of Regency in Mac Veagh's letter requesting payment, Isla de León, 3 April 1810.

75   AGMS, M-8 *Expediente* 72 Vizconde Macduff: Eusebio de Bardaxi, Inspector General of the Spanish Army to Council of Regency, Isla de León, 3 November 1810.

76   BOD North, c. 13, f. 87: Doyle to General José de Palafox, Madrid, 28 September 1808; AGMS, D-877 *Expediente* Carlos Guillermo Doile (sic, for Doyle): Memorial of services of *General* Carlos Doyle, Madrid, 26 August 1816.

77   AGMS, E-688 *Expediente* Patricio Campbell: Memorial of services of Patricio Campbell, 16 February 1815.

78   NA WO, 1/1120, ff. 175–6: Abstract of payments due to Patrick Campbell, Cadiz, 4 April 1810; AGMS, E-688 *Expediente* Patricio Campbell: Military record of Patricio Campbell up to the end of 1815.

79   Codrington Library, All Souls College, University of Oxford (ASL), Vaughan Papers, uncatalogued, reel 7 B1/11 and B2/3: 'Correspondence of Political and General Interest', 16 February to 25 October 1813; *Moore vs. Adam: Proceedings in a Cause Tried in the Court of King's Bench, December 21, 1815 for Special Damages in Consequence of an Assault Committed at Alicante, in Spain* (London, 1816), pp. 1, 7–8, 44–54, 61, 72, 154, 187.

80   Anthony Ludovici (ed.), *On the Road with Wellington: The Diary of a War Commissary in the Peninsular Campaigns by August Ludolf Friedrich Schaumann*

(London, 1924), pp. xiii–xv, 7, 353; Stephen George Peregrine Ward, *Wellington's Headquarters: A Study of the Administrative Problems in the Peninsula, 1809–1814* (London, 1957), pp. 72–5.

81 Marylin Butler, 'Romanticism in England', in Roy Porter and Mikula C. Teich (eds), *Romanticism in National Context* (Cambridge, 1988), pp. 40–4. For the volunteers' age, see Table 1.

82 Francisco de Miranda to John Downie, 9 July 1806, in Vicente Dávila (ed.), *Archivo del General Miranda* (24 vols., Caracas, 1929), XVIII, p. 78.

83 BL, Add. 40722, f. 190 John Downie to C. Dalrymple, 16 June 1809.

84 Ibid.

85 Ibid.

86 Wellington to General R. Crauford, Viseau, 23 March 1810, in John Gurwood (ed.), *The Dispatches of Field Marshall the Duke of Wellington during His Various Campaigns in India, Denmark, Portugal, Spain, the Low Countries, and France from 1799–1818* (13 vols., London, 1838), V, p. 588.

87 Wellington to W. Huskisson, Secretary to the Treasury, 22 September 1809, in Gurwood (ed.), *The Dispatches*, V, p. 174.

88 AGMS, D-1177 *Expediente* Juan Downie: Letter Canon Gavino Rodriguez, *Junta Suprema de Extremadura*, to Juan Downie, Badajoz, 10 March 1810 conferring Downie the rank of *coronel* under the Marquess de La Romana; AGM, *Fondo Blake*, Microfiche 2, *Caja* 2, ff. 26.2: Copy of note by Eusebio de Bardaxi, Inspector General of the Spanish Army, to Marquess de la Romana confirming Downie's rank in the Spanish army, Cadiz, 22 July 1810.

89 AGMS, D-1177 *Expediente* Juan Downie.

90 Sir Robert C. Steele, *The Marine Officer; or, Sketches of Service* (London, 1840), p. 270.

91 Colley, *Britons*, p. 287.

92 Steele, *The Marine Officer*, p. 271.

93 Arbuthnot, Carrol, Doyle, Downie, Kearney, Roche, Silvertop and Whittingham.

94 Steele, *The Marine Officer*, p. 272.

95 Landor to Southey, Falmouth, postmark 8 August 1808, in Forster (ed.), *The Works and Life*, I, pp. 115–16.

96 BL, Add. 58987, ff. 116–34: Correspondence Grenville with second Earl of Fife, 1808–1809.

97 Special Collections, King's College, Aberdeen University (AB), MS 3175/1433/1 Col. James Duff to Louisa Manners, 10 January 1806; Ibid., MS 3175/3553 Col. James Duff to second Earl of Fife, Norwich, 14 January 1806.

98 William Jerdan, *National Portrait Gallery of Illustrious and Eminent Personages of the Nineteenth Century: With Memoirs* (5 vols., London, 1830), II, pp. 140–1; AB, MS 3175/2262 Wilhelm Hammestein-Ecquord to Col. James Duff, undated; Ibid., MS 3175/1433/3 Undisclosed correspondent to Col. James Duff, Vienna, *circa* 1808; Constant von Wurzbach, *Biographisches Lexikon des Kaiserthums Oesterreich: enthaltend die lebensskizzen der denkwürdigen personen, welche seit 1750 in den österreichischen kronländern geboren wurden oder darin gelebt und gewirkt haben* (60 vols., Vienna, 1861), VII, pp. 291–3. I am grateful to Professor Robert Evans, Oriel College, University of Oxford, for translating some of this correspondence in German paleography and for his guidance in finding the background of the above-mentioned individuals.

99 Jerdan, *National Portrait*, II, pp. 140–1; 'Wrede, Carl Philipp', in Alfred Fierro, André Palluel-Guillard, Jean Tulard, *Histoire et Dictionnaire du Consulat et de L'Empire* (Paris 1995), p. 1165.

100 Alistair Norwich Tayler and Henrietta Tayler, *The Book of the Duffs* (2 vols., Edinburgh, 1914), I, p. 206.

101 G. E. Rothenberg, *Napoleon's Great Adversary: Archduke Charles and the Austrian Army, 1792–1814* (Staplehurst, 1995), p. 157; Walter Consuelo Langsam, *The Napoleonic Wars and German Nationalism in Austria* (New York, 1970), p. 16.

102 Jerdan, *National Portrait*, II, p. 205. The information could perhaps be considered as a first-person testimony, since in 1836, Duff recommended Jerdan's account of his life to a former British commissioner in Spain who was planning to write a history of the Peninsular War, see The National Library of Scotland (NLS), MS 4042, f. 287: fourth Earl of Fife to Barry O'Meara.

103 Ibid.

104 Langsam, *The Napoleonic Wars and German Nationalism*, p. 42.

105 Tayler, *The Book of the Duffs*, I, p. 234.

106 John Sinclair, *The Correspondence of the Right Honourable Sir John Sinclair, Bart. with Reminiscences of the Most Distinguished Characters Who have Appeared in Great Britain, and in Foreign Countries, During the Last Fifty Years* (2 vols., London, 1831), II, p. 131.

107 AB, MS 3715/2264: Report of the 10th Invernesshire Militia, Edinburgh, 1 March 1805.

108 A subsidiary dignity inherited when Duff's father became the third Earl of Fife on the death of the second Earl on 24 January 1809, see Tayler, *The Book of the Duffs*, I, p. 206.

109 AB, MS 3175/1410/3: Colonel James Duff to Gaspar Melchor de Jovellanos, Seville, 23 March 1809.

110 AGMS, M-8 *Expediente* 72 Vizconde Macduff: Bardaxi to Council of Regency, 3 November 1810.

111 Fransjohan Pretorius, 'Foreign volunteers with the Boer forces in the South African War of 1899–1902', in Krueger and Levsen (eds), *War Volunteering in Modern Times*, pp. 124–25. I am grateful to Professor Pretorius, of the University of Pretoria, for allowing me to consult his paper prior to its publication.

112 AGMS, L-702 *Expediente* Ricardo Lee: note of Francisco de Saavedra to Antonio Cornel, 21 December 1809.

113 Ibid. No record has been found suggesting that the Spanish authorities ever reconsidered his offer. Consequently, Richard Lee was not added to the list of volunteers surveyed by this book.

114 For more on this subject, see Chapter 5.

115 NA WO, 1/1123, 'Miscellaneous', ff. 315–16: Patrick Campbell to Lt. Col. Bunbury, 7 May 1811; AGMS, E-688 *Expediente* Patricio Campbell: Memorial of Patricio Campbell, 16 February 1815; AGMS, D-1176 *Expediente* Carlos Downie; AGMS, B-933 *Expediente* Benjamin Barrie.

116 AGMS, C-1704 *Expediente* Carlos Morgan; AGMS, C-1704 *Expediente* Miguel Carrol; Robertson, *A Long Way from Tipperary*, p. 31.

117 Sarah Virginia Percy, *Mercenaries: The History of a Norm in International Relations* (Oxford, 2007), pp. 50–3.

118 'Summary of politics', *Cobbett's Weekly Political Register* (London, England), Saturday, 16 July 1808. Cobbett's impatient desire to see political change in Spain echoed demands made by his radical friends, Major Cartwright and Sir Francis Burdett for political reform at home, see Hilton, *A Mad*, pp. 207–35.

119 AGMS, R-1365 *Expediente* Daniel Robinson; [Daniel Robinson] *The Political Constitution of the Spanish Monarchy Proclaimed in Cadiz, 19th March, 1812* (London, 1813); Robinson's pseudonym was revealed by John Watkins in his *A Biographical Dictionary of the Living Authors of Great Britain and Ireland, Comprising Literary Memoirs and Anecdotes of Their Lives* (London, 1816), p. 297.

120 Daniel Robinson, writing under the pseudonym *Philos Hispaniae*, in his dedication of the first full translation into English of the text of the liberal Cadiz Constitution; [Daniel Robinson] *The Political Constitution of the Spanish Monarchy Proclaimed in Cadiz, 19th March, 1812* (London, 1813).

Chapter 3

1 Conjured up with relish during crises that attracted international intervention, such as the French invasion that drew to an abrupt end the Liberal Triennium (1820–23), this phrase only appears to have faded away at the end of the Spanish Civil War (1936–39). See, for example, 'The friends and the enemies of the Spanish cause', *Liverpool Mercury*, 27 June 1823, p. 8; 'Spanish cause', *Morning Chronicle*, 9 August 1823, p. 2; Stanley Weintraub, *The Last Great Cause – The Intellectuals and the Spanish Civil War* (London, 1968); Hank Rubin, *Spain's Cause was Mine: A Memoir of an American Medic in the Spanish Civil War* (Carbondale, 1997); R. A. Stradling, *Wales and the Spanish Civil War: The Dragon's Dearest Cause?* (Cardiff, 2004).

2 A Google Book search of the term 'Spanish cause' for the period 1 May 1808 to 31 May 1814 produced 1,060 instances compared to only 5 during the precedent decade (1 May 1798 to 31 April 1808) and 25, mainly alluding to the Christian Reconquest of Spain, for the previous century, which included the period of the War of Succession, starting on 1 January 1700 and finishing on 1 April 1808 (search made on 2 April 2011). The comparatively small amount of Spanish texts available in Google Book tends to reduce the value of a similar search for the term 'la causa española'; nonetheless, the results for the same periods were zero before the war and 37 during the conflict. For archival evidence see, for example, *Gazeta de la Regencia de España y de las Indias*, 17 January 1811, p. 64; *Gaceta Extraordinaria del Gobierno de Mexico*, 4 November 1810, p. 911; *El gran proyecto de Bonaparte para agregar la España a la Francia* (Valencia, 1811), p. 21; Whittingham to Marquess Wellesley, Seville, 4 September 1809, British Library (BL), Additional Papers (Add.) 37287, f. 258; Marquess Wellesley to Garay, 8 September 1809, in Robert Montgomery Martin (ed.), *The Despatches and Correspondence of the Marquess Wellesley, K.G. During His Lordship's Mission to Spain as Ambassador Extraordinary to the Supreme Junta in 1809* (London, 1838), p. 113.

3 The vast majority of these studies have been inspired by Eric Hobsbawm's *Nations and Nationalism since 1780: Programme, Myth, Reality* (Cambridge, 1990) and by Benedict R. Anderson's *Imagined Communities: Reflections on the Origin and Spread of Nationalism* (London, 1983). See, for example, Alvarez Junco's acknowledgement in his 'La invención de la Guerra de la Independencia', p. 75; also Henry Kamen, *Imagining Spain: Historical Myth & National Identity* (London, 2008), pp. 10, 212.

4   See, for example, Jean René Aymes, *La guerre d'indépendance espagnole,*
    1808-1814 (Paris, 1973); Claudette Derozier, *La guerre d'indépendance espagnole*
    a travers l'estampe, 1808-1814 (Lille, 1976); Emmanuel Larraz, *La guerre*
    d'independance espagnole, 1808-1814, au théâtre: anthologie (Aix-en-Provence,
    1987); Marta Gine Janer, *La guerre d'indépendance espagnole dans la littérature*
    française du XIXe siecle: l'episode napoleonien chez Balzac, Stendhal, Hugo (Paris,
    2008).

5   Alvarez Junco, 'La invención de la Guerra de la Independencia', pp. 75–99;
    Carolyn P. Boyd, *Historia Patria: Politics, History, and National Identity in*
    Spain, 1875-1975 (Chichester, 1997), p. 72; Ricardo García Cárcel, 'El concepto
    de España en 1808', *Norba – Revista de historia*, 19 (2006), 176; Kamen,
    Imagining Spain, pp. 2–16. For a critique, see Francisco Carantoña Alvarez,
    'Un conflicto abierto. Controversias y nuevas perspectivas sobre la Guerra de
    la Independencia', *Alcores*, 5 (2088), 13–51, and from a late nineteenth to early
    twentieth centuries' perspective, Sebastian Balfour and Alejandro Quiroga,
    The Reinvention of Spain: Nation and Identity since Democracy (Oxford, 2007),
    pp. 19–21.

6   José Alvarez Junco, 'The nation-building process in nineteenth-century Spain',
    in Clare Mar-Molinero and Angel Smith (eds), *Nationalism and the Nation*
    in the Iberian Peninsula: Competing and Conflicting Identities (Oxford, 1996),
    pp. 89–105.

7   Charles Esdaile, 'War and politics in Spain, 1808-1814', *Historical Journal*, 31
    (1988), pp. 301–2, 316.

8   Esdaile, *The Duke of Wellington*, p. 3; *idem*, *Napoleon's Wars*, pp. 347–8.

9   Esdaile, *Napoleon's Wars*, pp. 347–8.

10 Ibid.

11 Esdaile, *Fighting Napoleon*, pp. 193–204.

12 Alejandro Quiroga, *Making Spaniards: Primo de Rivera and the Nationalization*
    of the Masses, 1923–30 (Basingstoke, 2007), pp. 29–31, 74–5, 116–22; José M.
    Nuñez Seixas, 'La memoria de la Guerra de la Independencia', in Sociedad
    Estatal de Conmemoraciones Culturales (ed.), *España 1808-1814 La Nación en*
    Armas (Madrid, 2008), pp. 396–7.

13 Fernández, *Mujeres en la Guerra de la Independencia*, p. 101. For a more detailed
    critique, see Carantoña Alvarez, 'Un conflicto abierto. Controversias y nuevas
    perspectivas sobre la Guerra de la Independencia', *Alcores*, 5 (2088), 13–51.

14 See, for example, BL, Add. 37286, f. 36: Martin de Garay to Canning, no
    day, April 1809; National Archives of the United Kingdom, Foreign Office

Papers (NA FO) 72/99, ff. 198–201: Carrol to Marquess Wellesley, Badajoz, no day, March 1810; NA WO, 1/1123, ff. 255–68: W. Parker Carrol to the Earl of Liverpool, Lisbon, 28 January 1811; Ibid., f. 515 Proclamation of John Downie, Cadiz, 28 July 1810; *El Redactor General*, 24 December 1811, p. 756; AGM, *Fondo Blake*, Microfiche 3, *Caja* 6, Nr. 6: Blake to H. Wellesley, no day, March 1811; AHN, *Estado* 43¹, *Legajo* 43, Nr. 187: Carlos Doyle to *Junta Central*, undated; AGM, *Fondo Guerra de la Independencia*, *Legajo* 2, *Carpeta* 2: Marquess de la Romana, 13 December 1810; NA FO, 72-99, ff. 161–3: Translation of letter of General Castaños to Marquess Wellesley, Algeciras, 3 January 1810.

15 BOD North, c. 16, f. 23: Copy letter Major Cox to Charles Doyle, Seville, 11 September 1808.

16 *Guía política de las Españas para el año 1813* (Cadiz, 1813), p. 1.

17 Francisco Xavier Cabanes, *Historia de las operaciones del Exército de Cataluña en la Guerra de la Usurpación o sea de la Independencia de España. Primera Campaña* (1st edn, Tarragona, 1809; 2nd edn, Mexico, 1810). The phrase 'viz the War of Spanish Independence' was removed from the title of a third edition published in Barcelona a year after the war ended (1815), but the content is the same.

18 Cabanes, *Historia de las operaciones* (2nd edn), p. 12; Pérez de Guzmán y Gallo, *El dos de mayo*, pp. 339, 358, 414.

19 Ronald Fraser, *Napoleon's Cursed War: Spanish Popular Resistance in the Peninsular War, 1808–1814* (London, 2008), pp. 68–71, 485–9.

20 Cabanes, *Historia de las operaciones* (2nd edn), pp. 36, 129–31, 149.

21 Cabanes, *Historia de las operaciones* (2nd edn), pp. 12, 115; *idem, Memoria acerca del modo de escribir la historia militar de la última guerra entre España y Francia, escrita en Madrid en 1814* (Barcelona, 1816), pp. 14–15.

22 BL, Add. 49490, f. 119: Captain Whittingham to Col. Gordon, Gibraltar, 4 June 1808.

23 Colonel Whittingham to Lieut.-Col. Hon. Henry Cadogan, Madrid, 6 October, 1808 in Whittingham (ed.), *A Memoir*, pp. 49–50.

24 *Trial of Lieutenant General John Whitelocke*, pp. 80–1, 86–8, 159–61; Whittingham, *A Memoir*, pp. 23–8; *The Times*, 16 March 1808, p. 1.

25 BL, Add. 49490, f. 121: Whittingham to Willoughby Gordon, Gibraltar, 5 June 1808.

26 Miguel Artola, *Los afrancesados* (Madrid, 1953), pp. 25–30, 236; Hans Juretschke, *Los afrancesados en la guerra de la Independencia: su genesis,*

desarrollo y consecuencias históricas (Madrid, 1962), pp. 196–7; Jean-Marc Lafon, *L'Andalousie et Napoléon: contre-insurrection, collaboration et résistances dans le midi de l'Espagne, 1808–1812* (Paris, 2007), p. 303; Jordi Canal i Morell (ed.), *Exilios: los éxodos políticos en la historia de España, siglo XV–XX* (Madrid, 2007), p. 143.

27   'Ne peut-on pas dire que la cause espagnole est désespérée?', *Mercure de France, journal littéraire et politique*, 40 (1810), 249; *Journal de l'Empire*, 13 October 1810, p. 2; Ibid., 17 May 1810, p. 4; Jean-René Aymes, 'La guerre d'Espagne dans la presse impériale, 1808–1814', *Annales historiques de la Révolution française*, 336 (2004), 129–45.

28   Juan López Tabar, *Los famosos traidores: los afrancesados durante la crisis del Antiguo Régimen, 1808–1833* (Madrid, 2001), pp. 31–46.

29   Joseph I to Queen Julie, 21 August 1810 in Albert Du Casse (ed.), *Mémoires et correspondance politique et militaire du roi Joseph: publiés, annotés et mis en ordre* (10 vols., Paris, 1853–54), VII, p. 318.

30   Richard Hocquellet (ed.), 'La invención de la modernidad por la prensa. La Constitución de la opinión pública en España al principio de la Guerra de la Independencia', in *La revolución, la política moderna y el individuo: Miradas sobre el proceso revolucionario en España (1808–1835)* (Saragossa, 2011), pp. 180–1.

31   Napoleon to Joseph I, Paris, 27 March 1809, in Vincent Haegele (ed.), *Napoléon et Joseph: correspondance intégrale 1784–1818* (Paris, 2007), p. 666.

32   Bartolomé Bennassar, *The Spanish Character: Attitudes and Mentalities from the Sixteenth to the Nineteenth Century* (Berkeley, 1979), p. 213; Julio Caro Baroja, *El mito del caracter nacional: meditaciones a contrapelo* (Madrid, 1970), pp. 86–91.

33   Rafael Fernández Sirvent, 'Notas sobre propaganda probonapartista: proclamas y Gazeta de Santander, 1809', *El Argonauta Español*, 3 (2006), 6.

34   Napoleon to Joseph I, Rambouillet, 11 March 1809, in Haegele, *Napoléon et Joseph*, p. 661.

35   Owen Connelly, *The Gentle Bonaparte: A Biography of Joseph, Napoleon's Elder Brother* (London, 1968), p. 170; Adrian Shubert, *Death and Money in the Afternoon: A History of the Spanish Bullfight* (Oxford, 1999), p. 156; Carrie Douglass, 'Toro muerto, vaca es: an interpretation of the Spanish bullfight', *American Ethnologist*, 11 (1984), 242–3.

36   Connelly, *The Gentle Bonaparte*, pp. 168–70; López Tabar, *Los famosos traidores*, pp. 31–46; Artola, *Los afrancesados*, p. 214.

37   General Doyle to Marquess de la Romana, *circa* December 1809, BOD North, d. 65, Doyle's Letterbook, pp. 31–9.

38 Michael Broers, *Napoleon's Other War: Bandits, Rebels and Their Pursuers in the Age of Revolutions* (Oxford, 2010), pp. 104–27.

39 BL, Add. 49491, f. 112: Copy of order by Martin de Garay, secretary of the *Junta Central* to Marquess de la Romana, undated, *circa* December 1809.

40 BOD North, c. 13, f. 9: Doyle to Arthur Wellesley, Astorga. 14 August 1808.

41 BL, Add. 49490, ff. 136–37: Whittingham to Major Coxe (sic, for Cox), Madrid, 5 September 1808. More on this subject in Chapter 4.

42 Juan Pérez Villamil, *Carta sobre el modo de establecer el Consejo de Regencia del Reino con arreglo a nuestra Constitución* (Madrid, 1808), p. 9; Portillo Valdés, *Crisis Atlántica*, p. 67.

43 AGMS, A-2104 *Expediente* Jaime Arbuthnot y Arbuthnot; AGMS Q-1 *Expediente* Felipe Qeating (sic, for Keating) Roche; AGMS, P-541 *Expediente* Guillermo Parker Carrol; AGMS, D-877 *Expediente* Carlos Guillermo Doile (sic, for Doyle); AGMS, E-688 *Expediente* Patricio Campbell; AGMS, V-43 *Expediente* Santiago Whittinghan (sic, for Whittingham).

44 Artola, *Los orígenes*, I, p. 167.

45 Hamnett, *La política española*, p. 64.

46 Whittingham to R. H. Davies, 11 August 1808, in Whittingham (ed.), *A Memoir*, p. 44.

47 Esdaile, *The Peninsular War*, p. 116. By contrast, see Manuel Moreno Alonso, *La Junta Suprema de Sevilla* (Sevilla, 2001), p. 225, where the incident is mentioned only as a footnote.

48 NA FO, 72/99, ff. 145–6: Whittingham to Marquess Wellesley, Gibraltar, 4 January 1810; see also Chapter 4.

49 NA WO, 1/241, ff. 267–9: Doyle to unknown, Granada, 17 April 1809.

50 See, for example, the proclamation of the Supreme *Junta* of Asturias, Oviedo, 30 June 1808 alluding to the 'pernicioso egoismo ó timidez' (pernicious egoism or timidity) of those who hesitated in giving their full support to the Patriots, in *Archivo Municipal de Oviedo* (AMO), Decretos Reales 1800–1810, E-4, f. 680.

51 Article 4 of the oath pledged by the members of the *Junta* of the Principality of Catalonia on 3 August 1808, published by the *Gaceta Ministerial de Sevilla*, 26 May 1808, pp. 205–6.

52 Jeremy Adelman, *Sovereignty and Revolution in the Iberian Atlantic* (Oxford, 2006), p. 176.

53 Antonio Peiró Arroyo, *Las Cortes aragonesas de 1808 – Pervivencias forales y revolución popular* (Saragossa, 1985), pp. 9–10.

54 BOD North, c. 13, f. 64: Doyle to Lord Castlereagh, 28 September 1808.

55 Peiró Arroyo, *Las Cortes aragonesas*, p. 101.

56 Henry Kamen, *The War of Succession in Spain 1700–15* (London, 1969), pp. 15–24.

57 AHN, Consejos 5519, *Expediente* 13, 50–2: Palafox to the Council of Castile, Saragossa, 14 August 1808.

58 BOD North, c. 13, f. 236: Doyle to José Palafox, 15 December 1808.

59 José de Palafox returned to Spain in 1814. Unlike his brothers, Francisco and Luis de Palafox, Marquess of Lazan, he backed the constitutional regimen of 1820–23 and remained a liberal supporter until his death in 1847, see 'Palafox y Melci, José Rebolledo de, duque de Zaragoza', *Gran Enciclopedia Aragonesa* (Zaragoza, 2009), online edn [www.enciclopedia-aragonesa.com/voz. asp?voz_id=9794, accessed 20 March 2009]. Confusing him with his siblings may explain why some historians have described him as an 'ambitious and bombastic dictator', see H. M. Stephens, 'Doyle, Sir (Charles) William (1770– 1842)', rev. Charles Esdaile, DNB, September 2004 [www.oxforddnb.com/view/ article/7997, accessed 11 February 2012].

60 AHN, Consejos 5519, *Expediente* 13, ff. 50–2: Palafox to Interim President of the Council of Castile, Arias Mon y Velarde, Saragossa, 21 August 1808.

61 Lasting 7 months, Gerona's second siege was the longest of the war. The 30-month-long assault suffered by the port city of Cadiz, often described as a siege, was, in fact, limited to a land blockade because the French were never able to bar the Patriots access to the sea.

62 *Diario de Gerona*, 23 September 1809, quoted by Ronald Fraser, *Napoleon's Cursed War*, p. 310; Joan Torrent, 'La prensa de Cataluña durante la Guerra de la Independencia', *Destino*, Barcelona, Nr. 1745 (1965), 52–5.

63 BL, Add. 37288, ff. 119–20: Colonel Rudolf Marshal to James Duff, consul in Cadiz, Gerona, 30 August 1809.

64 AHN, *Estado* 38 E, Nr. 371: *Real Orden de la Junta Central para que se socorra con dinero a Gerona ante el peligro de ser sitiada*, Seville, 12 May 1809; Ibid., Nr. 376 *Comunicación a la Junta Central desde Tarragona informando que se le enviará dinero a Gerona tan pronto como se le pueda hacer llegar*, Tarragona, 3 July 1809.

65 NA WO, 1/237, ff. 551–2: E. R. Green to Cooke 1 September 1809.

66 Balfour and Quiroga, *The Reinvention of Spain*, p. 26; Burdiel, 'Liberalism and Nationalism', pp. 61–4.

67 Francisco Xavier Cabanes, *Historia de las operaciones del Exército de Cataluña en la Guerra de la Usurpación o sea de la Independencia de España* (Tarragona, 1809); Fray Bruno Casals, *Tarragona sacrificada en sus intereses y vidas por la*

independencia de la nación y la libertad de su cautivo monarca Fernando Septimo (Tarragona, 1816). On the use of the term '*guerra del Francès*', see Lluís Maria de Puig i Oliver, *Girona francesa 1812–1814 L'anexió de Catalunya a França i el domini napoleònic a Girona* (Girona, 1976), pp. 9–10.

68 NA FO, 72/99, ff. 198–204: Carrol to Marquess Wellesley, Badajoz, no day, March 1810.

69 NA WO, 1/1123, ff. 371–3: Memorial of William Parker Carrol, Major in the British Army and *Brigadier General* in the Service of Spain to the Right Honourable the Earl of Liverpool His Majesty's Principal Secretary for the War Department, London, 30 July 1811.

70 NA FO, 72/99, ff. 198–204: Carrol to Marquess Wellesley, Badajoz, no day, March 1810.

71 Carrol to Spanish Ministry of War, 20 March 1823, and Carrol to Spanish Consul at Malta, Antonio Salinas de Vilches, 24 September 1822, in AGMS, P-541 Expediente Guillermo Parker Carrol. His offer was politely declined by a civil servant.

72 BL, Add. 49490, f. 121: Whittingham to Willoughby Gordon, Gibraltar, 5 June 1808.

73 NA FO, 72/99, ff. 198–204: Carrol to Marquess Wellesley, Badajoz, no day, March 1810.

74 BOD North, c. 13, ff. 20–3: C. W. Doyle to Duke of Infantado, Madrid, 20 August 1808.

75 BNE, R/63251 *Convocatoria dirigida a extremeños y españoles en general para que se alisten en la Leal Legión de Extremadura*, 28 July 1810; BOD North c. 17, f. 182: Proclamation in Spanish of General Doyle to the people of Valencia 3 December 1810; NAWO 1/1123 ff. 255–68: W. Parker Carrol to the Earl of Liverpool, Lisbon 28 January 1811.

76 Lorenzo Calvo de Rozas, *Proposición de Calvo de Rozas de convocatoria de las Cortes y elaboración constitucional*, 15 April 1809, in *Biblioteca Virtual Miguel de Cervantes* [www.cervantesvirtual.com/servlet/SirveObras/c1812/90251731092370596454679/p0000001.htm#I_1_, accessed 20 October 2008].

77 Ibid.

78 Ibid.

79 *Primera Exposición de Guillermo Hualde, el Conde de Toreno y otros al Consejo de Regencia, instando la rápida convocatoria de Cortes, 17 June 1810, in Biblioteca Virtual Miguel de Cervantes* [www.cervantesvirtual.com/

servlet/SirveObras/24616107767149619976613/index.htm, accessed 21 November 2008].

80 Winslow Copley Goodwin Jr, 'The political and military career of Don Pedro Caro y Sureda, Marqués de la Romana' (Florida University Ph.D. thesis, 1973), pp. 36–40.

81 AHN, *Estado* 2 D, images 145–83: Marquess de la Romana to *Junta Central*, 16 December 1809.

82 Ibid.

83 Ibid.

84 Balfour and Quiroga, *The Reinvention of Spain*, p. 18.

85 Tamar Herzog, *Defining Nations: Immigrants and Citizens in Early Modern Spain and Spanish America* (London, 2003); Mateo Ballester Rodríguez, *La identidad española en la Edad Moderna, 1556–1665: discursos, símbolos y mitos* (Madrid, 2010).

86 Jorge Cañizares-Esguerra, *How to Write the History of the New World: Histories, Epistemologies, and Identities in the Eighteenth-Century Atlantic World* (Stanford, 2001), pp. 8, 204–65; Scott Eastman, *Preaching Spanish Nationalism Across the Hispanic Atlantic, 1759–1823* (Louisiana, 2012), *passim*.

87 Kamen, *Imagining Spain*, pp. 2–16.

88 Hamnett, *La política española*, p. 164.

89 AGMS, P-541 *Expediente* Guillermo Parker Carrol; AGMS, M-8 *Expediente* 69 Reynaldo Macdonell.

90 BOD North, c. 16, ff. 14–16: Carrol to Charles Doyle, Herrera de Rio Pesuerga, 5 September 1808.

91 See Chapter 4, 'The so-called "Marquess de La Romana's coup"', pp. 87–112.

92 For examples of the use of this term, see Antonio Mordella y Spotorno, *Sacrificios y ejemplos que la Madre Patria presenta a la imitación de sus hijos. Publicalos D. Antonio Mordella y Spotorno vecino de Cartagena, quien los dedica al Excmo. Sr. Milor Doyle, Mariscal de Campo de los Reales Exercitos* (Valencia, 1808), pp. 1–4, 12–13; General Felipe Roche to Francisco Elio, Elche, 4 January 1813, in Andrés Ortega del Alamo (ed.), *Cartas inéditas del General Felipe Roche a los Generales Copons, Freyre y Elio* (Madrid, 1955), pp. 6–7; [Puigrubí, Miguel], *Respuestas a la pregunta de un criticón ¿Qué ha hecho el corregimiento de Figueras en defensa o favor de la Justa causa que sostiene la Nación española?* (Tarragona, 1813–1814), *passim*.

93 Michael Walzer, *Just and Unjust Wars: A Moral Argument with Historical Illustrations* (New York, 2006), pp. xvi–xvi, 54, 59–62, 75, 82, 90; A. J. Coates, *The Ethics of War* (Manchester, 1997), pp. 147–63.

94 Ibid., p. 114.

95 As in those resulting from the 'Declaración de Guerra Santa' (Declaration of
    Holy War) proclaimed by the *Junta Suprema de Extremadura*, 20 April 1809,
    reproduced in Ramón Gomez Villafranca (ed.), *Extremadura en la Guerra de la
    Independencia, memoria histórica y colección diplomática* (Badajoz, 1908), pp.
    184–5, and from the edict of the *Junta de Badajoz*, 29 April 1809, supporting the
    partidas de cruzadas (crusades) organized by priests and monks in that province
    and in Saragossa, see Lafoz Rabaza, *El Aragón Resistente*, pp. 150–1.

96 NA WO, 1/1123, f. 519: Proclamation of John Downie, Valencia de Alcantara,
    14 February 1811.

97 BNE, R/63251 Downie's Proclamation '*Extremeños! ¡Españoles!*', 28 July 1810.

98 Ibid.

99 NA WO, 1/230, ff. 33–5: Lord William Henry Cavendish Bentick to Hew
    Dalrymple, Memorandum, Madrid, 2 October 1808.

100 NA WO, 1/230, ff. 58–63: Reply Nr. 2 of General Castaños to questionnaire sent
    by Lord William Henry Cavendish Bentinck, Madrid, 2 October 1808.

101 Lords Sitting of Monday 4 July 1808', in Hansard, Thomas C., *Parliamentary
    Debates from the year 1803 to the present time* (41 vols., London, 1820), XI,
    cc. 1138–41.

102 Rory Muir, *Britain and the Defeat of Napoleon 1807–1815* (London, 1996),
    pp. 116–20.

103 First mentioned, as an in-passing reference, in an article on fears of the eventual
    recovery of the defeated French forces in Portugal, *The Morning Post*, 27
    November 1810, p. 2. This finding resulted from searching the online databases
    'Nineteenth Century British Library Newspapers', 'Ninenteenth Century UK
    Periodicals', 'British Periodicals, 1680s–1930s', 'Eighteenth Century Journals'
    and the digitalized archives of *The Times* for the period 1 May 1808 to 31 May
    1814.

104 AGMS, D-1177 *Expediente* Juan Downie: *Prospecto Plan de la Leal Legión de
    Extremadura, circa* January–February 1810.

105 Esdaile, *The Peninsular War*, p. 457.

106 Richard Hocquellet (ed.), 'Los dirigentes patriotas y su representación del poder
    durante la Guerra de la Independencia. Del *consensus populi* a la voluntad
    general', in *La revolución, la política moderna y el individuo: Miradas sobre el
    proceso revolucionario en España (1808–1835)* (Saragossa, 2011), p. 105.

107 This and subsequent quotes in this paragraph: NA FO 72-99 ff. 158–60: General
    Castaños to the Marquis of Wellesley, Algeciras, 13 January 1810.

Chapter 4

1 NA WO, 1/227, f. 1: Instructions of Lord Castlereagh to Lt. Col. Doyle, 2 July 1808; NA WO, 1/237, ff. 33–8: Copy Instructions of Lord Castlereagh to Col. Sir Thomas Dyer, Major Roche, Captain Patrick, 19 June 1808; Ibid., f. 155: Circular of Lord Castlereagh to Col. Sir T. Dyer, Major Roche and Capt. Patrick, at Asturias, and Lt. Col. Doyle, Capt. Carrol and Capt. Kennedy at Galicia, 4 August 1808.

2 NA WO, 1/233, ff. 359–67: Roche to Lord Castlereagh, Santander, 1 August 1808.

3 Ibid.

4 Ibid.

5 AGMS, Q-1 *Expediente* Felipe Qeating (sic, for Keating) Roche: Certified copy of rank of *coronel* granted by the *Junta* of Asturias, 17 August 1808.

6 NA WO, 1/233, ff. 359–67: Roche to Lord Castlereagh, Santander, 1 August 1808.

7 Adolfo Martínez Carrasco, 'El XIII Duque del Infantado, un aristócrata en la crisis del Antiguo Régimen', *Revista de la Universidad Complutense de Madrid*, 13 (2009), 321–6.

8 NA WO, 1/233, ff. 359–67: Roche to Lord Castlereagh, Santander, 1 August 1808.

9 NA WO, 1/233 ff. 415–42: Philip Keating Roche, Gijon, 8 August 1808.

10 Ibid.

11 NA WO, 1/233, ff. 443–4: Lord Castlereagh to Major Roche, Downing Street, 18 August 1808.

12 NA WO, 1/227, ff. 139–41: Doyle to Castlereagh, Astorga, 14 August 1808; BL, Add. 49490, ff. 136–7: Copy letter Whittingham to Major Coxe (sic, for Cox), military *attachée*, Seville, Madrid, 5 September 1808.

13 Esdaile, *The Peninsular War*, p. 126.

14 NA WO, 1/227, ff. 139–41: Doyle to Lord Castlereagh, Astorga, 14 August 1808.

15 BOD North, c. 13, ff. 20–3: Copy letter C.W Doyle to Duke de Infantado, 29 August, 1808.

16 NA WO, 1/227, ff. 139–41: Doyle to Lord Castlereagh, Astorga, 14 August 1808.

17 Ibid.

18 Ibid.

19 BOD North, c. 13, ff. 20–3: Copy letter C. W. Doyle to Duke de Infantado, 29 August 1808.

20 BL, Add. 49490, ff. 130–3: Whittingham to Col. Gordon, Madrid, 2 September 1808; Artola, *Los orígenes*, p. 134.

21 BOD North, c. 16, ff. 14–16: Carrol to Doyle, Herrera de Rio Pesuerga, 5 September 1808.

22 Ibid.

23 Ibid.

24 See *Amados españoles, dignos compatriotas* (Beloved Spaniards, honourable compatriots) a proclamation of the Council of Castile urging Spaniards to obey the new King, Joseph Bonaparte in *Gazeta Extraordinaria de Madrid*, 14 June 1808, pp. 576–78. Infantado is mentioned among the signatories, but he was not in Madrid at that time.

25 BOD North, c. 16, ff. 14–16: Carrol to Doyle, Herrera de Rio Pesuerga, 5 September 1808.

26 BOD North, c. 16, f. 21: Letter W. Carrol, Reynosa, 11 September 1808.

27 Ibid.

28 NA WO, 1/227, ff. 37–40: Cooke to Doyle, 31 August 1808.

29 Ibid.

30 NA WO, 1/231, ff. 325–30: Copy letter Doyle to Cox, Madrid, 1 September 1808.

31 BL, Add. 49490, ff. 136–7: Copy letter Whittingham to Major Coxe (sic, for Cox), military agent in Seville, Madrid, 5 September 1808.

32 NA WO, 1/231, ff. 323–5: Cox to Caslereagh, Seville 11 September 1808; Ibid., ff. 337 Francisco de Saavedra to Cox, Seville, 19 September 1808.

33 AHN, *Estado* 43[1], *Legajo* 184: Unsigned draft testimonial on behalf of Carlos Doyle, Seville, 1 October 1809; AGMS, D-877 *Expediente* Carlos Guillermo Doile (sic) version of same testimonial signed by Martin de Garay, 2 October 1809.

34 Martínez Carrasco, 'El XIII Duque del Infantado', pp. 321–6.

35 Charles Esdaile, 'The Marques de la Romana and the Peninsular War: A case study in Spanish civil-military relations' in Ellen Evans and John W. Rooney, Jr. (ed.), *The Consortium on Revolutionary Europe 1750–1850* (Florida, 1994), p. 374; Carr, *Spain 1808–1975*, p. 109; Alicia Laspra Rodriguez, *Intervencionismo y Revolución, Asturias y Gran Bretaña durante la Guerra de la Independencia (1808–1813)* (Oviedo, 1992), p. 184; Carlos Canales Torres, *Breve historia de la Guerra de la Independencia* (Madrid, 2006), p. 138.

36 Francisco Carantoña Alvarez, *Revolución liberal y crisis de las instituciones tradicionales asturianas* (Gijón, 1989), pp. 48–56; González Enciso et al., *Los Borbones*, p. 55.

37 André Fugier, *La Junte Supérieure des Asturies* (Paris, 1930), pp. 10–11; Alfonso Menendez González, *Elite y poder: la Junta General del Principado de Asturias 1594–1808* (Oviedo, 1989), pp. 146–7, 149.

38 Menendez González, *Elite y poder*, pp. 289–90.

39 Marta Friera Alvarez, *La Junta General del Principado de Asturias a fines del antiguo régimen (1760–1835)* (Oviedo, 2003), pp. 535–7.

40 Ibid.

41 Ibid., p. 536.

42 Ramón Alvarez Valdés, *Memorias del levantamiento de Asturias en 1808* (Gijón, 1988), p. 279.

43 Carantoña Alvarez, *Revolución liberal*, pp. 92–9.

44 Alvarez Valdés, *Memorias,* pp. 114–15.

45 AGMS, A-2104 *Expediente* Jaime Arbuthnot y Arbuthnot: Service records for May 1814, December 1832 and June 1843.

46 Alvarez Valdés, *Memorias*, pp. 109, 352.

47 Carantoña Alvarez, *Revolución liberal,* p. 99.

48 Report of Ignacio Florez and Gregorio de Jove Vales to the Marquess de la Romana, Oviedo, 8 April 1809, in Francisco Carantoña Alvarez, *La Guerra de laIndependencia en Asturias* (Gijón,1984), pp. 202–09.

49 Alvarez Valdés, *Memorias*, pp. 110–11.

50 Ibid.

51 A witness of these events, the liberal Ramón Alvarez Valdés stated that Campo Sagrado and Jovellanos were appointed because they had 'parientes y amigos' (relatives and friends) in the *junta*. Jovellanos's nephew, Baltasar Cienfuegos Jovellanos, was secretary of the *junta* (Alvarez Valdés, *Memorias,* p. 175).

52 Friera Alvarez, *La Junta General,* p. 582.

53 The rumour was credible because Jovellanos was among those who in the past had criticized this law arguing that would damage landowner – tenant relations, see Pedro Rodriguez Campomanes and Ana Alvarez Gonzalo, *Campomanes en su II centenario* (Madrid, 2003), p. 200; Carantoña Alvarez, *Revolución liberal,* p. 105.

54 AMO, Reales Ordenes 1800–1810, E.4, f. 731: *Bando de la Junta Suprema de Asturias del 29 de septiembre de 1808.*

55 Ibid.

56 Fugier, *La Junte Supérieure*, p. 14.

57 (Translation by the author of this thesis) Decree of *Junta Suprema* of 21 September 1808, Article 2, Appendix Nr. 59, in Alvarez Valdez, *Memorias*, p. 342.

58 Carantoña Alvarez, *Revolución liberal*, pp. 48–51.

59 Ibid., p. 33; González Enciso et al., *Los Borbones*, pp. 55–8.

60 Carantoña Alvarez, *Revolución liberal,* pp. 48–51; Friera Alvarez, *La Junta General,* p. 470.

61 NA WO, 1/241, ff. 369–71: Carrol to Lord Castlereagh, Gijon, 19 February 1809.

62 Colin Lucas, 'Nobles, bourgeois and the origins of the French Revolution' in Gary Kates (ed.), *The French Revolution: Recent Debates and New Controversies* (London, 1998), p. 58.

63 NA WO, 1/241, ff. 369–71: Carrol to Lord Castlereagh, Gijon, 19 February 1809.

64 Ibid.

65 AMO, Reales Ordenes 1800–10, E.4, f. 712: Proclamation of Guillermo Parker Carrol, 30 November 1808.

66 NA WO, 1/241, ff. 369–71: Carrol to Lord Castlereagh, Gijon, 19 February 1809.

67 Friera Alvarez, *La Junta General*, p. 470.

68 NA WO, 1/241, ff. 369–71: Carrol to Lord Castlereagh, Gijon, 19 February 1809. No mention was made of prior consultation with his immediate British military superior, General John Broderick, then on his way back to London, or with any British diplomatic representatives such as Charles Stuart in Lisbon and John Hookham Frere in Seville.

69 BL, Add. 49486, ff. 80–4: Memorandum of General Leith, *circa* September 1808.

70 NA WO, 1/241, ff. 369–71: Carrol to Castlereagh, Gijon, 19 February 1809.

71 Fugier, *La Junte Supérieure*, p. 13.

72 NA WO, 1/241, ff. 357–59: Carrol to Castlereagh, Oviedo, 2 February 1809 and NA FO, 72/80 f. 3: Parker Carrol to Canning, Gijon, 19 February 1809. Carrol mentioned Ballesteros's inability to move outside Asturias in an earlier letter to the secretary of the Duke of York, see BL, Add. 49491, ff. 103–05: Carrol to Gordon, Llanes, 24 December 1808.

73 Since the fourteenth century, the Leonese represented the Asturian principality in the national *Cortes*, see Friera Alvarez, *La Junta General*, pp. 504–05.

74 BL, Add. 49491, ff. 148–50: Translated copy of letter *circa* March 1809 sent by Carrol to the Supreme *Junta* of Asturias transmitting a request by the *Junta* of Leon; BL, Add. 49491, ff. 141–44: Carrol to Gordon, Gijon, 22 March 1809; similar letters on the same date at NA FO, 72/80 addressed to Canning and at NA WO, 1/241, ff. 405–15 addressed to Lord Castlereagh.

75 The *Gaceta de Oviedo* published the order on 7 October 1808, reproduced in Carantoña Alvarez, *Revolución liberal*, p. 108.

76 José Miguel Caso (ed.), *Gaspar Melchor de Jovellanos – Obras Completas* (7 vols., Gijon, 1990), V, pp. 145–46.

77 AHN, *Estado* 8 A, Nr. 75: *Real orden comunicada a las Juntas provinciales de Galicia, León y Asturias poniendo al frente de la organización de sus tropas al Marqués de la Romana*, Seville, 29 December 1809; BL, Add. 49491, f. 112: Copy of

order by Martin de Garay, secretary of the *Junta Central* to Marquess de la Romana, undated (*circa* December 1809); Esdaile, 'The Marques de la Romana', p. 367.

78　Ibid. This order was also mentioned in a proclamation issued by Romana on 18 December 1808, see AHN, *Estado* 42 A, Nr. 160 Personal files of Spanish generals: Marquess de la Romana. This was not the first time that La Romana received instructions from the central government to discipline rebellious provinces. In September 1801, First Minister Godoy dispatched Romana to Valencia to quash a rising in defence of provincial *fueros* considered in Madrid more dangerous to the Bourbon regime than the Esquilache riots of 1766. Repression was harsh, but order was restored; see Manuel Ardit, *Revolución liberal y revuelta campesina – Un ensayo sobre la desintegración del régimen feudal en el País Valenciano (1793–1840)* (Barcelona, 1977), p. 118; Esdaile, *The Spanish Army*, pp. 47–8.

79　BL, Add. 49491, ff. 108–10: Carrol to the Duke of York, Colombres, 28 December 1808.

80　BL, Add. 49491, ff. 3–5: Carrol to Gordon, 7 August 1808.

81　AHN, Diversos-Colecciones 110, N. 32: Guillermo Parker Carrol, *Teniente Coronel al Servicio de España*, Reynosa, 14 September 1808.

82　*Felix Farley's Bristol Journal*, 19 November 1808, p. 1.

83　BL, Add. 49486, f. 174: Copy letter Charles Lefevre, Captain of Engineers, to General Leith, Bilbao, 25 October 1808.

84　BL, Add. 49491, ff. 108–10: Carrol to the Duke of York, Colombres, 28 December 1808.

85　Ibid.

86　BOD, MS Eng. Lett., c. 666 Copy Book of Gral. John Broderick, ff. 1–4: General Broderick to W. Parker Carrol, 9 October 1808.

87　NA WO, 1/241, ff. 369–71: Carrol to Lord Castlereagh, Gijon, 10 February 1809.

88　General John Broderick's return to London and his immediate promotion to Major General were reported by *The Morning Chronicle*, 16 February 1809, p. 2.

89　NA WO, 1/241, ff. 381–4 and BL, Add. 49491, f. 116: Proclamation of Guillermo Parker Carrol, Oviedo, 2 February 1809.

90　NA WO, 1/241, ff. 389–94: Carrol to Lord Castlereagh, Gijon, 16 February 1809.

91　NA WO, 1/241, ff. 389–94: Carrol to Lord Castlereagh, 16 February 1809.

92　Ibid.

93　This was publicly acknowledged in an article published by the official newspaper of Asturias, the *Gaceta Extraordinaria de Oviedo*, 22 March 1809, pp. 197–9. Carrol was described as 'El Comisionado del Gobierno británico y Teniente

Coronel de nuestro exército D. Guillermo Parker y Carrol' (Commissioner of the British government and *Teniente Coronel* of our Army, Mr. *Guillermo* Parker Carrol).

94 BL, Add. 49491, f. 126: Translation of letter of *Teniente Coronel* Carrol to *Junta Suprema de Oviedo*, 8 February 1809.

95 Ibid.

96 Ibid.

97 Toreno, *Historia del levantamiento*, IV, p. 69; Christiansen, *The Origins of Military Power*, p. 13.

98 Fugier, *La Junte Supérieure,* p. 64; Enrique López Fernández, *Las Juntas del Principado durante la Guerra de la Independencia en Asturias* (Oviedo, 1999), p. 178.

99 BL, Add. 49491, ff. 141–4: Carrol to Gordon, Gijon, 22 March 1809; NA WO, 1/241, ff. 405–15: Carrol to Lord Castlereagh, Gijon, 22 March 1809.

100 Ibid.

101 Ibid.

102 Fugier, *La Junte Supérieure,* pp. 157–68.

103 BL, Add. 49491, ff. 141–4: Carrol to Gordon, Gijon, 22 March 1809; NA WO, 1/241 ff. 405–15: Carrol to Lord Castlereagh, Gijon, 22 March 1809.

104 Ibid

105 Ibid.

106 BL, Add. 49491, f. 159: English translation of the first letter addressed by Romana to Carrol, Paramo del Sil, 26 March 1809.

107 This and subsequent quotes: NA WO, 1/241, ff. 507–73: (original English translation) Carrol to Romana, Oviedo, 28 March 1809.

108 José María Patac de Las Traviesas and Magin Berenguer Alonso, *La guerra de la independencia en Asturias en los documentos del archivo del marqués de Santa Cruz de Marcenado: discurso leído por el autor en el acto de su solemne recepción académica el día 9 de noviembre de 1979* (Oviedo, 1980), p. 154.

109 Letter of Ignacio Florez Arango to Marquess de la Romana, 7 April 1809, in David Ruiz, *Asturias contemporanea, 1808–1975* (Madrid, 1981), pp. 17–18.

110 NA WO, 1/241, ff. 507–73 and BL, Add. 49491, f. 178: (original English translation) Carrol to Romana, Oviedo 28 March 1809.

111 Ibid.

112 Ibid.

113 BL, Add. 49491, f. 163: Carrol to Gordon, Oviedo 12 April 1809.

114 Esdaile, 'The Marques de la Romana', p. 373.

115 '. . . il y á neamoins plus á craindre peut etre, que l'autre en egard aus desordres qui regne dans la Junta celle-ci composée des gens desavoué du Public, sans opinion, sans force, et l'Objet de l'Execration de la plus saine partie de la Province: cependant je ne lui impute pas tout le tort comm'on veut me faire croire . . .' (original spelling in French), see BL, Add. 49491, f. 167: Copy letter sent in French by Marquess de La Romana to George Canning, Oviedo, 7 April 1809.

116 *Informe dado por la Junta Suprema de Asturias al Excmo. Sr. Marqués de la Romana sobre varios puntos*, Oviedo, 12 April 1809, in Alvarez Valdes, *Memorias*, Appendix Nr. 65, pp. 350–2.

117 *Informe dado al Exmo. Señor Marqués de la Romana por Ignacio Florez y D. Gregorio de Jove Valdes*, Oviedo, 8 April 1809, in Patac de Las Traviesas and Alonso, *La guerra de la independencia en Asturias*, pp. 145–51.

118 BL, Add. 49491, f. 175: Carrol to Gordon, Oviedo 7 May 1809.

119 BL, RB.23 b 4227–10 General Reference Collection Provenance Foreign and Commonwealth Office: 'Asturianos' – proclamation of Guillermo (William) Parker Carrol, 24 April 1809.

120 Ibid.

121 Ibid.

122 Ibid. The word 'liberal' was probably applied here in the sense of something that is bountiful and open-hearted rather than as a precursor of the modern political term believed to have been coined at the *Cortes* in Cadiz 2 years later, see María Cruz Seoane, *El primer lenguaje constitucional español: las Cortes de Cádiz* (Madrid, 1968), pp. 158–9. Vicente Lloréns Castillo, 'Sobre la aparición de "liberal"', in idem, *Literatura, historia, política (ensayos)* (Madrid, 1967), pp. 45–51.

123 Proclamation of Marquess de la Romana, Oviedo, 7 May 1809, in Gaspar Melchor de Jovellanos, *D. Gaspar de Jovellanos a sus compatriotas: Memoria en que se rebaten las calumnias divulgadas contra los individuos de la Junta Central y se da razón de la conducta y opiniones del autor desde que recobró la libertad* (Coruña, 1811), pp. 89–91.

124 Ibid.

125 Toreno, *Historia del levantamiento*, II, p. 190.

126 See Esdaile, 'The Marques de la Romana', p. 374; Canales Torres, *Breve historia*, p. 138; Laspra Rodriguez, *Intervencionismo y Revolución,* pp. 184–86; among others. Although an admirer of La Romana, Charles Oman thought that the 'petty *coup d'état*' bore 'an absurd resemblance to Cromwell's famous dissolution of the Long Parliament', see Oman, *A history of the Peninsular War*, II, pp. 375–6.

127 Friera Alvarez, *La Junta General*, p. 610.

128 Esdaile, 'The Marques de la Romana', p. 374.

129 Entry of 19 May 1809, in Ilchester (ed.), *The Spanish Journal*, p. 335.

130 Jovellanos to Holland, Seville 17 May 1809, in Jose Miguel Gonzalez Caso (ed.), *Gaspar Melchor de Jovellanos – Obras Completas* (7 vols., Gijon, 1990), V, Letter Nr. 1850, pp. 141–2.

131 Lord Holland to Jovellanos, Cadiz, 19 May 1809, in Ibid., Letter Nr. 1855, p. 148.

132 Jovellanos and Camposagrado to *Junta Central*, Seville, 29 May 1809, in Ignacio Fernández Sarasola (ed.), *Obras completas de Jovellanos: Escritos políticos* (11 vols., Oviedo, 2006), XI, pp. 663–4.

133 Letter Jovellanos and Camposagrado to *Junta Central*, Seville, 6 July 1809, in Ibid., pp. 666–9.

134 Letter Martin de Garay, secretary of the *Junta Central*, to Jovellanos and Camposagrado, 19 July 1809, in Ibid., p. 675.

135 AHN, *Estado 38 B, Nr. 113–18: Informe del marqués de Campo Sagrado y de Gaspar de Jovellanos sobre las quejas recibidas contra el marqués de la Romana y el General Ballesteros; y el estado miserable del principado y la extrema necesidad de socorros*, Oviedo, 16 October 1809; Ibid., Nr. 119–26 *Informes de Gaspar de Jovellanos sobre la extrema necesidad de socorros en que se haya el principado de Asturias y sus ejércitos*, Seville, 29 December 1809; AHN, Estado 2 D, Nr. 223: Flórez Estrada, Álvaro. Procurador del Principado de Asturias, Cadiz, 19 December 1809.

136 Carantoña Alvarez, *Revolución liberal,* p. 125; Menendez González, *Elite y poder,* p. 824.

137 Fugier, *La Junte Supérieure,* pp. 25–40.

138 Menendez González, *Elite y poder*, pp. 823–4; Friera Alvarez, *La Junta General*, pp. 685–91, 952–4, 1272–304.

139 Stanley G. Payne, *Politics and the Military in Modern Spain* (London, 1967), pp. 14–5.

140 Esdaile, 'The Marques de la Romana', p. 374.

141 Rodolfo G. de Barthelémy, *'El Marquesito' Juan Diaz Porlier – General que fue de los Ejércitos Nacionales (1788–1815)* (2 vols., Santiago de Compostela, 1995), I, p. 85. See also Laspra Rodriguez, *Intervencionismo y Revolución*, p. 184; Friera Alvarez, *La Junta General*, p. 588. On 15 April 1809, Carrol had been elevated to the rank of Major in the British army, but that was in reaction to an earlier request he made to have his services in Buenos Aires recognized with a promotion, see BL, Add. 49491, f. 1: Carrol to Gordon, headquarters of Galician Army, Astorga, 8 August 1808; *London Gazette*, 15 April 1809, p. 521.

142   NA WO, 1/241, ff. 581–2: Carrol to Lord Castlereagh, Coruña, 29 July 1809;
      Ibid., ff. 585–6: Romana to Carrol, same day, acknowledging Carrol's acceptance
      of the position.

143   Muir, *Britain and the defeat,* pp. 79–87.

144   Huw John Davies, 'British intelligence in the Peninsular War' (University of
      Exeter Ph.D. thesis, 2006), pp. 82–6. I am grateful to Dr. Davies for allowing me
      to quote from his unpublished research.

145   It seems that at some stage the Duke of York advanced the candidature of an
      uncle of the British volunteer Charles Doyle, Sir John Doyle, who was senior to
      Wellesley. But General Doyle was then serving in Guernsey and the letter with
      the offer went astray, see Muir, *Britain and the defeat,* pp. 85–7.

146   *The London Gazette,* 25 April 1809, p. 582.

147   Cambridge University Library (CU, Add.), Additional Manuscripts 7521, Copy
      of letters and orders upon service in the Peninsula addressed to Lieut. Gen. Sir
      Philip K. Roche, ff. 56–7: Lord Castlereagh to Philipe Keating Roche, Downing
      Street, 1 July 1809; NA WO, 1/241, ff. 333–39: 'Private', Doyle to Cooke,
      2 August 1809.

148   'London news, 29 May', *The Caledonian Mercury,* 1 June 1809, p. 4; *The Ipswich
      Journal* estimated Wellesley Spanish sojourn would last 3 months, see 'Sunday's
      Post', *The Ipswich Journal,* 3 June 1809, p. 2.

149   George Canning's Instructions to Marquess Wellesley, Foreign Office, 27 June
      1809 in Martin, *The Despatches,* pp. 189–90, 195.

150   Ibid.

151   Ibid.

152   BL, Add. 27286, f. 94: Letter 'secret and confidential' Canning to Wellesley,
      Foreign Office, 18 July 1809.

153   BL, Add. 37286, ff. 253–5: Canning to Marquess Wellesley, 12 August 1809.

154   Ibid.

155   Martin, *The Despatches,* p. 1.

156   From the very moment the British forces crossed the frontier, Sir Arthur
      bemoaned the lack of material assistance and soon accused the Spaniards of
      deliberately withholding supplies. Extremadura, the scene of operations, was
      one of the poorest regions of Spain and had suffered particularly from passages
      of the French army. The Spanish Army was not faring any better – indeed, the
      American ambassador in Cadiz believed that the Spaniards fared worse, see
      John Kenneth Severn, *A Wellesley Affair: Richard Marquess Wellesley and the
      Conduct of Anglo-Spanish Diplomacy, 1809–1812* (Tallahassee, 1981), p. 59.

157 Report of the Marquess of Wellesley to Canning regarding a meeting with Spanish Foreign Minister, Martin de Garay, Seville, 2 September 1809, in Martin, *The Despatches,* pp. 103–10.

158 William Jacob, *Travels in the South of Spain, in Letters Written A.D. 1809 and 1810* (London, 1811), p. 189.

159 Martin, *The Despatches*, p. 2.

160 BL, Add. 37286, ff. 186–90: 'General Doyle's letters': report undated, *circa* September 1809.

161 Ibid.

162 NA FO, 72/78, ff. 87–9: Roche to M. Wellesley, Headquarters Spanish Army of La Mancha, Daimiel, 3 October 1809.

163 NA FO, 72/78, ff. 100–03: Roche to M. Wellesley, Headquarters Spanish Army of La Mancha, Santa Cruz de Mudela, 19 October 1809.

164 Ibid.

165 Garay to Wellesley, Seville, 25 August 1809, point 1, in Martin, *The Despatches*, p. 75.

166 Wellesley to Canning, Seville, 15 September 1809, in Martin, *The Despatches*, pp. 119–35.

167 Christopher Alan Bayly, 'Wellesley, Richard, Marquess Wellesley (1760–1842)', DNB, September 2004; online edn, May 2009 [www.oxforddnb.com/view/article/29008, accessed 22 July 2009].

168 BL, Add. 37287, ff. 284–91: 'Private' Marquess Wellesley to Canning, 15 September 1809.

169 Whittingham (ed.), *A Memoir*, pp. 89–107

170 Whittingham to his brother-in-law, Seville, 4 November, 1809, in Whittingham (ed.), *A Memoir*, p. 117; Bristol Record Office, Richard Hart Davis Papers, 41593/Fam/1 and Fam/3 for biographical details of Richard Hart Davis and Whittingham's family.

171 Whittingham (ed.), *A Memoir*, pp. 105–09.

172 BL, Add. 37287, f. 258: Whittingham to Marquess Wellesley, Seville, 4 September 1809.

173 Ibid.

174 Ibid.

175 BL, Add. 37288, f. 33: Whittingham to Marquess Wellesley, Seville, 17 September 1809.

176 *The Morning Chronicle*, 18 October 1809, p. 2; *The Aberdeen Journal*, 15 November 1809, p. 3.

177 See NA FO, 72/80, f. 273: Letter of tradesman W. Hamleh to British Foreign Minister, Gibraltar, 27 November 1809; *Caledonian Mercury*, 25 November 1809, p. 2.

178 AHN, *Estado* 2 B: Draft Letter of *Junta Central* to Garay, 27 October 1809.

179 Ibid.

180 AHN, *Estado* 13 B: Proclamation *Junta Central*, Seville, 28 October 1809.

181 BL, Add. 37288, ff. 87–9: Whittingham to Marquess Wellesley, 24 September 1809.

182 *The Morning Chronicle*, 30 May 1809, p. 2.

183 BL, Add. 37288, ff. 87–9: Whittingham to Marquess Wellesley, 24 September 1809.

184 BL, Add. 37288, ff. 201–02: Whittingham to Marquess Wellesley, 29 October 1809.

185 Ibid.

186 Muir, *Britain and the defeat*, p. 106.

187 This and subsequent quotes in this paragraph: BL, Add. 37288, ff. 323–4: Whittingham to Marquess Wellesley, Seville, 4 November 1809.

188 Ibid.

189 NA FO, 72/99, ff. 145–69: Whittingham to Marquess Wellesley, Gibraltar, 4 January 1810, enclosing ff. 147–52: Copy of letter of Whittingham to Marquess Wellesley, Algeciras, 18 December 1809.

190 Manuel Moreno Alonso, *La Batalla de Bailén* (Madrid, 2008), p. 351; *idem*, *La Junta Suprema de Sevilla*, pp. 53–6.

191 Moreno Alonso, *La Batalla*, p. 351.

192 Antonio Alcalá Galiano, *Historia de España desde los tiempos primitivos hasta la mayoridad de la reina Doña Isabel II* (Madrid, 1846), p. 157; Toreno, *Historia del Levantamiento*, I, p. 186.

193 '(. . .) soumise à la volonté de deux hommes, l'un nommé Lorenzo Calvo, marchand de épicier de Sarragosse (. . .) L'autre étoit un nommé Tilly, condamné autrefois aux galéres comme voleur, frère cadet du nommé Guzmán, qui a joué un rôle sous Robespierre, dans le temps de la terreur', quoted in Alfred Morel-Fatio, 'Le révolutionnaire espagnol don Andrés Maria de Guzmán, dit "Don Tocsinos"', *Revue Historique*, CXXII, Mai-Juin (1916), p. 40. The report was highly tendentious. Lorenzo Calvo was no mere grocer, but one of the richest merchants in Spain, owner of several properties in the country and in Portugal, and a director of the first Spanish bank of issuance, the Banco de San Carlos, see 'Calvo de Rozas, Juan Lorenzo', in Alberto Gil Novales (ed.), *Diccionario Biográfico del Trienio Liberal* (Madrid, 1991), p. 116.

194 Fierro *et al.*, *Histoire et Dictionnaire du Consulat et de L'Empire*, pp. 1123–4.

195 In a spectacular example of political survival, Louis XVIII confirmed his nobility status in June 1814. During the Hundred Days, he pledged loyalty to Napoleon and was left in charge of the defence of Paris. Yet, the Bourbons allowed him to retire with no stain in his reputation. The name of Count de Tilly is among those engraved in the *Arc de Triomphe* in Paris, see Fierro *et al*, *Histoire et Dictionnaire du Consulat et de l'Empire*, p. 1124.

196 AHN, Consejos 49616, *Expediente* 17: Papers *Ministerio del Interior* (Joseph I).

197 AHN, *Estado* 52 A: Anonymous letters sent to the *Junta Central* 1808.

198 AHN, *Estado* 33 B: Personal file of Count de Montijo at the *Junta Central* 1808–10; AHN *Estado* 39: Montijo to *Junta Central*, 19 December 1808.

199 Landor to Southey, Clifton, November 1809, in John Forster, *Walter Savage Landor – A Biography* (2 vols., London, 1869), I, p. 146. For more on Landor, see Chapter 5.

200 AHN, *Estado* 45 A: Files on generals who were suspected of lack of patriotism: General Castaños.

201 AHN, *Estado* 39: Count de Tilly to *Junta Central*, 16 December 1808.

202 Jacob, *Travels in the south of Spain*, pp. 62–3; Joseph Blanco White 'Don Leucadio Doblado', *Letters from Spain* (London, 1822), pp. 326–7.

203 AHN, *Estado* 39 D: Mission of Count de Tilly in Morocco, Ceuta and Melilla, November 1808 to March 1809; Moreno Alonso, *La Batalla*, p. 351.

204 NA FO, 72/99, ff. 147–52: Copy letter Whittingham to Marquess Wellesley, Algeciras 18 December 1809 (mailed 4 January 1810).

205 Artola, *Los orígenes*, p. 211; 'Review of Toreno's history of the Spanish insurrection', *Blackwood's Edinburgh Magazine*, November 1836, p. 649.

206 *Dictamen de la Comisión de Cortes elevado a la Junta Central sobre la convocatoria de Cortes (junio de 1809) y exposiciones de los vocales – Voto disidente del conde de Tilly*, Seville, 16 July 1809, in *Biblioteca Virtual Miguel de Cervantes* [www.cervantesvirtual.com/servlet/SirveObras/1356073111213849 5222202/p0000001.htm?marca=conde%20de%20Tilly#26, accessed 25 March 2009].

207 NA FO, 72/99, ff. 147–52: Copy letter Whittingham to Marquess Wellesley, Algeciras, 18 December 1809 (mailed 4 January 1810).

208 He was alluding to Francisco Javier de Lizana y Beaumont (1750–1811), archbishop of Mexico and, from 19 July 1809 to 8 May 1810, viceroy of New Spain (modern Mexico). The *Junta Central* voted unanimously in favour of his appointment, see AHN, *Estado* 58 E, Nr. 43–59: Reports of Viceroy of New Spain.

209 NA FO, 72/99, ff. 147–52: Copy letter Whittingham to Marquess Wellesley.

210 Ibid.

211 Gould Francis Leckie, *An Historical Survery of the Foreign Affairs of Great Britain: For the Years 1808, 1809, 1810: With a View to Explain the Causes of the Disasters of the Late and Present Wars* (London, 1810), p. 352.

212 NA FO, 72/99, ff. 147–52: Copy of letter Whittingham to Marquess Wellesley, Algeciras, 18 December 1809 (mailed 4 January 1810).

213 Ibid.

214 NA FO, 72/99, ff. 153–5: Copy of letter Lord Wellington to Whittingham, Badajoz, 22 December 1809.

215 NA FO, 72/99, ff. 154–5: Whittingham to Wellington, Algeciras, 1 January 1809.

216 NA FO, 72–99, ff. 161–3: Translation of letter of General Castaños to Marquess Wellesley, Algeciras, 3 January 1810.

217 Ibid.

218 NA FO, 72–99, f. 159: Original letter in Spanish of General Castaños to Marquess Wellesley, Algeciras, undated (date added in margin in English: 3 January 1810).

219 Ibid.

220 NA FO, 72/99, ff. 147–52: Copy of letter Whittingham to Marquess Wellesley, Algeciras, 18 December 1809 (mailed 4 January 1810).

221 William Spence Robertson, *France and Latin-American independence* (Baltimore, 1939), pp. 52–3, 64–71.

222 NA FO, 72/99 ff. 147–52: Letter Whittingham to Marquess Wellesley, Gibraltar, 4 January 1810.

223 Whittingham to his brother-in-law, San Roque, 8 January 1810, in Whittingham (ed.), *A Memoir,* p. 121.

224 NA FO, 72/99, ff. 156–7: Whittingham to Marquess Wellesley, Gibraltar, 22 January 1810.

225 Fraser, *Napoleon's Cursed War,* p. 362.

226 AHN, *Estado* 3566, Caja 32: Report of Count de Tilly on proposal for Council of Regency, *circa* mid-late 1809 and AHN, *Estado* 2 B, Nr. 149 *Proyecto de creación de un Consejo de Regencia*: Reports of Riquelme and Tilly against project of concentration of power in a council, 10 October 1809.

227 *Acta de constitución del Consejo de Regencia,* 31 January 1810, in *Biblioteca Virtual Miguel de Cervantes* [www.cervantesvirtual.com/servlet/SirveObras/23584065433481630976891/p0000001.htm?marca=conde%20de%20Tilly#, accessed 29 March 2008].

228 NA FO, 72/99, ff. 166–67: Whittingham to Marquess Wellesley, Cadiz, 2 February 1810.

229 Ibid.

230 AHN, *Estado* 3566, Caja 2: Council of Regency's report on order of arrest of Count de Tilly, 23 February 1810.

231 Report of request addressed to the judge Conde de Pinar by Manuel de Santurio García Sala, legal representative of the family of the count de Tilly, in *El Redactor General*, 23 December 1811, pp. 753–4.

232 Robert Southey, *History of the Peninsular War* (6 vols., London, 1828), IV, p. 298; Toreno, *Historia del levantamiento*, II, p. 417; Moreno Alonso, *La Batalla*, p. 355; *idem, La Junta Suprema de Sevilla*, p. 53; Fraser, *Napoleon's Cursed War*, p. 363.

233 AGMS, V-43 *Expediente* Santiago Whittinghan (sic, for Samuel Ford Whittingham): Certificate signed by Juan Lozano de Torres, War Secretary, 5 February 1810, acknowledging receipt of Royal Order of 3 February conferring rank of *mariscal de campo* to Whittingham and of an order of the *Consejo de Regencia* approving Whittingham's plans for an academy in Mallorca, 28 November 1810. For more on this subject, see Chapter 6.

234 Fraser, *Napoleon's Cursed War*, pp. 390–432; Esdaile, *Fighting Napoleon*, pp. 52–60, 164–5; Tone, *The Fatal Knot,* pp. 93–126.

235 Thomas De Quincey to Mary Wordsworth, Wrington, 27 August 1810, in John Emory Jordan (ed.), *De Quincey to Wordsworth: A Biography of a Relationship* (Berkeley, 1962), pp. 258–9.

236 AGMS, R-1496 *Expediente* Felipe de la Roche (sic, for Roche): Order of *Consejo de Regencia*, signed by Minister José Heredia, 22 November 1810.

237 AGMS, Q-1 *Expediente* Felipe Qeating (sic, for Keating) Roche: *Diploma de Mariscal de Campo, Consejo de Regencia*, Isla de Leon, 31 December 1810.

238 Unsigned letter attributed to General Manuel Freyre, Lorca, 23 March 1811, and F. Roche to Freyre, Cartagena, 22 March 1811, both in Alamo, *Cartas inéditas*, pp. 5–10.

239 AGM, *Fondo de la Guerra de la Independencia, Legajo* 4, *Carpetas* 24–5, *Operaciones de Campaña*, f. 11: Antonio de la Cruz to General Blake, *circa* 17 September 1811.

240 Ibid f. 17: Joachin Blake to Antonio de la Cruz, Murvierzo, 19 September 1811.

241 Ibid.

242 AGMS, Q-1 *Expediente* Felipe Qeating Roche: *Diploma de Mariscal de Campo*, signed by Joachim Blake as head of the Second Council of Regency that followed Castaños's First Council of Regency, Isla de Leon, 31 December 1810;

AGM, *Fondo Blake, Caja* Nr. 7, Nr. 37 'Keating Roche': Draft Report of Joachim Blake, *Capitan General de los Reales Extos*, Madrid, 12 February 1815; Ibid., Report of Keating Roche, Valencia, 21 February 1815.

243   See, for example, correspondence with generals Freyre and Copons in Alamo, *Cartas inéditas*, pp. 1–14; AGM, *Fondo Blake, Caja* 7, Nr. 31: Henry Wellesley to Blake, Cadiz, 30 September 1810; CU, Add. 7521, ff. 306–07, 311–13, 324–5, 365–7, 371–3: Correspondence H. Wellesley-Roche, 1810–1816; NA WO, 1/1120, Miscellaneous: Correspondence H. Wellesly-Roche, 1810–1811; ASL, Vaughan Papers, E11/2, E/11.5, E/11.6 and C.118:5: Correspondence H. Wellesley-Roche, 1810–11.

244   He was replaced by General José San Juan, see *El Redactor General*, 27 February 1812, pp. 1011–2; María Luisa Alvarez y Cañas, 'El gobierno de la ciudad de Alicante en la crisis del Antiguo Regimen (1808–1814)', *Revista de historia moderna: Anales de la Universidad de Alicante*,8/9 (1988–90), p. 274.

245   AGMS, P-541 *Expediente* Guillermo Parker Carrol: Carrol to Spanish Minister of War, Miguel López Baños, 29 September 1822.

246   Downie congratulated the *Cortes* on their sitting, see *Diario de Sesiones,* III, p. 307; Doyle's regimental oath recorded on 30 May 1812, in Ibid., XIV, p. 333; Roche's, 1 January 1813, in Ibid., XVII, p. 26; Whittingham's, 14 August 1813, in Ibid., XXII, p. 240.

247   Esdaile, *The Peninsular War*, p. 281.

248   BOD North, c. 17, f. 182 and BL, Add. 15675, f. 53: '*Proclama a los Valencianos del General Doyle*', 3 December 1810.

249   BOD North, c. 16, f. 341: José Canga de Argüelles to Doyle, Cadiz, 13 July 1811; Gil Novales, *Diccionario del Trienio*, pp. 121–2.

250   AGMS, D-877 *Expediente* Carlos Guillermo Doile (sic): *Teniente General* Carlos Doyle to Spanish Minister of War, London, 21 December 1835.

251   AGMS, R-1365 *Expediente* Daniel Robinson.

252   Robinson's pseudonym was revealed in John Watkins, *A Biographical Dictionary of the Living Authors of Great Britain and Ireland, Comprising Literary Memoirs and Anecdotes of Their Lives* (London, 1816), p. 297.

253   [Daniel Robinson], *The Political Constitution of the Spanish Monarchy Proclaimed in Cadiz, 19 March 1812* (London, 1813), p. vii.

254   *Gaceta de Madrid*, 20 September 1822, p. 1379; Letter of Lieutenant-Colonel, Deputy Adjutant-General Spanish Staff Corps Daniel Robinson, London, 9 October 1823 to the Chairman and Members of the Spanish Committee in 'Cadiz', *The Morning Post*, 10 October 1823, p. 2; Return of the Officers of the

Royal Navy and Marines who are serving in the Army of the Queen of Spain, an in Receipt of the Half Pay, in 'Spain: arms and ammunitions', *The Morning Post*, 12 March 1836, p. 6.

255 Landor to Minister Cevallos, undated, *circa* 1814–16, quoted by Malcolm Elwin, *Landor: a replevin* (London, 1958), p. 119. Soon after returning from Spain, Landor published a small print run of correspondence he kept with a Spanish officer. Unfortunately, the only surviving copy of *Three Letters Written in Spain, to D. Francisco Riquelme, Commanding the Third Division of the Gallician Army* (Bath, 1809) has been mislaid. It was last mentioned in 1971, among the 18,000-book collection that Landor's biographer, the essayist and historian John Forster, bequeathed to the South Kensington Museum (now the National Art Library at the Victoria and Albert Museum). There is no record of the pamphlet in the National Art Library catalogue today, even when Thomas James Wise and Stephen Wheeler refered to it as being there registered with the number 5083 in their *A bibliography of the Writings in Prose and Verse of Walter Savage Landor* (Folkestone, 1971), pp. 33–4. Notwithstanding this loss, we know that the addressee of the letters was an officer of the Spanish navy who joined the army under General Joachim Blake, convinced that the scope for naval action had been diminished due to the reduction of the Spanish fleet after Trafalgar. Mortally wounded at the Battle of Espinosa de los Monteros, on 10 November 1808, Riquelme breathed his last – as Landor apparently relates in the preface of his publication – while being carried on board ship at Santander. We ignored why Riquelme was the recipient of Landor's views and the exact tenor of the poet's suggestions, but we do know that the pamphlet was organized in three parts: 'I – On the Means of supplying an adequate Force of Cavalry; II – A View of Parties in England, their Errors, and Designs, III – Our conduct at Ferrol, at Buenos Ayres, and at Cintra.' This information makes clear Landor's strong disapproval of British policy towards the Spanish world, but tells us very little of his views regarding the way the Spanish political landscape should have been shaped. Forster, who had access to the pamphlet and to Landor's complete correspondence, asserted that the poet was convinced that the best form of government for Spain was a 'federal republic adapted to the different *fueros* of the different kingdoms', see John Forster (ed.), *The Works and Life of Walter Savage Landor* (8 vols., London, 1876), I, p. 125. No evidence, however, has been found to confirm that this was a true reflection of Landor's opinion. See also Carlos Martínez-Valverde, *La Marina en la guerra de la Independencia* (Madrid, 1974), p. 46; Wise and Wheeler, *A Bibliography of the Writing*, pp. 33–4.

256 Whittingham (ed.), *A Memoir*, pp. 269–71.

257 Correspondence Francisco de Miranda and John Downie in Dávila (ed.),
     Archivo del General Miranda, XVIII, p. 78; Ibid., XXI, pp. 45–9, 55, 57, 59–61,
     69, 74, 76, 84–5, 113–14, 123–4, 127, 145, 157, 169–70, 183, 185, 195, 286, 288,
     290–4, 329, 337, 341, 346, 350, 357, 359; Memorial of Captain William Parker
     Carrol 'late British Hostage at Buenos Aires' to General Francisco de Miranda,
     London, 16 January 1808, in Ibid., XXI, pp. 158–64.

258 Landor to Southey, Clifton, August 1809, in Forster, *A Biography*, I, p. 146.

Chapter 5

1 Fernand Braudel, *On History* (Chicago, 1982), p. 10.

2 Donna T. Andrew, 'The code of honour and its critics: the opposition to duelling
   in England, 1700–1850', *Social History*, 5/3 (1980), p. 413.

3 The term 'Romanticism', the meaning of which remains much contested in
   historiography, refers here to the predominant culture of the period, see Murray
   Pittock, *Scottish and Irish Romanticism* (Oxford, 2008), pp. 1–28, 235; Roe,
   Romanticism, p. 10.

4 Pittock, *Scottish and Irish Romanticism*, pp. 59–76; Roe, *Romanticism*, pp.
   10, 40, 51–2, 63, 115, 129, 135, 165–81, 173–4, 575, 643–4, 665, 667; Butler,
   'Romanticism in England', pp. 44–5; Peter Womack, *Improvement and Romance –
   Constructing the Myth of the Highlands* (Basingstoke, 1989), pp. 20–4.

5 Good examples are provided by *The honour and advantage of agriculture. Being
   the twelfth discourse of the eighth volume of Feijoo's works, translated from the
   Spanish By a farmer in Cheshire* (London, 1760), and John Bowle, A letter to
   the Reverend Dr. Percy, concerning a new and classical edition of Historia del
   valeroso cavallero Don Quixote de la Mancha (London, 1777); see also David
   Howarth, The invention of Spain - Cultural relations between Britain and
   Spain 1770–1870 (Manchester, 2007), pp. 5–7.

6 Bruce Lenman, 'From Savage to Scot' via the French and the Spaniards:
   Principal Robertson's Spanish Sources', in Stewart J. Brown (ed.), *William
   Robertson and the Expansion of Empire* (Cambridge, 1997), p. 201; Richard B.
   Sher, 'Charles V and the book trade: an episode in Enlightenment print culture',
   in Ibid., p. 164; Howarth, *The invention of Spain*, pp. 5–7.

7 William Robertson, *The History of the Reign of the Emperor Charles V
   with a view of the progress of society in Europe, from the subversion of the*

Roman Empire, to the beginning of the sixteenth century (New York, 1836),
p. 5; Stewart J. Brown, 'William Robertson (1721–93) and the Scottish
Enlightenment', in *idem* (ed.), *William Robertson and the Expansion*, pp. 28–9;
Owen Dudley Edwards, 'Robertsonian Romanticism and realism', in Ibid.,
p. 116.

8 Lynda Pratt, 'Epic', in Roe, *Romanticism*, pp. 336–7; for an example of
eighteenth-century British citation of *El Cid*, see Eobald Toze, *The present state
of Europe: exhibiting a view of the natural and civil history of the Several countries
and kingdoms* (3 vols., London, 1770), p. 254. I am grateful to Profs W. A. Speck,
Lynda Pratt and particularly to Prof Diego Saglia for their guidance on assessing
the impact of *El Cid* in British culture in the long eighteenth century.

9 The term 'Quixotism', for example, was first recorded in the English language
in 1688, see Charles Talbut Onions (ed.), *The Shorter Oxford English Dictionary
on Historical Principles* (5 vols., Oxford, 1933), III, p. 1644.

10 Cyril Albert Jones, 'Spanish Honour As Historical Phenomenon: Convention
and Artistic Motive', *Hispanic Review*, 33 (1965), p. 38; Saglia, 'O My Mother
Spain!', pp. 363–93.

11 AGMS, D-1177 *Expediente* Juan Downie: Col. Juan Downie to unknown, Cadiz,
26 August 1812.

12 James Chandler, 'Moving Accidents: the Emergence of Sentimental Probability',
in Colin Jones and Dror Wahrman (eds.), *The Age of Cultural Revolutions:
Britain and France, 1750–1820* (London, 2002), pp. 137–8.

13 John George Peristiany and Julian Pitt-Rivers (eds.), *Honour and Grace in
Anthropology* (Cambridge, 1994), p. 4; see also Hans Speier, 'Honour and the
Social Structure', in *idem*, *Social Order and the Risks of War: Papers in Political
Sociology* (Cambridge, MA, 1952), pp. 36–52; and Ingrid Tague and Helen
Berry, 'Summary of Closing Plenary Discussion on "Honour and Reputation in
Early Modern England"', *Transactions of the Royal Historical Society*, 6 (1996),
pp. 247–8.

14 Langford, *A polite*, pp. 59–65, 463–93; Jonathan C. D. Clark, *English Society,
1660–1832: Religion, Ideology and Politics during the Ancien Regime* (Cambridge,
2000), pp. 200–12; John Greville Agard Pocock, *Virtue, Commerce, and History*
(Cambridge, 1985), pp. 113–15.

15 Good examples are Victor Gordon Kiernan, *The Duel in European History –
Honour and the Reign of Aristocracy* (Oxford, 1989) and James N. McCord, Jr.,
'Politics and Honour in Early-Nineteenth-Century England: The Dukes' Duel',
The Huntington Library Quarterly, 62, 1/2 (1999), pp. 88–114.

16 Stephen Banks, *A Polite Exchange of Bullets: The Duel and the English Gentleman 1750–1850* (Woodbridge, 2010), pp. 5–9, 26.

17 Andrew, 'The code of honour and its critics: the opposition to duelling in England, 1700–1850'; Banks, *A Polite Exchange of Bullets: The Duel and the English Gentleman 1750–1850*.

18 Banks, *A Polite Exchange of Bullets*, pp. 81–2.

19 Andrew, 'The code of honour', pp. 413–14.

20 Bartolomé Bennassar, *The Spanish Character: Attitudes and Mentalities from the Sixteenth to the Nineteenth Century* (Berkeley, 1979), p. 213; Julio Caro Baroja, *El mito del caracter nacional: meditaciones a contrapelo* (Madrid, 1970), pp. 86–91; Renato Barahona, *Sex Crimes, Honour, and the Law in Early Modern Spain: Vizcaya, 1528–1735* (Toronto, 2003), p. 120; Douglass, '*Toro muerto, vaca es*', p. 242.

21 'El honor', *El Redactor General*, 4 July 1811, p. 1.

22 Félix Arturo Lope de Vega Carpio, *Los Comendadores de Córdoba*, in idem, *Segunda parte de las comedias de Lope de Vega Carpio: que contiene otras doze, cuyos nombres van en la hoja segunda* (Barcelona, 1611), p. 3; James Mandrell, *Don Juan and the Point of Honour: Seduction, Patriarchal Society, and Literary Tradition* (Pennsylvania, 1992), pp. 57–8.

23 In the fifteenth century, the poet Jorge Manrique ranked honour above life since he marked out three states of existence for every human being: temporal life, which ends with the death of the body; the life of the reputation, longer and more glorious than physical life; and, finally, eternal life, see Bennassar, *The Spanish Character*, p. 213; Barahona, *Sex Crimes, Honour, Law*, p. 120.

24 Issues of 'blood purity' were also in play, particularly in Latin America, see Ramón A. Gutiérrez, 'Honour, Ideology, Marriage Negotiation, and Class-Gender Domination in New Mexico, 1690–1846', *Latin American Perspectives*, 12/1 (1985), p. 86.

25 Agesta, *Pensamiento del despotismo ilustrado*, pp. 146–7; Antonio Xavier Pérez y López, *Discurso sobre la honra y deshonra legal en que se manifiesta el verdadero mérito de la Nobleza de sangre, y se prueba que todos los oficios necesarios, y útiles al Estado son honrados por las Leyes del Reyno, según las quales solamente el delito propio difama* (Madrid, 1781).

26 Christopher Duffy, *The Military Experience in the Age of Reason* (London, 1987), p. 54.

27 Alvaro Navia Ossorio, Marquess de Santa Cruz de Marcenado, *Reflexiones militares del mariscal de Campo D. Vizconde del Puerto o Marques de Santa Cruz de Marcenado* (Turin, 1724), p. 415.

28 Esdaile, *The Spanish army,* p. 23.

29 Clemente Peñalosa y Zuñiga, *El honor militar, causas de su orígen, progresos y decadencia; O Correspondencia de dos hermanos desde el Exército de Cataluña de S.M.C.* (2 vols., Madrid, 1795–96), I, p. i.

30 Elwin, *A Replevin,* p. 119; Thomas James Wise and Stephen Wheeler, *A Bibliography of the Writings in Prose and Verse of Walter Savage Landor* (Folkestone, 1971), pp. 33–4.

31 Forster (ed.), *The Works and Life,* I, pp. 119–20; *The Aberdeen Journal,* 12 October 1808, p. 2.

32 Ibid.; ASL, Vaughan Papers, C: Landor to Vaughan, Villafranca, 15 September 1808.

33 Landor to Southey, undated, *circa* late 1808, quoted by Forster (ed.), *The Works and Life,* I, pp. 119–20.

34 Ibid., p. 120.

35 Elwin, *A Replevin,* p. 119; Wise and Wheeler, *A Bibliography of the Writings,* pp. 33–4.

36 Southey, who was writing his own version of the legend, told Landor that he felt as a disadvantage because Landor had been able to draw from his experiences in wartime Spain, see Forster (ed.), *The Works and Life,* I, p. 120.

37 Walter Savage Landor, *Count Julian: A Tragedy* in Wheeler, *The Poetical Works,* I, p. 174.

38 Ibid., pp. 161–2.

39 Artola, *Los afrancesados,* pp. 236–8.

40 Landor to Southey, Clifton, November 1809, in Forster, *A Biography,* I, p. 146.

41 Ibid.; Diego Saglia, *Poetic castles in Spain: British romanticism and figurations of Iberia* (Amsterdam, 2000), p. 156.

42 *Count Julian,* in Wheeler, *The Poetical Works,* I, pp. 176–88.

43 Forster (ed.), *The Works and Life,* I, p. 119.

44 Banks, *A Polite Exchange of Bullets,* p. 26.

45 ASL, Vaughan Papers, C, reel 6, *Copy of a Letter from Mr. Landor to Mr. Vaughan, Private Secretary to Mr. Stewart, Envoy at Corunna,* undated, *circa* late 1808.

46 Ibid.

47 Charles Stuart to Landor, Aranjuez, 14 November 1808, in Forster, *A Biography,* I, p. 156.

48 [Walter Savage Landor], *Count Julian: A Tragedy* (London, 1812); Thomas James Wise (ed.), *A Landor Library – A Catalogue of Printed Books, Manuscripts and Autograph Letters by Walter Savage Landor* (London, 1928), p. xvi.

49 Ibid.; Marchand, *Byron's Letters,* III, p. 36.

50 Wise (ed.), *A Landor Library*, p. xvi.

51 Robert Southey, *History of the Peninsular War* (3 vols., London, 1823). In 1814, Southey published his own version of the story of Count Julian, *Roderick, the Last of the Goths,* narrating the story also in reference to the French invasion of Spain in 1808, see Saglia, 'O My Mother Spain!', p. 370.

52 Landor made numerous references to Spain, for example, in his *Imaginary Conversations*, produced between 1821 and 1846, including those of 'General Lacy and Cura Merino', 'Lopez Baños and Romero Alpuente', 'Don Victor Saez and El Rey Netto' (sic, *El Rey Neto,* meaning 'the King pure and simple', the term shouted by partisans of Ferdinand VII in the risings of 1823), 'Odysseus, Tersitza, Acrive, and Trelawny' and 'Don Ferdinand and Don John-Mary-Luis' (for Ferdinand VII and the Portuguese King Joao VI), see Landor, *The works*, I, pp. 138–45, 211–17, 260–64, 397, 422–42.

53 Elwin, *A Replevin*, p. 218; Wheeler, *The Poetical Works*, I, p. iv; Inga Bryden, *The Pre-Raphaelites: Writings and Sources* (2 vols., London, 1998), II, p. 226.

54 Edmond Temple, *capitán* of the *Legión de Extremadura*, became a published author during the war. His semi-biographical satire of learned poetry and essays, *The Life of Pill Garlick; Rather a Whimsical Sort of Fellow*, was published in London in 1813. His *Travels in Various Parts of Peru, including a Year's Residence in Potosi* (2 vols., London, 1830) would become a classic of travel writing, see Jennifer Speake, *Literature of Travel and Exploration: An Encyclopedia* (3 vols., London, 2003), I, p. 24.

55 Ivy Lilian McClelland, *The Origins of the Romantic Movement in Spain: A Survey of Aesthetic Uncertainties in the Age of Reason* (2nd ed, Liverpool, 1975), *passim*; Jorge Campos, *Teatro y sociedad en España 1780–1820* (Madrid, 1969), pp. 158–75; Herr, *The Eighteenth-Century,* pp. 261–4.

56 Francisco Martinez Marina, *Ensayo histórico-crítico sobre la legislación y principales cuerpos legales de los reinos de León y Castilla especialmente sobre el código de las Siete Partidas de D. Alonso el Sabio* (Madrid, 1808); [Francisco Martinez Marina], *Carta sobre la antigua costumbre de convocar las Cortes de Castilla para resolver los negocios graves del Reino* (London, 1810) available at Biblioteca Virtual Miguel de Cervantes [http://www.cervantesvirtual.com/FichaObra.html?Ref=10589, accessed 20 May 2009].

57 Brian R. Hamnett, 'Constitutional Theory and Political Reality: Liberalism, Traditionalism and the Spanish Cortes, 1810–1814', *The Journal of Modern History*, 49/1 On Demand Supplement (March 1977), pp. D-1073, D-1075–D-1076.

58 'Numantia' and 'Sagunto', in John Roberts (ed.) *Oxford Dictionary of the Classical World* (Oxford, 2007), *Oxford Reference Online* [http://www.oxfordreference.

com/views/ENTRY.html?subview=Main&entry=t180.e1519, accessed 20 May 2009].

59 BL, Add. 37288, ff. 119–20: Rudolf Marshal to James Duff, consul in Cadiz, Gerona, 30 August 1809.

60 BL, Add. 49491, ff. 116: 'Asturianos – Proclama del teniente coronel Guillermo Parker Carrol', enclosed in letter Carrol to Gordon, Oviedo, 2 February 1809, also available in NA WO, 1/241, ff. 357–9.

61 NA FO, 72/99, ff. 266–7: John Downie to Marquess de la Romana, Almendralejo, 21 January 1810; Barrie, *Biografía del mariscal*, p. 4.

62 Ludovici, *On the road with Wellington,* pp. 180–1. According to Schaumann, a colleague of Downie in the British Commissariat, it was the successful interrogation of two prisoners captured by Downie in one of these expeditions that brought to the then Sir Arthur Wellesley the first news that he was about to be attacked at Talavera. I am grateful to Prof Charles Esdaile for drawing my attention to Schaumann's memoirs mentioned in his conference paper 'Guerrillas, Bandits, Adventurers and Commissaries: the Story of John Downie' presented at the 'Wellington Congress 2006', University of Southampton, 10–13 July 2006, later published in Chris M. Woolgar (ed.), *Wellington Studies IV* (Southampton, 2008), pp. 94–125; Downie's role regarding Talavera was also cited in a biography of Downie published by *The Royal Military Chronicle or British Officer's Monthly Register and Mentor*, July 1813, p. 173.

63 Downie's involvement with the Spanish *guerrillas* prior to joining the Spanish regular army was mentioned by the Marquess de la Romana in a letter to the Regency, Badajoz, 23 June 1810 (AGMS, D-1177 *Expediente* Juan Downie) and by Francisco Fernández Golfin, *coronel* in the Army of the Left and deputy for Extremadura in the *Cortes* at Cadiz, see *Diario de sesiones*, III, p. 308.

64 Proclamation of the *Junta Suprema de Extremadura*, 20 April 1809, in Gómez Villafranca (ed.), *Extremadura en la Guerra*, pp. 184–5.

65 Martin de Garay to *Junta Suprema de Extremadura*, Seville, 26 April 1809, in Gómez Villafranca, *Extremadura en la Guerra,* pp. 185–6. Manuel Jiménez Guazo, a civil servant at the *Junta Central*, raised a crusade in Seville, which he later regrouped in Cadiz to defend the hills of Ronda. Wounded in action, his deeds helped him to be elected for a seat in the *Cortes* as representative of Granada, see Manuel Gómez Imaz, *Los periódicos durante la Guerra de la independencia, 1808–1814* (Madrid, 1910), p. 113.

66 Robert Semple, *A Second Journey in Spain in the Spring of 1809* (London, 1st edition, 1809), p. 71; Downie's earlier visit to Seville was reported by the *Gazeta de la Regencia de España y de las Indias*, 17 January 1811, p. 64 and mentioned

by Downie himself in NA FO, 72/99, ff. 262–80: Downie to Secretary of the *Junta Central*, Francisco Saavedra, 20 January 1810.

67 AGMS, D-1177 *Expediente* Juan Downie: Canon Gavino Rodriguez, *Junta Suprema de Extremadura*, to Juan Downie, Badajoz, 10 March 1810 conferring Downie the rank of *coronel* under the Marquess de La Romana; AGM, *Fondo Blake*, Microfiche 2, *Caja* 2, ff. 26–2: Copy of order by Eusebio de Bardaxi, *Inspector General* of the Spanish Army to Marquess de la Romana confirming Downie's rank in the Spanish army, Cadiz, 22 July 1810.

68 AGMS, D-1177 *Expediente* Juan Downie: *Prospecto Plan de la Leal Legión de Extremadura*.

69 A translated version of the original proclamation published by *The Royal Military Chronicle or British Officer's Monthly Register and Mentor*, July 1813, pp. 180–1. The original in Spanish, 28 July 1810, is available at BNE, R/63251 and at NA WO, 1/1123, 'Miscellaneous', f. 515.

70 'Habitantes de Extremadura, ilustres descendientes de Pizarros y Cortes', proclamation of Francisco de Theran, Royal Commissionary of the province of Extremadura, Zafra, 7 January 1811 and 'Hijos valientes de Cortes y Pizarro: venganza y guerra', proclamation of the Council of Regency, Cadiz, no day, February 1812, both texts in Gómez Villafranca (ed.), *Extremadura en la Guerra*, pp. 376–8, 411–12, respectively.

71 I am grateful to Imke Heuer (University of York) for drawing this fact to my attention. More on this subject in Frederick Burwick, 'Gateway to Heterotopia: Elsewhere on Stage', in Jeffrey Cass and Larry H. Peer (eds.), *Romantic Border Crossings* (Ashgate, 2008), pp. 33–5; Michael Scrivener, *Seditious Allegories: John Thelwall and Jacobin Writing* (Pennsylvania, 2008), p. 239.

72 George Landmann, *Recollections of My military life by Colonel Landmann, Late of the Corps or Royal Engineers, author of 'Adventures and Recollections', &c.* (2 vols., London, 1854), I, p. 86.

73 NA WO, 6/206 and NA WO, 1/1120, 'Miscellaneous': Correspondence Downie with several officials at the War Department, 1810; NA FO, 72/99, ff. 266–80: Correspondence Downie with Marquess of Wellesley and others, 1810; NA WO, 1/1123, 'Miscellaneous': Correspondence Downie with several officials at the War Deparment, 1811; NA WO, 1/1126, 'Miscellaneous': *idem*, 1812; NA WO, 6/166: Copy Correspondence Downie with Secretary of State War Office, 1810–1814.

74 NA FO, 72/99, f. 278: Copy letter William Hamilton to Col. Downie, Foreign Office, 26 September 1810; AGMS, D-1177 *Expediente* Juan Downie: Secretary

of the *Junta Central* Bardaxi to Spanish Secretary of War Heredia, Isla de Leon, 6 November 1810.

75 Wellington to Earl of Liverpool, Cartaxo, 15 December 1810, in John Gurwood (ed.), *The Dispatches of Field Marshall the Duke of Wellington during His Various Campaigns in India, Denmark, Portugal, Spain, the Low Countries, and France from 1799-1818* (13 vols., London, 1837), VII, pp. 42–3; Wellington to Liverpool, Cartaxo, 28 January 1810, in Ibid., VII, pp. 198–9; Wellington to Beresford, 21 October 1811, Cartaxo, 29 January 1811, Ibid., VIII, pp. 199–200.

76 Four-thousand stands of arms and their corresponding equipment were dispatched to Downie in January 1811. Eight months later, Wellington authorized access to 200 sets of accoutrements to both General Castaños and Downie, see Wellington to Liverpool, Cartaxo, 12 January 1811, in Gurwood (ed.), *The Dispatches*, VII, p. 129; Wellington to R. H. Kennedy, Fuente Guinaldo, 21 August 1811, Arthur Richard Wellesley, Second Duke of Wellington (ed.), *Supplementary Despatches and Memoranda of Field Marshal Arthur, Duke of Wellington, K.G* (15 vols., London, 1858–60), p. 206.

77 Juan Downie to President of *Junta* of Extremadura, Valencia de Alcántara, 12 July 1811, in Gómez Villafranca (ed.), *Extremadura en la Guerra*, p. 392; NA WO, 1/1123, ff. 813–15: Charles Downie to Lord Liverpool, 28 October 1811; NA WO, 1/1120, 'Miscellaneous', ff. 605–7: Downie to Col. Bunbury, War Office, 6 November 1810; Ibid., ff. 633–7: Downie to Col. Bunbury, 17 November 1810; NA WO, 1/1126, ff. 349–52: Charles Downie, to the Earl of Liverpool, 1 April 1812; AGMS, D-1176, *Expediente* Carlos Downie: Juan Downie to Spanish Secretary of War, 3 August 1819 and Report of services of Carlos Downie, 25 July 1828; Barrie, *Biografía del mariscal*, pp. 4, 8; Wilson, *Private diary*, p. 17.

78 See [Sinclair, Sir John], *Particulars regarding The Merino Sheep imported by Charles Downie, Esq., of Paisley in Scotland: in answer to certain Queries transmitted by Sir John Sinclair, to the Spanish Shepherds who have the Charge of them from the Communications to the Board of Agriculture* (London, 1810), p. 1; AGMS, D-1176 Expediente Carlos Downie; Wellington to Liverpool, 5 January 1811, in Gurwood (ed.), The Dispatches, VII, p. 104.

79 *Diario de las Cortes*, III, session of 9 February 1811, p. 308.

80 Ibid.; Gil Novales, *Diccionario del Trienio*, p. 229.

81 'Francisco Fernández Golfin', in Mikel Urquijo Goitia (ed.), *Diccionario Biográfico de Parlamentarios Españoles – Cortes de Cadiz. 1810–1814* (3 vols., Madrid, 2010), I, pp. 781–93; Irene Castells, 'Le libéralisme insurrectionnel espagnol (1814–1830)', *Annales historiques de la Révolution française*, 336/1

(2004), p. 226. The Romantic painter Antonio Gisbert depicted Golfín's tragic
death, as the old man blindfolded before a firing squad on a desolate Spanish
beach in 1831, in his famous oil-on-canvas *Fusilamiento de Torrijos y sus
compañeros en las playas de Málaga* (1888).

82 *Diario de las Cortes*, III, p. 308; for Pérez de Castro's political sympathies, see
    Gil Novales, *Diccionario del Trienio*, p. 518, and 'Evaristo Pérez de Castro', in
    Urquijo Goitia (ed.), *Diccionario Biográfico de Parlamentarios Españoles*, I,
    pp. 173–83; for Castelló's, see Juan Ignacio Marcuello Benedicto, 'Las Cortes
    Generales y Extraordinarias: la organización y poderes para un gobierno de
    Asamblea', in Miguel Artola (ed.), *Las Cortes de Cádiz* (Madrid, 2003), p. 86, and
    'José Joaquín Castelló y Ferré', in Urquijo Goitia (ed.), *Diccionario Biográfico de
    Parlamentarios Españoles*, I, pp. 508–13.

83 For Vera y Pantoja's political affiliation, see Evaristo San Miguel, *Vida de Agustín
    Argüelles* (4 vols., Madrid, 1851), I, pp. 291–2, and 'Alonso María de la Vera
    y Pantoja', in Urquijo Goitia (ed.), *Diccionario Biográfico de Parlamentarios
    Españoles*, I, pp. 725–8.

84 Brian R. Hamnett, 'Joaquín Lorenzo Villanueva (1757–1837): de «católico
    ilustrado» a «católico liberal». El dilema de la transición', in Guy Thomson and
    Alda Blanco (eds.), *Visiones del liberalismo: política, identidad y cultura en la
    España del siglo XIX* (Valencia, 2008), pp. 19–42; Joaquín Lorenzo Villanueva,
    Mi viaje a las Cortes (4 vols., Madrid, 1860), *passim*.

85 Antonio Ramos Argüelles, *Agustín Argüelles (1776–1844): 'Padre del
    constitucionalismo español'* (2 vols., Madrid, 1991), *passim*; Gil Novales,
    Diccionario del Trienio, p. 48.

86 *Diario de las Cortes*, III, p. 308.

87 Ibid.; AGMS, D-1177 *Expediente* Juan Downie: Letter of Secretary of the *Cortes*
    Josef Aznarez to Juan Downie, 16 February 1811.

88 AGMS, D-1177 *Expediente* Juan Downie: Castaños to Secretary of War José de
    Heredia, Valencia, 19 August 1811.

89 Ibid.

90 Fraser, *Napoleon's Cursed War*, p. 251.

91 AGMS, D-1177 *Expediente* Juan Downie: Downie to the *Cortes*, Elvas, 10 and 11
    February 1811.

92 AGM, *Fondo Blake*, Microfiche 2, *Caja* 2, Nr. 26: *Plan de la Leal Legión
    Extremeña*.

93 NA WO, 1/1123, 'Miscellaneous', f. 517: Proclamation '¡Extremeños!
    ¡Españoles!', Badajoz, 1 January 1811 (also available at BNE, R/63251); NA WO,

1/1123, f. 519: Proclamation of Juan Downie addressed to Spaniards in occupied areas, Valencia de Alcantara, 14 February 1811; Ibid., f. 521: Proclamation addressed to *jefes de Partidas Manchegas*, Valencia de Alcantara, same date.

94 NA WO, 1/1123, f. 519: Proclamation, Valencia de Alcantara, 14 February 1811, and Ibid., f. 521: Proclamation to *guerrillas* in La Mancha, same date.

95 NA WO, 1/1123, f. 523: Proclamation of Martin la Carrera, *Jefe de Estado Mayor del Quinto Exército*, Badajoz, 13 February 1811.

96 AGMS, D-1177 *Expediente* Juan Downie: Castaños to Secretary of War José de Heredia, Valencia, 19 August 1811.

97 Report of Don Jose María de Carvajal, Secretary of War, Cadiz, 28 October 1813, published by *The Royal Military Chronicle or British Officers Monthly Register and Mentor*, July 1813, pp. 175–8.

98 AGMS, D-1177 *Expediente* Juan Downie: Downie to the *Cortes*, Elvas, 10 and 11 February 1811.

99 Benito Pérez Galdós, 'Cádiz', in *idem*, *Episodios Nacionales* (Primera Serie, Madrid, 1878), p. 52.

100 James Clayburn La Force, 'The Supply of Muskets and Spain's War of Independence', *The Business History Review*, 43 (1969), pp. 523–44.

101 'I have decided that part of my Legion's cavalry will be fitted out with lances, having been Your Excellency the first one to give me the idea of [using] the lance. . .', see Downie to Miranda, 4 June 1810, in Dávila (ed.), *Archivo del General Miranda*, XXIII, p. 456.

102 NA WO, 1/1123, f. 519: Proclamation Col. Juan Downie addressed to Spaniards in occupied areas, Valencia de Alcantara, 14 February 1811; Ibid., f. 521: Proclamation addressed to *jefes de Partidas Manchegas*, Valencia de Alcantara, same date.

103 Julian Sturgis (ed.), *A Boy in the Peninsular War: The Services, Adventures, and Experiences of Robert Blakeney, Subaltern in the 28 Regiment: An Autobiography* (London, 1899), p. 226. Blakeney's view of Downie and his legion has been embraced by Charles Esdaile for whom the Scot was nothing but a 'fantasist', a 'braggard and 'a fraud', see 'Prohombres, aventureros y oportunistas: la influencia del trayecto personal en los orígenes del liberalismo en España', in Thomson and Blanco, *Visiones del liberalismo*, pp. 76–85; *idem,* 'Guerrilas, bandits, adventurers and commissaries: the story of John Downie', in Woolgar, Chris M. (ed.), *Wellington Studies IV* (Southampton, 2008), pp. 94–125; *idem*, 'Guerrilleros, bandidos, aventureros y comisarios: la historia de Juan Downie,' *Alcores*, 5 (2088), pp. 109–32.

104   Sturgis (ed.), *A Boy in the Peninsular War,* pp. xii, 364.

105   Report of Isidoro Mir, officer of the 5th Army, to General Auditor of the Spanish
       War Department, Benito sobre Medellin, 7 March 1811, in Gómez Villafranca
       (ed.), *Extremadura en la guerra,* pp. 366–7.

106   *El Conciso*, 23 June 1811, pp. 3–4.

107   *Gazeta de la Regencia de España e Indias*, 12 September 1811, p. 944; AGMS,
       D-1177 *Expediente* Juan Downie: Report of Don Jose María de Carvajal,
       Secretary of War, Cadiz, 28 October 1813, published by *The Royal Military
       Chronicle or British Officers Monthly Register and Mentor*, July 1813, pp. 175–8.

108   AGMS, D-1177 *Expediente* Juan Downie: Report and Certificate of Services of
       Juan Downie by Spanish Secretary of War Juan O'Donojú, Cadiz, 16 August
       1813 and by *Estado Mayor de los Reales Exércitos*, Madrid, 19 June 1818; Letter
       Rolland Hill to his sister, Portalegre, 5 November 1811, in Edwin Sidney,
       The Life of Lord Hill, G. C. B., Late Commander of the Forces (London, 1845),
       pp. 171–2.

109   Hill's report to the *Consejo de Regencia* was reproduced in Spanish by *El
       Redactor General*, 22 November 1811, p. 625; AGMS, T-314 *Expediente*
       Edmundo Temple.

110   Dispatch of Lieutenant-General Hill to General Viscount Wellington, Merida,
       30 October 1811, in Gurwood (ed.), *The Dispatches*, VIII, pp. 380–4.

111   Hill's report in *El Redactor General*, 22 November 1811, p. 625; AGMS, T-314
       Expediente Edmundo Temple.

112   AGMS, D-1177 *Expediente* Juan Downie: Certificate of rank of *brigadier*
       awarded on 10 April 1812; Ibid., Report and Certificate of services of Juan
       Downie by Secretary of War Juan O'Donojú, Cadiz, 16 August 1813 and by
       Estado Mayor de los Reales Exércitos, Madrid, 19 June 1818; José Luis Isabel
       Sánchez (ed.), *Caballeros de la Real y Militar Orden de San Fernando (Infantería)*
       (5 vols., Madrid, 2001), I, pp. 25–35.

113   AHN, *Estado* 7368, Nr. 76: Extract Decree of Order of Charles III granted to
       Juan Downie, Cadiz, 18 October 1812.

114   AGMS, D-1177 *Expediente* Juan Downie: Report and Certificate of services of
       Juan Downie by Secretary of War Juan O'Donojú, Cadiz, 16 August 1813 and by
       Estado Mayor de los Reales Exércitos, Madrid, 19 June 1818.

115   Cristobal de Beña, *La lyra de la libertad* (London, 1813), pp. 61–4, in *Biblioteca
       Virtual Miguel de Cervantes* [http://www.cervantesvirtual.com/FichaObra.html?
       Ref=1364, accessed 9 February 2006].

116   Isidoro Montiel, *Ossian en España* (Barcelona, 1974), pp. 1–30.

117   Beña, *La lyra de la libertad,* pp. 23–4.

118 AGMS, D-1177 *Expediente* Juan Downie: Letter Juan Downie to Secretary of War regarding Beña's rank of *capitán* and his appointment as Downie's military secretary, 20 August 1811; Adolfo de Castro, *Cádiz en la Guerra de la Independencia – Cuadro histórico* (Cadiz, 1864), pp. 155–60; Montiel, *Ossian*, pp. 111–17.

119 Beña, *La lyra de la libertad* (London, 1813).

120 Rivas saw action in the war, but not under the Legion's colours, see Jorge Campos, 'El Duque de Rivas y el romanticismo español' in *idem* (ed.), *Obras completas del Duque de Rivas* (3 vols., Madrid, 1957), I, pp. vii–xlix; Leonardo Romero, *Panorama crítico del romanticismo español* (Madrid, 1994), p. 36.

121 Campos (ed.), *Obras Duque de Rivas,* I, p. 17.

122 *Aberdeen Journal*, 14 April 1813, p. 2; Ibid., 12 and 19 May 1813, p. 2; Ibid., 9 June 1813, p. 2.

123 *Caledonian Mercury,* 29 May 1813, p. 4.

124 *The Royal Military Chronicle, or British Officers Monthly Register and Mentor*, July 1813, p. 178.

125 *The London Gazette*, 18 May 1813, p. 966.

126 He joined instead Whittingham's division at Mallorca, under pressure from his uncle, British volunteer Patrick Campbell, who was Whittingham's second in command, NA WO, 1/1123, ff. 315–16: Patrick Campbell to Lord Liverpool, 7 May 1811.

127 AGMS, E-1596 *Expediente* Roberto Steele: Steele to Ministry of War, Madrid, 14 June 1814.

128 José María Marchesi, *Catálogo de la Real Armería* (Madrid, 1849), pp. 99–100; Castro, *Cádiz en la Guerra*, pp. 155–60.

129 Edmond Temple, *The Life of Pill Garlick; Rather a Whimsical Sort of Fellow* (Dublin. and London, 1813). It remains unclear whether the publications of this book coincided or not with Downie's visit (May–June 1813).

130 Temple, *The Life of Pill Garlick*, pp. 319–21.

131 AGMS, D-1177 *Expediente* Juan Downie: Report and Certificate of Services of Juan Downie by Secretary of War Juan O'Donojú, Cadiz, 16 August 1813 and Report of *Estado Mayor de los Reales Exércitos*, Madrid, 19 June 1818; Thomas Bunbury, *Reminiscences of a Veteran: Being Personal and Military Adventures in Portugal, Spain, France, Malta, New South Wales, Norfolk Island, New Zealand, Andaman Islands, and India* (London, 1861), pp. 141–2.

132 Lieutenant Coronel Augustus Simon Fraze to his family, Letter XCIX, Vera, 18 October 1813 and Letter CII, Vera, 1 November 1813, in Major-General Edward Sabine (ed.), *Letters of Colonel Sir Augustus Simon Frazer, K.C.B., commanding*

the Royal Horse Artillery in the Army under the Duke of Wellington Written during the Peninsular and Waterloo Campaigns (London, 1859), pp. 316–17, 328.

133 Ibid., Letter XCIX, p. 316.

134 AGMS, D-1177 *Expediente* Juan Downie: Report of Pedro Diaz de Rivera, Assistant Secretary of War, Madrid, 9 June 1814. Downie made his short trip to Britain while negotiations on his exchange were being held because he was prevented from taking the field again until an agreement was reached.

135 Sabine, *Letters of Colonel Frazer,* pp. 316–17.

136 Andrew, 'The code of honour', pp. 416–17; McCord, 'Politics and Honour', pp. 90–1.

137 Andrew, 'The code of honour', pp. 415, 434; Andújar Castillo, *Los Militares*, pp. 413–15; Bennassar, *The Spanish Character*, pp. 213–14.

138 Andújar Castillo, *Los Militares*, pp. 413–15; Bennassar, *The Spanish Character*, pp. 213–14.

139 ASL, Vaughan Papers, uncatalogued, reel 13: Report of session of the Spanish *Cortes*, 3 May 1812; for more on the subject of national identity, see Chapter 7.

140 John Lawrence Tone, 'El pueblo de las guerrillas', in Joaquín Alvarez Barrientos (ed.), *La guerra de la independencia en la cultura española (*Madrid, 2008), pp. 58–9.

141 Milburne, *A narrative of circumstances*, p. 110.

142 NA FO, 72/99, ff. 198–204: Carrol to Marquess Wellesley, Badajoz, no day, March 1810.

143 AB, MS 3175/1412/1 Whittingham to Earl of Fife, Palma, 13 September 1811.

144 Charles Richard Vaughan, *Narrative of the siege of Zaragoza* (London, 1809). For the impact of Vaughan's account, see Saglia, *Poetic castles*, pp. 195–7.

145 ASL, Vaughan Papers, D 11/11: Charles Vaughan to Dr. Vaughan, Madrid, 8 October 1808; BL, Add. 37888 ff. 77–83: Memorial of Charles Vaughan to undisclosed, London, 29 December 1808.

146 Vaughan, *Narrative*, p. 16; Doyle's admiration for Agustina had other far-reaching implications, see Chapter 6.

147 Vaughan, *Narrative*, p. 27.

148 Ibid., p. 4.

149 Ibid., p. 24.

150 Christopher D. Hall, *British Strategy in the Napoleonic War 1803–1815* (Manchester, 1992), pp. 62–3.

151 Vaughan, *Narrative*, p. iv.

152 C. A. Harris, 'Vaughan, Sir Charles Richard (1774–1849)', revised by H. C. G. Matthew, DNB, September 2004, online edn. [http://www.oxforddnb.com/view/article/28125, accessed 14 February 2006].

153 ASL, Vaughan Papers, B.1.7: Doyle to Vaughan, Seville, 3 October 1809; BOD North, c. 13, ff. 105–10: Copy of Doyle's account of the second siege of Saragossa.

154 See, for example, articles published by *Felix Farley's Bristol Journal* on 14 January 1809, p. 2; Ibid., 17 June 1809, p. 4; Ibid., 24 June 1809, p. 4.

155 Handwritten note signed by Charles R. Vaughan, 11 February 1837, added to the Preface of a copy of a first edition of his *Narrative of the siege of Zaragoza* donated to the library of his college at the University of Oxford, All Souls, where it remains to this day.

156 Saglia, 'O My Mother Spain!', p. 377.

157 *Childe Harold's Pilgrimage*, stanzas LIV to LVIII, in George Gordon N. Byron, *The Poetical Works of Lord Byron, Complete* (London, 1867), p. 145. In 1822, Byron alluded to Agustina as the 'maid waving her more than Amazonian blade', in the satire *The Age of Bronze*, stanza VII, in Ibid., p. 134; Leslie Alexis Marchand, *Byron: A Biography* (London, 1957), p. 191.

158 Jerome McGann (ed.), *The Complete Poetical Works of Lord Byron* (7 vols., Oxford, 1986), II, p. 186.

159 Tone, 'A Dangerous Amazon', pp. 548–61.

160 Ab, MS 3175/2356 Federico Moretti to Earl of Fife, 20 September 1813; Serafín Maria de Soto, Count de Clonard, *Historia orgánica de las armas de Infantería y Caballería Españolas desde la creación del ejército permanente hasta el dia* (16 vols., Madrid, 1851), VI, pp. 288–9.

161 Brian Jeffery, *Fernando Sor: Composer and Guitarist* (London, 1977); Michael Kennedy (ed.), *The Concise Oxford Dictionary of Music* (Oxford, 1980), p. 584.

162 Jeffery, *Fernando Sor*, p. 15.

163 *El Redactor General*, 10 January 1813, p. 2; Ibid., 15 and 16 May 1813, p. 2; AB MS 3175/2266 Disbursements of the passage of Sra. Mercandotti and Daughter to Cap. Dinell of the 'Spanish Patriot', which passage she lost and new passage in the Pasket to Falmouth, 1813.

164 J. Ebers, *Seven Years of the King's Theatre* (London, 1828), p. 134; Alberto Basso (ed.), *Musica in scena: storia dello spettacolo musicale* (6 vols., Torino, 1995), V, p. 674.

165 Jeffrey, *Fernando Sor*, p. 16.

Chapter 6

1   AHN, *Estado* 46, *Ordenes de la Junta sobre alistamientos y casos de exención*:
    Decree of 7 October 1808 summoning 350,000 men for infantry and 50,000 for
    cavalry regiments; Esdaile, *Spanish Army*, pp. 94–6; *idem, Fighting Napoleon*,
    pp. 67, 106.

2   BL, Add. 37288, f. 133: Memorandum of service rendered by Carlos Doyle in
    the Spanish service signed by Martin de Garay, War Minister, 21 October 1809.

3   Among those recruited by Doyle for his battalion on 1 December 1808 were
    capitán Eduardo Mac Cormick O'Neill, a descendant of the Irish 'Wild Geese'
    with 15 years of service in the Spanish army, and his compatriot, *teniente*
    Miguel Simon Val, see AGMS, M-59 *Expediente* Eduardo Mac Cormick O'Neill:
    Letter to Spanish War Ministry, 25 April 1810; AGMS, B-540 *Expediente* Simon
    Miguel Val.

4   Letter of Doyle to Francisco Palafox, 7 February 1809, in Mariano de Pano
    y Ruata, *El inglés Sir Carlos Guillermo Doyle y su plan de socorro a Zaragosa*
    (Madrid, 1909–10), pp. 86–9.

5   Milburne, *A Narrative*, pp. 11–14; AGMS, M-5080 *Expediente* Manuel O'Doyle
    (contains information regarding Juan Murphy) and O-101 *Expediente* Juan
    Murphy Porro.

6   This was the figure recorded by the French authorities in July 1809, see Jean-
    René Aymes, *Los Españoles en Francia 1808–1814: La deportación bajo el Primer
    Imperio* (Madrid, 1987), pp. 110–11, 186, 239, 243–5, 256.

7   The *Tiradores de Doyle* saw action again in Catalonia and Aragón and later
    joined the national *Ejército del Centro* (Army of the Center), see Alfonso
    Balderrábano and Juan Bautista de Maortua, *Instrucción de Guerrillas, sacada
    por la de los señores Blacke, O'Farril y San Juan. Compuesta y aumentada por
    el Teniente Coronel D. Alfonso Balderrábano, sargento mayor del Regimiento de
    Infantería ligera Tiradores de Doyle, y por D. Juan Bautista de Maortua, teniente
    del mismo* (Vitoria, 1813), pp. i–ii; Clonard, *Historia Orgánica*, VI, pp. 292–3.
    The future *guerrillero* and Liberal leader Francisco Espoz y Mina was briefly a
    recruit, Juana Maria Espoz y Mina (ed.), *Memorias del general don Francisco
    Espoz y Mina escritas por el mismo*, publ. J. M. de Vega, condesa de Espoz y Mina
    (5 vols., Madrid, 1851), I, p. 9.

8   Chapter 4.

9   Esdaile, *The Spanish Army*, pp. 22–3, 49; 'Real Academia Militar de Barcelona', in
    Inspección de Ingenieros, *Estudio histórico del Cuerpo de Ingenieros del Ejército*

(2 vols., Madrid, 1987), II, pp. 23–4; 'L' Academia Militar de Matemáticas', in Magda Fernández, *Passat i present de Barcelona: materials per l´estudi del medi urbá* (5 vols., Barcelona, 1985), II, pp. 53–6.

10 Esdaile, *The Spanish Army*, pp. 52–3; Chartrand, *Spanish Army*, pp. 6–7.

11 Esdaile, *The Spanish Army*, pp. 22–3.

12 Richard Glover, *Peninsular Preparation: The Reform of the British Army 1795–1809* (Cambridge, 1963), p. 234.

13 Esdaile, *The Spanish Army*, pp. 40–7; Andújar Castillo, *Los Militares*, pp. 27–8; Gil Muñoz, 'Revolución en las instituciones', pp. 848–9.

14 AHN, *Estado 46 A, Órdenes de la Junta sobre alistamientos y casos de exención:* Order of the *Junta Central*, 13 November 1808.

15 Gil Muñoz, 'Revolución en las instituciones', p. 855.

16 Fraser, *Napoleon's Cursed War*, p. 15.

17 Fiona MacCarthy, *Byron: Life and Legend* (London, 2004), p. 95.

18 Antonio Viñao Frago, 'Alfabetización, lectura y escritura en el Antiguo Régimen (siglos XVI–XVIII)', in Agustin Escolano and Robert F. Arnove (eds), *Leer y escribir en España: doscientos años de alfabetización* (Madrid, 1992), pp. 45, 579.

19 AGM, *Fondo Duque de Bailén*, Microfiche 8, *Legajo* 51 XLVIII Academias militares: *Exámenes Públicos de Aritmética, Algebra, Ordenanza y Táctica, que Tubieron el dia 9 de junio á las 9 de la mañana los alumnos de la Academia Militar de Palma establecida por el Comandante é Inspector General de la División Mallorquina Don Santiago Whittingham, bajo la dirección del Coronel Don Ramón Senseve, comandante del Batallón Segundo de Burgos de la Espresada División* (Palma, 1812), pp. 5–6; Whittingham to Vice-Admiral Sir Edward Pellew, Palma, 14 February 1812, in Whittingham (ed.), *A Memoir*, p. 169; Gil Muñoz, 'Revolución en las instituciones', p. 855.

20 BOD North, d. 65: Suggestions on the part of General Doyle to the *Junta Central*, Seville, 22 August 1809.

21 Major [Charles William] Doyle, *The Military Catechism for the Use of Young Officers* (London, 1804), p. A2; Major [Charles William] Doyle, *The Military Catechism for the Use of Covering or Supernumerary Serjeants* (London, 1804), p. ii.

22 BOD North, c. 17, f. 66: English translation of Doyle's letter to Marqués de la Romana, 26 November 1809.

23 Ibid.

24 Since its forced transfer to Cadiz in 1810, the Military Academy of Seville adopted the name of Military Academy of the Isla de Leon, see AGM, *Fondo*

Duque de Bailén, Microfiche 8 CLXXI *Reglamento que debe observarse en la Academia Militar compuesta de individuos del batallón de la real universidad de Toledo que de Real Orden se ha establecido en esta ciudad para proverer al ejército de oficiales instruídos* (Cadiz, 1810); José Cepeda Gómez, 'La creación de colegios militares durante la Guerra de la Independencia', in Martínez Sanz and de Diego García (eds), *El comienzo de la Guerra de la Independencia*, p. 193.

25 The most famous student of the Military Academy of the Isla de Leon was the future Liberal Progressive prime minister Joaquín Baldomero Fernández-Espartero. The ninth child of a carter, he passed his first exams in 1812, but a year later he was refused graduation because it was discovered that he had 'no right to approve the course', see Manuel Hiraldez de Acosta and José Trujillo, *Espartero, su vida escrita por D.M.H. y D.J.T* (2 vols., Barcelona, 1868), II, pp. 18–19. In 1813, access to this academy was still limited to children of officers with *limpieza de sangre* (good European lineage), see *Guía política de las Españas para el año 1813* (Cadiz, 1813), pp. 322–3.

26 James K. Hopkins, *Into the Heart of the Fire: The British in the Spanish Civil War* (Stanford, 1998), p. 322.

27 BCL, Rl Pr 2pb Biog. U–Z – B 4120; Glover, *Peninsular Preparation*, pp. 196–9.

28 Whittingham to Henry Wellesley, Palma, 6 January 1812 (extract), in Whittingham (ed.), *A Memoir*, p. 167.

29 French junior officers and the rank and file received little instruction until the Peace of Amiens provided an opportunity to introduce a degree of professionalization. Napoleon established a school at Fontainebleau for 1,000 students (500 recruits a year). But as war began, the one-year instruction was progressively reduced to six, two and even less than a month, see Jean Morvan, *Le soldat impérial 1800–1814* (2 vols., Paris, 1904), II, pp. 80–95; Rafe Blaufarb, *The French Army, 1750–1820: Careers, Talent, Merit* (Manchester, 2002), p. 176.

30 Samuel Ford Whittingham, *Sistema de maniobras de la línea* (London, 1815), p. 3.

31 Ibid., p. 5.

32 *Diario de Sesiones*, I, p. 89; AGM, *Fondo Duque de Bailén*, Microfiche 8, *Legajo* 32 LXXIII Libros de Ordenes del Ejercito del Centro: Order of 2 June 1810 registering Whittingham's Cavalry Division within the Army of Centre; Villanueva, 'Mi viaje a las Cortes', in Artola (ed.), *Memorias*, p. 48. In his diary, the future Argentine liberator Carlos Maria de Alvear made reference to the 'regimiento modelo del General Güitinghan (sic)' (the model regiment of General Whittingham), see Gregorio F. Rodríguez, *Historia de Alvear* (2 vols., Buenos Aires, 1913), I, p. 63.

33   AGMS, V-43 *Expediente* Santiago Whittingham: Order of *Consejo de Regencia*,
      Isla de Leon, 28 November 1810; NA FO, 72/109, ff. 133–4: Translation of letter
      by Jose de Heredia, Spanish Minister of War, to Major General Whittingham,
      22 November 1810; ibid., ff. 135–8: Translation of Whittingham's reply to the
      Regency, 25 November 1810; ibid., f. 138: Translation of letter of Heredia to
      Whittingham, Isla de Leon, 28 November 1810; AGM, *Fondo Duque de Bailén*,
      Legajo 52 LVIII Correspondence Roche (wrongly catalogued as 'La Roche'):
      Copy letter Heredia to Felipe Roche, Isla de Leon, 22 November 1810.

34   The organization of the Spanish army in the field armies of the Left, Centre,
      Right and Reserve in 1808 gave way in 1810 to six named after ordinal numbers
      (First, Second, Third, Fourth, Fifth and Sixth to which was added a Seventh
      in 1811), see Esdaile, *The Duke of Wellington*, p. 90.

35   NA FO, 72/109, ff. 133–4, 138; AGM, *Fondo Duque de Bailén*, *Legajo* 52 LVIII
      Correspondence Roche (wrongly catalogued as 'La Roche'): Heredia to Roche,
      22 November 1810.

36   Ibid.; AGM, *Fondo Duque de Bailén*, Microfiche 2 *Legajo* 51 XLVIII:
      Whittingham to Regency, Palma, 10 March 1812.

37   NA WO, 6/206, ff. 43–4, 69, 213, 304, and NA WO, 1/1120, 'Miscellaneous':
      Correspondence Downie with several officials at the War Department, 1810;
      NA FO, 72/99, ff. 266–80: Correspondence Downie with Marquess of Wellesley
      and others, 1810; NA WO, 1/1123, 'Miscellaneous', *idem*, 1811; NA WO, 1/1126,
      'Miscellaneous', *idem*, 1812; AGMS, P-541 *Expediente* Guillermo Parker Carrol:
      Notes on the re-establishment of the Irish Brigade, 2 October 1811.

38   Wellington to the Earl of Liverpool, Secretary of State, Richoso, 1 October 1811,
      in Gurwood (ed.), *The Dispatches*, VIII, pp. 313–14. See also Chapter 5.

39   The project failed because of the impossibility of removing the most numerous
      of the Irish regiments, the Ultonia, from the defence of Catalonia. Nevertheless,
      Carrol did receive British aid for the Hibernia regiment under his command, see
      AGMS, P-541 *Expediente* Guillermo Parker Carrol: Report of Inspector-General
      Manuel González Menchaca, 13 July 1811; Alicia Laspra Rodríguez, 'William
      Parker Carrol and the frustrated re-establishment of the Irish Brigade in Spain
      (1809–11)', *The Irish Sword*, XXVI, 104 (2008), p. 158.

40   NA FO, 72/109, ff. 133–4: Translation of letter by Jose de Heredia, Minister of
      War, to Major General Whittingham, 22 November 1810; AGM, *Fondo Duque
      de Bailén*, *Legajo* 52 LVIII: Correspondence Roche (wrongly catalogued as 'La
      Roche') Heredia to Roche, 22 November 1810.

41   NA FO, 72/109, ff. 133–4.

42 AGMS, E-688 *Expediente* Patricio Campbell: Certificate of Services of Patricio Campbell by commander Pedro Guerra, 12 January 1815; AGMS, S-2807 *Expediente* Carlos Silvertop: Certificate of services of Carlos Silvertop by General Whittingham, Saragossa, 8 September 1814; AGMS, U-6 *Expediente* Arturo Wavell: Testimony of *teniente coronel graduado* Arturo Wavell, Vich, 2 October 1815; NA WO, 1/1123, ff. 315–16: Patrick Campbell to Lt. Col. Bunbury, 7 May 1811.

43 NA FO, 72/109, ff. 148–50: Copy letter from Major General Whittingham to H. Wellesley, 2 January 1811; ibid., ff. 152–4: Copy letter H. Wellesley to Eusebio Bardaxi, Isla de Leon, 2 January 1811; ibid., f. 155: Translation of letter by Jose de Heredia, Minister of War, to Bardaxi, Isla de Leon, 5 January 1811; ibid., ff. 159–62: Copy letter of Whittingham to H. Wellesley, Isla de Leon, 12 January 1811; ASL, Vaughan Papers, E 3/12: Precis of Lord Wellington dispatches at the Cadiz legation, Freneda, 19 February 1813. For more on this subject, see Chapter 7.

44 NA FO, 72/109, ff. 133–4.

45 AGM, *Fondo Duque de Bailén*, *Legajo* 52 LVIII Correspondence Roche (wrongly catalogued as 'La Roche'): Heredia to Roche, Isla de Leon, 22 November 1810; ibid., E.M.G., Cadiz, 5 September 1812; ibid., Roche to Council of Regency, Elche 18 January 1813.

46 CU, Add. 7521, ff. 171–307: Letters of Gen. Sir Philip K. Roche, 29 January 1811 to 25 July 1812; AGM, *Fondo Duque de Bailén*, *Legajo* 51 XLVIII: *Exámenes Públicos de Aritmética, Algebra, Ordenanza y Táctica, que Tubieron el dia 9 de junio á las 9 de la mañana los alumnos de la Academia Militar de Palma establecida por el Comandante é Inspector General de la División Mallorquina Don Santiago Whittingham, bajo la dirección del Coronel Don Ramón Senseve, comandante del Batallón Segundo de Burgos de la Espresada División* (Palma, 1812), p. 36; BOD North, c. 16, f. 255: Roche to Doyle, Cartagena, 31 July, 1811; NA FO, 72/133, ff. 147–53: Roche to Castlereagh, Alicante, 20 April 1812.

47 CU, Add. 7521, ff. 113–14: Henry Wellesley to Roche, Cadiz, 28 April 1810; NA WO, 1/1120, ff. 613–15: Swiss Brigadier General Samuel de Turtaz to War Office, 12 November 1810; NA FO, 72/99, f. 176: Doyle to Marquess Wellesley, Alicante, 9 April 1810; BOD North, c. 15, f. 147: Doyle to Sir John Stuart, Tarragona, 21 January 1811; BOD North, c. 16, f. 331: Roche to Doyle, Cartagena, 29 May 1811; Hall, *British Strategy*, p. 13.

48 Division VIII, 'On the national military force' and Division IX 'On the Public Education' in [Robinson], *The Political Constitution of the Spanish Monarchy*, pp. 113–14, 115–17; 'Gil Muñoz, 'Revolución en las instituciones', p. 860.

49 AGMS, D-877 *Expediente* Carlos Guillermo Doile (sic): Report of services of Carlos Doyle, Madrid, 26 August 1816.

50 AGMS, D-877 *Expediente* Carlos Guillermo Doile (sic): *Reglamento de Constitución y Gobierno para el Depósito Militar de Instrucción a Establecerse en la Isla de León*, 1 October 1811; BOD North, c. 19, f. 45: Copy Letter of *Regencia* to Doyle, 12 October 1811.

51 Wilson, *Private Diary*, p. 12.

52 AGM, *Fondo Duque de Bailén, Legajo* LIII: Confirmation of Order of Regency re. Whittingham's academy, signed by Minister Carvajal, Cadiz, 21 April 1812.

53 AGM, *Fondo Duque de Bailén, Legajo* CLXXI: *Reglamentos de las escuelas militares*; ibid, *Legajo* LVII *Academias militares*; Fernando Fernández Bastarreche, *El Ejército español en el siglo XIX* (Madrid, 1978), p. 49.

54 Doyle's depot was closed on 11 August 1815; Whittingham's, on 21 September 1823. See BOD North, c. 16, f. 468: Minister of War Ballesteros to Doyle, 6 August 1815; AGMS, D-877 *Expediente* Carlos Doile (sic): Royal Order of 11 August 1815; Vicente Alonso Juanola and Manuel Gómez Ruiz (eds), *El ejército de los Borbones – Reinado de Fernando VII* (6 vols., Segovia, 1999), V, pp. 379–80.

55 AGM, *Fondo Duque de Bailén, Legajo* 51 XLVIII *Exámenes Públicos*, pp. 5–6.

56 AGMS, D-877 *Expediente* Carlos Guillermo Doile (sic): *Reglamento*.

57 BOD North, c. 15, f. 312: Doyle to O'Donojú, Isla de Leon, 2 April 1812.

58 AGMS, D-877 *Expediente* Carlos Guillermo Doile (sic): Report of services of *Carlos* Doyle, Madrid, 26 August 1816. No mention is made of the total of men instructed during the whole war. A cutting from an unidentified British newspaper found among Doyle's papers in the Bodleian Library claimed that they were over 12,000 (BOD North, b. 7, f. 113).

59 NA FO, 72/109, ff. 133–4; AGMS, D-877 *Expediente* Carlos Guillermo Doile (sic): Article 4 of *Reglamento de Constitución y Gobierno para el Depósito Militar*.

60 ASL, Vaughan Papers, E11/2: Henry Wellesley to Lord Wellesley, Cadiz, 12 December 1811; Esdaile, *The Peninsular War*, p. 341.

61 On 26 June 1811, *El Redactor General* carried on its front page the translation of an article allegedly published by an English newspaper criticizing the 'Old Spanish government' policies in Spanish America; see also Severn, *A Wellesley Affair*, pp. 176, 189.

62 José Luis Terrón Ponce, *Ejército y política en la España de Carlos III* (Madrid, 1997), p. 109.

63 NA FO, 72/109, ff. 133–4; AGMS, D-877, *Expediente* Carlos Guillermo Doile (sic): Article 4 of *Reglamento*.

64 AGMS, L-700 *Expediente* Francisco Lee; AGMS, E-1594 *Expediente* Roberto
    Steile (sic) and E-1596 *Expediente* Roberto Steele.

65 Nothing is known of his military background prior to joining the Spanish
    army, but by 1815 he was serving in the depot with the rank of *capitán*, see
    AGMS, R-1365 *Expediente* Gerónimo Robinson, and AGMS, L-700 *Expediente*
    Francisco Lee: Conde de Abisval to Ministry of War, 18 August 1815.

66 AGMS, M-2581 *Expediente* Juan Meélican (sic, for Mealican); BOD North, c. 16,
    ff. 414–16: John Mealican to General Doyle, Cadiz, 26 February 1814.

67 Mentioned in correspondence of colleagues Copping and Palmer, BOD North,
    c. 16, f. 389: Paul Palmer to General Doyle, San Carlos, 27 March 1813; ibid., f.
    390: Copping to Doyle, San Carlos 25 March 1813. No evidence has been found
    to link this O'Hara to the 'O'Hara' mentioned as one of the 'two gentlemen' who
    accompanied Landor on his trip to Galicia in 1808, see Chapter 2.

68 AGMS, P-267 *Expediente* Pablo Palmés (sic, for Palmer); BOD North, c. 16, ff.
    389–91: Paul Palmer to General Doyle, San Carlos 27–8 March 1813.

69 BOD North, c. 16, f. 390: Copping to Doyle, San Carlos, 25 March 1813. The
    first name of this volunteer is not mentioned in correspondence. On 29 March
    1814, *The London Gazette* reported the transfer of an Ensign 'Samuel Bloss'
    Copping from the Essex Militia to the 3rd Foot Regiment. But the military
    archives at Segovia recorded the services of a 'Jorge Coppy' (George Coppy,
    being the surname, perhaps, a Spanish interpretation of Copping) of whom it
    was only stated that he had joined as a *subteniente* the *Batallón Infantería de
    Irlanda* on 24 April 1812, after serving in the 87th Regiment, see AGMS, C-3283
    Expediente Jorge Coppy. However, no information has been found for a George
    Copping, or indeed 'Coppy' in British archives.

70 Ibid.

71 AGMS, E-1596 *Expediente* Roberto Steele; Steele to Ministry of War, Madrid,
    14 June 1814.

72 *El Redactor General*, 11 November 1811, pp. 583–4.

73 *El Redactor General*, 24 December 1811, p. 756.

74 Ibid.

75 NA FO, 72/109, f. 155: Translation of letter of Jose de Heredia, Spanish Minister
    of War, to Spanish Foreign Minister Bardaxi, re. Whittingham's division and
    academy, Isla de Leon, 5 January 1811; AGMS, D-877 *Expediente* Carlos
    Guillermo Doile (sic): Articles 16 and 20 of *Reglamento*.

76 AGMS, D-877 *Expediente* Carlos Guillermo Doile (sic): Article 20 of *Reglamento*.

77 AGM, *Fondo Duque de Bailén, Legajo* 51 XLVIII: *Exámenes Públicos*, p. 1;
    Gómez Ruiz (ed.), *El ejército de los Borbones*, V, p. 379.

78 BOD North, c. 16, f. 436: Memorandum on activities of depot in Cadiz, 15 May 1814.

79 BOD North, c. 16, f. 386: José María de Torrijos to General Doyle, Caceres, 17 May 1813; Luisa Saenz de Viniegra de Torrijos, *Vida del General José María de Torrijos y Uriarte* (2 vols., Madrid, 1860), I, pp. 16, 21.

80 AGM, *Fondo Duque de Bailén, Legajo* 51 XLVIII: *Exámenes Públicos*, pp. 5–6.

81 José Ángel Gallego Palomares and José Gregorio Cayuela Fernández, *La Guerra de la Independencia: historia bélica, pueblo y nación en España, 1808–1814* (Salamanca, 2008), pp. 327–44; Jean-René Aymes, *La guerra de la independencia en España (1808–1814)* (Madrid, 1986), pp. 68–9.

82 AGM, *Fondo Duque de Bailén, Legajo* 51 XLVIII: *Exámenes Públicos*, pp. 5–6.

83 Ibid.; BOD North, c. 16, f. 436.

84 AGMS, D-877, *Expediente* Carlos Guillermo Doile (sic): Article 13 of *Reglamento*; BOD North, c. 16, f. 436.

85 John E. Cookson, 'Regimental worlds: Interpreting the experience of British soldiers during the Napoleonic Wars', in Forrest, Hagemann and Rendall (eds), *Soldiers, Citizens and Civilians*, p. 32.

86 AGM, *Fondo Duque de Bailén, Legajo* 51 XLVIII *Exámenes Públicos*, p. 8; BOD North, c. 16, f. 436.

87 Gómez Ruiz (ed.), *El ejército de los Borbones*, V, p. 380; AGMS, D-877 *Expediente* Carlos Guillermo Doile (sic): Copy letter of Spanish Minister of War José de Heredia to Inspector General de Infanteria, Cadiz, 12 December 1811; on salaries, see ibid., Article 22 of *Reglamento*.

88 AGMS, D-877 *Expediente* Carlos Guillermo Doile (sic): Article 3 of *Reglamento*; AGM, *Fondo Duque de Bailén, Legajo* 51 XLVIII *Exámenes Públicos*, p. 36.

89 AGM, Fondo Duque de Bailén, Legajo CLXXI Reglamento formado para la Academia Militar de la Real Isla de Leon trasladada desde Sevilla, 28 June 1810.

90 AGM, *Fondo Duque de Bailén, Legajo* 51 XLVIII *Exámenes Públicos*, pp. 12–13.

91 BOD North, c. 16, f. 436.

92 Ibid.

93 Carlos Guillermo Doyle, *Manual para reconocimientos militares dispuesto por el Excmo. Sr. D. Carlos Guillermo Doyle, Teniente General de los Reales Exércitos, Comandante general del depósito militar de instrucción* (Cadiz, 1812).

94 Ibid., p. 16.

95 Ibid., p. 3.

96 Ibid.

97 *El Redactor General*, 2 February 1812, p. 906.

98   BOD North, c. 16, f. 372: Alberto de Megmo to General Doyle, Malta, 4 May 1812.

99   AGMS, D-877 *Expediente* Carlos Guillermo Doile (sic): Report of services of Carlos Doyle, Madrid, 26 August 1816; Doyle, *A Hundred Years of Conflict*, p. 106.

100 AGMS, D-1177 *Expediente* Juan Downie: Downie to Regency, 13 March 1812; BL, Add. 38366, f. 125: Certificate of Services of *teniente coronel* Robert Steele by *teniente general* Pedro Agustín Girón, Seville, 25 February 1815.

101 AGM, *Fondo Duque de Bailén*, *Legajo* 51 XLVIII: *Exámenes Públicos*, pp. 34–6; Clonard, *Historia orgánica*, XI, pp. 464–5.

102 Esdaile, *The Duke of Wellington*, pp. 182–9; Clonard, *Historia orgánica*, VI, pp. 281–2, 292–3; ibid., XI, pp. 464–5.

103 The other Spaniard was General Alava, *aide-de-camp* of Wellington, see John Palfrey Burrell (ed.), *Official Bulletins of the Battle of Waterloo in the Original Languages* (London, 1849), p. 66. The personal file of Mimussir in the Military Archive of Segovia was filed by error in the record folder of British volunteer Carlos Silvertop (AGMS, S-2807) until discovered by the author of this book. A file under Mimussir's name is now in the process of being created.

104 See, for example, NA FO, 72/78, ff. 100–3: Roche to M. Wellesley, Headquarters Spanish Army of La Mancha, Santa Cruz de Madela, 10 October 1809; NA FO, 72/99, ff. 198–204: Carrol to Marquess Wellesley, Head Quarters Army of the Left, Badajoz, no day, March 1810; NA FO, 72/99, ff. 156–7: Whittingham to Marquess Wellesley, Gibraltar, 22 January 1810; Milburne, *A Narrative*, p. 116.

105 BL, Add. 15675, ff. 29–30: Doyle to Rivas, Tarragona, 5 July 1810.

106 BOD North, c. 15, f. 27: Copy letter Doyle to Lord Wellesley, Tortosa, June 5 1810; BL, Add. 15675, ff. 29–30: Doyle to Rivas, Tarragona, 5 July 1810; AGM, *Fondo Duque de Bailén*, Microfiche 2, *Legajo LXV*: *Diario de Cervera*, 5 April 1809; CU, Add. 7521, ff. 338–44: *Memorandum from British and Foreign Consuls and British and Foreign Merchants resident in the City of Alicante to Philip Keatinge* (sic) *Roche, Esquire, Lieutenant General in the Service of His Catholic Majesty and Knight of the Royal Order of Charles The Third and Saint Ferdinand*, Alicante, 20 February, 1816.

107 David Hopkin, 'The World Turned Upside Down: Female Soldiers in the French Armies of the Revolutionary and Napoleonic Wars', in Forrest, Hagemann and Rendall (eds), *Soldiers, Citizens and Civilians*, p. 79.

108 Tone, 'A Dangerous Amazon', pp. 549, 556.

109 Fernández, *Mujeres en la Guerra de la Independencia*, pp. 21–2; 108. For a study of the present historiography regarding perceptions of Spanish womanhood

in the long eighteenth century, see Mónica Bolufer Peruga, *Las mujeres en la España del siglo XVIII: trayectorias de la investigación y perspectivas de futuro* (Valencia, 2009), in *Biblioteca Virtual Cervantes* [www.cervantesvirtual.com/servlet/SirveObras/p211/90250620980147265332679/p0000001.htm#I_0_, accessed on 29 October 2009].

110 Tone, 'A Dangerous Amazon', p. 557. The Golden Age offered the example of Catalina de Erauso (1592–1650?), also known as the *Monja Alférez* (The Nun Lieutenant), but in order to join first the navy and later the army in South America, she dressed as a man and called herself 'Francisco de Loyola', see Vicenta María Marquez de la Plata y Ferrandiz, *Mujeres de Acción en el Siglo de Oro* (Madrid, 2006), pp. 21–75.

111 See Chapter 5.

112 AGMS, *Personal Célebre, Caja* 176, *Expediente* 4, *Carpeta* 1, *Expediente* Agustina Zaragoza y Domenech: C. W. Doyle to Antonio Cornel, Cadiz, 20 July 1809; 'Carta de Recomendación del mariscal Doyle a favor de Agustina de Aragón, conocida por la Artillera', in Sociedad Estatal de Conmemoraciones Culturales (ed.), *España 1808–1814 La Nación en Armas* (Madrid, 2008), p. 289.

113 AGMS, *Personal Célebre, Caja* 176, Exp. 4, Carpeta 1, *Expediente* Agustina Zaragoza y Domenech, p. 35 a: Order of Francisco de Saavedra, secretary of the *Junta Central* to the Treasury, 30 August 1809.

114 Bernard A. Cook, *Women and War: A Historical Encyclopedia from Antiquity to the Present* (Santa Barbara, CA, 2006), pp. 5–6; Tone, 'A Dangerous Amazon', p. 552.

115 Tone, 'A Dangerous Amazon', p. 553; Agustina was a valuable icon of both Republican and Franquist propaganda during the Civil War, see *España 1808–1814: La Nación en Armas*, pp. 378–83; Jo Labanyi, 'Costume, identity and spectator pleasure in historical films of the early Franco period' in Parvati Nair and Steven Marsh (eds), *Gender and Spanish Cinema* (Oxford, 2004), pp. 34–50.

116 Sir John Carr, *Descriptive Travels in the Southern and Eastern Parts of Spain and the Balearic Isles in the Year 1809* (London, 1811), pp. 33–4.

117 Jacob, *Travels in the South of Spain*, p. 123.

118 Carr, *Descriptive Travels*, p. 30.

119 Ibid.; Carlota Cobo, *La ilustre heroina de Zaragoza o la célebre amazona en la Guerra de la Independencia* (Madrid, 1859), pp. 320–6. The author was Agustina's daughter.

120 Cobo, *La ilustre heroina*, pp. 335–46.

121 Hopkin, 'The World Turned Upside Down', p. 78.

122 ALS, Vaughan Papers B.1.7: Doyle to Vaughan, Seville, 3 October 1809 (original underlining).

123 Ramón Solís, *El Cadiz de las Cortes – La vida en la ciudad en los años de 1810 a 1813* (Madrid, 1987), p. 79.

124 AHN *Diversos-Colecciones*, 108, N. 34 *Reglamento de sueldos para los oficiales y demás clases del ejército que se retiran del servicio*, 1 January 1810.

125 César Herráiz de Miota, 'Los montepíos militares del siglo XVIII como origen del sistema de clases pasivas del Estado', *Revista del Ministerio de Trabajo y Asuntos Sociales*, 56 (2005), 178–82; Andrew Cunningham, Ole Peter Grell and Bernd Roeck (eds), *Health Care and Poor Relief in 18th and 19th Century Southern Europe* (Aldershot, 2005), pp. 101–4, 122–33.

126 Gloria Espigado Tocino, *Aprender a leer y a escribir en el Cádiz del ochocientos* (Cadiz, 1996), p. 67.

127 AGMS, R-1496 Felipe de la Roche (sic): Treasurer Carlos Rusconi to Governor of Alicante, Cayetano Iriarte, re. General Roche's assistance to troops of his division, 28 March 1811; AGMS, D-1177 Juan Downie: Manón González Menchaca to Inspector General, re. John Downie's personal financial assistance to *guerrilla* and soldiers of his legion, Cadiz, 3 September 1811.

128 AGMS, D-877 Carlos Guillermo Doile (sic): Acceptance of donation of salary of *mariscal de campo* of Carlos Doyle, 26 August 1809; ibid., Memorial of services of General Carlos Doyle, Madrid, 26 August 1816; BOD North, c. 15, f. 290: Doyle to *Regencia*, Isla de Leon, 12 December 1811.

129 A subsidiary dignity inherited when Duff's father became the third Earl of Fife on the death of the second Earl on 24 January 1809, see Tayler, *The Book of the Duffs*, I, p. 206.

130 *Biblioteca de Catalunya Arxiu*, Inventari del Fons Gonima/Janer, 1790 A-L (70/2): Registration of Kuhff, Grellet and Co. (London).

131 'Affairs of Spain', *The Hull Packet and Original Weekly Commercial, Literary and General Advertiser*, 6 September 1808, p. 2. The currency conversion from *reales* to pounds made in the article offers an estimation of 90 reales to the pound. Although exchange fluctuations were frequent during the war, this figure has been adopted as the benchmark for all currency conversions in this book, considering that it is not far from the average of 89 reales adopted by Charles Esdaile in his *The Duke of Wellington*, p. xi.

132 *Suplemento al Diario Mercantil de Cadiz*, 4 June 1810, p. 3; *Gazeta de la Regencia de España e Indias*, 31 July 1810, p. 454.

133 *Suplemento al Diario Mercantil de Cadiz*, 4 June 1810, pp. 2, 4.

134 Ibid.

135 *A List of the Subscribers to Lloyd's, September, 1814* (London, 1814), p. 14.

136 Charles Messenger, *Unbroken Service: The History of Lloyd's Patriotic Fund 1803–2003* (London, 2003), p. 121; 'Lloyd's Patriotic Fund: Report of the Charities Trust, 2009', available in the Charities Trust's website [www. charitiestrust.org/charities/LloydsPatrioticFund/index.html, accessed 20 November 2009].

137 'Fondo Patriótico, Lista de Suscripcion. Nr. 1', *El Diario Mercantil de Cádiz*, 24 June 1810, p. 3; 'Fondo Patriótico Lista Núm. 2', ibid., 28 June 1810, p. 4; 'Fondo Patriótico', *Gazeta de la Regencia de España e Indias*, 6 July 1810, pp. 373–4; 'Fondo Patriótico – Lista núm. 2', ibid., 31 July 1810, p. 454.

138 Including the sherry-producing family Alvear of which the future Argentine liberator Carlos María de Alvear was a member, see 'Fondo Patriótico, Lista de Suscripcion. Nr. 1', *El Diario Mercantil de Cádiz*, 24 June 1810, p. 3; Pedro E. Fernández Lalanne, *Los Alvear* (Buenos Aires, 1980), p. 8.

139 Article 2 of the statute of the *Fondo Patriótico* published in *Gazeta de la Regencia de España e Indias*, 24 July 1810, pp. 434–7.

140 Not to be confused with the Jansenist liberal priest and deputy of the *Cortes* Joaquín Lorenzo Villanueva.

141 *Gazeta de la Regencia de España e Indias*, p. 435.

142 Among the many clients of Duncan Shaw & Co. was the Venezuelan liberator Francisco de Miranda, see María Lourdes Díaz-Trechuelo Spínola, *Bolívar, Miranda, O'Higgins, San Martín: cuatro vidas cruzadas* (Madrid, 1999), pp. 79–80; Joseph F. Thorning, *Miranda: World Citizen* (Gainesville, 1952), pp. 278, 280–1. Shaw was also one of the subscribers of the published works of colonel David Humphreys, *aide-de-camp* to George Washington and former US ambassador to Madrid, see David Humphreys, *The Miscellaneous Works of David Humphreys: Late Minister Plenipotentiary to the Court of Madrid* (New York, 1804), p. 404.

143 Adolfo de Castro, *Cádiz en la Guerra*, p. 75; *Gazeta de la Regencia de España y de las Indias*, 14 September 1810, pp. 660, 824–6.

Chapter 7

1 BOD North, c. 13, f. 92: 'Pepe' (José) de Palafox to 'Carlos' Doyle, Madrid, 24 February 1831; BOD Nort c. 18 f. 93 Lorenzo Calbo to 'Carlos Doile, teniente

general del Ejército Español'. Palafox's fortunes improved when the liberals returned to power with the Regency of Queen Maria Cristina who granted him the title of First Duke of Saragossa (1834). He was reappointed Captain-General of Aragon and elected Senator. See 'Palafox y Melci, José Rebolledo de, duque de Zaragoza', *Gran Enciclopedia Aragonesa*.

2 'Recollections of Cadiz during the Siege 1810, 11, 12', *Blackwood's Edinburgh Magazine*, November 1836, p. 687. From a manuscript at the NLS it emerges that the author of this article, identified only as 'O', was Barry O'Meara, British Commissary General at Cadiz during the war. O'Meara asked Fife's permission to mention his involvement in the conflict. Fife agreed and provided these and other comments; see NLS, MS 4042, f. 287: Fife to Barry O'Meara, *circa* 1836.

3 Jacob, *Travels in the south of Spain*, pp. 359–60.

4 Aymes, *Los Españoles en Francia*, pp. 119–34.

5 Ibid.; Tomás Pérez Delgado, 'Españoles en campos de trabajo franceses. Amberes y Flesinga, 1811–1814', *Alcores*, 5 (2088), pp. 160–2.

6 AGMS, C-2843 *Expediente* Juan Clarke: Testimony of *teniente de navío* Manuel de Colombres and ten Bordeux merchants regarding Clarke's services in favour of Spanish PoWs, 11 July 1814.

7 Aymes, *Los Españoles en Francia*, p. 110.

8 *Archives Nationales de France* (ANF) F7/3312 Police files: Correspondence re. 'prisonniers Anglais et Espagnoles', 17–27 November 1813; Aymes, *Los Españoles en Francia*, pp. 72, 131.

9 AGMS, Q-1 *Expediente* Juan Quearney (sic, for Kearney) Donnelan.

10 AGMS, A-2104 *Expediente* Jaime Arbuthnot y Arbuthnot.

11 AGMS, *Expediente* Juan Clarke.

12 AGMS, Q-1; C-2843; A-2104.

13 See Chapter 5.

14 AGMS, U-6 *Expediente* Arturo Wavell.

15 Tayler, *The Book of the Duffs*, I, p. 206; 'Recollections of Cadiz', *Blackwood's Edinburgh Magazine*, p. 688.

16 Whittingham (ed.). *A Memoir*, pp. 89–106.

17 AGMS, D-877 *Expediente* Carlos Guillermo Doile (sic).

18 AAC, Census of Cadiz 1810: Padrón 1032 (address Los Pozos de la Nieve 165), p. 2.

19 BL, Add 49490, f. 138: Whittingham to Col. Gordon, 7 September 1808; BL, Add. 39199, f. 130: Roche to General Mackenzie, Cadiz, 28 February 1809; Esdaile, *The Peninsular War*, pp. 174, 193.

20   AAC, Census 1812: Padrón 1055 (Calle de la Carne), p. 1.

21   Gatherings held at private homes and considered as the first and foremost
     example of modern sociability in Spain, similar to that of the *salons* in France,
     see Francois-Xavier Guerra, *Modernidad e independencias: ensayos sobre las
     revoluciones hispánicas* (Madrid, 1992), p. 93.

22   AB, MS 3175/1410/3 Messages Strange family to viscount Macduff, 1809–1813;
     BOD North, c. 17, f. 362: List of Doyle's Spanish acquaintances; 'Recollections of
     Cadiz', *Blackwood's Edinburgh Magazine,* pp. 400–1.

23   ASL, Vaughan Papers, uncatalogued, reel 7: British envoy Charles Stuart to
     Vaughan, Lisbon, 6 May 1810 and 26 August 1810; AB, MS3175/2296: Letter
     William Miller to the fourth Earl of Fife, Canterbury, 29 June 1827 in which
     Miller mentioned an entry in his journal for 27 October 1812, Cadiz, re.
     meeting 'Major McDuff' at the theatre; Jerdan, *National portrait*, II, pp. 146–7;
     Jorge Campos, *Teatro y sociedad en España (1780–1820)* (Madrid, 1969), p. 163.

24   BOD North, c. 17, f. 360–1: List of Doyle's Spanish acquaintances.

25   Guerra, *Modernidad*, p. 123.

26   AB, MS3175/2276 and MS3175/2269: Correspondence Macduff and Antonia
     Acosta 1810–1813; Ibid., MS3175/2273: Roche to the Earl of Fife, Alicante,
     4 May 1813, re. 'Spanish fair lady'.

27   John Kearney married Carlota Price, daughter of the British consulate in
     Cartagena in 1817 [AGMS, Q-1 *Expediente* Juan Quearney (sic, for Kearney)
     Donnelan]. James O'Ryan tied the knot twice, in 1824 with Francisca Teresa
     Vidal and in 1827 with Ramona Buil y Ferrer [AGMS, O-548 *Expediente* Jayme
     O Rian (sic, for O'Ryan)]. James Arbuthnot married Dolores Zuaso y O'Carrol,
     daughter of the *capitán de fragata* Luis O'Carrol (AGMS, A-2104 *Expediente*
     Jaime Arbuthnot y Arbuthnot).

28   *Archivo General de Indias*, Fabrica_De_Tabacos, 1218: Pedro Creus Jiménez (sic, for
     Ximenes); AHN, FC-M° Hacienda 514 *Expediente* 2871: Marriage licence of Pedro
     Creus Jiménez (sic, for Ximenes), 1805; Whittingham (ed.), *A Memoir*, p. 121.

29   AGM, *Fondo Duque de Bailén* 1 BIS *Legajo* 52: 'Exposición del General Santiago
     Whittingham al Marques de Coupigny', Palma, 7 March 1812.

30   AB, MS3175/F41/2/3 Correspondence Viscount MacDuff (later Earl of Fife)
     with Patricio Wiseman, Peter Strange and Costello Brothers 1809–1813; BOD
     North, c. 17, f. 360–1: Doyle's Spanish acquaintances.

31   BOD North, c. 15, f. 150: Doyle to Sir John Stuart, Tarragona, 21 January 1811;
     Ibid., f. 151: Doyle to H. Wellesley, same date; Ibid., f. 159: *idem*, 1 February
     1811.

32 AGMS, Q-1 *Expediente* Juan Quearney (sic, for Kearney) Donnelan; NA WO,
     1/237, ff. 399–400: General John Hope to Lord Castlereagh, re. Spanish officers
     attached to Moore's army, London, 25 February 1809.

33 Matters would change after the war when they were forced to explain the reason
     of their prolonged absence in England to officials who wanted to bring to an end
     their careers in Spain, AGMS, C-3476 *Expediente* Diego Corrigan; AGMS, U-34
     Expediente Enrique Wilson.

34 BOD North, c. 16, f. 157: Blake to Doyle, Tortosa, 6 April 1809.

35 BOD North, c. 16, f. 381: Brigadier Pedro Patricio Sarsfield y Waters to General
     Doyle, Calatayud, 6 February 1813.

36 BL, Add. 49490, f. 138: Whittingham to Col. Gordon, Madrid, 7 September
     1808.

37 BOD North, c. 14, f. 63: Doyle to Green, Tortosa, 5 February 1809.

38 NA WO, 1/237, ff. 551–2: Green to Cooke, 1 September 1809; Green married
     Frances Cotton, in Cheshire, on 30 July 1810, see 'Edwin Rowland Joseph
     Green' in the free family history website FamilySearch (The Church of Jesus
     Christ of Latter-day Saints) [available at http://www.familysearch.org, accessed
     20 March 2007].

39 NA WO, 1/237, ff. 551–2: Green to Cooke, 1 September 1809.

40 NA WO, 1/237, f. 553: Certificate of Green's rank of *coronel de infantería* signed
     by General Reding, 29 January 1809; Ibid., ff. 552–4: Bunbury to Major Green,
     21 December 1810.

41 NA WO, 6/166, ff. 46–50: Bunbury to Hamilton explaining appointments of
     British agents by the Earl of Liverpool, 24 September 1811.

42 ASL, Vaughan Papers, uncatalogued, reel 12, OB. No. 25: *Relación de los Cuerpos
     de Infantería existentes en los Ex. Nacionales hoy día de la fecha con expresión
     de los Jefes y fuerza que cada uno contiene* (Cadiz, 1813); Clonard, *Historia
     orgánica*,VI, pp. 290–1.

43 See Chapter 6.

44 NA FO, 72/116, ff. 160–2: Whittingham to Wellesley, Palma, 29 October 1811;
     Whittingham (ed.), *A Memoir*, pp. 152–65.

45 *Diario de Palma*, 4 October 1811, pp. 114–15.

46 José María Massons, *Historia de la Sanidad Militar Española* (4 vols., Barcelona,
     1994), III, pp. 408–3.

47 The French also subscribed to the contagion theory and were similarly keen
     on enforcing *cordon sanitaires*. Ibid.; Mark Harrison, *Medicine in an age of*

commerce and empire: Britain and its tropical colonies, 1660–1830 (Oxford, 2010), pp. 255–86.

48 Letter of 'Dr. Enrique Milburne, miembro del real colegio de cirugía de Lóndres é inspector de los reales hospitales de España', Mahon, 24 September 1811, in *Diario de Palma*, 4 October 1811, pp. 114–15.

49 *Diario de Palma*, 23 October 1811, pp. 190–1.

50 National Archives of the United Kingdom, Admiralty Records (NA ADM) 51/2491–9 and 10 Captain's Logs HMS Invincible, 7 April 1810 to 30 September 1811 and 7 April 1812 to 27 January 1814; NA ADM 51/2068 – 10 and 11 Captain's Logs HMS Temeraire, 11 March 1811 to 19 March 1812.

51 *Diario de Sesiones*, XVIII, pp. 338–9.

52 The Royal Order changing the name of the regiment *Tiradores de Doyle* to that of *Regimiento de Barbastro* was published in the *Gaceta de Madrid*, 3 November 1814, p. 2123.

53 *Apuntes que dio a su abogado el primer ayudante del Estado Mayor General D. Luis de Landáburu y Villanueva estando preso en la cárcel de Madrid el año de 1814 por su amor a la Constitución* (Madrid, 1820), *passim*.

54 Francisco Ballesteros, *Respetuosos descargos que el Teniente General D. Francisco Vallesteros* [sic] *ofrece a la generosa nación española. En contestación á los cargos que S.A. la Regencia del Reyno se ha servido hacerle en su Manifiesto de 12 de Diciembre del año pasado de 1812 dirigido á la misma para su inteligencia* (Algeciras, 1813); AGMS, C-2843 *Expediente* Juan Clarke: Certificate of services of Juan Clarke by Francisco Ballesteros, *teniente General del Real Exercito*, Fregenal, 30 June 1814; AGMS, M-8 *Expediente* 69 Reynaldo Macdonnell: Certificate of services of Reynaldo Macdonnell by Francisco Ballesteros, 31 August 1814; AGMS, A-2104 *Expediente* Jaime Arbuthnot y Arbuthnot: Certificate of Services of Jaime Arbuthnot y Arbuthnot, May 1814.

55 Juan Romero Alpuente, *Wellington en España y Ballesteros en Ceuta* (Cadiz, 1813); 'Ingleses', *El Español Libre,* Cadiz, 4 May 1813, pp. 17–31; Gallego Palomares and Cayuela Fernández, *La Guerra de la Independencia*, p. 465.

56 *Semanario Patriótico*, 29 August 1811, p. 3; Seoane, *El primer lenguaje constitucional español*, pp. 158–9; Lloréns Castillo, 'Sobre la aparición de "liberal"', pp. 45–51.

57 Manuel Suárez Cortina, 'Las tradiciones culturales del liberalismo español 1808–1950', in *idem* (ed.), *Las máscaras de la libertad: el liberalismo español, 1808–1950* (Madrid, 2003), pp. 14–15; Marta Ruiz Jiménez, *El liberalismo*

exaltado: la confederación de comuneros españoles durante el Trienio Liberal
(Madrid, 2007), p. 15; Raul Morodo and Elias Diaz, 'Tendencias y grupos
políticos en las Cortes de Cadiz y en las de 1820', *Cuadernos Hispanoamericanos*,
201 (1966), pp. 651–5.

58 Isabel Martín Sánchez, 'El Conciso: un periódico liberal en tiempos de las
Cortes de Cádiz', *Trienio: ilustración y liberalismo: revista de historia*, 30 (1997),
pp. 23–46.

59 *El Conciso*, 4 November 1813, p. 8.

60 On O'Donojú's role as head of the War Department and his relationship with
'Jacobin' Spaniards, see Chapter 8.

61 *El Conciso*, 7 November 1813, p. 8.

62 Gil Novales, *Diccionario del Trienio*, p. 371.

63 Art. 223, Chapter VI 'De los Secretarios de Estado y del Despacho', in
*Constitución politica de la Monarquia Española: Promulgada en Cadiz á 19 de
Marzo de 1812* (Madrid, 1820), p. 68.

64 *El Duende de los Cafés*, 15 November 1813, p. 472.

65 ASL, Vaughan Papers, E.4.1: Memoradum Charles Vaughan to Sir H. Wellesley,
winter 1812. In 1816, O'Donojú was mentioned among those who plotted to kill
Ferdinand VII in the 'conspiracy of the triangle'. During the Liberal Triennium,
he was appointed Captain-General and Superior Political Chief of New Spain
(Mexico). He died soon after signing the Convention of Cordoba (24 August
1821) by which Spain recognized Mexico's autonomy and agreed to withdraw
troops. The Spanish government refused to ratify the treaty, see Alberto Gil
Novales, *Las sociedades patrióticas (1820–1823): las libertades de expresión
y de reunión en el origen de los partidos políticos* (2 vols., Madrid, 1975), II,
p. 898; Manuel Ortuño Martínez, *Expedición a Nueva España de Xavier Mina:
materiales y ensayos* (Pamplona, 2006), p. 258.

66 Gil Novales, *Diccionario del Trienio*, p. 700; *Diario de Sesiones*, XV, pp. 321–2.

67 Marta Lorente Sariñena, *Las infracciones a la Constitución de 1812: un
mecanismo de defensa de la constitución* (Madrid, 1988), pp. 216–17.

68 BOD North, c. 13, f. 321: Copy letter of Doyle to Juan Jacinto López,
17 November 1813.

69 *El Duende de los Cafés*, 18 November 1813, p. 484.

70 *Errores del señor Doyle, ligeramente advertidos por un español que siente los
insultos de su patria* (Cadiz, 18 November 1813), p. 1.

71 Hamnett, *La política española*, p. 170.

72 BOD North, c. 16, f. 404: Copy letter Doyle to Juan Jacinto López, 18 November
1813.

73 Emilio La Parra López, *La libertad de prensa en las Cortes de Cádiz* (Valencia, 1984), pp. 4–5.

74 Ironically in a matter of months, magistrates of the restored absolutist regime applied the same term ('subversive') when they sentenced López to death for incitement to commit regicide. López fled to Gibraltar before sentence could be carried out; see Gil Novales, *Diccionario del Trienio*, p. 371.

75 BOD North, c. 17, f. 278: Copy of the ruling of the *Junta de Censura*, Cadiz, 29 March 1814.

76 Gil Novales, *Diccionario del Trienio*, p. 12.

77 BOD North, c. 16, f. 421: Joaquín Aguilar to Carlos Doyle, Cadiz, 29 March 1814.

78 BOD North, c. 16, f. 97: Vaughan to Doyle, Madrid, 25 November 1808.

79 From 31,000 soldiers, only 8,200 survived. See Raymond Rudorff, *War to the death: the sieges of Saragossa, 1808–1809* (London, 1974), p. 227; José María Massons, *Historia de la Sanidad Militar Española* (4 vols., Barcelona, 1994), II, p. 73.

80 Inmortalized by Picasso's eponymous painting, the number of dead in Guernica, estimated at over 1,600, was smaller than that of Saragossa, but the plight of these towns turned into ruins by foreign attack similarly shocked the world, see Leonardo Romero Tobar, 'Los "Sitios de Zaragoza", tema literario internacional (1808–1814)', in Martínez Sanz and de Diego García (eds.), *El comienzo de la Guerra de la Independencia*, pp. 571–89; Herbert Rutledge Southworth, *Guernica! Guernica!: A Study of Journalism, Diplomacy, Propaganda, and History* (London, 1977), pp. 362–70.

81 NA WO, 1/227, ff. 527–8: Doyle to Lord Castlereagh, Saragossa, 18 November 1808.

82 BOD North, c. 16, f. 97: Vaughan to Doyle, Madrid, 25 November 1808.

83 Ibid.

84 AHN, *Estado* 43[1], *Legajo* 184, Documents of the *Junta Central*: Memorial of activities of Carlos Doyle, Seville, 1 October 1809.

85 BOD North, c. 13, f. 180: Doyle to José de Palafox, 27 November 1808.

86 BOD North, c. 17, f. 32: Doyle to José de Palafox, 3 December 1808.

87 Doyle to Francisco Palafox, Tortosa, 8 January 1809, Doyle to *Junta Central*, Tortosa, 3 February 1808; Doyle to Francisco Palafox, 5 February 1809; Doyle to Francisco Palafox, Mequinenza,7–14 February 1809 all in Pano y Ruata, *El inglés Sir Carlos Guillermo Doyle*, pp. 78–92.

88 Doyle to Francisco Palafox, Benicarló, 7 March 1809, in Ibid., p. 93.

89 NA WO, 1/227, f. 1: Instructions of Lord Castlereagh to Lt. Col. Doyle, 2 July 1808.

90 AHN, *Estado* 43¹, *Legajo* 184 Documents of the *Junta Central*: Memorial of activities of Carlos Doyle, 1 October 1809.

91 BOD North, c. 15, f. 75: Doyle to Roche, Valencia, 11 November 1810 in reply to Roche's letter, Cadiz, 8 October 1810.

92 Brian R. Hamnett, *The Mexican bureaucracy before the Bourbon reforms, 1700–1770: a study in the limitations of absolutism* (Glasgow 1979), p. 3; Patricia H. Marks, *Deconstructing legitimacy: viceroys, merchants, and the military in late colonial Peru* (London, 2007), p. 178; David Ringrose, *Spain, Europe, and the 'Spanish miracle', 1700–1900* (Cambridge, 1996), p. 256.

93 See Chapter 4.

94 Hew Strachan, *Wellington's legacy: the reform of the British Army, 1830–54* (Manchester, 1984), pp. 6, 8, 14.

95 Gurwood (ed.), *The Dispatches*, V, pp. 34–5, 62–4; Esdaile, *The Peninsular War*, pp. 212–15.

96 Gurwood (ed.), *The Dispatches*, V, p. 165.

97 Ibid., p. 166.

98 Ibid.

99 NA FO, 72/78, ff. 44–5: Roche to Marquess Wellesley, Headquarters Spanish Army, Deleytosa, 23 August 1809.

100 Ibid.

101 Gurwood (ed.), *The Dispatches*, V, p. 245; Whittingham (ed.), *A Memoir*, pp. 182–4.

102 BOD North, c. 16, f. 314: Banker Juan Fortaleza Ross to Doyle, 6 April 1811, re. loan granted for defensive operations; AGMS, R-1496 *Expediente* Felipe de la Roche (sic): Letter of members of the municipality of Alicante re. supplies for Roche's division, 30 March 1811; Whittingham (ed.), *A Memoir*, pp. 149–56, 184.

103 Fraser, *Napoleon's Cursed War*, p. 432.

104 Whittingham to H. Wellesley, Palma, 21 February 1812, in Whittingham (ed.), *A Memoir*, pp. 173–4.

105 Gurwood (ed.), *The Dispatches*, X, p. 24.

106 Ibid., pp. 57–8.

107 *Diario de Sesiones*, XX, pp. 49–50.

108 Wellington to Roche, Frenada, 12 March 1813, in Gurwood (ed.), *The Dispatches*, X, p. 184.

109 Whittingham to Wellington, Camp before Tarragona, 6 August 1813, and Wellington to Whittingham, Lesaca, 20 August 1813, in Whittingham (ed.), *A Memoir*, pp. 228–30, 237–8. There is no record of his resignation in his file at the military archive of Segovia, see AGMS, V-43 *Expediente* Santiago Whittingham.

110 Whittingham (ed.), *A Memoir*, pp. 187–9.

111 Ibid., p. 230.

112 Whittingham to Hart Davis, 22 August 1813, in Whittingham (ed.), *A Memoir*, pp. 230–2. In this edited version of recollections left by Whittingham, his resignation is attributed to a row with the Spanish authorities. While it is true that Whittingham was unhappy with the treatment received from the government in Cadiz, no mention of the episode has been found in the Spanish military archives. It is possible that the editor of the *Memoir*, Whittingham's first son, Ferdinand (his real name was Fernando Santiago Antonio Nicolas Whittingham) being at the time of publication a major in the British army found it embarrassing to show his father in direct confrontation with the much-admired Wellington.

113 Wellington to Whittingham, Lesaca, 20 September 1813 in Whittingham, *A Memoir*, pp. 237–9; Wellington to Clinton, St. Pé, 14 November 1813, in Gurwood (ed.), *The Dispatches*, XI, pp. 286–7.

114 ASL, Vaughan Papers, uncatalogue, reel 12, OB. No. 25: *Relación de los Cuerpos*.

115 Ibid.

116 Esdaile, *Wellington and the Spanish Army*, pp. 141–2, 161.

117 AGMS, C-1704 *Expediente* Carlos Morgan Carrol and *Expediente* Miguel Carrol; Ibid., P-541 *Expediente* Guillermo Parker Carrol, *Expediente* Richard Parker Carrol, *Expediente* Manuel Poe; Ibid., C-2843 *Expediente* Juan Clarke; Ibid., C-2843 Diego Corrigan; Ibid., D-877 Carlos Guillermo Doile (sic, for Doyle); Ibid., Q-1 Juan Quearney (sic, for Kearney) Donnelan and Felipe Qeating Roche (sic, for Keating Roche); Ibid., R-1496 Felipe de la Roche (sic); Ibid., L-700 Francisco Lee; Ibid., M-8 Exp. 60 Guillermo MacVeagh; Ibid., M-2581 Juan Méelican (sic, for Mealican); Ibid., P-267 Pablo Palmés (sic, for Palmer); Ibid., O-548 Jayme O Rian (sic, for James O'Ryan); Ibid., T-314 Edmundo Temple; Ibid., U-34 Enrique Wilson.

118 AGMS, A-2104 *Expediente* Jaime Arbuthnot y Arbuthnot; Ibid., B-933 Benjamin Barrie; Ibid., E-688 Patricio Campbell; Ibid., D-1176 Carlos Downie; Ibid., D-1177 Juan Downie; Ibid., M-8 Exp. 72 James (Vizconde) Macduff; Ibid., M-8 Exp. 69 Reynaldo Macdonell; Ibid., U-6 Arturo Goodall Wavell.

119 AGMS, L-288 *Expediente* Jorge Landmann; Ibid., R-1365 Daniel Robinson; Ibid., S-2807 Carlos Silvertop; Ibid., E-1594 Robert Steile [Steele] and E-1596 Roberto Steele; Ibid., V-43 Santiago Whittingham.

120 See for example, NA WO, 1/1123, ff. 511–12: John Downie to Lord Liverpool, Valencia de Alcantara, 14 February 1811; Whittingham (ed.), *A Memoir*, pp. 25, 163, 174, 177, 184, 229–30.

121 See, for example, AGMS, M-8 *Expediente* 60 Guillermo Mac Veagh: Military background of Guillermo MacVeagh, *teniente en el Ejército británico*, 27 November 1809; Whittingham (ed.), *A Memoir*, pp. 51, 93, 108, 174, 281, 496.

122 See, for example, Whittingham's account of Count Tilly's proposals in Chapter 4; also *Archivo General de Indias, Estado* 98, Nr. 40: Official Translation of an article of *The Morning Chronicle* regarding 'ingleses americanos', 25 October 1815; Leopoldo Alas 'Clarin', *La Regenta* (Madrid, 1900), p. 253.

123 See, for example, AMO, Reales Ordenes 1800–1810, E.4, f. 712: Proclamation of Irish volunteer William Parker Carrol, Oviedo 30 November 1808 entitled 'Asturianos: Un Oficial inglés tiene el honor de hablaros . . .' ('Asturians: An English officer has the honour of addressing you . . .').

124 Linda Colley, 'Britishness and Otherness: An Argument', *Journal of British Studies*, 31 (October 1992), pp. 311–29.

125 Colley, *Britons*, pp. 364–75.

126 BOD North, c. 14, f. 245: Doyle to Lord Castlereagh, Cadiz, 16 November 1809.

127 Roland Thorne, 'Stewart, Robert, Viscount Castlereagh and second marquess of Londonderry (1769–1822)', DNB, Sept 2004; online edn, May 2009 [http://www.oxforddnb.com/view/article/26507, accessed 19 February 2009].

128 See, for example, Roche, Doyle and Carrol's communications regarding Spanish unity in Chapter 4. After the war, the image of these three Irishmen bearing Spanish medals was a regular feature at social functions in Dublin and London. In 1817, Doyle became godfather to Carrol's first child, William Hutchinson Parker Carrol, see Robertson, *A long way*, pp. 89, 98–9, 113.

129 For example, Downie's friendship with the Earl of Fife, see AB, MS3175/1410/3 Downie to Fife, 4 July 1813; Ibid., 1433/1 *idem*, 24 October 1813; Ibid., 1412/1 *idem*, September 1814.

130 AGMS, D-1177 *Expediente* Juan Downie: Downie to members of the *Cortes*, Porto Alegre, 13 March 1812.

131 AGMS, S-2807 *Expediente* Carlos Silvertop: Silvertop to Elizondo, 13 September 1815.

132 AGMS, T-314 *Expediente* Edmundo Temple: Temple to Head of Spanish Royal Household, Madrid, 22 May 1814.

133 Whittingham, *A Memoir*, pp. ix, 101–2.

134 BOD North, c. 13, f. 236: Doyle to José Palafox, 15 December 1808.

135 See Chapter 3.

136 ASL, Vaughan Papers, uncatalogued, reel 13: Report of session of the Spanish *Cortes*, 3 May 1812.

137 AGMS, D-1177 *Expediente* Juan Downie: Rank of *brigadier* awarded on 10 April 1812 registered in main *hoja de servicio*, added report and certificate of services of Juan Downie by Secretary of War Juan O'Donojú, Cadiz, 16 August 1813 and by *Estado Mayor de los Reales Exércitos*, Madrid, 19 June 1818; Isabel Sánchez (ed.), *Caballeros de la Real y Militar Orden de San Fernando*, I, pp. 25–35.

138 *Diario de Sesiones*, III, pp. 307–8.

139 AGMS, D-1177 *Expediente* Juan Downie: Annotated report on secret committee sessions of the *Cortes* regarding Downie's request for Spanish nationality, 28 April 1812 and 3 May 1812.

140 BNE, R/63250/9 k *Documentos relativos a la vida y acciones militares durante la Guerra de la Independencia de D. Juan Downie*; Guzmán y Gallo, *El Dos de Mayo*, pp. 726–7.

141 Christian Demange, *El dos de mayo: mito y fiesta nacional, 1808–1958* (Madrid, 2004), pp. 136–40.

142 In this respect, their experience seems to back Linda Colley's view of British society as cohered around the Monarchy and the notion of British 'freedom', see Colley, *Britons,* pp. 30–42, 193–4, 201, 216–20, 354.

143 *El Universal*, 14 January 1814, pp. 54–5.

144 Brown, *Adventuring through Spanish Colonies*, p. 114.

145 R. J. Smith, *The Gothic Bequest: Medieval Institutions in British Thought, 1688–1863* (Cambridge, 2002), pp. 5, 39, 44–95; Stephanie L. Barczewski, *Myth and National Identity in Nineteenth Century Britain: The Legends of King Arthur and Robin Hood* (Oxford, 2000), pp. 11–123; David Armitage, *The Ideological Origins of the British Empire* (Cambridge, 2000), pp. 125–45.

146 See Chapter 6.

147 Whittingham (ed.), *A Memoir*, p. 128.

148 Pittock, *Scottish and Irish Romanticism*, pp. 28–9.

149 See Chapter 2.

150 BOD North, c. 15, f. 62: Doyle to Spanish minister Bardaxi, *circa* 1810.

Chapter 8

1 *El Redactor General*, 2 August 1812, p. 1636.

2 Ibid.

3 CU, Add. 7521, ff. 350–424: Correspondence General Baron de Rouelle and General Roche, Sagunto, 10 October 1813 to 24 May 1814; AGMS, Q-1

Expediente Felipe Qeating Roche: Certificate of services of Felipe Roche by
General Xavier Elío, 12 March 1815; Louis Gabriel Suchet, *Memoirs of the
War in Spain* (2 vols., London, 1829), II, p. 327; Jean Baptiste Pierre Jullien
De Courcelles, *Dictionnaire Historique et Biographique des Généraux Français
depuis le XIe siècle et 1823* (9 vols., Paris, 1823), IX, pp. 66–70.

4 BOD North, c. 16, f. 408–10: Vaughan to Doyle, Madrid, 3 January 1814. Those
covered by the term would not have considered themselves 'Jacobins' because
they were not advocates of direct democracy, see Hamnett, *La política española*,
pp. 131–2.

5 Oman, *A History of the Peninsular War*, VI, pp. 204–5; Esdaile, *Wellington and
the Spanish Army*, pp. 143–4.

6 CU, Add. 7521, ff. 328–31: General O'Donojú, Inspector General of the Spanish
Infantry to General Roche, Juan de Luz, 1 February 1814.

7 *Elogio histórico al Excmo. Señor D. Francisco Xavier Castaños con el motivo de
haberse publicado por su orden la constitución española en éste Principado de
Asturias* (Oviedo, 1812).

8 José Luis Comellas, *Los primeros pronunciamientos en España 1814–1820*
(Madrid, 1958), p. 104.

9 Castaños served under all Spanish regimes until his death in 1852, at the age of
96. Made Duke of Bailén by Ferdinand VII in 1833, he was appointed personal
tutor to his daughter, the future liberal Queen Isabel in 1843 and made a life
senator in 1845, see 'Necrología de Francisco Javier Castaños', *Eco literario de
Europa: Revista Universal* (Madrid, 1852), pp. 320–33.

10 Whittingham to his brother-in-law, Saragossa, 20 March, 1814, and *idem*,
Madrid, 21 May 1814, in Whittingham (ed.), *A Memoir*, pp. 253–4.

11 Whittingham to Hart-Davis, 11 July 1813, in Whittingham (ed.), *A Memoir*,
pp. 225–7.

12 BOD North, c. 16, f. 396: Duke of Infantado to General Doyle, 30 August 1813;
ibid., f. 436: Memorandum re. Doyle's depot, 15 May 1814.

13 Wellington to J. de Carvajal, Freneda, 7 March 1813 and Wellington to
H. Wellesley, Freneda, 16 April 1813, in Gurwood (ed.), *The Dispatches*, X,
pp. 169–70, 303; Gil Novales, *Diccionario del Trienio*, p. 4.

14 Two of the volunteers had been killed in action (Marshal and MacDougal),
nine left the Spanish service of whom four did so before the war ended (Carlo
Doyle, Landor, the Earl of Fife and Green). Of the remaining five (Richard
Parker Carrol, Meagher, Milburne and Reed) there are no further records. See
Biographical Notes.

15 The Scots James Arbuthnot, Benjamin Barrie, John and Charles Downie, the
Irish John Kearney and James O'Ryan, and the English Charles Silvertop. See
Biographical Notes.

16 AHN, *Estado* 7368, *Orden de Carlos III*: Extract Decrees Nr. 76 *Brigadier* Juan
Downie, 18 October 1812; ibid., Nr. 90 *Teniente Coronel* Juan Carthe (sic, for
Clarke), 4 April 1813; ibid., Nr. 181 *Teniente General* Carlos Guillermo Doyle,
24 October 1814; ibid., Nr. 190 *Mariscal de Campo* Guillermo Parker Carrol,
18 December 1814; ibid., Nr. 247 *Teniente Coronel* Carlos Downie, 2 April 1819;
ibid., Nr. 308 *Teniente General* Felipe Keating Roche, 22 May 1819; ibid., Nr.
399 *Teniente Coronel* Roberto Steele, 29 December 1819; ibid., Nr. 213 *Capitán*
Carlos [Morgan] Carrol, 3 February 1819; ibid., Nr. 215 *Capitán* Manuel Poe,
12 February 1819; ibid., Nr. 219 *Coronel* Patricio Campbell, 19 February 1819;
ibid., Nr. 221 *Brigadier* Reynaldo Macdonell, 26 February 1819; ibid., Nr. 222
Coronel Carlos Silvertop, 26 February 1819; AHN, *Estado* 7369 Order of Charles
III, Extract Decrees Nr. 13 Capitán Edmundo Temple, 23 April 1816; Nr. 16
Coronel [Edwin Rowlandson] Green, 26 April 1816; ibid., Nr. 115 *Teniente
Coronel* Francisco Lee, 29 December 1816; ibid., Nr. 173 *Teniente Coronel*
Arturo Wavel [sic], 11 December 1817. Order of Charles III granted to General
James Whitingam [sic, for Samuel Ford Whittingham] undated, mentioned in
Archivo General de Simancas, *Documentos relativos a Inglaterra: 1254–1834*
(Madrid, 1947), p. 412.

17 AHN, *Estado* 7368, *Orden de Carlos III*: Wavell, C. Downie, Roche, Steele,
C. M. Carrol, Poe, Campbell, Macdonell, Silvertop.

18 David Alan Guilmour Waddell, 'British neutrality and Spanish-American
independence: The problem of foreign enlistment', *Journal of Latin American
Studies*, 19/1 (1987), 1–13.

19 *The London Gazette*, 11 May 1813, p. 898.

20 Ibid., 9 May 1815, p. 872.

21 Both on the same day, ibid., 21 May 1816, p. 961.

22 Ibid., 15 February 1817, p. 334.

23 Ibid., 27 March 1817, p. 757.

24 BL, Add. 38265, ff. 8, 11, 228, 229, 230: Correspondence regarding Sir Robert
Steele's debts and imprisonment, March–June 1817.

25 Forster (ed.), *The Works and Life*, I, p. 120.

26 See Chapter 5.

27 AGMS, Q-1 *Expediente* Felipe Qeating (sic) Roche.

28 Ibid.

29 Obituary 'Sir P.K. Roche', *The Gentleman's Magazine*, April 1829, p. 372.

30 NA Records of the Prerogative Court of Canterbury (Prob): 11/1753 Will and Testament of Sir Philip Keating Roche. Much of his wealth was inherited from his wife, Elizabeth Salwey, who had died in 1799, see John Burke, *A Genealogical and Heraldic History of The Commoners of Great Britain and Ireland Enjoying Territorial Possessions or High Official Rank; but Uninvested with Heritable Honours* (4 vols., London, 1836), I, p. 155.

31 AGMS, S-2807 *Expediente* Carlos Silvertop: Note from *Comandancia General de Granada* to Carlos Silvertop, 21 August 1821, granting a period of leave to undertake mineralogical studies.

32 Charles Silvertop, *A Geological Sketch of the Tertiary Formation in the Provinces of Granada and Murcia, Spain with Notices Respecting Primary, Secondary, and Volcanic Rocks in the Same District and Sections* (London, 1836); Geological Society of London, *Proceedings of the Geological Society of London*, 1 (1826–34), pp. 1, 216, 235, 261, 293, 456, 465; ibid., 2 (1838), pp. 34, 80, 131, 135; ibid., 3 (1838–42), pp. 193, 260. See also Ellis F. Owen and Edward P. F. Rose, 'Early Jurassic Brachiopods from Gibraltar, and their Tethyan affinities', *Paleontology*, 40/2 (1997), 509; Juan-Carlos Braga, Agustin Martin-Algarra and Pascual Rivas, 'Hettangian and Sinemurian of Baños de Alhama de Granada reference section for the West-mediterranean Hettangian (Betic Cordillera, Southern Spain)', *Geobios*, 17/3 (1984), 271.

33 Silvertop, *A Geological*, p. ii.

34 Ibid. Silvertop died 'of inflamation of the lungs' on 10 June 1839, at Rennes, Britany, see *The Newcastle Courant*, 21 June 1839, p. 4.

35 BOD North, c. 16, f. 504: Lorenzo Vahajosa to Doyle, Caravaca, 4 March 1816; ibid., f. 508: Luis O Shea to Doyle, Caravaca, 10 March 1816; ibid., f. 507: Vahajosa to Doyle, Caravaca, 11 March 1816.

36 BOD North, c. 16, f. 468: Minister of War Francisco Ballesteros to General Doyle, Royal Palace, Madrid, 6 August 1815.

37 Ibid.

38 Gil Muñoz, 'Revolución en las instituciones', p. 866.

39 BOD North, c. 16, f. 396: Duke of Infantado to General Doyle, 30 August 1813.

40 AGMS, Q-1 *Expediente* Juan Quearney Donnelan (Kearney): Duke of Infantado, on behalf of the King, appointing Kearney director of the *Método de Enseñanza Mútua*, 4 April 1819; ibid., Secretary of State Agustin Argüelles to Secretary of War Pedro Diaz de Ribera backing Kearney's pedagogic role, 16 April 1820; *The Monthly Repository of Theology and General Literature*, October 1819, 649;

The Monthly Magazine, April 1820, p. 247; *The Friend of India*, Vol. 3, July 1820, 177–8; *The Christian Observer*, Vol. 20, October 1821, p. 808; *The Evangelical Magazine and Missionary Chronicle*, November 1821, p. 520; *The Missionary Herald*, April 1823, p. 121.

41 This method of education was established in 1801 by Joseph Lancaster, a Quaker minister, who benefited from the sponsorship of radical politicians James Mill, Henry Brougham and Samuel Whitbread, see G. F. Bartle, 'Lancaster, Joseph (1778–1838)', DNB, September 2004; online edn, January 2008 [www. oxforddnb.com/view/article /15963, accessed 19 April 2009].

42 Julio Ruiz Berrio, *Política escolar de España en el siglo XIX: (1808–1833)* (Madrid, 1970), pp. 58–9.

43 Bernabé Bartolomé Martínez, *Historia de la enseñanza en España y América: La educación en la España contemporánea (1789–1975)* (Madrid, 1994), pp. 145, 148, 151, 262; Marcelo Caruso, 'Disruptive dynamics: The spatial dimensions of the Spanish networks in the spread of monitorial schooling (1815–1825)', *Paedagogica Historica*, 43/2 (2007), 274–5.

44 BOD North, c. 16, f. 476: Correspondence regarding thermal baths at Archena and Mula, province of Murcia, Antonio de Elola, *Intendente* of Murcia to General Doyle, 22 January 1816; ibid., f. 482: Elola to Doyle, 31 January 1816; ibid., f. 483: Cosme Torreno, Caravaca, 4 February 1816; ibid., f. 489: Elola to Doyle, 10 February 1816.

45 Gil Novales, *Diccionario del Trienio*, p. 209.

46 BOD North, c. 16, f. 520: Elola to Doyle, Murcia, 24 April 1816.

47 AGMS, D-877 *Expediente* Carlos Guillermo Doile (sic): Certificate of extension of leave and permit for *Teniente General* Doyle to reside in Great Britain, Spanish Ministry of War, 21 May 1835.

48 ANF, LH/801/30, Register of the *Legion d'honneur*, f. 2: Dossier Nr. 23 'Charles Guilleaume Doyle, Général dans le Service du SMC', 8 October 1837. Although listed only under his Spanish rank, his status in the British army was acknowledged in the main text. He had been made a lieutenant general in the British army only 9 months earlier, see *The London Gazette*, 10 January 1837, p. 5.

49 No reason was recorded for the award in the Register of the Legion (ANF, LH/801/30). No file under Doyle's name has been found among those of the section O/3/840 Maison du Roi: *Dossier Legion d'honneur – Demandes D'Admission dans L'Ordre Royal de la Legion d'honneur*, also at the *Archives Nationales de France*, neither any documentation that could shed light on the subject in his correspondence at the Bodleian Library (North Collection).

50   Doyle died in Paris in 1842. There are doubts, however, regarding his date
     of birth. Three obituaries (*The Examiner*, 5 November 1842, p. 14; *John Bull*,
     5 November, 1842, p. 540; *The Age*, 6 November, p. 8) reported that he was
     62 years old at time of death. A manuscript report at the ANF backing his
     candidature to the *Legion d'honneur* stated that he was born in Dublin, 16 April
     1782 (ANF, LH/801/030): 'Charles Guillaume Doyle né en Dublin, le 16 avril
     1782, Lieutenant General dans le Service du SMC'. But the *Oxford Dictionary of
     National Biography* shows him as born 12 years earlier (1770), see 'Doyle', DNB,
     [www.oxforddnb.com/view/ article/7997, accessed 1 July 2005]. *FamilySearch*,
     the largest genealogy organization in the world run by The Church of Jesus
     Christ of Latter-day Saints, has no record of his birth.
51   Whittingham to his brother-in-law, Saragossa, 20 March 1814, in Whittingham
     (ed.), *A Memoir*, p. 253.
52   Whittingham to his brother-in-law, Madrid, 21 May 1814, in Whittingham
     (ed.), *A Memoir*, p. 255.
53   Ibid.
54   Session 1 March 1815, *Parliamentary Debates*, 1815, XXIX, col. 1126–66.
55   AGMS, V-43 *Expediente* Santiago Whittingham.
56   Whittingham (ed.), *A Memoir*, p. 269.
57   Whittingham to his brother-in-law, Madrid, 21 May 1814, in Whittingham
     (ed.), *A Memoir*, pp. 254–5.
58   AGMS, V-43 *Expediente* Santiago Whittingham; Ana María Berazaluce (ed.),
     Pedro Agustin Giron, Marques de las Amarillas – Recuerdos (1778–1837) (3 vols.,
     Pamplona, 1978), pp. 42–3; Isabel Sánchez (ed.), *Caballeros de la Real y Militar
     Orden de San Fernando*, I, pp. 14–16.
59   Ferdinand VII abolished the slave trade by means of an international treaty
     signed with Great Britain (23 September 1817) and ratified by a royal decree
     (19 December 1817). But the commerce continued with the complicity of the
     Spanish authorities until 1868, when slavery itself was ended in the colonies
     (Cuba, Puerto Rico, Philippines) by the liberal-conservative (Unionist)
     government of Francisco Serrano. See ASL, Vaughan Papers E/8/2: Charles
     Vaughan to Lord Castlereagh, re. Whittingham's lobbying against the slave trade,
     Madrid, 5 September 1816; BCL, Rl Pr 2pb Biog. U-Z – B 4120; Bristol Record
     Office, Hart Davis Papers, 41593/Co/11/47-48-50-51: Correspondence Hart
     Davis and William Wilberforce, 1815–21; 'Tratado entre los reyes de España y
     de la Gran Bretaña para la abolición del tráfico de negros: firmado en Madrid
     el 23 de setiembre de 1817', in Alejandro del Cantillo (ed.), *Tratados, convenios*

y declaraciones de paz y de comercio que han hecho con las potencias extranjeras los monarcas españoles de la Casa de Borbon desde el año de 1700 hasta el dia puestos en òrden è ilustrados muchos de ellos con la historia de sus respectivas negociaciones (Madrid, 1843), pp. 800–11; Arthur F. Corwin, *Spain and the Abolition of Slavery in Cuba, 1817–1886* (London, 1967), pp. 29–61, 218–19.

60 Whittingham (ed.), *A Memoir*, pp. 298–312; Thorne (ed.), *The House of Commons, 1790–1820*, IV, pp. 573–4.

61 AGMS, V-43 *Expediente* Santiago Whittingham: Address of *Teniente General* Whittingham to the King, Real Sitio de Sacedon, 19 July 1819.

62 See Chapters 1 and 5.

63 AGMS, D-1177 *Expediente* Juan Downie: Notification of Royal appointment of Downie as commander of Alcazar of Seville signed by Duke of San Carlos, 17 June 1814.

64 Ibid., Downie to the King, Seville, 12 November 1814.

65 [Daniel Robinson], *The Political Constitution of the Spanish Monarchy Proclaimed in Cadiz, 19th March, 1812* (London, 1813), pp. v–vi.

66 Alberto Gil Novales, *Las sociedades patrióticas (1820–1823): las libertades de expresión y de reunión en el origen de los partidos políticos* (2 vols., Madrid, 1975), I, pp. 581, 687.

67 AGMS, D-1177 *Expediente* Juan Downie: *Al Augusto Congreso Nacional – El Mariscal de Campo D. Juan Downie* (Seville, 24 May 1821).

68 *Diario de las Sesiones de Cortes Celebradas en Sevilla y Cadiz en 1823* (Madrid, 1858), Session of 11 June 1823, p. 242.

69 Thomas Steele, *Notes of the War in Spain Detailing Occurrences Military and Political in Galicia, and at Gibraltar and Cadiz from the Fall of Corunna to the Occupation of Cadiz by the French* (London, 1824), p. 135.

70 BNE, R/63248: *Manifiesto de Juan Downie*, Carraca, 16 June 1823; ibid., R/63241: *Manifiesto a los Españoles y compañeros de armas del Mariscal de Campo de los Reales Ejercitos Sir Juan Downie*, Seville, June–October 1823; *The Edinburgh Magazine and Literary Miscellany*, Vol. 2, July 1823, 109–10. With Ferdinand back on the throne, Downie was rewarded with yet more honours. He died penniless on 5 June 1826. Royal intervention prevented the embargo of his possessions, but the King ordered his brother to hand over the legendary sword of Pizarro to the Royal armouries, see BNE, R/63250/6 *Documentos relativos a la vida y acciones*: Royal Order of 2 November 1826; ibid., Copy letter Carlos Downie to the King, 18 December 1826; Marchesi, *Catálogo de la Real Armería*, pp. 99–100.

71   AGMS, L-700 *Expediente* Francisco Lee: Correspondence of *teniente coronel de los*
     Exercitos Nacionales Francisco Lee, 20 January 1821 to 8 September 1823; AGMS,
     R-1365, *Expediente* Daniel Robinson; *The Morning Post*, 10 October 1823, p. 2.

72   AGMS, P-541 *Expediente* Guillermo Parker Carrol: Carrol to Spanish Minister
     of War, Miguel López Baños, Malta, 20 September 1822.

73   AGMS, D-1176 *Expediente* Carlos Downie: Note of confirmation of adherence
     to the constitutional system signed by Nicolas Chacón, *coronel* Regiment of
     Murcia, September 1820; ibid., Juan Downie to the King, 10 October 1823; ibid.,
     Record of Carlos Downie's services, 6 December 1837; BNE, R/63250/9 h. Copy
     letter Juan Downie to the King, Seville, 3 February 1825.

74   Jaime Torras Elias, *Liberalismo y rebeldía campesina, 1820–1823* (Barcelona,
     1976), pp. 32–3.

75   Jean Baptiste Honoure Raymond Capefigue, *Récit des opérations de l'armée*
     française en Espagne, sous les ordres de S. A. R. Mgr. duc d'Angoulême:
     Accompagné de notices biographiques et géographiques; et suivi de considérations
     sur les résultats politiques de cette guerre (Paris, 1823), pp. xiii–xvi; William Penn
     Cresson, *The Holy Alliance: The European Background of the Monroe Doctrine*
     (New York, 1922), pp. 114–15.

76   'Convention between Sir Robert Wilson and the Spanish Government', in
     Thomas Steele, *Notes on the War*, pp. 256–61; 'Convenio entre don Juan Alvarez
     y Mendizabal por parte del general don Miguel Ricardo de Álava, ministro de
     Su Majestad Católica en Londres, y el mayor general sir Lnftus Otway (sic) por
     la del coronel de Lucy Evans M. P. para organizar una legión auxiliar británica
     al servicio de España; ajusfado (sic) y firmado en aquella corte en junio de 1835',
     in Alejandro del Cantillo (ed.), *Tratados, convenios y declaraciones de paz y de*
     comercio que han hecho con las potencias estranjeras los monarcas españoles de la
     casa de Borbón desde el año 1700 hasta el dia. Puestos en orden e ilustrados con la
     historia de sus respectivas negociaciones (Madrid, 1843), pp. 867–8. One veteran
     volunteer of the Peninsular War, Daniel Robinson, fought with the liberals in
     the Carlist wars, but not as a member of the British Legion, see 'Spain: arms and
     ammunitions', *The Morning Post*, 12 March 1836, p. 6.

77   Manuel Ortuño Martínez, *Expedición a Nueva España de Xavier Mina:*
     materiales y ensayos (Pamplona, 2006), *passim*; Riall, *Garibaldi*, pp. 41–5.

78   Ana Laura de la Torre Saavedra, *La expedición de Xavier Mina a Nueva España:*
     una utopía liberal imperial (Mexico, 1999), *passim*.

79   See Chapters 1 and 2.

80 Downie to Miranda, 4 June 1810, in Dávila (ed.), *Archivo del General Miranda*, XXIII, p. 456; Robert Harvey, *The Liberators: Latin America's Struggle for Independence, 1810–1830* (London, 2000), p. 58.

81 Sharp to Miranda enclosing note of John Downie, 20 August 1810, in Dávila (ed.), *Archivo del General Miranda*, XXIII, p. 521.

82 AGMS, S-1490 *Expediente* Justo Rufino de San Martín; BOD North, c. 16, ff. 200, 260: Correspondence Doyle re. Justo de San Martín, 1810; BOD North, c. 16, f. 378: Justo San Martín to Doyle, 7 January 1812; ibid., c. 15, ff. 29, 100, 168: Correspondence Doyle to Justo de San Martín, June 1810 to 11 February 1811; BL, Add. 15675, f. 19: Doyle re. Justo de San Martín, 22 June 1810.

83 BOD North, c. 16, f. 386: Torrijos to Doyle, 17 May 1813; AGMS, U-6 *Expediente* Arturo Wavell: Certificate of services signed by Jose María Torrijos, *coronel* of *Tiradores de Doyle*, 12 May 1812.

84 Irene Castells, *La utopía insurreccional del liberalismo: Torrijos y las conspiraciones liberales de la década ominosa* (Barcelona, 1989), *passim*; Vicente Lloréns Castillo, *Liberales y románticos. Una emigración española en Inglaterra, 1823–1834* (México, 1954), pp. 103–5.

85 Antonio Machado, 'Torrijos y sus compañeros', *Nuestra Bandera*, Barcelona, III, (March 1938) reproduced in Monique Alonso, *Antonio Machado: Poeta en el exilio* (Barcelona, 1985), pp. 213–17. Gisbert's painting has become the visual signature of the new extension of the *Museo del Prado* in Madrid.

86 Viniegra de Torrijos, *Vida del General Torrijos*, I, p. 21.

87 See Chapter 7.

88 John Miller, *Memorias del General Miller al Servicio de la República del Perú escritas en Inglés por Mr. John Miller y traducidas al castellano por el General Torrijos* (2 vols., London, 1829); Viniegra de Torrijos, *Vida del General Torrijos*, I, pp. 10–11, 15–16, 21–2, 36–7, 289.

89 AB, MS3175/2277: José de San Martín to Earl of Fife, undated, stamped with a Peruvian seal (*circa* 1821–23); AB, MS3175/2270: José de San Martín to Earl of Fife, Brussels, 19 March 1827.

90 AGMS, *Personal Célebre* 3S 6, *Expediente* José de San Martín Matorras.

91 ASL, Vaughan Papers, E11/2: Henry Wellesley to Lord Wellesley, Cadiz, 12 December 1811; Andres Angel de la Vega to the Duke of Ciudad Rodrigo, Cadiz, 28 April 1813, in Wellington (ed.), *Supplementary Despatches*, VIII, p. 181; María Teresa García Godoy, *Las Cortes de Cádiz y América: el primer vocabulario liberal español y mejicano (1810–1814)* (Sevilla, 1998), pp. 160–3, 175.

92 Jerdan, *National Portrait*, II, pp. 146–7.

93 See above, p. 197; Antonio Alcalá Galiano (ed.), *Memorias de D. Antonio Alcalá Galiano publicadas por su hijo* (2 vols., Madrid, 1886), I, p. 356.

94 AGMS, *Personal Célebre* 3S 6, *Expediente* José de San Martín Matorras: Heredia, Inspector General of the Spanish Cavalry to Captain San Martín, 9 September 1811.

95 John Miller, *Memoirs of General Miller, in the Service of the Republic of Peru* (2 vols., London, 1828), I, pp. 423–4; *idem, Memorias del General Miller*, I, pp. 402–3. Torrijos's translated account has been part of the canon of Latin American historiography since its adoption by the Argentine historian and statesman Bartolomé Mitre, see his *Historia de San Martín y de la emancipación sud-americana* (3 vols., Buenos Aires, 1887), I, pp. 119–21 and *idem, The Emancipation of South America, A Condensed Translation by W. Pilling of The History of San Martín* (London, 1893), p. 36.

96 Earl of Fife to San Martín, Edinburgh, 3 June 1817, in Museo Histórico Nacional, *San Martín – Su correspondencia 1823–1850* (Buenos Aires, 1911), p. 309; AB, MS3175/2277: San Martín to fourth Earl of Fife, Lima, undated, with seal bearing the inscription 'Renació el Sol de Peru' (The Peruvian sun reborn).

97 *The Morning Chronicle*, 4 May 1824, p. 2; *The Morning Post*, 6 May 1824, p. 2; *The Morning Chronicle*, 8 May 1824; *Caledonian Mercury*, 13 May 1824; 'Dinner to General San Martín', *The Morning Chronicle,* 23 June 1824, p. 3; *The Morning Chronicle*, 14 July 1824, p. 2; *Caledonian Mercury,*17 July 1824.

98 AB MS2727/2/94 Fife to R. Wharton Duff, 18 August 1824.

99 Aberdeen City Archives, Records of Royal Burgh of Banff (BH4) Freemen of the Burgh: 'José de San Martín, 19 August 1824'; John Lynch, *San Martín: Argentine Soldier, American Hero* (London, 2009), p. 204.

100 'Treaty of amity, commerce, and navigation, between His Majesty and the United Provinces of Rio de la Plata. Signed at Buenos Ayres, February 2, 1825', *House of Commons Papers; Accounts and Papers* (1825), XXVI, 21–9.

101 Lynch, *San Martín*, pp. 204–28; Tayler, *Book of the Duffs*, I, pp. 203–10; *The Scots Magazine and Edinburgh Literary Miscellany: Being a General Repository of Literature, History and Politics for 1817* (Edinburgh, 1817), p. 155; Richenda Miers, *Scotland* (London, 2006), p. 384.

102 In 1822, the Spanish consul in Gibraltar reported that *brigadier* Reginald Macdonnell had been seen at that port embarking in a Buenos Aires vessel. No further records of his life and career has so far been found in Spanish military records, see AGMS, M-8 *Expediente* 69 Reynaldo Macdonnell: Francisco Martinez de la Rosa to Military Headquarters, Cadiz, 5 April 1822.

103 Lynch, *San Martín*, pp. 147–57.

104 AGMS, C-1704 *Expediente* Carlos Morgan Carrol.

105 Basil R. N. Hall, *Extracts from a Journal Written on the Coasts of Chili, Peru and Mexico in the Years 1820, 1821, 1822* (London, 1840), pp. 328–34; Thomas Sutcliffe, *Sixteen Years in Chile and Peru from 1822 to 1839* (London, 1841), pp. 145–6, 150; Pedro Pablo Figueroa, *Diccionario biográfico de estranjeros* [sic] *en Chile* (Santiago, 1900), pp. 166–7; Tomás Guevara, *Historia de Curicó* (Santiago, 1890), Chapter IX, in *Biblioteca Virtual Miguel de Cervantes* [www.cervantesvirtual.com/servlet/SirveObras/80294996212796496754491/index.htm, accessed 10 October 2009].

106 The local newspaper *El Rancagüino*, for example, has its headquarters in the street Carlos María O'Carrol 518, Rancagua, Chile, see [www.elrancaguino.cl/news/ corporativo, accessed 20 March 2010].

107 Maria Graham, *Journal of a Residence in Chile, During the Year 1822; and a Voyage from Chile to Brazil, in 1823* (London, 1824), pp. 279–80; Thomas Sutcliffe, *Sixteen Years in Chile and Peru from 1822 to 1839* (London, 1841), p. 235.

108 AGMS, U-6 *Expediente* Arturo Wavell.

109 Manuel Bianchi, 'General Arthur Goodall Wavell – BBC Broadcast', in *idem*, *Chile and Great Britain* (London, 1944), pp. 34–6. His status of Chilean envoy was discredited by the British admiral Thomas Cochrane who, arriving a few days later, claimed that Wavell had no diplomatic credentials and that the stamp in his Chilean passport predated the declaration of Mexico's independence. This, however, appears to have been a case of sour grapes. Cochrane was angered by the cold reception he had met at Acapulco due to Wavell's account of his seizure of part of the Chilean navy to pursue his own campaign of piracy in the Pacific, see Henry McKenzie Johnson, *Missions to Mexico: A Tale of British Diplomacy in the 1820s* (London, 1992), pp. 38–9.

110 Arthur Goodall Wavell, *Notes and Reflections on Mexico, Its Mines, Policy, &c. by a Traveller, Some Years Resident in that and the Other American States* (London, 1827), p. 52; 'Maria de Guadaloupe Anna Antonia Robinson', in *Worldwide Greathead Family My One-Name Study* [www.greathead.org/greathead2-o/p104.htm, accessed 12 February 2012]; NA Prob. 11/2090: Will of Daniel Robinson.

111 McKenzie Johnson, *Missions to Mexico*, pp. 38–9, 243.

112 Arthur Goodall Wavell, *Táctica de la infantería de linea y ligera, y de las maniobras de linea, con reglas para el servicio de campaña* (London, 1823); Wavell, *Notes and Reflections*.

113 See Chapter 6.

114 Thomas W. Cutrer, *The English Texans* (San Antonio, 1985), pp. 41, 44.

115 AGMS, T-314 *Expediente* Edmundo Temple.

116 Henry English, *A General Guide to the Companies Formed for Working Foreign Mines with Their Prospectus, Amount of Capital, Number of Shares, Names of Directors, &c. and an Appendix Showing Their Progress since Their Formation, Obtained from Authentic Sources* (London, 1825), pp. 45–7, 70; Edmond Temple, *Travels in Various Parts of Peru, Including a Year's Residence in Potosi* (2 vols., Philadelphia, 1830), pp. 1–3.

117 Edmond Temple, *Travels in Various Parts of Peru*.

118 Speake, *Literature of Travel*, p. 24.

119 Temple, *Travels in Various Parts of Peru*.

120 See Chapter 7. AGMS, E-688 *Expediente* Patricio Campbell: Campbell to Spanish Minister of War, 30 April 1821.

121 Ibid.: Royal Order regarding Patricio Campbell, Madrid, Palacio, 5 May 1821.

122 *The Morning Post*, 23 October 1823, p. 2.

123 ASL, Vaughan Papers, C 25-4: Campbell to Vaughan, Bogotá, 27 March 1826; ibid., C24/4 Campbell to Vaughan, Bogotá, 28 November 1826; John Lynch, *Simón Bolívar: A Life* (London, 2006), pp. 229–30, 263–6.

124 Bolivar to Col. Patrick Campbell, Guayaquil, 5 August 1829, in David Bushnell (ed.), *El Libertador: Writings of Simón Bolivar* (Oxford, 2003), pp. 172–3.

125 'José de San Martín', *Encyclopædia Britannica Online Academic Edition*, Encyclopædia Britannica Inc. [www.britannica.com/EBchecked/topic/521474/Jose-de-San-Martín, accessed 14 February 2012]; John C. Metford, *San Martín, the Liberator* (Oxford, 1950), p. 29.

126 Stephen Conway, *Britain, Ireland, and Continental Europe in the Eighteenth Century: Similarities, Connections, Identities* (Oxford, 2011), pp. 266–78; Duffy, *The Military Experience*, p. 3.

127 He served the Spanish Army for 54 years, 8 months and 12 days, until his death in 1863, see AGMS, A-2104 *Expediente* Jaime Arbuthnot y Arbuthnot.

128 AHN, *Estado* 87, Nr. 33, f. 1a: Roche to Spanish Ambassador Fernán Nuñez, 1 July 1816; ibid., f. 1b: Popham to Roche, 30 June 1816; Hugh Popham, 'Popham, Sir Home Riggs (1762–1820)', DNB, September 2004; online edn, January 2008 [www.oxforddnb.com/view/article/22541, accessed 28 March 2008].

129 AGMS, D-1177 *Expediente* Juan Downie: Downie to the King, 12 November 1814.

130 See, for example, Downie's decision to incorporate Miranda's idea of resorting to the use of lances in his Legion of Extremadura (Chapter 5).

131 Juan Bautista Alberdi, *Escritos póstumos de J. B. Alberdi* (16 vols., Buenos Aires, 1895–1901), IV, p. 330; John Lynch, *San Martín: Argentine Soldier, American Hero* (London, 2009), pp. 46, 155.

132 See Chapters 2 and 3.

133 Lynch, *San Martín*, pp. 25, 222, 226–7; Simon Bolivar, 'An American's convictions' (a translation of Bolivar's 'Contestación de un americano meridional a un caballero de esta isla', Kingston, 6 September 1815) in John Lynch (ed.), *Latin American Revolutions, 1808–1826: Old and New World Origins* (London, 1994), pp. 308–20.

134 Earl of Fife to San Martín, Edinburgh, 3 June 1817, in Museo Histórico Nacional, *San Martín*, p. 309.

135 Fife's Spanish generalship and his role as 'heroe of the Spanish cause' were mentioned during his funeral on 19 March 1857, see *The Aberdeen Journal*, 25 March 1857, p. 7; James Imlach, *History of Banff and Familiar Account of its Inhabitants and Belongings; to which are added, Chronicles of the Old Churchyard of Banff* (Banff, 1868), p. 34.

136 Chapter 5.

137 Chapter 4.

138 Chapter 6.

139 José de San Martín to Peruvian President General Ramón Castilla, 11 September 1848, in *San Martín: su correspondencia 1823–1850*, p. 296; Jason Wilson, *The Andes: A Cultural History* (Oxford, 2009), pp. 182–3.

140 AB, MS 3175/1290/2: Samford Whittingham to the Earl of Fife, Calcutta, 20 January 1823.

Conclusion

1 Michael Glover, *The Peninsular War, 1807–1814: A Concise Military History* (Newton Abbot, 1974), p. 190; Fraser, *Napoleon's Cursed War*, p. 396.

2 See Table 1.

3 Javier Fernández Sebastián, 'Toleration and freedom of expression in the Hispanic world between enlightenment and liberalism', *Past and Present*, 211 (May 2001), p. 196.

4 Address to the Colombian Congress, 3 October 1821, in Vicente Lecuna (ed.), *Bolivar – Obras Completas* (3 vols., Havana, 1950), II, p. 1178.

Bibliography

Primary sources

Manuscripts and other archival sources:

. **Aberdeen City Archives, Aberdeen, Scotland:**
Records of Royal Burgh of Banff (BH4) Freemen of the Burgh.

. *Archives Nationales de France* (ANF), Paris, France:
F7 Police files (*Police Générale*).
LH/801/30 Register of the *Legion d'honneur(Dossiers des titulaires de l'Ordre de la Légion d'Honneur)*.
O/3/840 *Maison du Roi: Dossier Legion d'honneur – Demandes D'Admission dans L'Ordre Royal de la Legion d'honneur.*

. *Archivo de la Corona de Aragón*, Barcelona, Spain:
Diversos:*Junta Superior de Cataluña.*

. *Archivo del Ayuntamiento de Cadiz* (AAC), Cadiz, Spain:
Census 1805–13: *Padrones* 1032, 1034, 1055.

. *Archivo General de Indias,* Seville, Spain:
Fabrica_De_Tabacos, 1218.

. *Archivo General Militar de Madrid* (AGM), Madrid, Spain:
Colección Cuartel General del Ejército del Norte.
Colección del Fraile.
Fondo Blake.
Fondo Duque de Bailén.
Fondo Guerra de la Independencia.
Historiales de Regimientos.

. *Archivo General Militar de Segovia* (AGMS), Segovia, Spain:
Sección Primera:
A-2104 *Expediente* Jaime Arbuthnot y Arbuthnot.
B-540 *Expediente* Simon Miguel Val.
B-933 *Expediente* Benjamin Barrie.
C-1704 *Expediente* Carlos Morgan Carrol.
C-1704 *Expediente* Miguel Carrol.

C-2843 *Expediente* Juan Clarke.

C-3283 *Expediente* Jorge Coppy (for Copping?).

C-3476 *Expediente* Diego Corrigan.

C-3713 *Expediente* Guillermo Cox.

D-1136 *Expediente* Carlos Donovan.

D-1176 *Expediente* Carlos Downie.

D-1177 *Expediente* Juan Downie.

D-1237 *Expediente* Diego Duff.

D-752 *Expediente* Tomas Ricardo Dyer.

D-877 *Expediente* Carlos Guillermo Doile (sic, for Doyle).

E-1594 *Expediente* Roberto Steile (sic, for Steele).

E-1596 *Expediente* Roberto Steele.

E-688 *Expediente* Patricio Campbell.

J-811 *Expediente* Jose Jones.

L-228 *Expediente* Jorge Landmann.

L-700 *Expediente* Francisco Lee.

L-702 *Expediente* Ricardo Lee.

M-2581 *Expediente* Juan Meélican (sic, for Mealican).

M-5080 *Expediente* Juan Murphy Porro.

M-59 *Expediente* Eduardo Mac Cormick O'Neill.

M-8 *Expediente* 69 Reynaldo Macdonnell.

M-8 *Expediente* 72 Vizconde Macduff.

M-8 *Expediente* 60 Guillermo Mac Veagh.

O-61 *Expediente* Tomás O'Colgan.

O-101 *Expediente* Manuel O'Doyle (contains material regarding Juan Murphy).

O-548 *Expediente* Jayme O Rian (sic, for O'Ryan).

P-267 *Expediente* Pablo Palmés (sic, for Palmer).

P-541 *Expediente* Guillermo Parker Carrol (contains personal files of Manuel Poe, Timothy 'Timotheo' Meagher and some information relating to Charles 'Carlos' Morgan Carrol, Richard 'Ricardo' Carrol and Michael 'Miguel' Carrol).

Q-1 *Expediente* Felipe Qeating (sic, for Keating) Roche.

Q-1 *Expediente* Juan Quearney (sic, for Kearney) Donnelan.

R-1496 *Expediente* Felipe de la (sic) Roche.

R-1365 *Expediente* Daniel Robinson.

R-1365 *Expediente* Gerónimo Robinson.

S-1490 *Expediente* Justo Rufino de San Martín.

S-1493 *Expediente* Manuel Tadeo de San Martín.

S-2066 *Expediente* Pedro Sarsfield.

S-2807 *Expediente* Carlos Silvertop.

T-314 *Expediente* Edmundo Temple.

U-34 *Expediente* Enrique Wilson.

U-6 *Expediente* Arturo Wavell.

V-43 *Expediente* Santiago Whittinghan (sic, for Whittingham).

Personal Célebre (Celebrities):

Caja 176, *Expediente* 4, Carpeta 1 *Expediente* Agustina Zaragoza & Domenech.

3S 6, *Expediente* José de San Martín Matorras.

. *Archivo Histórico Nacional* (AHN), Madrid, Spain:

Consejos 49616, 5519.

Diversos-Colecciones 108, 110.

Sección Estado 2 B; 2 D; 8 A; 13 B; 33 B; 38 B; 38 E; 39; 39 B; 42 A; 43; 43[1]; 45 A; 46 A;
52 A; 58 E; 87; 3566; 7368; 7369.

FC-Mº Hacienda 514.

. *Archivo Municipal de Oviedo* (AMO), Oviedo, Spain:

Decretos Reales 1800–10.

. *Biblioteca de Catalunya Arxiu*, Barcelona, Spain:

Inventari del Fons Gonima/Janer.

. *Biblioteca Nacional de España* (BNE), Madrid, Spain:

R/60246 (3) *Colección de documentos interesantes que pueden servir de apuntes para la
historia de la revolución de España* (Valencia, 1809).

R/63241 *Manifiesto a los Españoles y compañeros de armas del Mariscal de Campo de los
Reales Ejercitos Sir Juan Downie.*

R/63248 *Manifiesto de Juan Downie.*

R/63250 *Documentos relativos a la vida y acciones militares durante la Guerra de la
Independencia de D. Juan Downie.*

R/63251 *Convocatoria dirigida a extremeños y españoles en general para que se alisten en
la Leal Legión de Extremadura.*

. Bodleian Library (BOD), University of Oxford, England:

North Collection (BOD North): b. 3.4; c. 13; c. 14; c. 15; c. 16; c. 17; c. 19; d. 65.

MS Eng. Lett. c. 666 Copy Book of Gral. John Broderick.

. Bristol Central Library (BCL), Bristol, England:

Rl Pr 2pb Biog. U-Z – B 4120 Extract of biographical notes of Samford Whittingham
published by the *Bristol Mercury*, 15 January 1870, with handwritten notes.

. Bristol Record Office, Bristol, England:

Richard Hart Davis Papers.

. British Library (BL), London, England:

RB.23 b 4227 – 10 General Reference Collection Provenance Foreign and
Commonwealth Office.

Spanish Tracts – Nr. 18.

Additional Manuscripts (Add.) 15675, 37286, 37287, 37288, 37888, 38265, 38366,
39199, 40722, 49486, 49490, 49491, 58987.

. Cambridge University Library (CU), Cambridge, England:

Additional Manuscripts (Add.) 7521 Copy of letters and orders upon service in the Peninsula addressed to Lieut. Gen. Sir Philip K. Roche.

. Codrington Library, All Souls College, University of Oxford (ASL), England:

Vaughan Papers: Series A, B, C, D, E; uncatalogued material in microfiche format in reels 6 (contains some material of 'C series'), 7, 11, 12, 13, 14, 19 (contains some material of 'D series'), 27.

. King's College, Special Collections, Aberdeen University (AB), Aberdeen, Scotland:

MS 3175 Duff Family Papers.

. National Archives of the United Kingdom (NA), London, England:

Admiralty Records (ADM): Captain's Logs of HMS Invincible and HMS Temeraire.

Foreign Office Papers (FO): 72 – General Correspondence relating to Spain, including Spanish America for the earlier period (1781–1905).

Home Office Papers (HO): 50/59 – Military Correspondence, Internal Defence (Milita and Volunteers) Banffshire.

Records of the Prerogative Court of Canterbury (Prob): 11/1753 Will and Testament of Sir Philip Keating Roche; 11/2090 Will and Testament of Daniel Robinson.

War Office Papers (WO): 1 – Papers of the Secretary-at-War and the Secretary of State for War (1794–1865); 6 – Out-letters Secretary of State for War and Secretary of State for War and the Colonies (1793–1859).

. National Library of Scotland (NLS), Edinburgh, Scotland:

MS 4042 Blackwoods correspondence.

Printed primary sources

A List of the Subscribers to Lloyd's, September, 1814 (London, 1814).

Alamo, Andrés Ortega del (ed.), *Cartas inéditas del General Felipe Roche a los Generales Copons, Freyre y Elio* (Madrid, 1955).

Alas 'Clarín', Leopoldo, *La Regenta* (Madrid, 1900).

Alberdi, Juan B., *Escritos póstumos de J. B. Alberdi* (16 vols., Buenos Aires, 1895–1901).

Alcalá Galiano, Antonio (ed.), *Memorias de D. Antonio Alcalá Galiano publicadas por su hijo* (2 vols., Madrid, 1886).

Alcalá Galiano, Antonio, *Historia de España desde los tiempos primitivos hasta la mayoridad de la reina Doña Isabel II* (Madrid, 1846).

Allibone, Samuel A., *Allibone's Dictionary of English Literature and British and American Authors Living and Deceased from the Earliest Accounts to the Latter Half of the Nineteenth Century* (3 vols., London, 1871).

Alpuente, Juan R., *Wellington en España y Ballesteros en Ceuta* (Cadiz, 1813).

Alvarez Valdés, Ramón, *Memorias del levantamiento de Asturias en 1808* (Gijón, 1988).

Apuntes que dio a su abogado el primer ayudante del Estado Mayor General D. Luis de Landáburu y Villanueva estando preso en la cárcel de Madrid el año de 1814 por su amor a la Constitución (Madrid, 1820).

Archivo General de Simancas, *Documentos relativos a Inglaterra: 1254–1834* (Madrid, 1947).

Archivo Histórico Nacional, *San Martín: su correspondencia 1823–1850* (Buenos Aires, 1911).

Balderrábano, Alfonso and Maortua, Juan B. de, *Instrucción de guerrillas sacada por la de los Señores Blacke, O-farril y San Juan. compuesta y aumentada, por el Teniente Coronel, Don Alfonso Balderrábano, Sargento Mayor del Regimiento de Infantería Ligera, Tiradores de Doyle, y por Juan Bautista de Maortua, teniente del mismo* (Vitoria, 1813).

Ballesteros, Francisco, *Respetuosos descargos que el Teniente General D. Francisco Vallesteros [sic] ofrece a la generosa nación española. En contestación á los cargos que S.A. la Regencia del Reyno se ha servido hacerle en su Manifiesto de 12 de Diciembre del año pasado de 1812 dirigido á la misma para su inteligencia* (Algeciras, 1813).

Barrie, Enrique, *Biografía del mariscal de campo de los Exercitos Españoles Don Juan Downie* (Madrid, 1887).

Bissell Pope, Willard (ed.), *The Diary of Benjamin Robert Haydon* (5 vols., Cambridge, MA, 1963).

Blanco White 'Doblado Don Leucadio', Joseph, *Letters from Spain* (London, 1822).

Bolivar, Simón, 'An American's convictions' [a translation of Bolivar's 'Contestación de un americano meridional a un caballero de esta isla', Kingston, 6 September 1815], in John Lynch (ed.), *Latin American Revolutions, 1808–1826: Old and New World Origins* (London, 1994), pp. 308–20.

Bowle, John, *A Letter to the Reverend Dr. Percy, Concerning a New and Classical Edition of Historia del valeroso cavallero Don Quixote de la Mancha* (London, 1777).

Buckley, Roger N. (ed.), *The Napoleonic War Journal of Captain Thomas Henry Browne 1807–1816* (London, 1987).

Bunbury, Thomas, *Reminiscences of a Veteran: Being Personal and Military Adventures in Portugal, Spain, France, Malta, New South Wales, Norfolk Island, New Zealand, Andaman Islands, and India* (London, 1861).

Byron, George G. N., *The Poetical Works of Lord Byron, Complete* (London, 1867).

Cabanes, Francisco Xavier, *Historia de las operaciones del Exército de Cataluña en la Guerra de la Usurpación o sea de la Independencia de España* (Tarragona, 1809).

—, *Memoria acerca del modo de escribir la historia militar de la última guerra entre España y Francia, escrita en Madrid en 1814* (Barcelona, 1816).

Cadalso, José Juan, *El buen militar a la Violeta – lección póstuma del autor del Tratado de los Eruditos* (Sevilla, 1790).

Capefigue, Jean-Baptiste H. R., *Récit des opérations de l'armée française en Espagne, sous les ordres de S. A. R. Mgr. duc d'Angoulême: Accompagné de notices biographiques et géographiques; et suivi de considérations sur les résultats politiques de cette guerre* (Paris, 1823).

Carr, Sir John, *Descriptive Travels in the Southern and Eastern Parts of Spain and the Balearic Isles in the Year 1809* (London, 1811).

Casals, Fray B., *Tarragona sacrificada en sus intereses y vidas por la independencia de la nación y la libertad de su cautivo monarca Fernando Septimo* (Tarragona, 1816).

Caso Gonzalez, Jose M. (ed.), *Gaspar Melchor de Jovellanos – Obras Completas* (7 vols., Gijon, 1990).

Constitución politica de la Monarquia Española: Promulgada en Cadiz á 19 de Marzo de 1812 (Madrid, 1820).

'Convenio entre don Juan Alvarez y Mendizabal por parte del general don Miguel Ricardo de Alava, ministro de Su Majestad Católica en Londres, y el mayor general sir Lnftus Otway por la del coronel de Lucy Evans M. P. para organizar una legión auxiliar británica al servicio de España; ajusfado [sic] y firmado en aquella corte en junio de 1835', in Alejandro del Cantillo (ed.), *Tratados, convenios y declaraciones de paz y de comercio que han hecho con las potencias estranjeras los monarcas españoles de la casa de Borbón desde el año 1700 hasta el dia. Puestos en orden e ilustrados con la historia de sus respectivas negociaciones* (Madrid, 1843).

Dávila, Vicente (ed.), *Archivo del General Miranda* (24 vols., Caracas, 1929).

de Las Cases, Emmanuel-Auguste-Dieudonne, Count, *Journal of the Private Life and Conversations of the Emperor Napoleon at Saint Helena* (4 vols., London, 1823).

Diario de las Sesiones de Cortes Celebradas en Sevilla y Cadiz en 1823 (Madrid, 1858).

Diario de Sesiones y Actas de las Cortes Generales y Extraordinarias (23 vols., Cadiz, 1810–13).

Donaldson, James [J.], *Recollections of an Eventful Life Chiefly Passed in the Army* (Glasgow, 1825).

Doyle, Carlos Guillermo, *Manual para reconocimientos militares dispuesto por el Excmo. Sr. D. Carlos Guillermo Doyle, Teniente General de los Reales Exércitos, Comandante general del depósito militar de instrucción* (Cadiz, 1812).

Doyle, Colonel Arthur, *A Hundred Years of Conflict Being Some Records of the Services of Six Generals of the Doyle Family 1756–1856* (London, 1911).

Doyle, Major [Charles William], *The Military Catechism for the Use of Covering or Supernumerary Serjeants* (London, 1804).

—, *The Military Catechism for the Use of Young Officers* (London, 1804).

Du Casse, Albert (ed.), *Mémoires et correspondance politique et militaire du roi Joseph: publiés, annotés et mis en ordre* (10 vols., Paris, 1853–54).

Ebers, John, *Seven Years of the King's Theatre* (London, 1828).

The Edinburgh Annual Register (Edinburgh, 1811).

Elogio histórico al Excmo. Señor D. Francisco Xavier Castaños con el motivo de haberse publicado por su orden la constitución española en éste Principado de Asturias (Oviedo, 1812).

Elwin, Malcolm, *Landor: A Replevin* (London, 1958).

English, Henry, *A General Guide to the Companies Formed for Working Foreign Mines with Their Prospectus, Amount of Capital, Number of Shares, Names of Directors, &c. and an Appendix Showing Their Progress Since their Formation, Obtained from Authentic Sources* (London, 1825).

Errores del señor Doyle, ligeramente advertidos por un español que siente los insultos de su patria (Cadiz, 1813).

Espoz y Mina, Juana M. (ed.), *Memorias del general don Francisco Espoz y Mina escritas por el mismo, publ. J. M. de Vega, condesa de Espoz y Mina* (5 vols., Madrid, 1851).

Fernández Sarasola, Ignacio (ed.), *Obras completas de Jovellanos: Escritos políticos* (11 vols., Oviedo, 2006).

Forster, John (ed.), *The Works and Life of Walter Savage Landor* (8 vols., London, 1876).

Forster, John, *Walter Savage Landor – A Biography* (2 vols., London, 1869).

Geological Society of London, *Proceedings of the Geological Society of London*, (3 Vols, London, 1826–42).

Gill, Stephen (ed.), *William Wordsworth: The Major Works* (Oxford, 2000).

Gómez Villafranca, Ramón (ed.), *Extremadura en la Guerra de la Independencia, memoria histórica y colección diplomática* (Badajoz, 1908).

Graham, Maria, *Journal of a Residence in Chile, during the Year 1822; and a Voyage from Chile to Brazil, in 1823* (London, 1824).

Guía política de las Españas para el año 1813 (Cadiz, 1813).

El gran proyecto de Bonaparte para agregar la España a la Francia (Valencia, 1811).

Gurwood, John (ed.), *The Dispatches of Field Marshall the Duke of Wellington during His Various Campaigns in India, Denmark, Portugal, Spain, the Low Countries, and France from 1799–1818* (13 vols., London, 1837 and 1838).

Haegele, Vincent (ed.), *Napoléon et Joseph: correspondance intégrale 1784–1818* (Paris, 2007).

Hall, Basil R. N., *Extracts from a Journal Written on the Coasts of Chili, Peru and Mexico in the Years 1820, 1821, 1822* (London, 1840).

Hansard, Thomas C., *Parliamentary Debates from the Year 1803 to the Present Time* (41 Vols., London, 1820).

The Honour and Advantage of Agriculture. Being the Twelfth Discourse of the Eighth Volume of Feijoo's Works, Translated from the Spanish By a Farmer in Cheshire (London, 1760).

Humphreys, David, *The Miscellaneous Works of David Humphreys: Late Minister Plenipotentiary to the Court of Madrid* (New York, 1804).

Ilchester, The Earl of (ed.), *The Spanish Journal of Elizabeth Lady Holland* (London, 1910).

Jacob, William, *Travels in the South of Spain, in Letters Written A.D. 1809 and 1810* (London, 1811).

Jerdan, William, *National Portrait Gallery of Illustrious and Eminent Personages of the Nineteenth Century: With Memoirs* (5 vols., London, 1830).

Johnston, Colonel William, *Roll of Commissioned Officers in the Medical Service of the British Army who Served on Full Pay Within the Period between the Accession of George II and the Formation of the Royal Army Medical Corps 20 June to 23 June 1898* (London, 1917).

Jordan, John E. (ed.), *De Quincey to Wordsworth: A Biography of a Relationship* (Berkeley, 1962).

Jovellanos, Gaspar M. de, *D. Gaspar de Jovellanos a sus compatriotas: Memoria en que se rebaten las calumnias divulgadas contra los individuos de la Junta Central y se da razón de la conducta y opiniones del autor desde que recobró su libertad* (Coruña, 1811).

Landmann, George, *Recollections of My Military Life by Colonel Landmann, Late of the Corps or Royal Engineers, Author of 'Adventures and Recollections', &c.* (2 vols., London, 1854).

[Landor, Walter S.], *Count Julian: A Tragedy* (London, 1812).

Landor, Walter S., 'Count Julian: A tragedy', in Stephen Wheeler (ed.), *The Poetical Works of Walter Savage Landor* (Oxford, 1937), pp. 161–224.

—, *The Works of Walter Savage Landor* (2 vols., London, 1846).

Leckie, Gould F., *An Historical Survey of the Foreign Affairs of Great Britain: For the Years 1808, 1809, 1810: With a View to Explain the Causes of the Disasters of the Late and Present Wars* (London, 1810).

Lecuna, Vicente (ed.), *Bolivar – Obras Completas* (3 vols., Havana, 1950).

Lillie, John S., *A Narrative of the Campaigns of the Loyal Lusitanian Legion under Sir Robert Wilson* (London, 1812).

The London Kalender or Court and City Register for England, Scotland, Ireland, and the Colonies (London, 1808).

Lope de Vega Carpio, Félix A., *Segunda parte de las comedias de Lope de Vega Carpio: que contiene otras doze, cuyos nombres van en la hoja segunda* (Madrid, 1611).

Ludovici, Anthony (ed.), *On the Road with Wellington: The Diary of a War Commissary in the Peninsular Campaigns by August Ludolf Friedrich Schaumann* (London, 1924).

Marchand, Leslie A. (ed.), *Byron's Letters and Journals* (12 vols., London, 1973).

Marchesi, José M., *Catálogo de la Real Armería* (Madrid, 1849).

Martin, Robert M. (ed.), *The Despatches and Correspondence of the Marquess Wellesley, K. G. During His Lordship's Mission to Spain as Ambassador Extraordinary to the Supreme Junta in 1809* (London, 1838).

Martinez Marina, Francisco, *Ensayo histórico-crítico sobre la legislación y principales cuerpos legales de los reinos de León y Castilla especialmente sobre el código de las Siete Partidas de D. Alonso el Sabio* (Madrid, 1808).

[Mayne, William], *A Narrative of the Campaigns of the Loyal Lusitanian Legion under Brigadier General Sir Robert Wilson, aide-de-camp to his Majesty, and Knight of the Order of Maria Theresa, and of the Tower and Sword with some Accounts of the Military Operations in Spain and Portugal during the Years 1809, 1810 & 1811* (London, 1812).

Milburne, Henry, *A Narrative of Circumstances Attending the Retreat of the British Army under the Command of the Late Lieut. Gen. Sir John Moore, K. B., with a Concise Account of the Battle of Corunna; in a Letter Addressed to the Right Honourable Lord Viscount Castlereagh, one of His Majesty's Principal Secretaries of State* (London, 1809).

Miller, John, *Memoirs of General Miller, in the Service of the Republic of Peru* (2 vols., London, 1828).

—, *Memorias del General Miller al Servicio de la República del Perú escritas en Inglés por Mr. John Miller y traducidas al castellano por el General Torrijos* (2 vols., London, 1829).

Mitre, Bartolome, *Historia de San Martín y de la emancipación sud-americana* (3 vols., Buenos Aires, 1887).

—, *The Emancipation of South America, a Condensed Translation by W. Pilling of The History of San Martin* (London, 1893).

[Moore, Thomas], *Moore vs. Adam: Proceedings in a Cause Tried in the Court of King's Bench, December 21, 1815, for Special Damages, in Consequence of an Assault Committed at Alicant, in Spain* (London, 1816).

Mordella y Spotorno, Antonio, *Sacrificios y ejemplos que la Madre Patria presenta a la imitación de sus hijos. Publicalos D. Antonio Mordella y Spotorno vecino de Cartagena, quien los dedica al Excmo. Sr. Milor Doyle, Mariscal de Campo de los Reales Exercitos* (Valencia, 1808).

Navia Ossorio, Alvaro, Marquess de Santa Cruz de Marcenado, *Reflexiones militares del mariscal de Campo D. Vizconde del Puerto o Marques de Santa Cruz de Marcenado* (Turin, 1724).

O'Connell, Maurice R. (ed.), *The Correspondence of Daniel O'Connell* (8 vols., Dublin, 1977).

Palfrey Burrell, John (ed.), *Official Bulletins of the Battle of Waterloo in the Original Languages* (London, 1849).

Pano y Ruata, Mariano de, *El inglés Sir Carlos Guillermo Doyle y su plan de socorro a Zaragosa* (Madrid, 1909–1910).

Peñalosa y Zuñiga, Don C., *El honor militar, causas de su orígen, progresos y decadencia; O Correspondencia de dos hermanos desde el Exército de Cataluña de S.M.C.* (2 vols., Madrid, 1795–96).

Pérez Galdos, Benito, *Episodios Nacionales* (Primera Serie, Madrid, 1874).

Pérez Villamil, Juan, *Carta sobre el modo de establecer el Consejo de Regencia del Reino con arreglo a nuestra Constitución* (Madrid, 1808).

Pérez y López, Antonio X., *Discurso sobre la honra y deshonra legal en que se manifiesta el verdadero mérito de la Nobleza de sangre, y se prueba que todos los oficios necesarios, y útiles al Estado son honrados por las Leyes del Reyno, según las quales solamente el delito propio difama* (Madrid, 1781).

[Puigrubí, Miguel], *Respuestas a la pregunta de un criticón ¿Qué ha hecho el corregimiento de Figueras en defensa o favor de la Justa causa que sostiene la Nación española?* (Tarragona, 1813–14).

Robertson, June O'Carroll, *A Long Way from Tipperary* (Upton-upon-Severn, 1994).

[Robinson, Daniel], *The Political Constitution of the Spanish Monarchy Proclaimed in Cadiz, 19th March, 1812* (London, 1813).

Rodríguez, Gregorio F. (ed.), *Historia de Alvear* (2 vols., Buenos Aires, 1913).

Ruiz Rivera, Julian B., *El consulado de Cádiz. Mátricula de Comerciantes 1730–1823* (Cadiz, 1988).

Sabine, Major-General Edward (ed.), *Letters of Colonel Sir Augustus Simon Frazer, K.C.B., Commanding the Royal Horse Artillery in the Army under the Duke of Wellington Written during the Peninsular and Waterloo Campaigns* (London, 1859).

The Scots Magazine and Edinburgh Literary Miscellany:Being a General Repository of Literature, History and Politics for 1817 (Edinburgh, 1817).

Semple, Robert, *A Second Journey in Spain in the Spring of 1809* (London, 1st edn, 1809).

Sidney, Edwin, *The Life of Lord Hill G.C.B, Late Commander of the Forces* (London, 1845).

Silvertop, Charles, *A Geological Sketch of the Tertiary Formation in the Provinces of Granada and Murcia, Spain with Notices Respecting Primary, Secondary, and Volcanic Rocks in the Same District and Sections* (London, 1836).

Sinclair, John, *The Correspondence of the Right Honourable Sir John Sinclair, Bart. with Reminiscences of the Most Distinguished Characters Who have Appeared in Great Britain, and in Foreign Countries, During the Last Fifty Years* (2 vols., London., 1831).

[Sinclair, Sir John], *Particulars Regarding The Merino Sheep Imported by Charles Downie, Esq., of Paisley in Scotland: In Answer to Certain Queries Transmitted by Sir John Sinclair, to the Spanish Shepherds who have the Charge of Them from the Communications to the Board of Agriculture* (London, 1810).

Southey, Robert, *History of the Peninsular War* (3 vols., London, 1823 and 1828).

Steele, Sir Robert C., *The Marine Officer; or, Sketches of Service* (2 vols., London, 1840).

Steele, Thomas, *Notes of the War in Spain Detailing Occurrences Military and Political in Galicia, and at Gibraltar and Cadiz from the Fall of Corunna to the Occupation of Cadiz by the French* (London, 1824).

Sturgis, Julian (ed.), *A Boy in the Peninsular War: The Services, Adventures, and Experiences of Robert Blakeney, Subaltern in the 28th Regiment: An Autobiography* (London, 1899).

Suchet, Louis G., *Memoirs of the War in Spain* (2 vols., London, 1829).

Sutcliffe, Thomas, *Sixteen Years in Chile and Peru from 1822 to 1839* (London, 1841).

Temple, Edmond, *The Life of Pill Garlick; Rather a Whimsical Sort of Fellow* (Dublin and London, 1813).

—, *Travels in Various Parts of Peru: Including a Year's Residence in Potosi* (2 vols., London, 1830).

Thiébault, Paul-Charles-François, *Relation de l'expédition du Portugal: faite en 1807 et.1808, par le 1er corps d'observation de la Gironde, devenu armée de Portugal* (Paris, 1817).

Toreno, José Maria Queipo de Llano Ruiz de Saravia, Count de, *Historia del levantamiento, guerra y revolución de España* (4 vols., Madrid, 1848).

Toze, Eobald, *The Present State of Europe, Exhibiting a View of the Natural and Civil History of the Several Countries and Kingdoms* (3 vols., London, 1770).

'Tratado entre los reyes de España y de la Gran Bretaña para la abolición del tráfico de negros: firmado en Madrid el 23 de setiembre de 1817', in Alejandro del Cantillo (ed.), *Tratados, convenios y declaraciones de paz y de comercio que han hecho con las potencias extranjeras los monarcas españoles de la Casa de Borbon desde el año de 1700 hasta el dia puestos en òrden è ilustrados muchos de ellos con la historia de sus respectivas negociaciones* (Madrid, 1843), pp. 800–11.

'Treaty of amity, commerce, and navigation, between His Majesty and the United Provinces of Rio de la Plata. Signed at Buenos Ayres, February 2, 1825', in *House of Commons Papers; Accounts and Papers* (1825), vol. XXVI, pp. 21–9. [Available at: http://gateway.proquest.com/openurl?url_ver=Z39.88-2004&res_dat=xri:hcpp&rft_dat=xri:hcpp:rec:1825-009727]

Trial of Lieutenant General John Whitelocke, Commander-in-chief of the Expedition Against Buenos Ayres, Taken Verbatim by a Student of Middle Temple (London, 1808).

Vaughan, Charles R., *Narrative of the Siege of Zaragoza* (London, 1809).

Villanueva, Joaquín L., *Mi viaje a las Cortes* (Madrid, 1860).

—, 'Mi viaje a las Cortes', in Miguel Artola (ed.), *Memorias de tiempos de Fernando VII* (2 vols., Madrid, 1957).

Viniegra de Torrijos, Luisa S. de, *Vida del General José María de Torrijos y Uriarte* (2 vols., Madrid, 1860).

Watkins, John, *A Biographical Dictionary of the Living Authors of Great Britain and Ireland, Comprising Literary Memoirs and Anecdotes of Their Lives* (London, 1816).

[Wavell, Arthur Goodall], *Notes and Reflections on Mexico, its Mines, Policy, &c. by a Traveller, Some Years Resident in that and the Other American States* (London, 1827).

Wavell, Arthur Goodall, *Táctica de la infantería de linea y ligera, y de las maniobras de linea, con reglas para el servicio de campaña* (London, 1823).

Wellesley, Arthur R., Duke of Wellington, *Supplementary Despatches and Memoranda of Field Marshal Arthur, Duke of Wellington, K. G.* (15 vols., London, 1858–60).

Wheeler, Stephen (ed.), *Letters of Walter Savage Landor, Private and Public* (London, 1899).

—, *The poetical Works of Walter Savage Landor* (3 vols., Oxford, 1937).

Whittingham, C. B. Major-General Ferdinand (ed.), *A Memoir of the Services of Lieutenant-General Sir Samuel Ford Whittingham, K.C.B., K.C.H., G.C.F., Colonel of the 71st Highland Light Infantry, Derived Chiefly from His Own Letters and from those of Distinguished Contemporaries* (London, 1868).

Whittingham, Samuel Ford, *Sistema de maniobras de la línea* (London, 1815).

Wilson, Sir Robert T., *Private Diary of Travels, Personal Services, & Public Events* (2 vols., London, 1861)

Wise, Thomas J. and Wheeler, Stephen, *A Bibliography of the Writings in Prose and Verse of Walter Savage Landor* (Folkestone, 1971).

Newspapers and magazines

The Aberdeen Journal

The Age

Blackwood's Edinburgh Magazine

Bombay Courier

Caledonian Mercury

The Christian Observer

Cobbett's Weekly Political Register

Diario de Palma

El Conciso

El Diario Mercantil de Cadiz (including *Suplemento al Diario Mercantil de Cadiz,* 4 June 1810)

El Duende de los Cafés

Eco literario de Europa: Revista Universal

The Edinburgh Magazine and Literary Miscellany

El Español Libre

The Evangelical Magazine and Missionary Chronicle

The Examiner

Felix Farley's Bristol Journal

The Friend of India

Gaceta Extraordinaria de Oviedo

Gaceta Ministerial de Sevilla

Gazeta de la Regencia de España y de las Indias

Gazeta de Madrid

The Gentleman's Magazine

The Hull Packet and Original Weekly Commercial, Literary and General Advertiser

The Ipswich Journal

John Bull

Journal de l'Empire

The London Gazette

Mercure de France, journal littéraire et politique

The Missionary Herald

The Monthly Magazine

The Monthly Repository of Theology and General Literature

The Morning Chronicle
The Morning Post
The Newcastle Courant
The Newfoundland Mercantile Journal
The Newfounlander
North Wales Chronicle
Notes and Queries
The Ordeal: a Critical Journal of Politicks and Literature
El Rancagüiño
El Redactor General
The Royal Military Chronicle or British Officer's Monthly Register and Mentor
El Semanario Patriótico
The Times
El Universal

Primary sources available in electronic form

Acta de constitución del Consejo de Regencia, 31 January 1810, in *Biblioteca Virtual Miguel de Cervantes* [www.cervantesvirtual.com/servlet/SirveObras/2358406543348 1630976891/p0000001.htm?marca=conde%20de%20Tilly#].

Beña, Cristobal de, *La lyra de la libertad* (London, 1813), in *Biblioteca Virtual Miguel de Cervantes* [www.cervantesvirtual.com/FichaObra.html?Ref=1364].

Dictamen de la Comisión de Cortes elevado a la Junta Central sobre la convocatoria de Cortes (junio de 1809) y exposiciones de los vocales – Voto disidente del conde de Tilly, Seville, 16 July 1809, in *Biblioteca Virtual Miguel de Cervantes* [www.cervantesvirtual.com/servlet/SirveObras/13560731112138495222202/p0000001.htm?marca=conde%20de%20Tilly#26].

Calvo de Rozas, Lorenzo, *Proposición de Calvo de Rozas de convocatoria de las Cortes y elaboración constitucional*, 15 April 1809, in *Biblioteca Virtual Miguel de Cervantes* [www.cervantesvirtual.com/servlet/SirveObras/c1812/90251731092370596454679/p0000001.htm#I_1_].

FamilySearch (The Church of Jesus Christ of Latter-day Saints, www.familysearch.org) Ancestral Files: 'Edwin Rowland Joseph Green', accessed 20 March 2007; 'Neil Macdougall', accessed 5 March 2008; 'Patrick Campbell', Campbell Branches of Ardkinglass – microfilm of MS at Inverary Castle, Argyll, Scotland, accessed 12 March 2008.

'Maria de Guadaloupe Anna Antonia Robinson' in *Worldwide Greathead Family My One-Name Study* [www.greathead.org/greathead2-o/p104.htm, accessed 12 February 2012].

[Martinez Marina, Francisco], *Carta sobre la antigua costumbre de convocar las Cortes de Castilla para resolver los negocios graves del Reino* (London, 1810), in

Biblioteca Virtual Miguel de Cervantes [www.cervantesvirtual.com/FichaObra.
   html?Ref=10589].
*Primera Exposición de Guillermo Hualde, el Conde de Toreno y otros al Consejo de
   Regencia, instando la rápida convocatoria de Cortes, 17 June 1810,* in *Biblioteca
   Virtual Miguel de Cervantes* [www.cervantesvirtual.com/servlet/SirveObras/2461610
   7767149619976613/index.ht].
Records of Sandpits Cemetery in Gibraltar, in *Malta Family History* website [website.
   lineone.net/~stephaniebidmead/gibralter.htm].

Secondary sources

Printed secondary works and electronic resources

Aaslestad, Katherine, 'Paying for war: Experiences of Napoleonic rule in the Hanseatic
   Cities', *Central European History,* 2006, 39/4, pp. 641–75.
Adelman, Jeremy, *Sovereignty and Revolution in the Iberian Atlantic* (Oxford, 2006).
Almirante, José, *Bibliografía militar de España* (Madrid, 1876).
Alonso Baquer, Miguel, *El modelo español de pronunciamiento* (Madrid, 1983).
Alonso, Monique, *Antonio Machado: Poeta en el exilio* (Barcelona, 1985).
Alvárez Barrientos, Joaquín (ed.), *La Guerra de la Independencia en la cultura española*
   (Madrid, 2008).
Alvarez Junco, José and Shubert, Adrian, *Spanish History Since 1808* (London, 2000).
Alvarez Junco, José, *Mater dolorosa – La idea de España en el siglo XIX* (Madrid,
   2001).
—, 'The nation-building process in nineteenth-century Spain', in Clare Mar-Molinero
   and Angel Smith (eds), *Nationalism and the Nation in the Iberian Peninsula:
   Competing and Conflicting Identities* (Oxford, 1996), pp. 89–107.
Alvarez y Cañas, María L., 'El gobierno de la ciudad de Alicante en la crisis del Antiguo
   Regimen (1808–1814)', *Revista de historia moderna: Anales de la Universidad de
   Alicante,* 8/9 (1988–90), pp. 273–88.
Anderson, Benedict R., *Imagined Communities: Reflections on the Origin and Spread of
   Nationalism* (London, 1983).
Andrew, Donna T., 'The code of honour and its critics: the opposition to duelling in
   England, 1700–1850', *Social History,* 5/3 (1980), pp. 409–34.
Andújar Castillo, Francisco, *Los Militares en la España del siglo XVIII – Un estudio social*
   (Granada, 1991).
Ardit Lucas, Manuel, *Revolución liberal y revuelta campesina: un ensayo sobre la
   desintegración del régimen feudal en el País Valenciano (1793–1840)* (Barcelona,
   1977).
Argüelles, Antonio R., *Agustín Argüelles (1776–1844): 'Padre del constitucionalismo
   español'* (2 vols., Madrid, 1991).

Armillas Vicente, José (ed.), *La guerra de la independencia – Estudios* (2 vols., Saragossa, 2001).

Armitage, David, *The Ideological Origins of the British Empire* (Cambridge, 2000).

Artola, Miguel (ed.), *Las Cortes de Cádiz* (Madrid, 2003).

—, *Memorias de tiempos de Fernando VII* (2 vols., Madrid, 1957).

Artola, Miguel, *Los afrancesados* (Madrid, 1953).

—, *Los orígenes de la España contemporánea* (2 vols., Madrid, 1959).

Asociación de Voluntarios de Bailén – Internet website and forum [voluntariosdebailen. mforos.com].

Aymes, Jean-René; Morange, Claude; Brey, Gérard; Lacour, Annie and Dérozier, Albert, *La Révolution francaise: ses conséquences et les réactions du 'public' en Espagne entre 1808 et 1814* (Paris, 1989).

Aymes, Jean-René, 'La guerre d'Espagne dans la presse impériale, 1808–1814', *Annales historiques de la Révolution française*, 336 (2004), pp. 129–45.

—, *La guerra de la independencia en España (1808–1814)* (Madrid, 1986).

—, *La guerre d'indépendance espagnole (1808–1814)* (Paris, 1973).

—, *Los Españoles en Francia 1808–1814: La deportación bajo el Primer Imperio* (Madrid, 1987).

Bagot, Captain Josceline (ed.), *George Canning and his friends containing hitherto unpublished letters, jeux d´esprit, etc.* (2 vols., London, 1909).

Bainbridge, Simon, *British Poetry and the Revolutionary and Napoleonic Wars: Visions of Conflict* (Oxford, 2003).

—, *Napoleon and English Romanticism* (Cambridge, 1995).

Balfour, Sebastian and Quiroga, Alejandro, *The Reinvention of Spain: Nation and Identity Since Democracy* (Oxford, 2007).

Ballester Rodríguez, Mateo, *La identidad española en la Edad Moderna,1556–1665: discursos, símbolos y mitos* (Madrid, 2010).

Banks, Stephen, *A Polite Exchange of Bullets: The Duel and the English Gentleman 1750–1850* (Woodbridge, 2010).

Barahona, Renato, *Sex Crimes, Honour, and the Law in Early Modern Spain: Vizcaya, 1528–1735* (Toronto, 2003).

—, *Vizcaya on the Eve of Carlism, Politics and Society 1800–1833* (Nevada, 1989).

Barczewski, Stephanie L., *Myth and National Identity in Nineteenth Century Britain: The Legends of King Arthur and Robin Hood* (Oxford, 2000).

Baroja, Julio C., *El mito del caracter nacional: meditaciones a contrapelo* (Madrid, 1970).

Barthélémy, Rodolfo G. de, *'El Marquesito' Juan Diaz Porlier – General que fue de los Ejércitos Nacionales (1788–1815)* (2 vols., Santiago de Compostela, 1995).

Bartle, George F., 'Lancaster, Joseph (1778–1838)', *Oxford Dictionary of National Biography*, Oxford University Press, September 2004; online edn, January 2008 [www.oxforddnb.com/view/article/15963].

Bartlett, Thomas and Jeffery, Keith, 'An Irish military tradition?', in idem (eds), *A Military History of Ireland* (Cambridge, 1996), pp. 1–25.

Bartlett, Thomas and Jeffery, Keith (eds), *A Military History of Ireland* (Cambridge, 1996).

Basso, Alberto, *Musica in scena: storia dello spettacolo musicale* (6 vols., Torino, 1995).

Basurto Larrañaga, Román, *Comercio y burguesia mercantil de Bilbao en la Segunda Mitad del Siglo XVIII* (Bilbao, 1983).

Baxell, Richard, *British Volunteers in the Spanish Civil War: The British Batallion in the International Brigades, 1936–1939* (London, 2004).

Bayly, Christopher A., 'Wellesley, Richard, Marquess Wellesley (1760–1842)', *Oxford Dictionary of National Biography*, Oxford University Press, September 2004; online edn, May 2009 [www.oxforddnb.com/view/article/29008].

Bell, David A., *The First Total War – Napoleon's Europe and the Birth of Modern Warfare* (London, 2007).

Bence-Jones, Mark, *The Catholic Families* (London, 1992).

Bennassar, Bartolomé, *The Spanish Character: Attitudes and Mentalities from the Sixteenth to the Nineteenth Century* (Berkeley, 1979).

Berazaluce, Ana M. (ed.), *Pedro Agustin Giron, Marques de las Amarillas – Recuerdos (1778–1837)* (3 vols., Pamplona, 1978).

Best, Geoffrey, *War and Society in Revolutionary Europe, 1770–1870* (Oxford, 1986).

Bethell, Leslie (ed.), *The Cambridge History of Latin America* (11 vols., Cambridge, 1984).

Bianchi, Manuel, *Chile and Great Britain* (London, 1944).

Blaufarb, Rafe, *The French Army, 1750–1820: Careers, Talent, Merit* (Manchester, 2002).

Boase, Federic, *Modern English Biography Containing Many Thousand Concise Memoirs of Persons who have Died Between the Years 1851–1900 with an Index of the Most Interesting Matter* (6 vols., London, 1897).

Bolufer Peruga, Mónica, *Las mujeres en la España del siglo XVIII: trayectorias de la investigación y perspectivas de futuro* (Valencia, 2009), in *Biblioteca Virtual Miguel de Cervantes* [www.cervantesvirtual.com/servlet/SirveObras/p211/90250620980 147265332679/p0000001.htm#I_0_].

Boyd, Carolyn P., *Historia patria: politics, history, and national identity in Spain, 1875–1975* (Chichester, 1997).

Braga, Juan-Carlos; Martin-Algarra, Agustin and Rivas, Pascual, 'Hettangian and Sinemurian of Baños de Alhama de Granada reference section for the West-mediterranean Hettangian (Betic Cordillera, Southern Spain)', *Geobios*, 17/3 (1984), pp. 269–79.

Braudel, Fernand, *On History* (Chicago, 1982).

Breña, Roberto, *El primer liberalismo español y los procesos de emancipación de América: 1808–1824: una revisión historiográfica del liberalismo hispánico* (México, 2006).

Brewer, John, *The Sinews of Power: War, Money and the English State, 1688–1783* (London, 1989).

Brockliss, Laurence and Eastwood, David (eds), *A Union of Multiple Identities: The British Isles, c1750–c1850* (Manchester, 1997).

Broers, Michael, 'Napoleon, Charlemagne, and Lotharingia: Acculturation and the boundaries of Napoleonic Europe', *Historical Journal*, 44 (2001), pp. 135–54.

—, *Napoleon's Other War: Bandits, Rebels, and Their Pursuers in the Age of Revolution* (Oxford, 2010).

—, 'Cultural imperialism in a European context? Political culture and cultural politics in Napoleonic Italy', *Past & Present*, 170 (2001), pp. 152–80.

Brown, Matthew, *Adventuring through Spanish Colonies: Simón Bolivar, Foreign Mercenaries and the Birth of New Nations* (Liverpool, 2006).

Brown, Stewart J. (ed.), *William Robertson and the Expansion of Empire* (Cambridge, 1997).

Bryden, Inga, *The Pre-Raphaelites: Writings and Sources* (2 vols., London, 1998).

Bulloch, John M., *Territorial Soldiering in the North-East of Scotland during 1759–1814* (Aberdeen, 1914).

Burdiel, Isabel and Casey, James (eds), *Identities: Nations, Provinces and Regions 1550–1900* (Norwich, 1999).

Burdiel, Isabel and Pérez Ledesma, Manuel (ed.), *Liberales, agitadores y conspiradores* (Madrid, 2000).

Burke, John (ed.), *A Genealogical and Heraldic History of The Commoners of Great Britain and Ireland Enjoying Territorial Possessions or High Official Rank; But Uninvested with Heritable Honours* (4 vols., London, 1836).

Bushnell, David (ed.), *El Libertador: Writings of Simón Bolivar* (Oxford, 2003).

Caldwell, Ronald E. (ed.), *The Consortium on Revolutionary Europe 1750–1850* (Florida, 1994).

Campbell Barker, Eugene and Fuller Austin, Stephen, *The Life of Stephen F. Austin, Founder of Texas, 1793–1836. A Chapter in the Westward Movement of the Anglo-American People* (Austin, 1969).

Campomanes, Pedro R. and Alvarez, Gonzalo A., *Campomanes en su II centenario* (Madrid, 2003).

Campos, Jorge (ed.), *Obras completas del Duque de Rivas* (3 vols., Madrid, 1957).

Campos, Jorge, *Teatro y sociedad en España (1780–1820)* (Madrid, 1969).

Canal i Morell, Jordi (ed.), *Exilios: los éxodos políticos en la historia de España, siglo XV–XX* (Madrid, 2007).

Canales Torres, Carlos, *Breve historia de la Guerra de la Independencia* (Madrid, 2006).

Canella Secades, Fermin, *Memorias Asturianas del Año Ocho* (Oviedo, 1908).

Cañizares-Esguerra, Jorge, *How to Write the History of the New World: Histories, Epistemologies, and Identities in the Eighteenth-Century Atlantic World* (Stanford, 2001).

Carantoña Alvarez, Francisco, *La Guerra de la Independencia en Asturias* (Gijón, 1984).

—, *Revolución liberal y crisis de las instituciones tradicionales asturianas* (Gijón, 1989).

—, 'Un conflicto abierto. Controversias y nuevas perspectivas sobre la Guerra de la Independencia', *Alcores*, 5 (2088), pp. 13–51.

Cardwell, Richard A. (ed.), *The Reception of Byron in Europe* (2 vols., London, 2004).

Carnall, Geoffrey, 'Landor, Walter Savage (1775–1864)', *Oxford Dictionary of National Biography*, online edn. September 2004 [www.oxforddnb.com/view/article/15980].

Carr, Raymond, *Spain, 1808–1975* (Oxford, 1982).

—, *Spain: A History* (Oxford, 2000).

Carrasco Martínez, Adolfo, 'El XIII Duque del Infantado, un aristócrata en la crisis del Antiguo Régimen', *Revista Universidad Complutense de Madrid*, 13 (2009), pp. 305–35.

Caruso, Marcelo, 'Disruptive dynamics: the spatial dimensions of the Spanish networks in the spread of monitorial schooling (1815–1825)', *Paedagogica Historica,* 43/2 (2007), pp. 271–82.

Cass, Jeffrey and Peer, Larry H. (eds), *Romantic Border Crossings* (Aldershot, 2008).

Castells, Irene, *La utopía insurreccional del liberalismo: Torrijos y las conspiraciones liberales de la década ominosa* (Barcelona, 1989).

—, 'Le libéralisme insurrectionnel espagnol (1814–1830)', *Annales historiques de la Révolution française*, 336/1 (2004), pp. 221–33.

Castro, Adolfo de, *Cádiz en la Guerra de la Independencia – Cuadro histórico* (Cadiz, 1864).

Chandler, James, 'Moving accidents: the emergence of sentimental probability', in Colin Jones and Dror Wahrman (eds), *The Age of Cultural Revolutions: Britain and France, 1750–1820* (London, 2002), pp. 132–70.

Chartrand, René, *Spanish Army of the Napoleonic Wars* (London, 1998).

Chenevix Trench, Charles, *Grace's Card: Irish Catholic Landlords 1690–1800* (Dublin, 1997).

Chichester, Henry M., 'Gurwood (ed.), John (1790–1845)', rev. James Lunt, *Oxford Dictionary of National Biography*; Oxford University Press, 2004; online edn, January 2008 [www.oxforddnb.com/view/article/11778].

—, 'Pakenham, Sir Edward Michael (1778–1815)', rev. Roger T. Stearn, *Oxford Dictionary of National Biography*, Oxford University Press, 2004; online edn, May 2006 [www.oxforddnb.com/view/article/21138].

Christiansen, Eric, *The Origins of Military Power in Spain, 1800–1854* (London, 1967).

Clark, Jonathan C. D., *English Society, 1660–1832: Religion, Ideology and Politics during the Ancien Regime* (Cambridge, 2000).

Clary, David A., *Adopted Son: Washington, Lafayette, and the Friendship That Saved the Revolution* (New York, 2007).

Clonard, Serafin Maria de Soto, Count de, *Historia orgánica de las armas de Infanteria y Caballeria Españolas desde la creación del ejército permanente hasta el dia* (16 vols., Madrid, 1851).

Coates, Anthony J., *The Ethics of War* (Manchester, 1997).

Cobo, Carlota, *La ilustre heroina de Zaragoza o la célebre amazona en la Guerra de la Independencia* (Madrid, 1859).

Colley, Linda, 'Britishness and otherness: an argument', *Journal of British Studies*, 31 (1992), pp. 309–29.

—, *Britons: Forging the Nation, 1707–1837* (London, 2003).

Comellas, José L. (ed.), *Historia general de España y América* (Madrid, 1981).

—, *Los primeros pronunciamientos en España 1814–1820* (Madrid, 1958).

Connell, Kenneth H., *The Population of Ireland 1750–1845* (Oxford, 1950).

Connelly, Owen, *The Gentle Bonaparte: A Biography of Joseph, Napoleon's Elder Brother* (London, 1968).

Conway, Stephen, *Britain, Ireland, and Continental Europe in the Eighteenth Century: Similarities, Connections, Identities* (Oxford, 2011).

—, *War, State and Society in Mid-Eighteenth-Century* (London, 2006).

Cook, Bernard A., *Women and War: A Historical Encyclopedia from Antiquity to the Present* (2 vols., Santa Barbara, 2006).

Cookson, John E., *The British Armed Nation, 1793–1815* (Oxford, 1997).

—, 'Regimental worlds: interpreting the experience of British soldiers during the Napoleonic wars', in Alan Forrest, Karen Hagemann and Jane Rendall (eds), *Soldiers, Citizens and Civilians: Experiences and Perceptions of the Revolutionary and Napoleonic Wars 1790–1820* (London, 2009), pp. 23–42.

Corona Baratech, Carlos, *Revolución y reacción en el reinado de Carlos IV* (Madrid, 1957).

Corwin, Arthur F., *Spain and the Abolition of Slavery in Cuba, 1817–1886* (London, 1967).

Craske, Matthew, *Art in Europe 1700–1830: A History of the Visual Arts in an Era of Unprecedented Urban Economic Growth* (Oxford, 1997).

Cresson, William P., *The Holy Alliance: The European Background of the Monroe Doctrine* (New York, 1922).

Cunningham, Andrew; Grell, Ole P. and Roeck, Bernd (eds), *Health Care and Poor Relief in 18th and 19th Century Southern Europe* (Aldershot: Ashgate, 2005).

Cutrer, Thomas W., *The English Texans* (San Antonio, 1985).

De Courcelles, Jean Baptiste Pierre Jullien, *Dictionnaire Historique et Biographique des Généraux Français depuis le XIe siècle et 1823* (9 vols., Paris, 1823).

De la Torre Saavedra, Ana L., *La expedición de Xavier Mina a Nueva España: una utopía liberal imperial* (Mexico, 1999).

Demange, Christian (ed.), *Sombras de mayo: mitos y memorias de la Guerra de Independencia en España (1808–1908)* (Madrid, 2007).

Demange, Christian, *El dos de mayo: mito y fiesta nacional, 1808–1958* (Madrid, 2004).

Dérozier, Albert, *Manuel José Quintana y el nacimiento del liberalismo en España* (Madrid, 1978).

Devine, Thomas M., *Scotland's Empire, 1600–1815* (London, 2003).

Díaz-Trechuelo Spínola, María L., *Bolívar, Miranda, O'Higgins, San Martín: cuatro vidas cruzadas* (Madrid, 1999).

Dippel, Horst (ed.), *Constitutions of the World: From Late 18th Century to the Middle of the 19th Century Europe, Spain* (13 vols., Berlin, 2010).

Douglass, Carrie, 'Toro muerto, vaca es: An interpretation of the Spanish bullfight', *American Ethnologist*, 11/2 (1984), pp. 242–58.

Duffy, Christopher, *The Military Experience in the Age of Reason* (London, 1987).

Dunlop, Robert, 'Hutchinson, Christopher Hely (1767–1826)', rev. Thomas Bartlett, *Oxford Dictionary of National Biography*, Oxford University Press, 2004; online edn, January 2008 [www.oxforddnb.com/view/article/12881].

Eastman, Scott, *Preaching Spanish Nationalism Across the Hispanic Atlantic, 1759–1823* (Louisiana, 2012).

Elliott, John H., 'Atlantic history: A circumnavigation', in Michael J. Braddick and David Armitage (eds), *The British Atlantic World, 1500–1800* (Basingstoke, 2002), pp. 233–50.

Elwin, Malcolm, *Landor: A Replevin* (London, 1958).

Escolano, Agustin and Arnove, Robert F. (eds), *Leer y escribir en España: doscientos años de alfabetización* (Madrid, 1992).

Esdaile, Charles, 'El Archivo Histórico Nacional como fuente de la Guerra de la Independencia española 1808–1814', in Francisco Miranda Rubio (ed.), *Fuentes documentales para el Estudio de la Guerra de la Independencia* (Pamplona, 2002), pp. 121–31.

—, *Fighting Napoleon: Guerrillas, Bandits, and Adventurers in Spain, 1808–1814* (London, 2004).

—, 'Guerrilleros, bandidos, aventureros y comisarios: la historia de Juan Downie', *Alcores*, 5 (2088), pp. 109–32.

—, *Napoleon's Wars - An International History, 1803–1815* (London, 2007).

—, *Popular Resistance in the French Wars: Patriots, Partisans and Land Pirates* (Basingstoke, 2005).

—, 'Prohombres, aventureros y oportunistas: la influencia del trayecto personal en los orígenes del liberalismo en España', in Guy Thomson and Alda Blanco (eds), *Visiones del liberalismo: política, identidad y cultura en la España del siglo XIX* (Valencia, 2008).

—, *Spain in the Liberal Age: From Constitution to Civil War, 1808–1939* (Oxford, 2000).

—, *The Duke of Wellington and the Command of the Spanish Army, 1812–14* (Basingstoke, 1990).

—, 'The Duke of Wellington and the Spanish Revolution', *Wellington Archive Exhibition* (University of Southampton, 2001) [www.archives.lib.soton.ac.uk/wellington/peninsularwar/essays/ess_esdaile.htm].

—, 'The Marques de la Romana and the Peninsular War: A case study in Spanish civil-military relations', in Ellen Evans and John W. Rooney, Jr. (eds), *The Consortium on Revolutionary Europe 1750–1850* (Florida, 1993), pp. 366–74.

—, *The Peninsular War: A New History* (London, 2003).

—, *The Spanish Army in the Peninsular War* (Manchester, 1988).

—, 'War and politics in Spain, 1808–1814', *Historical Journal*, 31 (1988), pp. 295–317.

Espigado Tocino, Gloria, *Aprender a leer y a escribir en el Cádiz del ochocientos* (Cadiz, 1996).

Fagan, Patrick, *Catholics in a Protestant Country – The Papist Constituency in Eighteenth-Century Dublin* (Dublin, 1998).

Fehrenbach, Charles W., 'Moderados and Exaltados: the liberal opposition to Ferdinand VII, 1814–1823', *The Hispanic American Historical Review*, 50/1 (1970), pp. 52–69.

Fernández, Elena, *Mujeres en la Guerra de la Independencia* (Madrid, 2009).

Fernández, Magda, *Passat i present de Barcelona: materials per l'estudi del medi urbá* (5 vols., Barcelona, 1985).

Fernández Bastarreche, Fernando, *El Ejército español en el siglo XIX* (Madrid, 1978).

Fernández Jiménez, María A., 'La mujer en la guerra', in Sociedad Estatal de Conmemoraciones Culturales, *España 1808–1814 La Nación en Armas* (Madrid, 2008).

Fernández Lalanne, Pedro E., *Los Alvear* (Buenos Aires, 1980).

Fernández Sebastián, Javier, 'Toleration and freedom of expression in the Hispanic world between enlightenment and liberalism', *Past and Present*, 211 (2001), pp. 160–97.

Fernandez Sirvent, Rafael, 'Notas sobre propaganda probonapartista: proclamas y Gazeta de Santander, 1809', *El Argonauta Español*, 3 (2006), pp. 2–14. [Available at http://argonauta.imageson.org/document69.html]

Fierro, Alfred; Palluel-Guillard, André and Tulard, Jean, *Histoire et Dictionnaire du Consulat et de L'Empire* (Paris, 1995).

Figueroa, Pedro P., *Diccionario biográfico de estranjeros* [sic] *en Chile* (Santiago de Chile, 1900).

Fontana, V. J. L., 'The political and religious significance of the British/Irish militias interchange, 1811–1816', *Journal of the Society for Army Historical Research*, 84/338 (2006), pp. 131–57.

Forrest, Alan, *The Soldiers of the French Revolution* (Durham, 2003).

Förster, Stig and Chickering, Roger (eds), *War in an Age of Revolution, 1775–1815* (Cambridge, 2010), pp. 243–59.

Fortescue, John W., *A History of the British Army* (13 vols., London, 1910).

Franklin, Alexandra; Philp, Mark and Navickas, Katrina, *Napoleon and the Invasion of Britain* (Oxford, 2003).

Fraser, Ronald, *La Maldita Guerra de España: Historia Social de la Guerra de la Independencia 1808–1814* (Barcelona, 2006).

—, *Napoleon's Cursed War: Spanish Popular Resistance in the Peninsular War, 1808–1814* (London, 2008).

Friera Alvarez, Marta, *La Junta General del Principado de Asturias a fines del antiguo régimen (1760–1835)* (Oviedo, 2003).

Fugier, André, *La Junte Supérieure des Asturies* (Paris, 1930).

Gaines, James R., *For Liberty and Glory: Washington, Lafayette, and their Revolutions* (London, 2007).

Gallego Palomares, José Á. and Cayuela Fernández, José G., *La Guerra de la Independencia: historia bélica, pueblo y nación en España, 1808–1814* (Salamanca, 2008).

García Cárcel, Ricardo, 'El concepto de España en 1808', *Norba – Revista de historia*, 19 (2006), pp. 175–89.

García Godoy, María T., *Las Cortes de Cádiz y América: el primer vocabulario liberal español y mejicano (1810–1814)* (Sevilla, 1998).

Gates, David, *The Spanish Ulcer: A History of the Peninsular War* (London, 2002).

Gee, Austin, *The British Volunteer Movement, 1794–1814* (Oxford, 2003).

Gil Novales, Alberto (ed.), *Diccionario Biográfico del Trienio Liberal* (Madrid, 1991).

Gil Novales, Alberto, *Las sociedades patrióticas (1820–1823): las libertades de expresión y de reunión en el origen de los partidos políticos* (2 vols., Madrid, 1975).

Glover, Michael, *A Gentleman Volunteer: Letters of George Hennell from the Peninsular War, 1812–1813* (London, 1979).

—, *A Very Slippery Fellow: The Life of Sir Robert Wilson, 1777–1849* (Oxford, 1978).

—, *The Peninsular War, 1807–1814: A Concise Military History* (Newton Abbot, 1974).

Glover, Richard, *Peninsular Preparation: The Reform of the British Army, 1795–1809* (Cambridge, 1963).

Gómez Arteche y Moro, José, *Guerra de la Independencia. Historia militar de España de 1808 a 1814* (14 vols., Madrid, 1895).

—, *La mujer en la Guerra de la Independencia* (Madrid, 1906).

Gomez Imaz, Manuel, *Los periódicos durante la Guerra de la Independencia (1808–1814)* (Madrid, 1910).

González Enciso, Agustín; Enciso Recio, Luis M.; Egido López, Teófanes; Barrio Gozalo, Maximiliano and Torres Sánchez, Rafael, *Los Borbones en el Siglo XVIII (1700–1800)* (Madrid, 1991).

Goodwin Jr., Winslow C., 'The politicial and military career of Don Pedro Caro y Sureda, Marqués de la Romana' (Florida University Ph.D. thesis, 1973).

Goodwin, Albert (ed.), *The European Nobility in the Eighteenth Century – Studies of the Nobilities of the Major European States in the Pre-Reform Era* (London, 1953).

Grasset, Aphonse, *La guerre d'Espagne (1807–1813)* (Paris, 1914).

Guerra, Francois-Xavier (ed.), *Revoluciones Hispánicas: Independencias Americanas y Liberalismo Español* (Madrid, 1995).

Guerra, Francois-Xavier, *Modernidad e independencias: ensayos sobre las revoluciones hispánicas* (Madrid, 1992).

Guevara, Tomás, *Historia de Curicó* (Santiago, 1890), in *Biblioteca Virtual Miguel de Cervantes* [www.cervantesvirtual.com/servlet/SirveObras/02949962127964967544 91/index.htm].

Guillamón Alvarez, Javier, *Honor y honra en la España del siglo XVIII* (Madrid, 1981).

Guimerá Ravina, Agustín, *Burguesia extranjera y comercio atlántico: la empresa comercial irlandesa en Canarias (1703-1771)* (Santa Cruz de Tenerife, 1985).

Gutiérrez, Ramón A., 'Honor, ideology, marriage negotiation, and class-gender domination in New Mexico, 1690-1846', *Latin American Perspectives*, 12/1 (1985), pp. 81-104.

Guzmán y Gallo, Juan P. de, *El Dos de Mayo de 1808 en Madrid* (Madrid, 1908).

Hall, Christopher D., *British Strategy in the Napoleonic War, 1803-15* (Manchester, 1992).

Hamilton, Henry B., *Historical Record of the 14th (King's) Hussars 1715-1900* (London, 1901).

Hamnett, Brian R., 'Constitutional theory and political reality: liberalism, traditionalism and the Spanish cortes, 1810-1814', *The Journal of Modern History*, 49/1 On Demand Supplement (1977), pp. D1071-D1110.

—, 'Joaquín Lorenzo Villanueva (1757-1837): de «católico ilustrado» a «católico liberal». El dilema de la transición', in Guy Thomson and Alda Blanco (eds), *Visiones del liberalismo: política, identidad y cultura en la España del siglo XIX* (Valencia, 2008), pp. 19-41.

—, *La política española en una época revolucionaria, 1790-1820* (Mexico, 1985).

—, 'Las rebeliones y revoluciones iberoamericanas en la época de la Independencia. Una tentativa de tipología', in Francois-Xavier Guerra (ed.), *Revoluciones Hispánicas: Independencias Americanas y Liberalismo Español* (Madrid, 1995), pp. 47-70.

—, *Roots of Insurgency: Mexican Regions, 1750-1824* (Cambridge, 1986).

—, *The Mexican Bureaucracy Before the Bourbon Reforms, 1700-1770: A Study in the Limitations of Absolutism* (Glasgow, 1979).

Hargreaves-Mawdsley, William N. (ed.), *Spain Under the Bourbons, 1700-1833 – A Selection of Documents* (London, 1973).

Hargreaves-Mawdsley, William N., *Eighteenth Century Spain (1700-1789)* (London, 1979).

Harlow, Vincent, *The Founding of the Second British Empire 1763-1793* (2 vols., London 1964).

Harris, C. A., 'Vaughan, Sir Charles Richard (1774-1849)', rev. Henry Colin Grade Matthew, *Oxford Dictionary of National Biography*, September 2004, online edn [www.oxforddnb.com/view/article/28125].

Harris, Ronald W., *Romanticism and the Social Order, 1780-1830* (London, 1969).

Harrison, Mark, *Medicine in an Age of Commerce and Empire: Britain and Its Tropical Colonies, 1660-1830* (Oxford, 2010).

Harvey, Robert, *The Liberators: Latin America's Struggle for Independence, 1810-1830* (London, 2000).

Hasbrouck, Alfred, *Foreign Legionaries in the Liberation of Spanish South America* (New York, 1928).

Heredero y Roura, Federico, Marques de Desio and de Cadenas y Vicent, Vicente (eds), *Archivo General Militar de Segovia – Indice de Expedientes Personales* (9 vols., Madrid, 1959).

Herr, Richard, *The Eighteenth-Century Revolution in Spain* (London, 1958).

Herráiz de Miota, César, 'Los montepíos militares del siglo XVIII como origen del sistema de clases pasivas del Estado', *Revista del Ministerio de Trabajo y Asuntos Sociales*, 56 (2005), pp. 107–208.

Herzog, Tamar, *Defining Nations: Immigrants and Citizens in Early Modern Spain and Spanish America* (London, 2003).

Hilton, Boyd, *A Mad, Bad & Dangerous People? England, 1783–1846* (Oxford, 2006).

Hiraldez Acosta, Manuel de and Trujillo, José, *Espartero, su vida escrita por D.M.H. y D.J.T* (2 vols., Barcelona, 1868).

Hobsbawm, Eric, *Nations and Nationalism Since 1780: Programme, Myth, Reality* (Cambridge, 1990).

Hocquellet, Richard, *La revolución, la política moderna y el individuo: Miradas sobre el proceso revolucionario en España (1808–1835)* (Saragossa, 2011).

Hopkin, David, 'The world turned upside down: Female soldiers in the French armies of the Revolutionary and Napoleonic wars', in Alan Forrest, Karen Hagemann and Jane Rendall (eds), *Soldiers, Citizens and Civilians: Experiences and Perceptions of the Revolutionary and Napoleonic Wars 1790–1820* (London, 2009), pp. 77–95.

Hopkins, James K., *Into the Heart of the Fire: The British in the Spanish Civil War* (Stanford, 1998).

Howarth, David, *The Invention of Spain – Cultural Relations Between Britain and Spain 1770–1870* (Manchester, 2007).

Hunt, Margaret, *The Middling Sort: Commerce, Gender, and the Family in England, 1680–1780* (London, 1996).

Iglesias Rogers, Graciela, 'War volunteering in the 19th and 20th centuries. Heinrich-Fabri-Institut, Blaubeuren, 6–8 September 2007', *Militärgeschichtliche Zeitschrift*, 67/1 (2008), pp. 147–52.

Imlach, James, *History of Banff and Familiar Account of its Inhabitants and Belongings; to Which are Added, Chronicles of the Old Churchyard of Banff* (Banff, 1868).

Inspección de Ingenieros, *Estudio histórico del Cuerpo de Ingenieros del Ejército* (2 vols., Madrid, 1987).

Iriye, Akira and Saunier, Pierre-Yves (eds), *The Palgrave Dictionary of Transnational History* (London, 2009).

Isabel Sánchez, José L. (ed.), *Caballeros de la Real y Militar Orden de San Fernando (Infantería)* (5 vols., Madrid, 2001).

Jean, Carlo, 'Garibaldi e il volontariato nel Risorgimento', *Rassegna Storica del Risorgimento*, 69/4 (1982), pp. 399–419.

Jeffery, Brian, *Fernando Sor: Composer and Guitarist* (London, 1977).

Jiménez Codinach, Estela G., *La Gran Bretaña y la independencia de México, 1808–1821* (México, 1991).

Jones, Cyril A., 'Spanish honour as historical phenomenon: convention and artistic motive', *Hispanic Review*, 33 (1965), pp. 32–9.

Jones, Colin and Dror, Wahrman (eds), *The Age of Cultural Revolutions: Britain and France, 1750–1820* (London, 2002).

Juanola, Vicente A. and Gómez Ruiz, Manuel (eds), *El ejército de los Borbones – Reinado de Fernando VII* (6 vols., Segovia, 1999).

Junta de Iconografía Nacional, *Retratos: Guerra de la Independencia* (Madrid, 1935).

Juretschke, Hans, *Los afrancesados en la guerra de la Independencia: su genesis, desarrollo y consecuencias históricas* (Madrid, 1962).

Kamen, Henry, *Imagining Spain: Historical Myth & National Identity* (London, 2008).

—, *The War of Succession in Spain 1700–15* (London, 1969).

Kates, Gates, *The French Revolution: Recent Debates and New Controversies* (London, 1998).

Kennedy, Michael (ed.), *The Concise Oxford Dictionary of Music* (London, 1980).

Kenyon-Jones, Christine (ed.), *Byron: The Image of the Poet* (Cranbury, 2008).

Kidd, Colin, *Subverting Scotland's Past: Scottish Whig Historians and the Creation of an Anglo-British Identity, 1689–c.1830* (Cambridge, 1993).

Kiernan, Victor G., *The Duel in European History – Honour and the Reign of Aristocracy* (Oxford, 1989).

Kinsbruner, Jay, *Independence in Spanish America: Civil Wars, Revolutions, and Underdevelopment* (Albuquerque, 2000).

Kramer, Lloyd, *Lafayette in Two Worlds: Public Cultures and Personal Identities in an Age of Revolutions* (London, 1996).

Krueger, Christine G. and Levsen, Sonja (eds), *War Volunteering in Modern Times: From the French Revolution to the Second World War* (Basingstoke, 2010).

Labanyi, Jo, 'Costume, identity and spectator pleasure in historical films of the early Franco period', in Parvati Nair and Steven Marsh (eds), *Gender and Spanish Cinema* (Berg, 2004), pp. 33–51.

La Force, James C., 'The supply of Muskets and Spain's war of independence', *The Business History Review*, 43 (1969), pp. 523–44.

La Parra López, Emilio, *La libertad de prensa en las Cortes de Cádiz* (Valencia, 1984).

Lafon, Jean-Marc, *L'Andalousie et Napoléon: contre-insurrection, collaboration et résistances dans le midi de l'Espagne, 1808–1812* (Paris, 2007).

Lambert, Eric, *Voluntarios británicos e irlandeses en la gesta bolivariana* (2 vols., Caracas, 1980).

Lamikiz, Xabier, *Trade and Trust in the Eighteenth-Century Atlantic World: Spanish Merchants and their Overseas Networks* (London, 2010).

Langford, Paul, *A Polite and Commercial People: England, 1727–1783* (Oxford, 1989).

Langsam, Walter C., *The Napoleonic Wars and German Nationalism in Austria* (New York, 1970).

Laspra Rodriguez, Alicia, *Intervencionismo y Revolución, Asturias y Gran Bretaña durante la Guerra de la Independencia (1808–1813)* (Oviedo, 1992).

—, 'William Parker Carrol and the frustrated re-establishment of the Irish Brigade in Spain (1809–11)', *The Irish Sword*, XXVI, 104 (2008), pp. 151–70.

Linch, Kevin B., 'A citizen and not a soldier: the British volunteer movement and the war against Napoleon', in Alan Forrest, Karen Hagemann and Jane Rendall (eds), *Soldiers, Citizens and Civilians: Experiences and Perceptions of the Revolutionary and Napoleonic Wars 1790–1820* (London, 2009), pp. 205–21.

—, 'The recruitment of the British Army 1807–1815' (University of Leeds Ph.D. thesis, 2001).

Lloréns Castillo, Vicente, *Liberales y románticos. Una emigración española en Inglaterra, 1823–1834* (México, 1954).

—, *Literatura, historia, política (ensayos)* (Madrid, 1967).

—, 'Sobre la aparición de 'liberal'', in idem, *Literatura, historia, política (ensayos)* (Madrid, 1967).

Lloyd's Patriotic Fund: Report of the Charities Trust, 2009, available in the Charities Trust's website [www.charitiestrust.org/charities/Lloyds PatrioticFund/index.html].

López Fernández, Enrique, *Las Juntas del Principado durante la Guerra de la Independencia en Asturias* (Oviedo, 1999).

López Tabar, Juan, *Los famosos traidores: los afrancesados durante la crisis del Antiguo Régimen (1808–1833)* (Madrid, 2001).

Lorente Sariñena, Marta, *Las infracciones a la Constitución de 1812: un mecanismo de defensa de la constitución* (Madrid, 1988).

Lucas, Colin, 'Nobles, bourgeois and the origins of the French Revolution', in Gary Kates (ed.), *The French Revolution: Recent Debates and New Controversies* (London, 1998), pp. 33–50.

Lucena-Giraldo, Manuel, 'The limits of reform in Spanish America' in Gabriel B. Paquette (ed.), *Enlightened Reform in Southern Europe and its Atlantic Colonies, c.1750–1830* (Farnham, 2009), pp. 307–20.

Lynch, John (ed.), *Latin American Revolutions, 1808–1826: Old and New World Origins* (London, 1994).

Lynch, John, *Bourbon Spain 1700–1808* (Oxford, 1989).

—, 'British policy and Spanish America, 1783–1808', *Journal of Latin American Studies*, 1/1 (1969), pp. 1–30.

—, *Latin America Between Colony and Nation: Selected Essays* (Basingstoke, 2001).

—, *San Martín: Argentine Soldier, American Hero* (London, 2009).

—, *Simón Bolívar: A Life* (London, 2006).

—, *The Spanish American Revolutions, 1808–1826* (New York and London, 1986).

MacCarthy, Fiona, *Byron: Life and Legend* (London, 2004).

Mandrell, James, *Don Juan and the Point of Honor: Seduction, Patriarchal Society, and Literary Tradition* (Pennsylvania, 1992).

Marchand, Leslie A., *Byron: A Biography* (3 vols., London, 1957).

Marcuello Benedicto, Juan I., 'Las Cortes Generales y Extraordinarias: la organización y poderes para un gobierno de Asamblea', in Miguel Artola (ed.), *Las Cortes de Cádiz* (Madrid, 2003), pp. 67–104.

Marks, Patricia H., *Deconstructing Legitimacy: Viceroys, Merchants, and the Military in Late Colonial Peru* (London, 2007).

Marquez de la Plata y Ferrandiz, Vicenta M., *Mujeres de Acción en el Siglo de Oro* (Madrid, 2006).

Martín Sánchez, Isabel, 'El Conciso: un periódico liberal en tiempos de las Cortes de Cádiz', *Trienio: ilustración y liberalismo*, 30 (1997), pp. 23–46.

Martínez Carrasco, Adolfo, 'El XIII Duque del Infantado, un aristócrata en la crisis del Antiguo Régimen', *Revista de la Universidad Complutense de Madrid*, 13 (2009), pp. 321–6, online edn [revistas.ucm.es/ghi/02143038/articulos/ELEM0606220305A. PDF].

Martínez Sanz, José L. and Diego, Emilio de (eds), *El comienzo de la Guerra de la Independencia – Congreso Internacional del Bicentenario* (Madrid, 2009).

Martínez, Bernabé B., *Historia de la enseñanza en España y América: La educación en la España contemporánea (1789–1975)* (Madrid, 1994).

Martínez-Valverde, Carlos, *La Marina en la guerra de la Independencia* (Madrid, 1974).

Massie, Alastair W., 'Doyle, Sir John, baronet (1756–1834)', *Oxford Dictionary of National Biography*, Oxford University Press, September 2004; online edn, May 2006 [www.oxforddnb.com/view/article/8002].

Massons, José M., *Historia de la Sanidad Militar Española* (4 vols., Barcelona, 1994).

Matthew, Henry Colin Grade and Harrison, Brian, 'James Duff, fourth Earl of Fife', in *Oxford Dictionary of National Biography* (60 vols., Oxford, 2004), XVII, p. 129.

Matthew, Henry Colin Grade and Harrison, Brian (eds), *Oxford Dictionary of National Biography* (60 Vols, Oxford, 2004).

McClelland, Ivy L., *The Origins of the Romantic Movement in Spain: A Survey of Aesthetic Uncertainties in the Age of Reason* (Liverpool, 1975).

McCord, James N., Jr., 'Politics and honor in early-nineteenth-century England: the Dukes' Duel', *The Huntington Library Quarterly*, 62 (1999), pp. 88–114.

McDayter, Ghislaine, *Byromania and the Birth of Celebrity Culture* (Albany, 2009).

McGann, Jerome (ed.), *The Complete Poetical Works of Lord Byron* (7 vols., Oxford, 1986).

McKenzie Johnson, Henry, *Missions to Mexico: A Tale of British Diplomacy in the 1820s* (London, 1992).

Menendez González, Alfonso, *Elite y poder: la Junta General del Principado de Asturias 1594–1808* (Oviedo, 1989).

Messenger, Charles, *Unbroken Service: The History of Lloyd's Patriotic Fund 1803–2003* (London, 2003).

Metford, John C., *San Martín, The Liberator* (Oxford, 1950).

Miers, Richenda, *Scotland* (London, 2006).

Minta, Stephen, 'Byron and Mesolongi', *Literature Compass*, 4/4 (2007), pp. 1092–108.

Mitchell, Leslie, *Holland House* (London, 1980).

Moliner Prada, Antonio, *La guerrilla en la Guerra de la Independencia* (Madrid, 2004).

Montiel, Isidoro, *Ossian en España* (Barcelona, 1974).

Morel-Fatio, Alfred, 'Le révolutionnaire espagnol don Andrés Maria de Guzmán, dit "Don Tocsinos"', *Revue Historique*, CXXII Mai-Juin (1916), pp. 34–44.

Moreno Alonso, Manuel, *Ingleses, franceses y prusianos en España (entre la Ilustración y el Romanticismo)* (Sevilla, 2004).

—, *La Batalla de Bailén* (Madrid, 2008).

—, *La forja del liberalismo en España: los amigos españoles de Lord Holland (1793–1840)* (Madrid, 1997).

—, *La generación española de 1808* (Madrid, 1989).

—, *La Junta Suprema de Sevilla* (Sevilla, 2001).

—, *Los españoles durante la ocupación napoleónica – La vida cotidiana en la vorágine* (Malaga, 1997).

Mori, Jennifer, *Britain in the Age of the French Revolution, 1785–1820* (Harlow, 2000).

Morodo, Raul and Diaz, Elias, 'Tendencias y grupos políticos en las Cortes de Cadiz y en las de 1820', *Cuadernos Hispanoamericanos*, 201 (1966), pp. 637–75.

Morvan, Jean, *Le soldat impérial (1800–1814)* (2 vols., Paris, 1904).

Muir, Rory (ed.), *At Wellington's Right Hand: The Letters of Lieutenant-Colonel Sir Alexander Gordon 1808–1815* (London, 2003).

—, *Britain and the Defeat of Napoleon, 1807–1815* (London, 1996).

—, *Inside Wellington's Peninsular Army 1808–1814* (Barnsley, 2006).

Murtagh, Harman, 'Irish soldiers abroad (1600–1800)', in Thomas Bartlett and Keith Jeffery (eds), *A Military History of Ireland* (Cambridge, 1996), pp. 294–314.

Napier, William F. P., *History of the War in the Peninsula and in the South of France, from the Year 1807 to the Year 1814* (4 vols., Philadelphia, 1842).

Noel, Charles C., 'In the house of reform: the Bourbon Court of eighteenth-century Spain' in Gabriel Paquette (ed.), *Enlightened Reform in Southern Europe and its Atlantic colonies, c.1750–1830* (Farnham, 2009), pp. 145–66.

Nuñez Seixas, José M., 'La memoria de la Guerra de la Independencia', in Sociedad Estatal de Conmemoraciones Culturales, *España 1808–1814 La Nación en Armas* (Madrid, 2008), pp. 385–97.

Ocerin, Enrique (ed.), *Indice de los expedientes matrimoniales de militares y marinos que se conservan en el Archivo General Militar (1761–1865)* (2 vols., Madrid, 1959).

Oliver y Tolrá, Miguel de los Santos, *Mallorca durante la primera revolución, 1808–1814* (3 vols., Barcelona, 1982).

Oman, Charles W. C., *A History of the Peninsular War* (9 vols., London, 1922).

—, *Wellington's Army, 1809–1814* (London, 1912).

Onions, Charles T., *The Shorter Oxford English Dictionary on Historical Principles* (5 vols., Oxford, 1933).

Ortuño Martínez, Manuel, *Expedición a Nueva España de Xavier Mina: materiales y ensayos* (Pamplona, 2006).

Owen, Ellis F. and Rose, Edward P. F., 'Early Jurassic Brachiopods from Gibraltar, and their Tethyan affinities', *Paleontology*, 40/2 (1997), pp. 497–513.

Pakenham, Thomas, Fifth Earl of Longford (ed.), *Pakenham Letters, 1800 to 1815* (London, 1914).

Palacio Atard, Vicente (ed.), *De Hispania a España – el Nombre y el Concepto a través de los siglos* (Madrid, 2005).

Palacio Buñuelos, Luis, *España, del liberalismo a la democracia (1808–2004)* (Madrid, 2004).

'Palafox y Melci, José Rebolledo de, duque de Zaragoza', *Gran Enciclopedia Aragonesa* (Zaragoza, 2009) online edn [www.enciclopediaaragonesa.com/voz.asp?voz_id = 9794].

Paquette, Gabriel, 'Empire, enlightenment and regalism: New directions in eighteenth-century Spanish history', *European History Quarterly*, 35/1 (2005), pp. 107–17.

—, (ed.), *Enlightened Reform in Southern Europe and Its Atlantic Colonies, c.1750–1830* (Farnham, 2009).

—, 'The intellectual context of British diplomatic recognition of the South American Republics, c.1800–1830', *Journal of Transatlantic Studies*, 2/1 (Spring) (2004), pp. 75–95.

Parra Pérez, Caracciolo, *Miranda et la Revolution Francaise* (Caracas, 1989).

Patac de las Traviesas, José M., and Berenguer Alonso, Magin, *La guerra de la independencia en Asturias en los documentos del archivo del marqués de Santa Cruz de Marcenado: discurso leído por el autor en el acto de su solemne recepción académica el día 9 de noviembre de 1979* (Oviedo, 1980).

Payne, Stanley G., *Politics and the Military in Modern Spain* (London, 1967).

Pearce, Adrian J., *British Trade with Spanish America, 1763–1808* (Liverpool, 2007).

Peiró Arroyo, Antonio, *Las Cortes aragonesas de 1808 – Pervivencias forales y revolución popular* (Zaragoza, 1985).

Pérez Delgado, Tomás, 'Españoles en campos de trabajo franceses. Amberes y Flesinga, 1811–1814', *Alcores*, 5 (2088), pp. 157–88.

Peristiany, John G. and Pitt-Rivers, Julian A. (eds), *Honor and Grace in Anthropology* (Cambridge, 1992).

Philp, Mark (ed.), *Resisting Napoleon: The British Response to the Threat of Invasion, 1797–1815* (Aldershot, 2006).

Pittock, Murray, *Scottish and Irish Romanticism* (Oxford, 2008).

Pocock, John G. A., *Virtue, Commerce, and History* (Cambridge, 1985).

Popham, Hugh, 'Popham, Sir Home Riggs (1762–1820)', *Oxford Dictionary of National Biography*, September 2004; online edn, January 2008 [www.oxforddnb.com/view/article/22541].

Porter, Roy and Teich, Mikula C. (eds), *Romanticism in National Context* (Cambridge, 1988).

Portillo Valdés, José M., *Crisis atlántica: autonomía e independencia en la crisis de la monarquía hispana* (Madrid, 2006).

Puig i Oliver, Lluís M. de, *Girona francesa 1812–1814 L'anexió de Catalunya a França i el domini napoleònic a Girona* (Girona, 1976).

Quiroga, Alejandro, *Making Spaniards: Primo de Rivera and the nationalization of the masses, 1923–30* (Basingstoke, 2007).

Rabaza, Helminio L., *El Aragón resistente – la Junta Superior de Aragón y parte de Castilla 1809–1813* (Zaragoza, 2007).

Racine, Karen, 'Miranda, Francisco de (1750–1816)', *Oxford Dictionary of National Biography*, September 2004; online edn, May 2006 [www.oxforddnb. com/view/article/89687].

Rapport, Michael, *Nationality and Citizenship in Revolutionary France – The Treatment of Foreigners 1789–1799* (Oxford, 2000).

Riall, Lucy, *Garibaldi: Invention of a Hero* (London, 2007).

Ringrose, David R., *Spain, Europe, and the 'Spanish miracle', 1700–1900* (Cambridge, 1996).

Roberts, John (ed.), *Oxford Dictionary of the Classical World* (Oxford, 2007).

Rodríguez, Gregorio F., *Historia de Alvear* (2 vols., Buenos Aires, 1913).

Rodriguez, Moises E., *Freedom's Mercenaries – British Volunteers in the Wars of Independence of Latin America* (Oxford, 2006).

Roe, Nicholas (ed.), *Romanticism – An Oxford Guide* (Oxford, 2005).

Romero Tobar, Leonardo, 'Los "Sitios de Zaragoza", tema literario internacional (1808–1814)', in José Luis Martínez Sanz and Emilio de Diego García (eds), *El comienzo de la Guerra de la Independencia – Congreso Internacional del Bicentenario* (Madrid, 2009), pp. 571–87.

Romero, Leonardo, *Panorama crítico del romanticismo español* (Madrid, 1994).

Rothenberg, Gunther E., *Napoleon's Great Adversary: Archduke Charles and the Austrian Army, 1792–1814* (Staplehurst, 1995).

—*The Napoleonic Wars* (London, 1999).

Rubin, Hank, *Spain's Cause was Mine: A Memoir of an American Medic in the Spanish Civil War* (Carbondale, 1997).

Rudorff, Raymond, *War to the Death: The Sieges of Saragossa, 1808–1809* (London, 1974).

Ruiz Berrio, Julio, *La enseñanza en Madrid en tiempos de Fernando VII* (Madrid, 1967).

—, *Política escolar de España en el siglo XIX: (1808–1833)* (Madrid, 1970).

Ruiz, David, *Asturias contemporanea, 1808–1975* (Madrid, 1981).

Ruiz Fernández Jiménez, Marta, *El liberalismo exaltado: la confederación de comuneros españoles durante el Trienio Liberal* (Madrid, 2007).

Ruiz Rivera, Julián Bautista, *El consulado de Cádiz 1730–1823* (Cadiz, 1988).

Rutledge Southworth, Herbert, *Guernica! Guernica!: A Study of Journalism, Diplomacy, Propaganda, and History* (London, 1977).

Sack, James, 'Lord Grenville and the Peninsular War', in Ronald Ed Caldwell (ed.), *The Consortium on Revolutionary Europe 1750–1850* (Florida, 1994), pp. 146–52.

Saglia, Diego, '"O My Mother Spain!" The Peninsular War, family matters, and the practice of romantic nation-writing', *ELH*, 65/2 (1998), pp. 363–93.

—, *Byron and Spain: Itinerary in the Writing of Place* (Lampeter, 1996).

—, 'Nationalist texts and counter-texts: Southey's Roderick and the dissensions of the annotated romance', *Nineteenth-Century Literature*, 53/4 (1999), pp. 421–51.

—, *Poetic Castles in Spain: British Romanticism and Figurations of Iberia* (Amsterdam, 2000).

'San Martín, José de', *Encyclopædia Britannica Online Academic Edition*, Encyclopædia Britannica Inc. [www.britannica.com/EBchecked/topic/521474/Jose-de-San-Martin].

San Miguel, Evaristo, *Vida de Agustín Argüelles* (4 vols., Madrid, 1851).

Sanchez Agesta, Luis, *El pensamiento político del despotismo ilustrado* (Madrid, 1953).

Sánchez-Blanco, Francisco, *La mentalidad ilustrada* (Madrid, 1999).

Santos, Madrazo, *El sistema de transportes en España, 1750–1850: El Tráfico y los Servicios* (2 vols., Madrid, 1984).

Scrivener, Michael H., *Seditious Allegories: John Thelwall and Jacobin Writing* (Pennsylvania, 2008).

Seoane, María C., *El primer lenguaje constitucional español: las Cortes de Cádiz* (Madrid, 1968).

Severn, John K., *A Wellesley Affair: Richard Marquess Wellesley and the Conduct of Anglo-Spanish Diplomacy, 1809–1812* (Tallahassee, 1981).

—, *Architects of Empire: The Duke of Wellington and His Brothers* (Norman, OK, 2007).

Sheehan, Edward H., *Nenagh and Its Neighbourhood* (Tipperary, 1949).

Shubert, Adrian, *Death and Money in the Afternoon: A History of the Spanish Bullfight* (Oxford, 1999).

—, *A Social History of Modern Spain* (London, 1990).

Smith, Roger John, *The Gothic Bequest: Medieval Institutions in British Thought, 1688–1863* (Cambridge, 2002).

Sociedad Estatal de Conmemoraciones Culturales (ed.), *España 1808–1814 La Nación en Armas* (Madrid, 2008).

Solís, Ramón, *El Cadiz de las Cortes – La vida en la ciudad en los años de 1810 a 1813* (Madrid, 1987).

Speake, Jennifer, *Literature of Travel and Exploration: An Encyclopedia* (3 vols., London, 2003).

Speck, William A., *Robert Southey: Entire Man of Letters* (London, 2006).

Speier, Hans, *Social Order and the Risks of War: Papers in Political Sociology* (Cambridge, MA, 1952).

Spence Robertson, William, *France and Latin-American Independence* (Baltimore, 1939).

Spence, Peter, *The Birth of Romantic Radicalism: War, Popular Politics and English Radical Reformism, 1800–1815* (Aldershot, 1996).

Spiers, Edward M., 'Army organization and society in the nineteenth century', in Thomas Bartlett and Keith Jeffery (eds), *A Military History of Ireland* (Cambridge, 1996), pp. 335–9.

Stephens, H. M., 'Doyle, Sir (Charles) William (1770–1842)', rev. C. Esdaile, *Oxford Dictionary of National Biography* (Oxford, 2004) [www.oxforddnb.com/view/article/7997, accessed 11 February 2012].

Strachan, Hew, *Wellington's Legacy: The Reform of the British Army, 1830–54* (Manchester, 1984).

Stradling, Robert A., *Wales and the Spanish Civil War: The Dragon's Dearest Cause?* (Cardiff, 2004).

Suárez Cortina, Manuel, *Las máscaras de la libertad: el liberalismo español, 1808–1950* (Madrid, 2003).

Super, Robert H., *Walter Savage Landor – A Biography* (London, 1957).

Tague, Ingrid and Berry, Helen, 'Summary of Closing Plenary Discussion on "Honour and Reputation in Early Modern England"', *Transactions of the Royal Historical Society*, 6 (1996), pp. 247–48.

Tayler, Alistair N. and Tayler, Henrietta, *The Book of the Duffs* (2 vols., Edinburgh, 1914).

Taylor, Maurice, *The Scots College in Spain* (Valladolid, 1971).

Terrón Ponce, José L., *Ejército y política en la España de Carlos III* (Madrid, 1997).

Thompson, Irving Anthony A., *Guerra y decadencia. Gobierno y administración en la España de los Austrias, 1560–1620* (Barcelona, 1981).

Thomson, Guy and Blanco, Alda (eds), *Visiones del liberalismo: política, identidad y cultura en la España del siglo XIX* (Valencia, 2008).

Thorne, R. G. (ed.), *The House of Commons, 1790–1820* (5 vols., London, 1986).

Thorne, Roland, 'Stewart, Robert, Viscount Castlereagh and second marquess of Londonderry (1769–1822)', *Oxford Dictionary of National Biography*, September 2004; online edn, May 2009 [www.oxforddnb.com/view/article/26507, accessed 19 February 2009].

Thorning, Joseph F., *Miranda: World Citizen* (Gainesville, 1952).

Tone, John L., 'A dangerous Amazon: Agustina Zaragoza and the Spanish Revolutionary War, 1808–1814', *European History Quarterly*, 37/4 (2007), pp. 548–61.

—, 'Partisan warfare in Spain and Total War', in Förster, Stig and Chickering, Roger (eds), *War in an Age of Revolution, 1775–1815* (Cambridge, 2010), pp. 243–59.

—, *The Fatal Knot: The Guerrilla War in Navarre and the Defeat of Napoleon in Spain* (London, 1994).

Torras Elias, Jaime, *Liberalismo y rebeldía campesina, 1820–1823* (Barcelona, 1976).

Torrent, Joan, 'La prensa de Cataluña durante la Guerra de la Independencia', *Destino*, Barcelona, Nr. 1745 (1965), pp. 52–63.

Tortella, Teresa, *A Guide to Sources of Information on Foreign Investment in Spain 1780–1850* (Amsterdam, 2000).

Uriarte Ayo, Rafael, 'Anglo-Spanish trade through the port of Bilbao during the second half of the eighteenth century: Preliminary findings', *International Journal of Maritime History*, 4/2 (1992), pp. 193–217.

Urquijo Goitia, Mikel (ed.), *Diccionario Biográfico de Parlamentarios Españoles – Cortes de Cadiz. 1810–1814* (3 vols., Madrid, 2010).

Ventós, Xavier R. de, *El laberinto de la hispanidad* (Barcelona, 1987).

Vetch, Robert Hamilton, 'Landmann, George Thomas (1780–1854)', rev. John Sweetman, *Oxford Dictionary of National Biography*, Oxford University Press, 2004; online edn [www.oxforddnb.com/view/article/15976, accessed 23 February 2011].

Vicens Vives, Jaime; Nadal, Jordi and López-Morillas, Frances M., *An Economic History of Spain* (Princeton, 1969).

Vilar, Pierre, *Hidalgos, amotinados y guerrilleros – pueblo y poderes en la historia de España* (Barcelona, 1982).

Villar Garcia, Maria B. (ed.), *La emigración irlandesa en el siglo XVIII* (Malaga, 2000).

Villa-Urrutia, Wenceslao R. de, *Relaciones entre España e Inglaterra durante la Guerra de la Independencia – Apuntes para la Historia diplomática de España de 1808 a 1814* (3 vols., Madrid, 1911).

Waddell, David A. G., 'British neutrality and Spanish-American independence: the problem of foreign enlistment', *Journal of Latin American Studies*, 19/1 (1987), pp. 1–18.

Walzer, Michael, *Just and Unjust Wars: A Moral Argument with Historical Illustrations* (New York, 2006).

Ward, Stephen G. P., *Wellington's Headquarters: A Study of the Administrative Problems in the Peninsula, 1809–1814* (London, 1957).

Ward, Wilfrid P., *The Life and Times of Cardinal Wiseman* (2 vols., London, 1897).

Weintraub, Stanley, *The Last Great Cause – The Intellectuals and the Spanish Civil War* (London, 1968).

Whitridge, Arnold, 'Washington's French volunteers', *History Today*, 24/9 (1974), pp. 593–603.

Wilson, Jason, *The Andes: A Cultural History* (Oxford, 2009).

Wise, Thomas J. (ed.), *A Landor Library – A Catalogue of Printed Books, Manuscripts and Authograph Letters by Walter Savage Landor* (London, 1928).

Woley, Laurence, *Guide de Recherches en Histoire de la Legion d'honneur* (Paris, 2002).

Woudhuysen, H. R., 'Sidney, Sir Philip (1554–1586)', *Oxford Dictionary of National Biography*, 2004; online edn, May 2005 [www.oxforddnb.com/view/article/25522, accessed 15 December 2010].

Womack, Peter, *Improvement and Romance – Constructing the Myth of the Highlands* (Basingstoke, 1989).

Wood, Gordon, *The Radicalism of the American Revolution* (New York, 1993).

Woolf, Stuart J., *Napoleon's Integration of Europe* (London, 1991).

Woolgar, Chris M. (ed.), *Wellington Studies IV* (Southampton, 2008).

Wurzbach, Constant von, *Biographisches Lexikon des Kaiserthums Oesterreich: enthaltend die lebensskizzen der denkwürdigen personen, welche seit 1750 in den österreichischen kronländern geboren wurden oder darin gelebt und gewirkt haben* (60 vols., Vienna, 1861).

Unpublished thesis

Davies, John Huw, 'British intelligence in the Peninsular War', (University of Exeter Ph.D. thesis, 2006).

Index

Due to different conventions of the languages and periods represented in this book, readers are advised that if they cannot find a person under their second surname, they should also look under their first. Variations of the volunteers' names are offered in Table 1 and in Biographical Notes.

Lightning Source UK Ltd.
Milton Keynes UK
UKOW07f0630141114

241605UK00005B/111/P